Veracruz

Estado de Oaxaca

Chiapas

Golfo de Tehuantepec

Pacífico

SEASONS OF
MY HEART

SEASONS OF MY HEART

A Culinary Journey Through Oaxaca, Mexico

SUSANA TRILLING

Companion to the National Public Television Series

BALLANTINE BOOKS • NEW YORK

A Ballantine Book
Published by The Ballantine Publishing Group

Copyright © 1999 by Susana Trilling

Grateful acknowledgment is made to the following for permission to reprint recipes:

Editorial Diana: Recipe for "Manchamanteles Oaxaqueña" from *Cocina oaxaqueña* by Josefina Velázquez de León, published by Editorial Diana.

Editorial Trillas: Recipes for "Alegrías," "Casuelitas de Tamarindo," and "Palanquetas" from *Y la comida se hizo de dulces y postres,* by Beatrice Fernández.

Junior League of Monroe, Louisiana: Recipe for "Italian Cream Cake" from *The Cotton Country Collection,* Junior League of Monroe, Louisiana, P.O. Box 7138, Monroe, LA 71211, (800) 256-4888.

Alfred A. Knopf, a division of Random House, Inc., and Collier Associates: Recipe for "Capirotada—Mexican Bread Pudding" from *The Book of Latin American Cooking* by Elisabeth Lambert Ortiz. Copyright © 1979 by Elisabeth Lambert Ortiz. Reprinted by permission of Alfred A. Knopf, a division of Random House, Inc., and Collier Associates.

Library of Congress Cataloging-in-Publication Data
Trilling, Susana.
    Seasons of my heart : a culinary journey through Oaxaca, Mexico / Susana Trilling. — 1st ed.
        p.   cm.
    "Companion to the national public television series."
    Includes bibliographical references and index.
    ISBN 0-345-42596-0 (hc. : alk. paper)
    1. Cookery, Mexican.   2. Cookery—Mexico—Oaxaca.   3. Oaxaca (Mexico)—Social life and customs.   I. Title.
    TX716.M4T78   1999
    641.5972'74—dc21   99-31048
                                                                                              CIP

Text design by Patricia Fabricant
Endpapers by Hector Hara
Cover photos:
Front cover: Breakfast at Rancho Aurora. Clockwise from upper left corner: *Pan Dulce, Chocolate con Leche, Canasta de Frutas, Plantanada, Ensalada de Piña, Jícama, y Aguacate, Chilaquiles Verdes, Ejotes con Huevos, Cecina Enchilada* with *Tlayudas,* and *Tamales de Dulce*
Spine: *Panuchos*
Flaps: View from the outdoor kitchen in the dry season, Rancho Aurora
Back cover: Top: *Tamales* "how to": Hermelinda spreading the *masa,* Susana spooning *Mole Negro* on the pork, Rebecca folding the banana leaves in thirds, and Cheryl completing the package and tying the *tamales* (Marcela Taboada)
Bottom: Late-afternoon *comida* for two: *Flor de Calabaza Rellena con Requesón* (center), *Mezcal con Sal de Guasanito de Limón, Crema de Poblano, Loma con Piña, Arroz con Chepil,* and *Pastel de Tres Leches con Moca*
Pages ii–iii: Vegetable sellers in the Playa Mercado de Abastos, Oaxaca City (Alfredo Díaz Mora)
Page vi: Susana with Anamaría Mendoza de Ruíz waiting for the *tamales* to steam, Teotitlán del Valle, Tlacolula (Alfredo Díaz Mora)
Manufactured in the United States of America

First Edition: November 1999

10   9   8   7   6   5   4   3   2   1

This book is dedicated to my grandmother,
Marie Antoinette Chavana Flores,

in memory of my father, Jack A. Trilling,

and to the children of Centro de Atención Infantil Piña
Palmera, who brought me to Oaxaca.

©Alfredo Díaz Mora

CONTENTS

ACKNOWLEDGMENTS

This book and television series are the results of the collective effort of many different people who have one passion in common: great food. So many people contributed their knowledge, recipes, time, and energy to document Oaxaca's fine cuisine. I am deeply indebted to every one of them.

First, I would like to thank my family, who helped in so many ways: Eric Ulrich and our children Kaelin, Jesse Beau, Lider, Serafin (and Abel), who have all been loving and supportive. They contributed good ideas, comforted me, and made me laugh when I felt completely overwhelmed. I am grateful to my sister-in-law, Ine Van Aerle, my mother, Melanie Trilling, who always encouraged me, and Phyllis Gosfield, who always has an answer and has been a constant inspiration to make good, wholesome food. I want to thank my grandmother, Marie Antoinette Chavana Flores, Aunt Dorothy and Uncle Burford Westlund, Aunt Renée Levin, and Helen Zwart.

I would like to thank my wonderful assistants, Cheryl Camp, Valy Nadeau, and Gretchen Wirtz, who contributed so much of their time and energy. I send a warm *gracias* to Marieke Bekkers de Díaz Cruz, Norma García, Jacqueline Kauffer, Shawna Haynes, Claudia Burr, Patty Santiago Cruz, Roger Brooks, and especially Víctor Velasco, who researched, translated, and edited for the book.

My teachers, peers, and fellow cookbook writers have influenced and inspired me throughout the years and encouraged me to find my own voice and express it. Although I can't name everyone here, I am grateful to Doug Newbold, Tom Neuhaus, Miguel Rávago, Diana Kennedy, Rick Bayless, Elaine González, Betty Fussell, Helen Studley, Marilyn Tausend, Elisabeth Lambert Ortiz, Nancy Zaslavsky, Shelton Wiseman, Susan Baldassano, and Ricardo Muñoz. Special thanks to the *maestras* of the Oaxacan kitchen: María Concepción Portillo de Carballido, Ana María Gúzman de Vásquez Colmenares, and Soledad Díaz Altimarano.

I am most happy to thank the wisest, best agent anyone could have, Janis Donnaud, and thanks to longtime friend Alan Kannof of the William Morris Agency for representing my best interests.

I would like to acknowledge the staff at the Ballantine Publishing Group for their professionalism and attention to every detail, especially Amy Scheibe, editor, who believed in the book from the start, and Elizabeth Zack, senior editor, who took over the project with style and has been great fun to work with along with Allison Dickens, her assistant. I am grateful to Carole Berglie, copy editor, Eileen Gaffney, managing editor, Patricia Fabricant, text designer, Kristine V. Mills-Noble, cover designer, and Alex Klapwald, production director.

I loved working with my talented photographers, Marcela Taboada, Barbara Lawton, and Alfredo Díaz Mora, and their assistants, Angie and Rebecca Lerma.

I appreciate my traveling comrades who came on my many research trips and adventures, always making them fun while discovering and rediscovering the beautiful state of Oaxaca, and the wonderful people we met. I never could have done without my support system at home, including Josefina Avendaño Cruz, Irene Sánchez Santiago, Hermelinda Sánchez Santiago, Fermina Arellanes Martínez, and Alma Bautista Vásquez.

No cookbook would be complete without recipe testers. They helped me overcome the difficulties of writing this book in another country, especially because I used different ingredients and worked at high altitudes. I appreciate their input greatly. I am grateful to my sisters, Nancy Moyer, Jacqui Sattler, and Melanie Mumbauer, and to Phyllis Gosfield, Claudia Raab, Roedean Landeaux, Jessica Reisman, Ineke Grondstra, and Roger Brooks. I am truly grateful to all the employees of Seasons of My Heart Cooking School, and our intern from Elgin Community College, Dana Thomas. My thanks to the staff and volunteers from WMHT: Marjorie Ward, Audrey Donner, Joyce Stah, Leslie Maiello, Melissa Mangino, Phoebe Van Scoy, Stacy Malloran, and Dan Dufresne. A warm thanks to all the students of Seasons of My Heart Cooking School who contributed their comments and tested many recipes, especially Marian Miller, who came for a class and left six weeks later.

I would like to thank our friends who gave sound advice over these years: Jane and Thorny Robison, our compadres, the staff at Casa Colonial, Mary Jane Gagnier, Arnulfo Mendoza, the staff at La Mano Mágica, Dr. Marcus Winter, Shawn Spitzer, Anna Johannson, Balbino Cano, Jan and Ineka Grondstra, Paulina Salas, Phyllis and Gene Gosfield, Liz Garnier, the Garnier family, Guido and Myra Lesser, Roy Murphy, Helen McNeil, Roedean Landeaux, Tommy Lawry, Kathy Card, Virginia Wood, Fran Moody, Pamela Nevarez, Familia José Cuauhtémoc Marmolejo, Karen Blockman Carrier, Chris Gilheany, Christopher King, Kathryn Milan, Roger Hernández, and Justin Moreau.

The catalyst that made this wonderful project happen was WMHT Public Television station in Schenectady, New York. I want to express my heartfelt thanks to Donn Rogosin, executive producer, who really believed in me, Glenda Bullock, publicist, Stephen Honeybill, a marvelous and fun producer, Barbara Lawton, production assistant, Mike Melita, the good-humored videographer, and Gary Carter, audio.

In the studio, I was grateful for the humor and expertise of cameramen and audiomen William "Woody" Forst, Dominic Figliomini, and Rick Meed, Dan Toma, and Matt Elie. I want to thank set builders Ron McGowty and Kenny Girard, Paul Hoagland, production manager; David Nicosia, engineering manager; David French, Tim Stah, Dan Dufresne, Bruce G. Cole, Audrey Donner, and Beth Morrison. You all did a great job!

Estoy muy cariñosamente agradecida to the Oaxacan Department of Tourism, especially Secretary of Tourism Martín Ruiz Camino and his wife, Tonny Zwollo, Alfredo Díaz Mora, Luis Barreda, Guadalupe Harp, Liz Baños, Gloria Toledo, and Arturo Espinoza. Thank you to Rosario Marza and the Oaxacan film commission and *un abrazo caluroso* to Gloria Carrasco, who became a friend and inspiration. A special thanks goes to the ex-governor of the state of Oaxaca, Diódoro Carrasco Altamirano.

We couldn't have done without our wonderful sponsors: Azteca Foods, manufacturer of fine Mexican foods; JD Henkels, who make the best knives in the world; and Mexicana Airlines, especially Captain Jan Albright and Jorge Guytotulla. I was happy to have the support of Le Creuset, KitchenAid, Kohler, Culture Stone Corporation, Best Tile Distributors, Inc., Faddegon's Nursery, and Bob's Trees. I tip my hat and send a big thank-you to all the hotels and restaurants who offered a warm bed or meal to the crew and myself while we were filming on location. A special thanks to all the drivers (especially David and Julio Sánchez) who got us through raging rivers, fires, and more.

I'd like to thank each person who has contributed recipes for this book or the television series.

Special thanks to Bertola Morales and Fidel Pereda of Organización de Derechos Humanos de la Mujer Chinanteca and their associates, who are fun and gracious people. I want to thank Stephen Morales, the community of Nuevo Arroyo Camarón, María del Carmen Vásquez, Tomasa Ruiz, and the Casa de Cultural Tuxtepec.

It was a great privilege to know and to work with Roberto Vásquez López of the Papaloapan Regional Producers of Vanilla, especially the growers of Santo Domingo del Río. In the Cañada and Mazatec region, I'd like to thank the INI de Huatla de Jiménez, Rosalba Terán Carrera, Inés Cerqueda García, Orefelia Meza Muñoz, Silvia Carrera Gamboa, Señora Beatriz Avendaño, Felipa Hernández Avendaño, and Ofelia Carrera Hernández.

I feel grateful to our friends on the Pacific coast, and I want to say thanks to all of them, especially Suzana López, friends at Centro de Atención Infantil Piña Palmera, Tina Coaché Chacón, Jim Clouse, Valentina Gopar Vásquez, the Torres family, Gustavo, María Isabel and Claudia Scherenberg, Mamá Goya, Carmen Herrera Silva, and Juana Ramírez.

The Mixtecan people are very warm and giving, and I am indebted to Doña Sofía Hernández Cervantes, María Mora Santos and the people of Santa María Tindú, Ester Cervantes, Julia and Antonio Martinez, Vincenta and Aurelia Hernández, Gonzalo Cruz Ramírez, Alicia Hernández, and the weavers of Santiago Jamiltepec.

I greatly appreciate everyone who opened their hearts in the Isthmus of Tehuantepec, and I'd like to thank Lupe Rodríguez de Barbieri, her grandmother Tía Cándida Blas Aguilar and family, Gustavo López, Julín Contreras, María Elena Mimiage

Sosa, Teófila Palafox, Chica Mon, Francisca López Liña, Margarita Molino de la Rosa, Teresa Morales Matus, Geralda Mattis Jiménez, Milka, Esteban Espinoza Gurayab, Florentina, Angel and Oresta Serefino, and the Salt Collective of La Colorada.

I received a warm reception in the Sierras throughout Oaxaca, and I send a big *gracias* to Tino Garrido and Gudelia Santiago Rosales, Plácido Hernández, Isabel Pérez, Ernesto Avendaño Cruz, and Norma of Ecotur, Ixtlán. In the Sierra Mixe, I am grateful to Salomón Martínez Gómez, the INI de Ayutla, the village *cocineras* of Santa María Tlahuitoltepec, María Alcantara Gómez de Bernal, Juan Areli and Elda Bernal, Dr. Salomón Nahmad, Hermenegildo "Gordo" Rojas Ramírez, Josefina García, Swilma Pérez García, and Isabel Aguilar María.

Closer to home, it is an ongoing pleasure to work with and know the people who live in the Valles Centrales. These old friends have taught me the language and the customs and all about Oaxacan food: Vicenta Vásquez Ramírez, Paula Martínez, Chico Machine, Carlota Santos, María, Salomón, Germán Castro Santiago, Aurelio Galván, Augustina Jiménez, Bertha, Juana Galván, Yolanda Girón, Antonio and Flavia, Luz Elena Moctezuma Torre, Galdino and Ramona Lázaro, María and Fraulein Galván Taboada, Pancha, Pedro Ortiz, Minerva Mendez, Juan Díaz, Laura Vásquez, María Tabaoda, Eugenio Gónzalez Ortíz, his mother Rafaela, Romero Gónzalez Ortíz, Rosa Matadamas, Claudia Muñoz Mejia, Teresa Mejia, Tía Martina, Christina Arturo Vásquez Núñez, Margarita Vásquez Núñez, the women in the Etla market, especially the Morales sisters, Minerva Morales, Conchita Castellanos González, Doña Josefa Sánchez, Elias, Samari Carrasco Sánchez, Inés Pérez, Guadalupe Ruiz, Chuchu and Rafaela Cruz, Paula Cortez, Leticia Aragón Núñez, Audelia, Leonel, Marvi Peterson, and la Familia Mendoza Ruiz: Ana María, Hermilio, Graciela, and Juana.

In Oaxaca City, I thank Biblioteca Vasconcelos Bustamante, Frank Howell, INAH, Dr. Marcus Winter, CII DIR, IPN, Gladys Manzanero Medina, Esther Mora Villar, María Luisa, Mari and Antonio Cárdenas, all the *señoras* who have given me recipes in Mercado de Abastos, Sisters Marilú, Irma Moguel de Sorroza, Eliseo Ramírez Hernández, Don Paulo and Doña Irene, Molinos del Sol, Teresa García, Irene García, Edith López Gómez, Patricia Chagoya, and Cecilia Acevedo de Torres.

I'd like to thank all the farmers who grow the food to nourish our bodies, the artists and musicians who nourish our hearts, and the Virgen de Guadalupe, Buddha, and God, who nourish our souls. I thank you all!

INTRODUCTION

Although I have explored many different types of cooking in my twenty years of being a chef, the Cocina Mexicana is most certainly the closest to my heart. My mother's parents are Mexican, and my grandmother used to run a little restaurant in the Hospital of Santa Rosa in San Antonio, Texas, to feed the Mexican workers. Her food was Tex-Mex, based on the most incredibly chewy flour tortillas, pinto beans with crispy corn *chalupa* shells and exceptional hot *tamales*. Her cupboard was full of her famous homemade jams, made from the large variety of fruit trees she nurtured in her yard. As a child, I thought her kitchen was the center of the universe. Something about the smells there and the language spoken by my grandparents over steaming cups of hot coffee seemed exotic and mysterious, and I embraced it wholeheartedly.

Years later, when I began to train professionally, I started to cook in Mexican restaurants. I have been lucky enough to work for great chefs who were also hands-on mentors. This has influenced me in my own teaching about Mexican food. Fonda San Miguel Restaurant in Austin, Texas, sent me to Mexico for the first time in 1977 to study the roots of the cuisine. I was so strongly impressed by the cultures I explored that I have continued to study cooking in this manner ever since. It is not surprising that most of the professionals who come to my cooking school are looking to learn about the daily traditions that are still very much alive in the southern Mexican state of Oaxaca, where I live and teach.

Oaxaca invites a deep appreciation of Mexican culture. Here time has stood still in the small village where I went to visit my husband for the first time. I was enchanted with every burro laden with corn going to the mill, every horse-drawn cart filled with alfalfa for the cows and horses; I was filled with laughter at the sight of the native *guajolote*, or wild turkey, puffing up his chest to impress his mate. I loved the women who could balance huge trays with watermelon slices as well as countless other products on their heads, carry babies on their backs in *rebozos* (woven shawls), and take time to arrange beautiful altars for their patron saints in their homes or in their market stalls. Now, after living here for eleven years, I see many subtle changes, but still feel the magic, see the beauty, and am eager to always learn more about the history embedded here.

When I came to live here full time, I was introduced to the other end of the food chain. I had always been a chef, but had never grown a thing in my life. I actually thought that beans grew on trees! What a revelation to grow, harvest, and clean our own produce. We have generous neighbors who taught us not only how to grow tomatoes but also how to select and pack them according to the Oaxacan standard.

I made friends with the women in the market and in my village and thus nurtured my biggest passion—the Oaxacan kitchen and its delicacies.

Our ranch (Rancho Aurora) is located between two small villages—San Lorenzo Cacaotepec and San Felipe Tejalapan. San Felipe is a Zapotec village where handmade tortillas are the major cottage industry. I felt I really became a part of the community when my husband, Eric, started growing native crops of corn, beans, squash, and tomatoes during the rainy season and flowers for big fiestas such as the *Día de Muertos* (Day of the Dead). While selling them door to door with a friend, I naturally showed a sincere curiosity about the local foods. Consequently, village women proudly showed me how they used their ingredients and shared with me the traditions that surround their holidays. We planted a variety of crops and learned the hard way that people here are very traditional and are not interested in trying new foods. The cooking techniques here are ancient—customs in some villages have been preserved for over 1,000 years, and that is what gives the food its unique flavor. Crops are picked in their mellow, ripe stage to allow the flavors to reach a delicious peak. Every dish has its own magic, and its own traditional sauce to make it even more special. Oaxacans are proud of their food, and rightly so, for its flavor can be subtle or very intense, but always pure Oaxaqueño.

To help with our harvest of watermelon and cantaloupe, we brought a twelve-year-old boy, Serafín, from the Centro de Atención Infantíl Piña Palmera (the Palm Grove Children's Center), where Eric and I had worked. He came for two weeks and never went back, finding in us the family he wanted, and we found happiness with him. A year later, our son Kaelin was born. When he arrived, some of the neighborhood women sent me corn *atole* to produce breast milk, and others came to make an herbal bath or *temazcal* for me to cleanse my body and soul. We had bonded over food, working in the *campo*, and now, in childbirth.

After Kaelin's birth, I revived "Seasons of My Heart" (my old catering business established in 1980) as a cooking school. Here I teach international cooking to local women and Oaxacan cooking to foreigners. Nutritional foods and vegetable dishes became very popular with the young local women who were trying to improve their diets. Some of our guests at the bed-and-breakfast Eric had built wanted to participate in the classes, so we started a weekend bed-and-breakfast course. With this addition, people can come down for a long weekend and be immersed in the culture as they learn the traditional foods of Oaxaca.

Just as success with the cooking school and the bed-and-breakfast was approaching, all the females in the house (dog, cat, banana tree, and myself) got pregnant. I thought we should put a warning in our brochure about the fertility of the place! Son number three, Jesse Beau, was born, and immediately after, another young man, Lider, came from the Piña Palmera to be our fourth son.

Worldwide fascination with the culinary delights of Mexican cuisine has continued to grow, and as a result Oaxaca has earned recognition as a very special place with a unique cooking style. The food arts of Oaxaca have a mystique owing to the complicated cooking methods and the intense and subtle depth of flavors. I have adapted many of the recipes in this book for the American home cook by using a mixture of older techniques, such as grilling or toasting the ingredients to enhance the flavors. I've also incorporated modern timesaving equipment available in the United States, such as the blender or spice grinder to replace the pre-Hispanic *metate*, still used in Oaxaca today.

One of my purposes in writing this book is to share what I have learned about old Mexico, and the centuries-old traditions that are still part of Oaxacan life today. I also want to tell of my experiences as a chef, woman, wife, and mother here in our village and introduce you to my neighbors and friends. In my eleven years here, I have grown to love and deeply appreciate the people of Oaxaca and am constantly impressed by the pride they have in their cuisine. In every one of the many interviews I've conducted with local cooks, I've learned something special—sometimes about a dish from a remote area of this mountainous land or sometimes about a unique memory of someone's mother in her *cocina* (kitchen). The indigenous peoples, their dialects, their fiestas, and the dishes, like the various *huipiles* and styles of dress, weave a tapestry that makes up the fabric of the state of Oaxaca and its cuisine. Come, join me on a culinary tour of the seven regions of Oaxaca—grab an apron, get your ingredients, or find a good armchair, turn on some Mexican *ranchero* music, and *adelante*!

©Alfredo Díaz Mora

CHAPTER ONE

The Seven Regions and Gastronomic Culture of Oaxaca

Agave on
the road to
Totontopec,
Mixe (Barbara
Lawton)

Overleaf:
Sierra Mixe
(Barbara
Lawton)

Oaxaca is one of the most distinctive states in all of

Mexico and boasts some of the most original and widely

known food in the country. It contains an enormous variety

of natural resources, gorgeous terrain, and an array of

both pre-Hispanic and colonial archaeological remains.

It has a broad cultural diversity because of the fourteen

different indigenous groups living here and a wealth of

popular traditions. From a culinary point of view, it has an

outstanding array of dishes that make up the subtle but

complex cuisine of the Oaxacan kitchen. From the simple squash vine soup to the most complex sauces, or *moles*, this food is traditional yet very sophisticated because of the variety of ingredients used and the manner in which these ingredients are prepared.

The state of Oaxaca is divided into seven regions that represent seven geographical areas: Los Valles Centrales (Central Valleys), La Cañada, Tuxtepec, La Costa, La Mixteca, La Sierra, and El Istmo. Each region has its own specific products and style of cooking, primarily governed by the foods produced in that area. The culture and dialects in each area differ, changing with the various indigenous peoples who live there. Each region also has its own style of dress, music, dance, and rituals that contribute to its unique character.

The geography of the state is mostly mountainous, with two giant Sierra Madre mountain ranges dominating the terrain and dotted with many different micro-climates hosting a variety of food products. The farms are generally small tracts of land, with most people growing crops for their own use during the *temporada de lluvias* (rainy season). In the Central Valleys, farmers grow primarily maize, beans, and squash, which are the basis of the diet, while more commercial farmers grow tomatoes, greens, onions, garlic, and various chiles. Other mountainous crops like coffee and potatoes are grown in the high-altitude areas of the Sierra, Costa, or Cañada, while in the tropical lowlands of Tuxtepec, sugarcane, bananas, pineapples, and tobacco are abundant. La Costa, the area near the Pacific Ocean that forms the state's southern shore, provides a large array of seafood, fish, and even reptiles to eat. The fish and seafood are eaten fresh, smoked, salted, and dried in the Isthmus region. Most of the produce grown is consumed locally and is dictated by the region's traditions and holidays. All of the produce brought in by farmers or gathered by the sellers themselves is harvested at the peak of ripeness and taken to market. These markets are a special feature of Oaxacan culture and have been the center of commerce for many centuries, with people previously utilizing cacao, maguey, and other things of value as trade items instead of money.

Oaxacan cuisine is a blend of pre-Hispanic dishes and Spanish-influenced Mexican food. The indigenous ingredients of the Oaxacan kitchen range from the "holy trinity" of corn, beans, and squash to the tomatoes, *tomatillos,* and chiles used to flavor them. There is an array of native plants used to enhance the diet and add flavor to the food: greens such as nopal cactus; pungent herbs like *chepiche, chepil,* and *yerba de conejo*; plus the medicinally useful culinary herbs *hierba santa, verdolagas,* and *epazote.* Trees such as *guaje* (leucaena) and *granada* (pomegranate) give their seeds to thicken sauces or adorn them, while plants such as the maguey and *guayabas* are used to make nectars. A favorite food of Oaxacans still is the ancient dish of toasted grasshoppers, or *chapulines.* Legend has it that if visitors eat *chapulines* on a visit to Oaxaca, they will always return.

The Spanish addition of domesticated animals changed the local people's diet considerably by the time the first generation of Oaxacan *mestizos* were actually combining foods from the Old and New Worlds. When an animal is slaughtered, all parts of the animal are used, from the head to the feet. Parts that cannot be used right away are salted and air-dried to be used later. In the case of pork, the fat is rendered to make lard and the skin is cooked to make *chicharrón*. Only in recent times have cooks changed to oil for frying, but traditional recipes dictate the use of lard. Chicken eggs are very popular and used on many occasions as a protein source when meat is scarce. Oaxacan cheese is world famous, with the three cow's milk cheeses being the *queso fresco* (fresh cheese), *quesillo* (string cheese), and a wonderfully rich farmer cheese called *requesón* made from the whey of *queso fresco*.

Probably Mexico's most important contributions to the world cuisine are cacao and tomatoes. Although cacao is originally from the state of Tabasco, it is being cultivated in the tropical parts of Oaxaca (as is vanilla, another indigenous flavoring) and used extensively in the Oaxacan kitchen. Cacao is used to make chocolate, Chinatecan *popo*, and *tejate*, pre-Hispanic drinks that were originally called "food of the gods" and are still used as primary tradition-bound offerings in fiestas today. Oaxaca is the only state in Mexico where people, using family recipes, still go to their local village mill to grind their own cacao, cinnamon, almonds, and sugar to make chocolate. A drink like *tejate*, where the oils of the mamey seed are extracted and whipped with boiled corn and toasted cacao to make a foamy refreshing drink, is a good example of the alchemy that occurs in the Oaxacan kitchen. This highly nutritious drink is ceremonially enjoyed in our village each year on March 6, when everyone cleans out their wells. It provides energy, and is said to give men *fuerza* (strength) to make lots of children. It is also served to women in childbirth and those with malnutrition.

Some Oaxacan dishes are complex, including many layers and levels of flavors. I think one of the ways this flavor intensity developed was through the making of tortillas, which can take up a good part of the morning. One of the key expressions in Oaxaca is *aprovechar*, which means "to take advantage of." Whenever women are cooking, they'll always say "take advantage of the coals" or "take advantage of the hot *comal*," meaning put the onions, tomatoes, and chiles under the *comal* to cook directly on the coals while the tortillas are cooking on top. Later, the vegetables will be peeled and have a more intense flavor than if used raw or boiled.

All the regional similarities and differences converge in the city of Oaxaca, where people from all seven regions live together and have developed a cooking style of their own. Called by the locals "Oaxaca City," this colonial town was a gift to Hernán Cortés by the king of Spain. Located in a large lovely valley, it owes its fame to the beauty of its churches and buildings, wealth of traditions, and variety of regional cuisines. Some say the focal point of the city is the central plaza, or *zócalo*, but I feel the pulse of the city is in the Mercado de Abastos, the largest market in the city. People come to it from all seven regions of Oaxaca to buy and sell their wares. There is also a livestock market, where folks buy and sell animals, especially before big fiestas or holidays. Women sell ready-made food, and there are countless stalls, or *puestos*, where great food is made to order using the freshest ingredients possible. It is very exciting to be at the wholesale market, which begins before dawn, and watch huge piles of cabbages, tomatoes, and chiles dwindle as the morning sun begins to shine. Money is tight for most Oaxacans, who take shopping very seriously, searching for the best and finest ingredients and not accepting less than perfect quality. There is an overall pride in the food from Oaxaca, which I consider "the heart of Mexican cooking," and each woman develops her own special touches, but they all agree that whatever the dish, it starts with the best ingredients. The most revered comment that one woman can bestow upon her neighbor is that she has *buen sazón*, which simply means good taste buds or palate, combined with a good hand for seasoning. In my travels I have met many such women and hope that they have influenced my own *sazón*, which I share with you here.

"Corn fairies," Totontopec, Mixe (Marcela Taboada)

CHAPTER TWO

The Central Valleys
(Los Valles Centrales)

Meat counter at Mercado de Abastos, Oaxaca City (Stephen Honeybill)

Overleaf: Susana selecting beans at Mercado de Abastos, Oaxaca City (Barbara Lawton)

Since pre-Hispanic times, the region around the capital city of Oaxaca has been part of an important commercial trade route in Mesoamerica. At the time of the Spanish conquest, Oaxaca City was an Aztec outpost. Aztecs controlled the trade route that opened the way to the Isthmus of Tehuantepec and beyond to Central and South America. The flat plains of the Central Valleys stretch out in three directions below the ancient city of Monte Albán, which is located 500 feet above the valley floor.

Today that area consists of the Etla Valley, the Tlacolula Valley, and the market centers, which include Zimatlán, Ejutla, Miahuatlán, Ocotlán, and Zaachila. Subsistence farming and commercial agriculture play leading roles in the daily lives of the people here. The valleys are very fertile and thus more productive than the surrounding mountains. From time immemorial the Central Valleys were destined to be a crossroads for people, culture, and trade.

The largest indigenous group is the Zapotec, whose culture is symbolized by the great archaeological site of Monte Albán and the other impressive ruins in the valleys. Another main ethnic group is the Mixtecs. Their cultures and customs, like those of other indigenous groups, are reflected in the markets. The market system is a network of sellers that visit each municipality on a different day of the week so that everyone has a chance to buy and sell in his or her own area as well as travel around to others. The markets have individual appeal: Zaachila is noted for a huge variety of beans, nuts, and seeds, as well as a variety of *mole* pastes; Ocotlán features an animal market as well as baskets near the newly restored church; Tlacolula has *pataxtle*, which is calcified cacao, an ingredient in *chocolate atole*. Bargaining is expected, and in the firewood market of Zaachila, the barter system is still used.

Known for its cheeses, *barbacoa,* and the green cantera stone of its buildings, the Wednesday market in Etla is a real treat and one of my favorites. Rancho Aurora is in the Etla Valley, so we have gone to shop here for years. It's a small market that has everything rural folk need for their lives in the *campo*. Outside the market, the *ollas*, *comales*, *jarras*, and other green earthenware from Atzompa line the stone steps, as do ice cream vendors and fruit, vegetable, and *cal* (lime) sellers. Men hawk their wares with and without microphones, selling buckets, blankets, clothes, and burro saddles; they even tell the crowd they have just the right herbal potion to give vitality. On the steps to the market women are selling red *gusanos de maguey* (worms), alive and wiggling, or dried, toasted, and ground with salt and chile. Local women display baskets of fried *chapulines* (grasshoppers) that are caught in the local alfalfa and corn fields.

At the main entrance to the Etla market sits Carmen Campos, an appropriate name for a woman who grows and sells her own vegetable and herb seeds. She also sells local spices and herbs, ashes to soften dried corn for *nixtamal,* and beautiful braids of tiny garlic bulbs. Cecilia, a young woman with blond hair and green eyes, has the big garlic heads I like. Maricela, the medicinal herb lady, has dried and fresh plants to cure every ill, from diabetes to heartburn. She sits on the floor, her straw mat covered with special charms to protect children from the evil eye, Buddhas for good luck, and mysterious powders that promise to help you achieve your desires. The packages of herbs are illustrated with before and after shots of the "cure"! One of the healthiest habits of Oaxaqueños is to drink fresh fruit blends or vegetable tonics made with water or milk. The juice lady makes concoctions of fruits and vegetables in any combination requested: people tell her what hurts and she has just the right mixture for them. I usually get the alfalfa drink for energy, an example of the natural curing and preventative medicine that is quite common here.

Going down the next aisle, one finds the *atoles*: *de granillo*, *de panela*, and *champurrado* (the special corn gruel made with chocolate). At the end of the aisle are the *tamal* stands. All major varieties are represented, plus a *tamal* with squash flowers and ground herbs mixed in the dough. The combination of *atole* and *tamales* for an early-morning breakfast has been the tradition here since pre-Hispanic times.

I always buy my chickens from Carmelita Pérez, because she raises them from chicks and is gentle with them. People always ask me why the chickens are so yellow here. It's because the chicks are fed chicken feed that is dyed with marigold coloring. There is truth to the saying "You are what you eat." (Eric and I grew marigolds as a cash crop for about two years, but it wasn't much of a money-maker, although the ranch did look beautiful in orange.) Next to Carmelita is the cheese area. I buy from four different women, just to spread the money around a bit. The first is Juanita, from Reyes, Etla, with *quesillo*, *queso*, squash seeds, *mole* paste, and tostadas. The next two young women are substitutes, because their mothers are sick and haven't come for a few weeks. I buy cheeses from them and another from Minerva, and send my *saludos* to the sick ones. All these women make their cheese from their own cows' milk. Almost everyone in the valley of Etla has cows, either to sell the milk or to make cheese. Down this aisle, natural rennet from the cow's stomach and woven palm or plastic cheese molds are also sold.

On the sweeter side, Neveria Angelita sells the best ice cream in the whole valley. The oldest lady, Angelita, is the *jefa* (boss). Her daughters and granddaughters help dish out the ices made from *tuna*, lime, pecan, burnt milk, and *rompope*. Dulcerías de Etla has a stand on the corner near the ice cream. Owner Señora Lidia has been making *dulces* such as *conos de lechecilla*, *casquito* (meringue in a cookie crust), and *borrachos* (bright red with a mezcal syrup) for over twenty years in her bakery down the street.

At the end of the row are Candelaria, Juana, and Justina, who are all related and are from San Juan Guelache. They have an assortment of goodies: *limalimones*, *guayabas*, limes, watercress, *chepiches*, and *plátanos*. They are the "gatherer" merchants. The other gatherers have *limas*, peaches, and nectarines from their trees and *epazote*, *chepiles*, and tiny native potatoes from the mountains. Josefina is here with *chiles de agua*, tomatoes, and *tomatillos*. I have known her since she started buying chiles from Eric, when he grew *chiles de agua*. Across the aisle are the *barbacoa* stands. Rosenda has both lamb and goat *barbacoa* slathered with chile paste. Her *consomé* (a goat broth) and *masa* (rough-ground corn steamed with the meat when it is cooked in a pit in the ground) accompany the meat tacos she sells.

Near the west entrance, women from Guacamaya—Inés Pérez and Guadalupe Ruíz—sell fresh flowers, bay leaves, chiles, watercress, *picapájaro* (a flower grown for bird feed), and *poleo* (Oaxacan savory). *Poleo* is an important herb, always given to guests when they arrive at a *fiesta*. Legend has it that if it is carried throughout the party, one can drink all one wants and never get drunk. Of course, it is also the cure

Bread assortment at Mercado de Abastos, Oaxaca City (Alfredo Díaz Mora)

for a hangover. On a table to the right, Jovita makes *tejate*. She's from San Andres Huayapan, on the other side of Oaxaca City, a lovely pueblo known for this special drink. It is here that the aromatic *rosita de cacao* flower is grown. Jovita's concoction is made from cacao, dried corn, mamey seed (a salmon-colored fruit shaped like a football), *rosita de cacao*, and wood ash. I always say that this pre-Hispanic drink kept the race alive because of its nutritional value.

Amalia and Eufrocinia Morales, in a corner grocery store in the market, look as if their picture should be on a jar of hot sauce. They are so pretty and healthy looking—they owe it all to homeopathic medicine, they tell me. Their store, Abarrotes General, has cooking oil, vinegar, canned goods, chiles, liquor, salt, nuts, sugar, eggs, cereal, and other dry goods. Then, up a short flight of steps, are long boards and huge baskets of bread on one side of the room and small *fondas* (restaurants) lining the opposite wall. The breads of Etla are fascinating, indeed. *Pan de manteca*, *mollete*s made with *piloncillo, pan de yema* (egg bread), and all kinds of *pan dulce* are found here, but my favorite is the *hojaldra*, in the shape of a bunny. In my village, people always ask "*¿Adónde vas?*" ("Where are you going?"). When I say, "Etla," I receive the standard reply, "Bring me a bunny."

Before I leave I always have a snack with Conchita Cástellanos González at her *fonda*. Conchita boasts that she has fed my kids even while they were still in the womb, and continues to do so now. Her beans are wonderful, as well as her *entomatadas*.

All of the markets in the Central Valleys have their own special charm, but this particular market has a hometown feeling for me. All week long I look forward to Wednesdays and my shopping excursion in the Etla market.

IN THIS CHAPTER

SOPA DE TORTILLA
Country-Style Tortilla Soup

Tortilla soup is one of those great examples from the "land of no waste," my nick-name for Mexico. As the soft tortilla (blanda) ages, it needs to be eaten, so it is fried and used in other dishes such as tortilla soup or chilaquiles. This is recycling at its best, using old tortillas and adding a broth or sauce and fresh garnishes. The tortilla becomes reborn with a new identity, flavor, and name. In Oaxaca, I have had tortilla soup two ways—this version and another with a brown bean puree as the base.

MAKES 6 TO 8 SERVINGS

1¼ pounds tomatoes (3 medium–large round or 10–13 plum)

½ cup peanut, sunflower, or vegetable oil

4–6 tortillas, cut into strips (about 2 cups)

1 medium white onion, chopped

½ head of garlic, cloves separated and finely chopped

12 cups well-flavored chicken stock (page 343)

Salt and pepper to taste

10 chiles chipotles en adobo (page 332)

1 Haas avocado, peeled and cut into chunks

¼ pound queso fresco, cut into ½-inch chunks (see page 346; manchego or Muenster may be substituted)

1 cup shredded poached chicken

½ cup finely chopped cilantro leaves

On a 10-inch dry *comal*, griddle, or in a cast-iron frying pan, roast the tomatoes over medium heat 10 to 12 minutes until soft and the skin starts to slough off. Allow to cool, then peel and discard the skins. Puree the tomatoes in the blender until smooth.

Heat the oil in an 8-inch cast-iron frying pan until it smokes. Add the tortilla strips. Fry for 3 to 5 minutes over medium heat or until brown, and drain on paper towels. Remove the remaining oil, reserving 2 tablespoons.

Put the 2 tablespoons oil in a heavy 4-quart stockpot and sauté the onion in the oil until clear, about 3 minutes. Add the garlic and continue to cook 2 minutes longer. Add the tomato puree and fry well, about 10 minutes.

Add the chicken stock, lower the heat to a simmer, and cook, covered, for ½ hour. Add salt and pepper.

Put *chile chipotle*, a few avocado chunks, some cheese cubes, shredded chicken, chopped cilantro, and fried tortilla strips in each bowl. Add the soup and serve.

CALDO DE GATO
Clear Beef Broth with Summer Vegetables

It's Thursday, market day in Zaachila, one of the most traditional Zapotec villages in the Central Valleys. We have a favorite fonda (restaurant) in the market where I enjoy this Caldo de Gato. Although cat (gato) meat is not used, there are big chunks of beef and lots of vegetables cooked in the light broth. Many cooks add the chile pasilla oaxaqueño right to the soup; this fonda serves the traditional salsa de chile pasilla (page 151) on the side and lots of fresh lime halves.

MAKES 8 SERVINGS

For the broth:

1 pound stewing beef, cut into
    chunks
1 pound beef bones
1 medium white onion, quartered
1 small head of garlic
3 bay leaves

For the vegetables:

¼ pound dried garbanzo beans
    soaked overnight or canned
    (if canned, omit the baking soda
    and add at the end of the
    cooking time)
Pinch of baking soda
½ medium white onion, chunked
½ head of garlic, cloves separated
    and finely chopped
1 pound husked corn on the cob,
    cut into thick rounds (8 pieces)
4 carrots, cut into lengthwise strips
2 chayotes, cut into long wedges
    (see page 326)
1 pound small potatoes
½ pound green beans, cut into
    3-inch pieces

FOR THE BROTH:
Put the beef, beef bones, onion, garlic, and bay leaves in a heavy 4-quart stockpot or *olla* with 3 quarts of water. Bring to a boil over high heat. Skim off the foam that rises to the top, lower the heat, and simmer, covered, for 2 hours or until the beef is tender. Remove and discard the bones. Keep broth with beef warm.

FOR THE VEGETABLES:
In a 2-quart saucepan, cook the dried garbanzo beans with the baking soda in 1 quart of water for 20 minutes over moderate heat. Drain and place some of the beans on one half of a terry cloth towel. Fold the towel over the beans and rub vigorously. The skins will separate from the beans. Remove the skins and discard. Repeat with remaining beans. Rinse the beans in cold water. Put the garbanzos, onion, garlic, and 2 quarts of water in a large saucepan. Bring to a boil over high heat, then reduce heat to a simmer, cover, and cook for 1½ hours or until beans are almost soft. (If using canned garbanzos, skip this step.)

Drain the garbanzos, add them to the stockpot, and cook over low heat for ½ hour. Add the corn, carrots, chayotes, potatoes, beans, and tomatoes to the broth. If using canned garbanzos, rinse them well, then add to the broth. Simmer for 20 minutes. Add the *hierbabuena*, cilantro, salt, and pepper. Serve with limes.

¼ pound tomatoes (3–4 plum),
  peeled and chopped
¼ cup hierbabuena leaves
  (see page 336)
¼ cup cilantro leaves
2 tablespoons salt, or to taste
1 tablespoon black pepper
4 limes, cut into halves or wedges,
  depending on size

Hint: If you use hybrid sweet corn, add it 10 minutes after you put in the carrots and other vegetables.

MOLOTES
Spicy Fried Corn Masa Fritters

Every evening at 6 P.M. under the big clock that towers over the taxi stand in San Lorenzo Cacaotepec, Raquel García comes out to sell her molotes. *They are fried on the spot in a big cauldron of oil set over large chunks of* carbón. *My respect for her increased tenfold when I tried to make them for the first time. Serve a few for a light supper with rice, or one or two as a* botana, *or snack, with a cold beer.*

MAKES 16 *MOLOTES*

For the fritters:
1 chile guajillo, *stemmed (see
  page 331)*
1 whole allspice
2 black peppercorns
¼ pound chorizo, *casings removed
  (see page 342)*
¼ medium white onion, *finely
  chopped*
3 garlic cloves, *finely chopped*
½ pound potatoes, *cooked in their
  skins, peeled, and mashed*
Salt *(about ¼ teaspoon)*
1 pound prepared masa *for tortillas or 1¾ cups* masa harina
  for tortillas

FOR THE FRITTERS:
Bring ½ cup water to a boil. Prepare the *chile guajillo* by wiping it off with a damp cloth, then toast it on a hot, dry *comal* or heavy griddle until it browns, blisters a bit, and gives off its scent. Place it in the hot water to soak for 10 minutes. Meanwhile, on the same hot *comal*, toast the allspice and peppercorns. Grind the allspice and peppercorns in a *molcajete*, or blender, then add the chile and grind into a paste. (You can do this all together in a blender if you wish.)

In an 8-inch cast-iron frying pan, fry the chorizo over medium heat until dry. If there is not enough fat in the chorizo, you can add 1 teaspoon oil so it won't stick. Drain if there is excess fat. Add the onion and fry until clear, about 5 minutes. Add the garlic and continue frying a minute more. Add the chile paste and stir in well with a wooden spoon. Add the mashed potatoes and mix well. Add salt to taste. Set aside to cool.

(continued)

For black bean sauce:

2 chiles de árbol *(see page 330)*

1 avocado leaf *(hoja de aguacate; see page 338)*

1 cup cooked Frijoles Negros de Olla *with broth, pureed in blender (page 146)*

1 tablespoon sunflower or vegetable oil

2 tablespoons finely chopped white onion

Salt

To assemble:

1½ cups sunflower, corn, or peanut oil, for frying

12–14 lettuce leaves

1 cup finely shredded green cabbage

Salsa de guacamole *(page 57)*

½ cup queso fresco, queso ranchero, *or another crumbly cheese (see page 346)*

If using prepared *masa*, massage the dough until soft, adding a few drops of water so it doesn't "crack" when you knead it. Add a bit of salt to taste. If using *masa harina*, mix the *harina* with 1 cup plus 2 tablespoons warm water to make a soft dough. Add salt to taste and allow the dough to sit and rest 15 minutes, covered with a damp cloth.

Roll the *masa* into 16 balls, flatten them out to form thick disks, and cover with a damp cloth. Press them out between two sheets of plastic in a tortilla press, if you have one, or spread them out evenly with your fingertips or the heel of your hand until they are 5 inches in diameter and ⅛ inch thick. Remove the top sheet of plastic from the tortilla. Lay it gently on top of the tortilla and invert the tortilla, leaving the plastic on both sides. Peel off the plastic on top and place 1 table-spoon of the chorizo mixture onto the middle of the circle and spread it out in a rectangular shape in the center of the tortilla, leaving 1 inch on either end. Fold down the sides of the tortilla and envelop the mixture in the remaining tortilla dough. Pick up the *molote* from the plastic, place it between both of your hands, and roll the *molote* back and forth between your palms and fingertips to make an oblong fritter with pointed ends and a fat middle. Score the *molote* with a knife with two or three diagonal slashes on each side. Repeat with the remaining disks. Add a little water, if needed, as the dough dries out.

FOR THE BLACK BEAN SAUCE:
Toast the *chiles de árbol* and avocado leaf on a dry *comal*, frying pan, or griddle 3 to 5 minutes, over low heat, until they start to brown and give off their aromas. Hold the avocado leaf by the stem and crumble both sides of the leaf into a blender. Discard the stem. Add the chiles and grind for a few seconds, then add the beans and the bean liquid. Puree well.

In a medium frying pan, heat the oil and fry the onion until clear, about 5 minutes. Add the bean puree and heat through for 5 minutes. Add salt to taste. Keep warm.

TO ASSEMBLE:
Heat the oil in a large frying pan until smoking hot. Fry the *molotes* until they float and are golden brown in color, about 8 to 10 minutes. Remove them from the pan and drain on paper towels.

To serve, place each *molote* on a lettuce leaf and spread 1 tablespoon of the black bean sauce on top. Top with a vertical pinch of shredded cabbage and drizzle *salsa de guacamole* on top. Sprinkle the cheese over all and serve immediately.

CALABAZAS HORNEADAS
Baked Squash with Chiles, Corn, and Cream

This combination of corn, squash, chiles, and cream is a comfort food for me, and this method is one of my favorite ways to make it. It is best eaten in corn tortillas as a taco filling served with soup for a light supper. It is also a good dish to serve with Liebre en Adobo (page 176) or Albóndigas Estilo Ejutla (page 29), as the cream and the sweetness of the corn help cut the intensity of those chile-based sauces.

MAKES 6 TO 8 SERVINGS

5 ears fresh corn on the cob

3 chiles poblanos (see page 329)

2½ medium white onions, thinly sliced

2 tablespoons butter

1 pound calabaza, cut into 1-inch wedges (see page 325), or zucchini, cut in half lengthwise, then into wedges

13 garlic cloves, finely chopped

36 flor de calabaza (see page 326)

2 sprigs epazote, leaves only, or 2 teaspoons dried (see page 336)

1 cup Mexican crema (see page 345), crème fraîche, or sour cream

Salt and ground white pepper to taste

½ pound queso fresco, crumbled, or quesillo, manchego, or Muenster cheese (see pages 345 and 346), grated

Remove the kernels from the corncobs and reserve the cobs. You should have about 3 cups of kernels. Put the cobs in a 4-quart stockpot with 1 quart of water. Bring to a boil and reduce the heat to medium. Cook for 30 minutes. Strain the stock.

Grill the chiles over an open flame until they are charred. Put them in a plastic bag to sweat, about 5 minutes. When the chiles are cool enough to handle, peel off their skins and discard. Do not rinse the chiles with water or you will wash the oil off and reduce the flavor. Cut the chiles into ¼-inch strips, or *rajas*.

Preheat the oven to 350°F.

In a 4-quart heavy stockpot, *cazuela*, or deep cast-iron frying pan over medium heat, fry the onions in the butter until transparent, about 2 minutes. Add the corn kernels, squash wedges, and garlic. Continue frying for 10 minutes, stirring occasionally.

Add the chiles and cook for 10 minutes longer.

Gently stir 1 cup of the corn stock into the corn-chile mixture.

Add the *flor de calabaza* and *epazote*, and cook for 5 minutes longer. Add the *crema* and season with salt and pepper.

(continued)

Top with the cheese and bake for 15 minutes. Serve with fresh hot tortillas.

Hint: You can make this in a deep frying pan, then transfer the mixture to an ovenproof casserole, top with the cheese, and bake; or just add the cheese, cover the pan, and simmer 15 minutes on top of the stove.

TACOS DE HUITLACOCHE
Corn Fungus Tacos

Every year during the rainy season, we look in the corn patches for signs of huitlacoche. *This is a corn fungus with a subtle musty, earthy taste that is quite delicious. In the village, the family of Chico Machine, his wife Paula, their children, and grandchildren all live in the compound of his mother, Señora Vicenta Vásquez Ramírez, who is one of the best foragers I know. She taught me this dish and the sauce, which nearly knocked my socks off. Instead of the* salsa de chile piquín, *you could use* salsa de chilito verde *(page 175).*

MAKES 6 SERVINGS

2 ears fresh huitlacoche *(see page 320; see Hint) or 4 cups canned*

3 ears fresh corn on the cob

2 tablespoons sunflower or vegetable oil

¾ cup finely chopped white onion

15 garlic cloves, finely chopped

1 cup mint leaves, tightly packed

Salt

12 soft corn tortillas, 8 inches in diameter

For the salsa de chile piquín:

1 tablespoon sunflower or vegetable oil

13 garlic cloves

Scrape the *huitlacoche* kernels off the cobs with a knife, as you would fresh corn; you should have about 4 cups kernels. Place on a cutting board and chop finely. Scrape the kernels off the regular cobs with a knife; you should have about 2 cups kernels.

In a 12-inch cast-iron frying pan, heat the oil over medium heat. Add the onion and fry until transparent, about 5 minutes. Add the fresh corn, *huitlacoche*, and garlic and sauté about 20 minutes. Add the mint and continue to cook, covered, for 10 minutes. Add salt to taste. Serve the *huitlacoche* in a bowl with hot, soft tortillas on the side, or roll the *huitlacoche* into the tortillas and serve individually prepared.

FOR THE *SALSA DE CHILE PIQUÍN*:

In a small frying pan, heat the oil over medium heat. Add the garlic cloves and fry until garlic is clear, about 2 minutes. Add the chiles and cook for 1 minute longer.

Mash the mixture in a *molcajete* or blender. Add salt to taste and the lime juice. Mix in a few drops of water.

2 tablespoons chile piquín (see
    page 331)
Salt
1 tablespoon lime juice

Caution: This sauce is extremely hot and will go straight up
your throat and into your head with the heat! Serve sauce
with the *huitlacoche*, hot corn tortillas, and eggs for a
summer breakfast.

Hints: The fresh *huitlacoche* must be dry and grayish white.
If it is already black and wet, it is too far gone. If unavailable,
you can substitute canned or frozen (see Sources). The corn
mix keeps well in the refrigerator once cooked.

To use the corn mix as a squash filling for a vegetarian
course, hollow out a *criolla* or zucchini squash and blanch
the shell in salted water until tender, about 5 minutes.
Chop the squash pulp and fry in a little butter for 5 minutes, then add the *huitlacoche* mixture. Stuff the squash and
top with manchego cheese. Bake at 400°F for 15 minutes.

TLAYUDAS CON FRIJOLES
Giant Black Bean Tostadas

The giant, well-cooked tortillas of Oaxaca are still called by their pre-Hispanic name,
tlayudas. Tlayudas *are cooked longer than the soft* blanda *tortillas, and are not as cooked
and crispy as tostadas. The flavor of the* asiento *(leftover* chicharrón *drippings) permeates
this dish, giving it a unique flavor.* Tlayudas *are one of the most popular snacks in Oaxaca.*

MAKES 8 LARGE *TLAYUDAS*

For the bean paste:
9 avocado leaves (hoja de agua-
    cate), *fresh or dried (see
    page 338), or 1 tablespoon
    ground aniseed*
9 chiles de árbol *(see page 330),
    stemmed, seeded, and deveined,
    or dried Chinese or Thai chiles*
2½ cups Frijoles Negros de Olla
    with their juice (page 146)
Salt

FOR THE BEAN PASTE:
Toast the avocado leaves and the *chiles de árbol* on a 10-inch
dry *comal*, griddle, or in a cast-iron frying pan 3 to 5 minutes
over low heat until they start to brown and give off their
aromas. Hold the avocado leaves by the stem and crumble
both sides of the leaves into a blender. Discard the stems.
Add the chiles. Grind for a few seconds and then add the
beans and the bean liquid. Puree well. Add salt to taste.
Set aside.

(continued)

For the salsa verde:

½ *pound* tomatillos *(5–6 medium), husks removed*

½ *small white onion, chunked*

3 *chiles jalapeños or 7 chiles serranos (see page 329)*

2 *garlic cloves*

1 *small bunch of cilantro, about 17 sprigs*

1 *teaspoon salt*

½ *teaspoon sugar*

For the tlayudas:

8 *tlayudas, 12 inches in diameter, or tostadas*

5 *tablespoons* asiento *(see page 342) or bacon drippings (optional)*

2 *cups shredded or crumbled* quesillo *or* queso fresco *(see pages 345 and 346), or Muenster, Monterey Jack, or fresh mozzarella*

2 *cups thinly shredded green cabbage*

FOR THE *SALSA VERDE:*

In a 2-quart saucepan over high heat, boil the *tomatillos* in ½ cup water until they change color, about 15 minutes. Place the *tomatillos* with their cooking liquid in a blender with the onion, chiles, garlic, cilantro, salt, and sugar. Blend well. Set aside.

FOR THE *TLAYUDAS:*

In a 2-quart saucepan, heat the bean puree over medium heat until it starts to bubble, then remove from heat. On a 10-inch dry *comal*, griddle, or in a cast-iron frying pan, over medium heat, heat a *tlayuda* on both sides, rotating it every 30 seconds so it won't burn. When it's hot, quickly spread 2 teaspoons of the *asiento* over the top of the *tlayuda*. Then spread 4 tablespoons of the bean paste on top of the *asiento*, followed by ¼ cup of the cheese. When the cheese starts to melt, remove the *tlayuda* from the griddle and top with ¼ cup of the cabbage. Make remaining *tlayudas*. Spoon *salsa verde* over the top and serve immediately.

Hint: You can serve the *tlayudas* with *salsa de chile de árbol* (page 57) or *salsa de guacamole* (page 57), or a combination of the two sauces.

EMPANADAS DE BETABEL
Savory Beet and Corn Turnovers

The beets here in Mexico have an exceptional taste. Being a die-hard beet fan from my borscht days, I got excited when I heard about Doña Josefa Sánchez's beet empanadas. Every weekend she and Don Elías turn their country home in San Agustín Etla into a restaurant for pork carnitas and empanadas filled with mushrooms or beets. They can be made with or without cheese.

For the filling:

1 pound beets, trimmed of leaves
    and up to 1 inch of stem

1 medium white onion, finely
    chopped

1 tablespoon sunflower or vegetable
    oil

1 tablespoon butter

1 tablespoon finely chopped garlic

1 cup corn kernels (from 2 ears)

1 teaspoon salt, or to taste

1 teaspoon ground black pepper

½ cup fresh epazote leaves (see
    page 336) or 3 tablespoons dried
    or fresh parsley

10 ounces quesillo, shredded, or
    manchego, Gouda, or Muen-
    ster cheese (see page 345), grated

For the masa:

1½ pounds prepared masa for tor-
    tillas, or 3 cups masa harina for
    tortillas

¾ teaspoon salt

FOR THE FILLING:

In a 2-quart saucepan, heat 2 cups water and bring to a boil. Add the beets, making sure there is enough water to cover. Cook for 50 minutes or until tender. Drain and set aside to cool. Peel the beets when they are still warm. Chop them finely and set aside.

In an 8-inch cast-iron frying pan over medium heat, fry the onion in the oil and butter for 5 minutes. Add the garlic and cook for 5 minutes. Add the corn kernels and cook for 10 minutes. Add the beets, salt, pepper, and *epazote*. Cook for 15 minutes. Set aside.

FOR THE *MASA*:

Preheat a 10-inch *comal*, griddle, or cast-iron frying pan over medium heat.

If using fresh *masa*, break up the *masa* in a mixing bowl with your fingers. Knead the *masa* with salt and add 6 table-spoons warm water, if needed, to make a soft dough. If using *masa harina*, mix the *masa harina* with 1¾ cups warm water to make a soft but not dry dough. Cover with a damp cloth and allow the dough to rest 15 minutes. Add 6 table-spoons warm water and the salt. Knead for about 1 minute to make a soft even dough.

Divide the dough into 10 balls. Shape each ball into a log 5 inches long and 1½ inches wide. Place a log between two sheets of plastic placed inside a tortilla press and press down; an oval shape will appear. If you don't have a tortilla press, spread the log out evenly with your hand and create the same dimensions. Rotate the oval and press again. Remove the plastic from the top and place 3 to 4 tablespoons of cheese in the middle. Top with 2½ tablespoons of the beet filling. Place a little bit of water around the edge of the tor-tilla with your finger, fold the empanada over, and press to seal it closed. Lift the empanada from the plastic and place in the middle of the *comal*, griddle, or frying pan. Cook 3 to 5 minutes on each side, until it starts to brown and removes easily from the *comal* without breaking. Turn it over and cook on the second side.

Serve at once. Continue making the balls until the *masa* is gone. If you must, keep them warm by wrapping them completely in a cloth napkin until serving time.

SALSA DE QUESO DE ROSA MATADAMAS

Rosa Matadamas's Fresh Cheese in Tomato Sauce

A student at our Long Weekend Bed & Breakfast course wrote me, "Of all the tastes I remember from the trip, it's Rosa's Salsa de Queso that haunts me in my dreams." Rosa is our neighbor and a cheese maker who produces a wonderful pressed queso fresco. *She prepared this dish for me several years ago, while I was mixing a cake for her daughter Laura's fifteenth birthday, which is a huge* celebración *in Mexico. As I was beating enough batter by hand to make a birthday cake for 350 people, Rosa invited me to sit down and eat* almuerzo, *a late, but hearty breakfast. My mixing arm was numb, but still I managed to lift the tortilla to my lips. It was so simple, so pure, and a wonderful way to present her cheese.*

MAKES 6 SERVINGS

4½ pounds tomatoes (9 medium–large round or 32–36 plum)

2 large chiles de agua (see page 328)

2 tablespoons sunflower or vegetable oil

½ medium white onion, finely chopped

Salt

12 ounces queso prensado, queso fresco, or fresh mozzarella cheese, cut into 1-inch-thick wedges (see page 346; see Hint)

2 sprigs epazote, leaves only, or 2 teaspoons dried (see page 336)

Corn tortillas

On a dry *comal*, in a cast-iron frying pan, or on a griddle, blacken the tomatoes over medium heat. Turn the tomatoes in the pan every few minutes until all sides are blackened and the tomatoes soften, about 20 minutes. Set aside to cool. (We always roast the tomatoes directly on the coals if there is a fire handy.)

Grill the chiles in the same way, 5 to 10 minutes, taking care not to burn the delicate chiles. Remove the chiles from the heat and place them immediately in a plastic bag or under the lid of a pot to "sweat." When the chiles are cool enough to handle, peel them and discard the peel, seeds, and stems.

Peel the blackened skins from the tomatoes and discard. Place the chiles and tomatoes in a blender and coarsely grind.

In a 4-quart heavy pot or deep cast-iron frying pan, heat the oil over medium heat. When the oil is hot, add the onion and fry about 5 minutes, stirring constantly so that the onion does not brown. Add the tomato and chile puree and simmer for 5 minutes, stirring often. Add salt to taste. Add the cheese wedges to the sauce and cook for 5 minutes more over low heat, covered. Add the *epazote*, remove from the heat, and serve in shallow bowls with tortillas, torn in pieces and used as spoons.

Hint: You cannot use *queso fresco* that has been made that day or it will fall apart in the sauce. It must be at least one day old or have been pressed for at least three hours.

ENTOMATADAS
Cortillas Dipped in Spicy Tomato Sauce with Fresh Cheese

One of Eric's partners in his tomato-growing operation in 1993 was Chucho Cruz, from Jalapa de Valle. The harvest days back then were memorable. Chucho's wife Rafaela would meet me in the campo *(field) and make food to serve all the workers for* comida *(midday meal). I have a vivid recollection of standing in the field under a tree, the wind blowing from the east while we assembled the* entomatadas *that had been made from tomatoes just picked, stewed on the spot, and ground by hand on the stone* metate. *These meals in the* campo *have been some of the best I have ever eaten in Oaxaca. Serve these* entomatadas *with Frijoles Negros de Olla (page 146) and a fried egg for breakfast or, for a heartier meal, with a piece of grilled* tasajo *(page 342), cecina (page 342), or chicken. I also serve just one* entomatada *as an appetizer.*

MAKES 8 SERVINGS

For the salsa:

- 2 pounds ripe tomatoes (4 medium–large round or 16–20 plum)
- 4 chiles de árbol, *seeded and stemmed (see page 330)*
- 1 piece of Mexican cinnamon, *2 inches long (see page 337)*
- 1 whole allspice
- 3 black peppercorns
- ½ teaspoon cumin seeds (optional)
- 1½ tablespoons lard, sunflower oil, *or vegetable oil*
- 1 medium white onion, diced

FOR THE SALSA:

Peel the tomatoes by making an x on the bottom of each and cooking them in 1 quart boiling water for about 4 minutes. Remove them from the pot and let them cool. Reserve the water. Remove the tomato skins and discard.

Toast the chiles on a 10-inch dry *comal*, griddle, or in a cast-iron frying pan over medium heat, turning once. When their scent is released and they are toasted, place them to soak in the leftover tomato water about 5 minutes, or until they are soft. Toast the cinnamon stick, allspice, peppercorns, and cumin seeds on the *comal* briefly so they don't burn but their flavor is enhanced. Set them aside to cool.

Grind the tomatoes on a *metate* (or in a blender), adding ½ cup of the tomato water. Grind the soaked chiles and spices in the *molcajete* or blender using ¼ cup of the tomato water. Add to the tomato mixture. *(continued)*

1 small head of garlic, cloves
     separated and minced
Pinch of piloncillo or brown sugar
     (see page 348)
1 sprig Oaxacan oregano, or
     1 teaspoon dried (see page 336)
1 bay leaf
Salt

To prepare entomatadas:
3 tablespoons sunflower or
     vegetable oil
16 corn tortillas
8 ounces queso fresco (see
     page 346), crumbled
1 medium white onion, halved
     and thinly sliced
8 sprigs flat-leaf parsley, leaves
     only

Heat the lard or oil until smoking in a deep 8-inch heavy frying pan over medium-high heat. Add the onion and fry until transparent. Add the garlic and cook for 5 minutes. Add the tomato mixture, then the sugar, oregano, and bay leaf. Stir once or twice, and heat the sauce for about 5 minutes, until reduced somewhat. Add salt to taste.

TO PREPARE ENTOMATADAS:
In an 8-inch cast-iron frying pan, heat the oil and fry each tortilla quickly until soft, then turn over with tongs to fry on both sides and drain; do not fry the tortillas too long, or they will harden.

Place each tortilla in the tomato sauce and coat both sides with sauce. Place it on a plate and fold it in half, then in half again to make a triangle. Repeat so that each serving has two tortillas. Spoon a bit more sauce on top, then garnish each plate with some crumbled cheese, onion slices, and parsley leaves.

Hint: In Oaxaca, the tortillas are not fried because fresh hot tortillas are available. These fresh tortillas are made from *nixtamal* and can be folded and put in the sauce without falling apart. Tortillas made with *masa harina* will fall apart if they are not fried first.

Offering tejate *in the market in* Ocotlán (Marcela Taboada)

TAMALES DE MOLE AMARILLO
Yellow Mole Tamales

I first ate these tamales when we were invited to the house of Hermilio Ruíz Mendoza, a rug weaver from Teotitlán del Valle, to celebrate Día de Muertos. His wife, Ana María, took me upstairs to her roof kitchen, where she had a huge vat simmering over a charcoal fire. She lifted the lid to show me the tamales—and what an aroma hit me in the face! There was the scent: of the "fresh cooked tamal" as well as the green corn scent from the leaves that enclosed each tamal. I held a huge clay platter for her as she piled them before me. As I unfolded my first tamal like a flag, I noticed the finely ground masa and the chicken filling in mole amarillo. If you don't have corn growing nearby to cut fresh leaves, you may have to substitute dried cornhusks, available at Mexican specialty stores everywhere. Serve these with Chocolate de Agua (page 281) or Atole de Maíz (page 160).

MAKES 12 *TAMALES*

12 fresh corn leaves or 2 packages dried cornhusks, soaked for ½ hour

1 pound prepared corn masa for tortillas or 2 cups masa harina for tortillas

¾ teaspoon salt, or more if needed

2½ cups boned and shredded cooked chicken

2¾ cups mole amarillo (½ recipe, page 346)

Soak the corn leaves or cornhusks in warm water to soften them, about 30 minutes.

If using prepared *masa*, break it up with your fingers in a mixing bowl. Mix the *masa* with the salt and massage well with sufficient water to make a soft dough. Mix the dough with your hands until the dough is soft. If using *masa harina*, mix in a mixing bowl with 1¼ cups warm water until the dough is soft; let the dough rest 15 minutes.

Divide the *masa* into 12 balls about 1½ inches in diameter. Cover with a damp cloth.

Fill a steamer with salted water to the level of the rack and bring to a boil over high heat.

Remove the corn leaves or cornhusks from the water and dry them off with a cloth. Using a tortilla press with two pieces of plastic wrap (a plastic bag cut in half is best), press out the balls. If you do not have a tortilla press, you can flatten the dough between two sheets of plastic by using the heel of your hand. Press once, then make a quarter turn and make another press. Remove the top piece of plastic from

Selecting onions at Mercado de Abastos, Oaxaca City (Stephen Honeybill)

the *masa*, lay it lightly back on the *masa*, and turn it over. Remove the second piece of plastic and set aside. Hold the "tortilla" in your left hand (still on the piece of plastic) and put two or three little pieces of chicken right in the middle. Spoon a generous amount of sauce on top and fold the top third down over the filling. Fold the bottom third up and you should have a long rectangular tortilla.

If using the corn leaf, lay the *tamal* seam side down on the wide end of the leaf, leaving a border about 1 inch wide. Fold the leaf over lengthwise to cover the *tamal*. Make a quarter turn with the remaining leaf and wrap the *tamal* to completely enclose it, then tuck in the pointed end of the leaf to secure. If using cornhusks, blot 30 husks dry with a tea towel. Shred 6 cornhusks into ½-inch ties and tie them together in pairs. Lay two husks together, wide end to wide end, and place on the table horizontally. Place each *tamal* seam side down in the middle of the husks. Fold one side down to cover the *tamal*, then the other side up to completely enclose it. Fold in the pointed ends to overlap, then secure with the ties. Repeat with the rest of the *masa*, chicken, and filling.

Cover the steamer rack with the extra husks or leaves, and place the *tamales* on the rack. Cover tightly and weigh the lid down with a heavy object to keep it snugly closed. Steam over a slow rolling boil for about an hour, or when the *tamal* falls easily from the husk and "smells like *tamales*." Serve hot.

CHILES RELLENOS DE PICADILLO
Stuffed Fresh Green Chiles Floating on a Light Tomato Sauce

My grandmother always told me that a good woman should know how to make a great chile relleno to keep a man happy. The first time I learned how to make one was not from her, but from Miguel Ravago, a chef in Austin, Texas. Even though I have changed the filling and chiles, I still owe the basic method and the batter recipe to the generosity of Miguel and his teachings. The idea of the sauce underneath comes from Patricia Chagoya of Oaxaca, who, after listening to me complain that my chiles rellenos were too oily, told me to make a caldillo underneath to catch the grease and offset the chiles. It works beautifully. This is one of my favorite dishes of all time. Serve with Arroz con Chepil (page 52) or Arroz Criollo Mexicano (page 299). You can use any extra picadillo for a taco filling or as a Memela topping (page 323).

MAKES 6 TO 7 SERVINGS, DEPENDING ON THE SIZE OF THE CHILES

For the chiles:
12–14 large chiles de agua, *or*
    6 chiles poblanos *(see page 329)*

For the picadillo:
2 tablespoons sunflower or
    vegetable oil
1 small white onion, halved and
    thinly sliced
5 garlic cloves, finely chopped
½ cup coarsely chopped tomato
Pinch of sugar
1½ cups shredded cooked chicken,
    pork, or beef
1½ tablespoons pitted and finely
    chopped green olives
1½ tablespoons raisins

FOR THE CHILES:
On an open fire or burner over medium heat, char the chiles until their skins are black and blistered, being careful not to burn the flesh. Remove the chiles from the heat and put them in a plastic bag to sweat, about 5 minutes. When the chiles are cool enough to handle, peel off their skins, taking care not to rip the flesh. Make a slit in the side and carefully remove the seeds with a small paring knife, keeping the chiles intact with the stems on. Do not rinse with water or you will wash the oil off and reduce the flavor.

FOR THE *PICADILLO*:
In an 8-inch cast-iron frying pan, heat the oil and fry the onion until transparent, about 5 minutes. Add the garlic and sauté a moment longer. Add the tomato and sugar; cook for 5 minutes. Add the shredded meat, and heat thoroughly over medium heat. Add the olives, raisins, almonds, capers, herbs, and cinnamon. Add the pepper and salt. Stir in the stock if needed to moisten the filling. Allow to cook for 5 minutes more, then let the mixture cool.

(continued)

1½ tablespoons toasted and finely
    chopped blanched almonds

1 tablespoon capers, either whole if
    small or chopped if large

1 small sprig fresh thyme, leaves
    only, or a pinch of dried

¼ cup finely chopped fresh parsley
    leaves

1 piece of Mexican cinnamon,
    1 inch long, toasted and ground
    (see page 337)

½ teaspoon ground black pepper

Pinch of salt

¼–½ cup chicken stock (page 343;
    optional)

For the tomato sauce:

2 pounds tomatoes (4–5
    medium–large round or
    16–20 plum)

¼ medium white onion, thickly
    sliced

3 garlic cloves

1 chile de árbol (see page 330)

1 tablespoon sunflower or vegetable
    oil

Salt to taste

1 tablespoon fresh epazote leaves,
    or 1 teaspoon dried (see page 336)

To assemble the chiles:

24 fresh epazote leaves (see
    page 336; optional)

½ cup flour, mixed with salt and
    pepper to taste

4 large eggs, at room temperature
    for at least 30 minutes

Pinch of salt

2½ cups peanut, sunflower, or
    vegetable oil

FOR THE TOMATO SAUCE:

On a 10-inch dry *comal*, griddle, or in a cast-iron frying pan, grill the tomatoes, onion, and garlic until the tomatoes blacken slightly and the onion and garlic become transparent. Toast the *chile de árbol* on the *comal* until it turns brown and gives off its scent, about 2 minutes.

Remove the tomato skins and discard. Put the tomatoes, onion, and garlic in a blender and puree until smooth.

Heat the oil until smoking in a heavy saucepan over medium heat. Fry the tomato mixture in the oil about 5 minutes, stirring with a wooden spoon. Add the chile to the sauce, lower the heat, stir once more, cover, and let the sauce simmer for 20 minutes. Add the salt and *epazote*.

TO ASSEMBLE THE CHILES:

Stuff the cleaned chiles with the *picadillo* mixture, being careful not to fill them too much so that they can close well without bulging. Line the inside seam with the *epazote* leaves to hold the filling in. Dredge the chiles in flour; shake off the excess flour. Press with your hands to seal the chiles shut.

Separate the egg yolks and whites into two bowls. Beat the whites with the salt with an electric mixer on high until stiff peaks form. Add the yolks all at once, and beat 30 seconds more or until the yolks are completely incorporated, no more.

Preheat the oven to 350°F.

In a large frying pan or wok, heat the oil until smoky. Pass each chile through the batter, holding on to the chile by the stem and covering it completely with batter. Place the chile directly in the pan and fry. With the back of a metal spatula, flick oil over the top of the chile to form its shape. Using two spatulas, turn carefully to cook on all sides. By holding the chile up on its side with the spatula, it will come out rounded, not flat. Remove from the pan and drain on paper towels. Keep warm in the oven. Continue to cook remaining chiles, one or two at a time.

Ladle ½ cup of the tomato sauce into each flat extended bowl. Place each chile over the sauce and serve.

ALBÓNDIGAS ESTILO EJUTLA
Meatballs Ejutla Style

I met Leticia Aragón Nuñez and her novio *Rodolfo through Eric's tomato farming. They would come to visit us on a Sunday, bringing along assorted ingredients, and we would spend hours in the kitchen cooking traditional dishes from Lety's hometown of Ejutla. She is modern and beautiful, but her food portrays an ancient past. One of her best dishes is these meatballs. We took turns grinding the meat mixture on the metate—a lot of physical work—to give it a well-ground consistency. You can do this in your blender or food processor, but try to let some sweat fall into the feed tube. It makes the food taste so much better! Serve with Arroz Blanco con Plátanos Fritos (page 53) and Calabazas Horneadas (page 17) and, of course, soft corn tortillas.*

MAKES 6 SERVINGS

For the meatballs:
½ teaspoon cumin seeds
3 whole cloves
3 whole allspice
3 black peppercorns
1 tablespoon minced garlic
Salt to taste
½ cup mint leaves
1½ pounds ground beef
2 eggs, beaten
¼ cup bread crumbs
Salt to taste, about 1 teaspoon
2 eggs, hard boiled and cut into
    small pieces
¼ cup sunflower or vegetable oil

FOR THE MEATBALLS:
On a 10-inch dry *comal*, griddle, or in a cast-iron frying pan, over medium heat, toast the cumin seeds, cloves, allspice, and peppercorns together quickly, until they give off their scents. Remove to a *molcajete* or spice grinder to cool. Grind the spices, then add the garlic and salt and continue to grind into a paste. Add the mint leaves and incorporate well into the mixture. You can do this in the blender if you like.

In a meat grinder or food processor, grind the meat fine with the spices. Remove to a bowl. Add the eggs and bread crumbs, mixing in well. Add the salt. Make meatballs of about 2 tablespoons of mixture and put a small piece of egg inside each one, making sure they are completely covered with the meat mixture.

Heat the oil in a deep, heavy 8-inch frying pan with a lid and fry some of the meatballs until browned, about 2 minutes. Remove them from the pan and set aside. Continue with the remaining meatballs until all of them are browned. Set pan aside.

(continued)

For the sauce:

7 chiles guajillos, *seeded,
    stemmed, and deveined (see
    page 331*

2 chiles pasillas oaxaqueños,
    *seeded, stemmed, and deveined
    (see page 331), or 3 chiles
    chipotles en adobo (page 332),
    or 3 dried chiles chipotles (see
    page 330)*

1½ *pounds* tomatillos *(15–18
    medium; see page 327)*

7 *garlic cloves*

1½ *teaspoons salt*

FOR THE SAUCE:

Bring 2 cups of water to a boil in a medium saucepan. On a
dry *comal*, toast the chiles on both sides until they blister and
give off their scent. Allow them to soak in the hot water
until soft, about 10 minutes. Boil the *tomatillos* in 3 cups of
water until they change color from a bright green to a dull
green. Put the chiles, *tomatillos*, and garlic in a blender and
blend well.

In the frying pan used to brown the meatballs, heat the
oil remaining in the pan or add an additional tablespoon, if
needed. When hot, pour the chile sauce through a strainer
and fry about 5 minutes. Return the meatballs to the sauce.
Lower the heat to a simmer, cover, and cook 25 minutes
longer. Serve.

Hint: These meatballs last a week and taste even better the
next day. They would also be good made smaller and served
at a cocktail buffet.

SEGUEZA DE CONEJO
Toasted Corn Stew with Rabbit

*Segueza is one of the pre-Hispanic stews still being made in Oaxaca. It is usually
served with pork and chicken, but I have eaten variations of the same dish with beef,
rabbit, and native red beans that grow wild mixed up in the cornstalks every
summer. If you don't have a neighbor who raises rabbits, you can use a combination
of pork ribs and chicken parts or just beef stewing meat and the stocks from each to
give it flavor. The corn has to have texture. If you do not have a* metate *or grain mill,
you can toast it first, then place it in the food processor and pulse it bit by bit. You
want to be careful not to turn it into corn flour, but to have real texture to the corn.
Serve this with Arroz con Chepil (page 52).*

For the rabbit stock:

2½ pounds of rabbit portioned into
  6 pieces, head reserved for stock

1 medium white onion

1 head of garlic

5 bay leaves

Salt to taste

3 tablespoons sunflower or vegetable oil

For the segueza:

4 chiles chilcostles, *stemmed and
  seeded (see page 330)*

4 chiles guajillos, *stemmed and
  seeded (see page 331)*

½ pound tomatoes
  (1 medium–large round or
  4–5 plum)

2 large tomatillos, *husks removed
  (see page 327)*

7 garlic cloves, *peeled*

3 black peppercorns

2 whole cloves

½ pound dried corn (maíz; *see
  page 320)*

1 tablespoon lard or sunflower oil

2 leaves hierba santa *(see
  page 336)*

1½–2 tablespoons salt

FOR THE STOCK:

Make a rabbit stock by placing the reserved rabbit head (if available), the onion, garlic, and bay leaves in a 6-quart stockpot with 3 quarts of water. Bring to a boil and add the rabbit pieces. Lower the heat to a simmer and cook for 1 hour, covered, until the meat is soft. Remove the onion and garlic.

FOR THE *SEGUEZA*:

In a small saucepan, bring about 3 cups of water to a boil. On a hot 10-inch dry *comal*, griddle, or in a cast-iron frying pan, roast the chiles on both sides over medium heat until they blister and give off their scent. Place them in a bowl and cover with the hot water to soften. Soak for 20 minutes.

On the same *comal*, roast the tomatoes and *tomatillos* until soft. Also roast the garlic until translucent. Add the peppercorns and cloves and toast quickly; set aside. With the *comal* or griddle empty, toast the corn until brown, moving it constantly with a wooden spoon for about 8 to 12 minutes. When it is puffed and toasted, remove the corn from the *comal* and set aside to cool completely.

When the chiles are soft, place them and the tomatoes, *tomatillos*, garlic, and spices in a blender with ¼ cup of the chile water and blend until smooth. Pass this mixture through a sieve or a food mill.

In an 8-inch cast-iron frying pan, heat the lard or oil until it smokes. Add the chile-tomato mixture and stir. Fry for 20 minutes, then add to the rabbit stock.

Grind the cooled corn kernels until coarse (like rough cornmeal) on a *metate*, in a *molcajete* (bit by bit), a hand grinder, or in a food processor, pulsing (see Hint). Add the corn and the *hierba santa* leaves to the rabbit mixture and cook until thickened, about 45 minutes. Add salt to taste.

Serve in wide bowls with fresh tortillas.

Hint: There is an attachment available for KitchenAid mixers that can grind corn coarsely.

PIPIÁN ROJO
Chicken and Vegetables in a Red Sesame Seed Sauce

Hermelinda Sánchez Santiago and her daughter have been working with our family for a few years. Of all the various jobs Hermelinda does, she loves gardening most of all. Once in a blue moon, we get her to come in the kitchen and cook one of her old family favorites, which gets raves from us all. She calls this "pipián," although I was under the impression that sauces with that name had to include squash seeds. Whatever the name, I hope you find it sabroso!

MAKES 6 SERVINGS

½ pound small new potatoes in their skins

½ pound green beans

4 chiles anchos rojos, *stemmed, seeded, and deveined (see page 330)*

11 garlic cloves

½ medium white onion, quartered

1 pound tomatoes (2 medium–large round or 8–10 plum)

½ teaspoon cumin seeds

2 teaspoons Mexican cinnamon bits (see page 337)

¾ cup sesame seeds

1 cup chicken stock (page 343)

3 pounds chicken, cut into 6 pieces, skin removed

3 tablespoons sunflower or vegetable oil

Salt

Heat about 3 cups of water in a 2-quart saucepan. Add the potatoes and boil for 15 minutes covered or until soft. Remove and set aside. Boil the beans in the potato water for 7 minutes. Remove and plunge into cold water, then drain. Set aside. Reserve the hot water.

On a 10-inch dry *comal*, griddle, or in a cast-iron frying pan, toast the chiles until they give off their aroma. Place in a small bowl and pour the reserved vegetable water over the top. Let soak for 10 minutes. On the same *comal*, grill the garlic and onion until soft and transparent, about 5 minutes. Remove and place in a blender and set aside.

On the *comal*, grill the tomatoes for about 10 to 15 minutes, or until soft. Remove and when cool enough to handle, peel the tomatoes and discard the skins. Add the tomatoes along with the soaked chiles to the blender. On the *comal*, toast the cumin and cinnamon quickly, until they give off their scents, and add to the blender. Lower the heat and toast the sesame seeds on the *comal*, stirring constantly, until they turn light brown. Remove from the heat and allow to cool. Blend the tomato mixture well for 2 to 3 minutes. Pour the mixture through a strainer into a bowl.

Grind the sesame seeds slowly on the *metate*, *molcajete*, or in a spice grinder until smooth. It is important to grind them slowly so the full flavor is released. Add to the tomato mixture. (If you don't have the time or the patience to do this, just add the toasted seeds to the blender with 1 cup stock. Blend well, then pour through a strainer into the tomato mixture.)

In a heavy 6-quart stockpot, brown the chicken in the oil over medium-high heat for 15 minutes. Remove from the pan and set aside. If there is excess oil in the stockpot, drain off all but 1 tablespoon and fry the tomato sauce for 15 minutes. Place the chicken in the sauce and cook for 20 minutes, covered, over low heat. Add the potatoes and string beans. Heat thoroughly, 5 to 10 minutes. Add salt to taste. Serve with hot corn tortillas.

ESTOFADO DE POLLO
Spanish Chicken Stew with Capers and Olives

This recipe is Oaxaca's salute to Spain and is prepared many different ways. Sometimes it's red, sometimes green; this version is a beautiful orange color. The color varies depending on the type of chiles used, how ripe the tomatoes are, and the proportion to tomatillos used. My husband, Eric, loves this dish. We take turns grinding the ingredients on the metate—the three-legged grinding stone used since pre-Hispanic times. The first time we ground the sauce by hand was when the electricity went out during a cooking class.

MAKES 8 SERVINGS

2¼ pounds tomatoes (about 4½ medium–large round or 18–23 plum)

3–4 large tomatillos, husks removed (see page 327)

3 chiles anchos rojos, dried, stemmed, seeded, and deveined (see page 330)

½ cup sesame seeds

4 tablespoons lard or sunflower or vegetable oil

In a heavy 4-quart stockpot, boil about 1½ quarts of water. Add the tomatoes and tomatillos and cook until they just change color, about 8 minutes. Reserving the water, remove the tomatoes and tomatillos to a colander, and when they are cool enough to handle, remove and discard the skins. Set the tomatoes and tomatillos aside.

On a 10-inch dry *comal*, griddle, or in a cast-iron frying pan, toast the *chiles anchos* over medium heat for about 2 minutes on each side, until the skins blister and bubble and they give off their aroma. Remove from the heat and place them in the leftover hot tomato water to soak for 20 minutes. Set aside.

(continued)

½ cup almonds

½ cup raisins

½ head of garlic, cloves separated

½ medium white onion, sliced

1–3 whole cloves, or to taste

Piece of Mexican cinnamon,
  1½ inches long (see page 337)

½ teaspoon black peppercorns

2 sprigs Oaxacan oregano, or
  1 teaspoon dried (see page 336)

1 sprig thyme, or a pinch of dried

4 cups chicken stock (page 343)

2 chickens (3 pounds each), cut
  into 8 pieces (reserve the back
  and neck, and feet, if possible,
  for stock)

2 tablespoons capers, with 1
  tablespoon of the juice

¼ cup green olives, pitted

Salt

½ cup chiles serranos en
  escabeche (page 329)

In an 8-inch cast-iron frying pan, fry the sesame seeds in 1 tablespoon oil over low heat for 10 minutes. Remove, let cool, and grind bit by bit in a spice grinder or a metate. Set aside. In the same frying pan, add 1 tablespoon oil and fry the almonds, raisins, garlic, onion, cloves, cinnamon, peppercorns, oregano, and thyme over medium heat until brown and the onion is transparent and aromatic. Set aside to cool.

Place the tomatoes, *tomatillos*, and soaked chiles in a blender with 1 cup of the chicken stock. Blend for 3 minutes. Pour the tomato and chile mixture through a food mill or sieve to remove any seeds and the chile skins. Set aside. Blend the almonds, raisins, onion, garlic, and seasonings in the blender with 1½ cups chicken stock until smooth. Set aside.

In a heavy 6-quart pot, heat the remaining 2 tablespoons oil and brown the chicken pieces well, but do not cook them through, about 10 minutes. Remove from the pan. Pour off all but 1½ tablespoons of the oil and fry the tomato and chile mixture with the seasoning mixture over medium heat for 10 minutes, stirring constantly. Add the ground sesame seeds and stir until well incorporated, about 10 minutes. Return the chicken to the bubbling sauce and continue cooking over low heat, covered, for 20 minutes more. Add the remaining 1½ cups chicken stock, thinning it so that the sauce is just thick enough to coat the back of a spoon. Add the capers, caper juice, and olives to the sauce. Let the chicken simmer, covered, 15 minutes more.

Add salt to taste. Place the *chiles serranos* directly into the sauce just before serving or put in each bowl as a garnish. Serve immediately with fresh corn tortillas.

Hint: If the sesame seeds jump around a lot in the frying pan, add a pinch of salt and keep stirring. We grind the sesame seeds by hand on a metate, but you can also grind them in a spice grinder. It takes a bit of time, but it is the only way to grind them fine enough. If you don't care if the sauce has a little texture, grind the seeds in a blender and strain through a wire-mesh strainer.

HIGADITOS DE FANDANGO
Fiesta Eggs with Pork Liver

Higaditos, *meaning "little livers," is an egg dish served on the morning of a big celebration in the Central Valleys of Oaxaca. There are basically two types. The first is sort of a scrambled egg soup that I've eaten in Teotitlán del Valle. This recipe, inspired by Eusebia Pacheco, is a dry version fried in lots of oil, then drained and served. Sometimes it contains chicken livers or a mixture of livers and meat, and there are even versions with no livers at all. At a village fiesta, people make it with up to 400 eggs at one time.*

MAKES 8 SERVINGS

For the salsa de chile de agua:
½ pound tomatoes
    (1 medium–large round or
    4–5 plum), roasted
2 chiles de agua, roasted
    (see page 328; see Hint)
3 garlic cloves
Salt to taste
3 sprigs cilantro, finely chopped

For the higaditos:
1 cup sunflower or vegetable oil
1 medium white onion, finely
    chopped
1 pound tomatoes (2 medium–large
    round or 8–10 plum), finely
    chopped
½ pound tomatillos (5–6 medium),
    husked and finely chopped
½ head of garlic, cloves separated
    and finely chopped
¼ pound pork liver, boiled and
    finely chopped (you can substi-
    tute chicken livers)
½ cup flat-leaf parsley leaves, finely
    chopped

FOR THE *SALSA DE CHILE DE AGUA:*
Peel the roasted tomatoes and discard the peels. Peel the chiles and remove the stems and seeds. In a *molcajete* or a mortar and pestle, grind the garlic with the salt. Add the chiles one by one and grind well. Add the tomatoes and grind them, leaving the resulting sauce a little chunky. Add the cilantro and ½ cup of water. Set aside.

FOR THE *HIGADITOS:*
In a deep, heavy 8-inch frying pan, heat the oil over medium heat. Add the onion, tomatoes, and *tomatillos* and cook until soft. Add the garlic, liver, parsley, and oregano and continue to cook about 10 minutes more. Add salt and pepper and stir well.

Meanwhile, beat the eggs in a medium bowl and whip well. Add salt and pepper to taste to the egg mixture and mix in well. Raise the heat under the frying pan and add the eggs, mixing in gently. There must be enough oil to rise to the same level as the eggs. Pull the eggs away from the sides of the pan as they start to set. After 10 to 15 minutes, as eggs start to set, form a square with the egg mixture and divide into quarters with your spatula. Carefully flip over each section and continue to cook on the other side. When eggs are evenly browned and no longer loose, remove from the pan carefully and drain off any oil. Place on a serving platter and serve hot with *salsa de chile de agua* and tortillas or bread.

(continued)

1 teaspoon dried Oaxacan oregano
   (see page 336)
1 teaspoon salt, or more as needed
½ teaspoon ground black pepper
15 eggs
Salt and pepper to taste

Hints: In our village, this is always served with enchiladas on the side. In San Pablo Huixtepec, where the Señora Eusebia is from, people serve it with a roasted tomato sauce made with the local *chiles de agua*.

If you don't have *chiles de agua*, substitute *chiles jalapeños* or *chiles habaneros*.

PAY DE QUESO
Farmer Cheese Pie

The inspiration for this recipe comes from my friend Minerva Morales, who has a cheese stand in the Etla market. The Wednesday Etla market is known for its special cheeses. Minerva always has wonderful requesón made by her mother, who also makes queso fresco and quesillo. Requesón literally means "re-cheesed," and is made from the whey that remains after queso fresco is produced.

MAKES 8 TO 10 SERVINGS

For the crust (one 11-inch pie):
18 plain vanilla wafers, known in
   Mexican food stores as
   "Marías"
2 tablespoons pecan pieces, toasted
¼ teaspoon ground cinnamon
4 tablespoons (½ stick) butter

For the Filling:
½ cup raisins
2 tablespoons coffee-flavored
   mezcal, rum, or other liquor of
   your choice (see page 350)
½ pound requesón (see page 346),
   fresh farmer cheese, or ricotta
   cheese
3 ounces cream cheese
4 large eggs

FOR THE CRUST:
Preheat the oven to 350°F.

In a food processor or a blender, finely grind the wafers and the pecans. Place them in a medium mixing bowl and add the cinnamon.

In a small saucepan over low heat, melt the butter and add it to the wafer and nut mixture, stirring with a fork. Thinly line the inside of an 11-inch pie pan with the mixture, reserving 1 tablespoon to sprinkle on top.

FOR THE FILLING:
Heat the raisins over low heat in a small saucepan along with the mezcal and 2 tablespoons water until they plump up and are soft, about 10 minutes. Drain.

In a blender, combine the cheeses, eggs, milk, vanilla extract, orange extract, and grated rind. Blend for 1 minute, then remove to a medium mixing bowl. Add the raisins and guava to the bowl and mix with a spoon. Pour the fruit mixture into the pie crust and sprinkle the top in the center with the remaining tablespoon of crust mixture.

1 cup sweetened condensed milk

1 teaspoon vanilla extract

½ teaspoon orange extract

1 teaspoon finely grated orange or lime rind

½ pound guavas, seeded and cubed, but unpeeled (½ cup cleaned fruit; see Hint)

Bake pie for 55 minutes to 1 hour, or until the filling is set and is light golden brown on top or a knife inserted into the center comes out clean. Let cool for at least 1 hour before slicing. The pie can be served either at room temperature or cold.

Hint: If you cannot find fresh guavas, canned will do in a pinch, or use some other fresh fruit such as peaches or apricots.

PANQUÉ DE TÍA ELENA
Aunt Helen's Sour Cream Pound Cake

Tía Elena Zwart is the madrina (godmother) of my sister Jacqui. For as long as I can remember, she has been making this sour cream pound cake, which is the best panqué I know. If you don't have sour cream, you can substitute yogurt with good results. Here in Oaxaca, it is popular to put raisins or pecans in the batter. For a change I like to make the marbleized version (see Hint). This is another good keeper; it can last two weeks or more if the kids don't get to it.

MAKES 12 TO 16 SERVINGS

1 cup (2 sticks) butter or margarine, softened

2½ cups granulated sugar

6 eggs

½ teaspoon vanilla extract

½ teaspoon orange extract

½ teaspoon lemon extract

Preheat the oven to 350°F. Butter a Bundt or 10-inch tube pan on all sides, including the tube in the center.

In a large mixing bowl, cream the butter until it is light and fluffy. Add the sugar and continue to beat. Beat in the eggs one at a time. Continue beating for 5 minutes. Stir the extracts into the sour cream.

Sift the flour, baking soda, and salt. Alternately add the flour mixture and sour cream mixture to the butter mixture, starting and ending with the flour. Beat for 5 minutes. Pour the batter into the prepared pan and bake for 1¼ to 1½ hours. Leave the cake to cool in the pan for about 15 minutes after removing from oven. Loosen the sides with a knife and flip over to remove from the pan. Dust the top with confectioners' sugar, if desired.

(continued)

Hint: Add cinnamon and sugar or ¼ cup chopped pecans to the greased pan before pouring in the batter. If you want a marbleized cake, add ½ cup cocoa or grated Mexican chocolate to half of the batter. When filling the pan, place large spoonfuls of batter into it, alternating the vanilla and chocolate batters.

REGAÑADAS
Flaky Broiled Bread

The literal translation of the word regaño *means "burst crust," which is essentially what these sweet, thin breads are like. They are almost all crust that bubbles up and has caramelized sugar on top. In the adobe oven at the home of Galdino and Ramona Lázaro, where I first learned to make and eat* regañadas, *they achieved this by burning an egg carton on one side of the oven to create a flame to broil the sugar. Re-creating them at home in my gas oven, I place them under the broiler for 30 seconds to a minute, depending on their location on the baking sheet. Keep them in a dry jar and they will last for days. These are eaten as a dessert or in the evening or early-morning breakfast with coffee, tea, or champurrado (page 349).*

MAKES 12 *REGAÑADAS*

1¾ cups all-purpose flour
¼ teaspoon salt
1 teaspoon sugar
½ teaspoon active dry yeast
½ cup vegetable shortening
½ cup sugar, on a plate

Preheat the oven to 475°F.

In a large mixing bowl, combine the flour, salt, sugar, and yeast. Mix in the vegetable shortening with your fingers. Make a well in the center of the mix. Add ½ cup warm water and mix in well with your hands. Knead for 3 to 5 minutes. The dough will be soft.

Divide the dough into 12 balls. Put ample flour on a board and place a ball of dough on top. (You can do two at a time once you have experience.) Roll out the dough to make an oval 8 inches long and 3 to 4 inches wide. Dust more flour on the top and fold in fourths lengthwise to make a long strip. Tie the strip in a knot with the ends tucked inside and pat down on a flour surface to make a little flat ball. Continue with all the remaining dough.

Roll each flat ball out again and make ovals 8 inches long and 4 inches wide. Spread oil or melted lard on top with a brush and dip in the sugar, oiled side down. Place on ungreased baking sheets and bake 7 minutes. Remove from the oven and place under the broiler 30 seconds to 1 minute to caramelize the sugar. They should be crispy.

JUGO DE PIÑA, ALFALFA, Y NARANJA
Pineapple, Alfalfa, and Orange Juice

In the rainy season, the ejido lands around Rancho Aurora are green with corn, beans, squash, and lots of alfalfa. The alfalfa is for the large number of cows and horses in the Etla Valley, where we are located. This is a family recipe that Serafin, one of our adopted kids, made up when he and Eric grew a big field of alfalfa on our ranch. Always a master of jugos and licuados, Serafin says this combination gives us energy. "People give alfalfa to the horses to make them frisky," he said, "why not us?"

MAKES 6 TO 7 CUPS

4 cups fresh pineapple chunks
4 cups alfalfa leaves
4 cups fresh orange juice

Put all the ingredients in a blender and blend well. Serve well chilled.

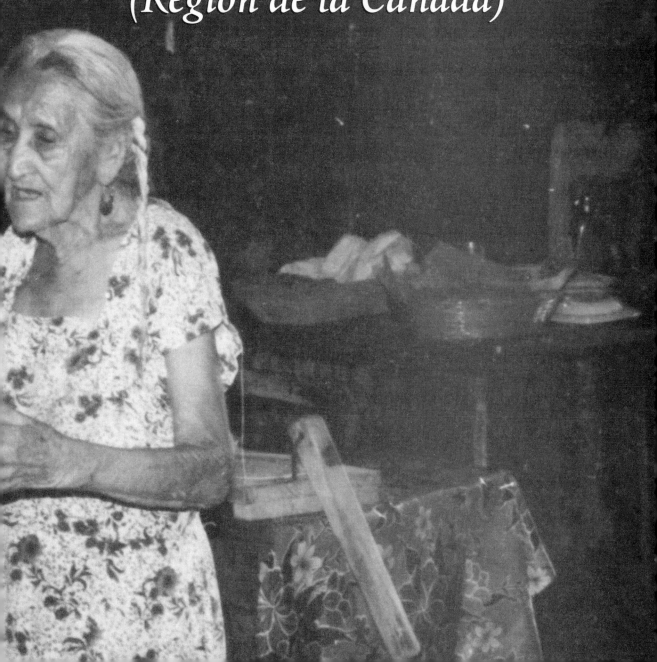

CHAPTER THREE

The Cañada Region
(Región de la Cañada)

Enchiladas de Pollo
to go (Barbara Lawton)

Overleaf:
La Abuelita *teaching Susana how to make* Empanadas de Mole Amarillo Cuicatlán *(Barbara Lawton)*

Ꝺne of the most beautiful spring rituals in our village is to take the early-morning Oaxaca-Puebla train that passes through Cuicatlán. Our local train station in Hacienda Blanca is alive with women bundled up in rebozos to ward off the morning chill. They are laden with baskets of home-made cheeses or rustic pottery from nearby Atzompa, and they take these items either to sell on the train or to use as barter for the mangoes and other fruits in Cuicatlán, our destination. Gliding through the fertile valley of Etla, we see the local *campesinos* cutting their alfalfa, loading burro-drawn carts waiting nearby. If there is a lot of rain in the spring, you may see entire families in the fields planting their annual crops of corn, beans, and squash. The man leads the ox-drawn yunta (Egyptian plow), making furrows in the soil as the women and children plant the seeds behind him. It is a scene out of ancient times.

In Etla, local women get on the train to sell traditional early-morning fare: cheese, breads, *tamales*, *arroz con leche*, and *gelatinas*, to be washed down with drinks of coffee and various flavored *atoles*. In between selling and collecting tickets, the conductor gets in on the action, too, selling candies, peanuts, gum, and other munchies. After the stop in Telixtlahuaca, the train slowly begins to ascend the Sierra Juárez. The weather becomes warmer as the morning sun burns through the mist and the landscape changes. As we climb, the vegetation becomes more sparse and the air is dry and cool.

At El Progreso, more women board the train, bringing potato and rice tacos, empanadas, *memelitas*, and drinks flavored with fruits like watermelon, *jamaica* (hibiscus flower), and cantaloupe. Carrying their baskets on their heads, they make the trek to the train down tiny mountain paths through hills dotted with little adobe houses guarded by cactus fences. After the train begins to move again the large organ cacti, along with myriad wildflowers and wild frangipani trees, whiz by as we descend into the canyon. From the train we can see the Río Grande racing down the canyon and we begin to enter the wet and fertile microclimate of the Cañada Chica.

At the next stop, it is chaos as women board the train carrying *tlayudas* and *nopales* (cactus paddles) prepared in more ways than you can imagine: *nopales* with eggs, *nopal* salad, grilled *nopales* with lime and salsa, and hot *nopal tacos* cooked with the yellow *chile manzano* that is so hot. With yellow flesh, shaped like an apple, and hosting dark black seeds inside, it is one of the spiciest chiles I have ever eaten.

Approaching Cuicatlán, we pass an abundance of lime, papaya, banana, and *chicozapote* orchards. Above them all, the mango trees are umbrellas of shade laden with their green and yellow fruit. We arrive at the station and say hello to my friends at La Abuelita, a beautiful old restaurant with two large kitchens, one with traditional wood fires and a modern one fired with gas. Señora Beatriz Avendaño, a sweet, barefoot little woman over a hundred years old, *is* the Abuelita, the namesake of the restaurant. Her daughter, Felipa Hernández Avendaño, who is eighty-six, recently retired from the restaurant and handed the reins to La Abuelita's granddaughter, Ofelia Carrera Hernández. Promising to come back later to eat, we go in search of fruit. Cuicatlán is in the Cañada, the smallest region of Oaxaca, set between two beautiful rivers. Its altitudes and climates vary dramatically. The Cañada Chica is a fascinating microclimate that hosts many varieties of mango, papaya, banana, and other exotic fruit-bearing trees, such as *zapote* and *chicozapote*.

Nearby, the famous chiles native to Oaxaca, the *chilcostles* and the revered *chihuacles negros,* are grown. My friend Teodoro, from the village of La Unión Nacaltepec, harvests over nine and a half acres of *chihuacles negros* and *rojos* every fall. The chiles mature on the vine and then are dried on the ground on *petates*, or woven palm mats. These chiles are an important ingredient of the *mole negro* that is prepared for *Día de Muertos* celebrated throughout the state.

Past Cuicatlán, traveling through the Cañada, is Teotitlán de Flores Magón, otherwise known as Teotitlán del Camino. I stopped unexpectedly at this small, friendly village at the base of the Sierra Mazateca during a recent trip. My destination had been Huautla de Jiménez, but a large landslide, quite frequent in these mountainous parts, blocked the only road. Returning to Teotitlán, I discovered a unique style of cooking here and was able to meet and learn from Señora Silvia Correra Gamboa, a local chef and the owner of Restaurant Silvia for over thirty years.

Señora Orefelia Meza Muñoz, owner of the Hotel Orefelia in Teotitlán del Camino, taught me to make *Tesmole de Gallina,* which is actually a *pipián* made with ground pumpkin and *chiltepec* seeds. The recipe comes from Santa María Chilchotla, a village in the largest *Pergamino* coffee-producing zone of Oaxaca. Coffee is the largest crop produced for export in this high-altitude region near the border of Puebla, but the area needs the resources to start new plantations and better roads to get the coffee to market.

In the Sierra Mazateca, the highlands of the Cañada, is the town of Huautla de Jiménez, home of the Mazateca people. Advanced in herbal healing and shamanism, they use magic mushrooms to cure the ills of their bodies and souls. The most famous of these shamans, María Sabina, has died, but her legend lives on and her knowledge of plants is shared through her grandson.

Our guide and friend, Rosalba Terán, a beautiful Mazateca woman who works for the National Institute of Indigenous People, speaks both Spanish and Mazateco. She introduces us to Señora Inés Cerqueda García, who is one of the most respected cooks in the area, who teaches us to make *Pílte de Pollo Mazateco* (page 67), the most famous dish of this village, as well as the typical *tamales de tesmole con frijol bayo,* wrapped in banana leaves.

Rosalba also describes some of the area's most cherished fiestas. The biggest fiesta in the village is on the third Friday in Lent, when all the women come down from the surrounding mountains to participate in a procession wearing their distinctive *huipiles.* The night before Easter, everyone goes to the cemetery to light candles, much like the celebration of *Día de Muertos* in and around Oaxaca City.

Santo Domingo del Río, where the Mazateca region meets the Chinanteca (Tuxtepec region), truly captures my heart. It is a friendly village situated under Cerro Rabón, an unusually high mesa above an area of fertile rolling hills and orchards. It is here that Oaxaca's vanilla and cacao trees grow, as well as fruits of all varieties. When I first visited this village, I was accompanied by Fidel Pereda and Roberto Vásquez López, of the Papaloapan Regional Producers of Vanilla. This organization helps to unite and educate the 4,200 vanilla producers of Tuxtepec, Choapan, and Cuicatlán.

Climbing the hills on this later visit, with about twenty children following behind me, I feel like the Pied Piper. I fantasize about building a little adobe home on top of the hill overlooking the fertile valley, with its river winding gently through it. It seemed for that moment that living under the sacred Cerro Rabón would be a dream come true.

Mango seller in Cuicatlán (Barbara Lawton)

IN THIS CHAPTER

SOPA DE HABA
Savory Fava Bean Soup

During Lent, the people in the Cañada—and in the rest of Oaxaca, for that matter—observe many days without eating meat. On the designated days of abstinence, like Ash Wednesday and each Friday in Lent, culminating on Good Friday, many vegetable caldillos *(light broths) are served. Sopa de Haba is one of the broths served during this time.*

MAKES 6 SERVINGS AS A FIRST COURSE, 4 AS A MAIN COURSE

1 pound fresh fava beans (see Hint)

1 medium white onion, finely chopped, and ½ medium onion, chunked

12 garlic cloves, 7 finely chopped and 5 left whole

2 sprigs hierbabuena *(see page 336)*

1 teaspoon salt, or to taste

1 pound tomatoes (2 medium–large round or 8–10 plum), boiled, peeled, and finely chopped (reserve 1 cup cooking water)

2 teaspoons sunflower oil

½ cup cilantro leaves, finely chopped

In a 4-quart saucepan, bring 1½ quarts of water to a boil. Add the fava beans, chopped onion, chopped garlic, and *hierbabuena* and cover the pan. Lower the heat and cook until the beans are soft, about 45 minutes. Add the salt.

In a blender, combine the tomatoes, chunked onion, and whole garlic with 1 cup of the reserved tomato water. Blend until smooth. Heat the oil in a medium frying pan and fry the tomato mixture for 5 minutes. Add to the fava beans and stir in. Add the cilantro, adjust the seasoning, and serve.

Hint: You can substitute fresh peas for the fava beans.

CREMA DE CHILE POBLANO

Roasted Chile Poblano Bisque

I had this soup for the first time at a fancy wedding in San Felipe del Agua, the ritziest section of Oaxaca. The soup was delicious—creamy but not picante at all. One day I started craving chiles poblanos, and we made the soup for a cooking class. We had just been to the Etla market, where I had bought some requesón (farmer cheese), so we added it to thicken the soup, adding another dimension. The corn tortilla topping contributes a flavor contrast with the poblano. If the soup is too picante, you can double the amount of cheese.

MAKES 6 SERVINGS

7 chiles poblanos *(see page 329)*

1 tablespoon butter

2 medium white onions, thickly sliced

½ head of garlic, cloves separated

Salt and black pepper to taste

3 sprigs epazote, or 1½ teaspoons dried *(see page 336; optional)*

1 quart chicken stock *(page 343)*

1½ cups milk

2 ounces requesón *(about ⅓ cup; see page 346)* or ricotta or farmer cheese (with salt)

To serve:

3 teaspoons Mexican fresh crema *(see page 345),* heavy cream, or crème fraîche

4 corn tortillas, 8 inches in diameter, cut into strips and fried, or tostadas, toasted

In a 10-inch dry *comal,* griddle, or in a cast-iron frying pan or over an open flame, roast the chiles until they blister, turning to roast all sides. Place in a plastic bag to "sweat" and set aside for 15 minutes. Peel and remove stems and seeds. Cut the clean flesh into strips; these are called *rajas.*

In a heavy 4-quart stockpot, melt the butter over medium heat and sauté the onions until transparent. Add the garlic and continue to cook about 5 minutes longer, but do not brown it. Add the chile strips and continue to cook about 20 minutes longer, stirring. Add the salt and pepper and *epazote* to the mixture, then follow with the chicken stock. Simmer 15 minutes longer, covered, over low heat.

Puree the chile mixture in a blender until smooth. Return the puree to the pot and add the milk. Heat through. Remove ½ cup of the puree and blend with the *requesón* in a mixing bowl until smooth. Return mixture to the soup and heat through. Adjust salt to taste.

TO SERVE:

Place the *crema* in a mixing bowl and beat with a whisk until smooth. Thin with a little milk if necessary to make a thin stream. Pour the *crema* into a small plastic bag or squirt bottle. Place a ladle of soup in each bowl. Squirt about ½ teaspoon of *crema* onto each serving in a free-form fashion. Add a handful of tortilla strips on top in a vertical fashion or serve tostadas on the side.

Hint: Sometimes I sauté corn kernels in the chile mixture and puree it all to make a corn and *poblano* bisque; or I sauté the kernels on the side and add them whole to the pureed bisque.

SOPA DE GARBANZO
Garbanzo Bean Bisque

This soup can be made with either the whole garbanzos, as I have here, or toasted garbanzo bean powder, which may be harder for people outside Mexico to find. I have eaten this soup in several mountainous areas, like Ixtlán in the Sierra Juárez or Huautla de Jiménez in the Cañada, where the cloud cover lies low over the town and the weather is foggy and chilly. This soup gives a homey and satisfying feeling to the stomach and heart. I can appreciate the Mexican saying "Panza llena, corazón feliz" (Full stomach, happy heart) when this is served.

MAKES 4 TO 6 SERVINGS

1 tablespoon sunflower or vegetable oil

1 cup finely chopped white onion

½ tablespoon finely chopped garlic

1½ tablespoons finely chopped or crumbled mint leaves, fresh or dried

3½ cups cooked garbanzo beans and their liquid (Guisado de Garbanzo Istmeño, *page 203*)

2 cups chicken stock (*page 343*), or more if needed

½ teaspoon salt, or to taste

½ teaspoon white pepper

Butter or oil, for spreading on bread slices

2 bolillos or French bread, cut into 4–6 slices each

In a heavy 4-quart soup pot, heat the oil and sauté the onion over medium heat until translucent and slightly brown, about 10 minutes. Stir occasionally. Add the garlic and mint and continue to cook 5 minutes more, or until the garlic is soft.

Puree 2½ cups of the cooked garbanzos in a blender with their cooking liquid to a smooth consistency. Add it to the onion mixture, stirring constantly. Blend the remainder of the garbanzos roughly (using the pulse button on the blender) with 1 cup of the chicken stock. Add the remaining 1 cup chicken stock and the garbanzos to the soup. Cook over low heat, covered, at least 1 hour. Add salt and pepper.

Butter or oil each slice of bread and toast them until brown. Serve the soup with 2 toasted croutons in the center of each serving, floating on top.

Hints: This soup is very good chilled, but totally untraditional served like that.

(continued)

If you want to use the garbanzo bean flour, mix ¾ cup garbanzo bean flour with 1 cup cold water. Then add this mixture to 2½ cups chicken stock and stir to a smooth paste. Follow the directions and substitute the paste for the pureed beans. Add the 2 cups of chicken stock as directed and more if it thickens the soup too much.

ENSALADA DE BERENJENA
Eggplant Salad

This salad comes from the Cañada region near Puebla, where people grow fields of eggplant. I always make eggplant in a different way, so I was delighted to learn this new preparation. Serve the salad with crackers or tostadas around it, or over lettuce leaves.

MAKES 4 TO 6 SERVINGS

2–2¼ pounds eggplant

½ medium white onion, finely chopped

2 chiles serranos, *thinly sliced* (see page 329)

3 garlic cloves, finely chopped

1 tablespoon fresh lime juice

2 tablespoons chopped parsley leaves

2 tablespoons cilantro leaves

1 teaspoon salt, or to taste

½ teaspoon fresh ground black pepper

Toast the eggplant over a flame, turning frequently until completely charred and soft. Peel and cut into ½-inch pieces and put into a medium bowl. Add the onion, chiles, and garlic and mix in well. Squeeze the lime juice over all and add the parsley and cilantro. Season with salt and pepper. Serve cold or at room temperature.

ENSALADA DE NOPALES ASADOS
Grilled Nopales Salad

I had never liked the nopales salad found in the markets and homes around Oaxaca. The boiled, limp cactus paddles seemed boring and the lack of seasoning bothered me. One day I came home to find an older couple harvesting and drying the black beans that they had grown on our ranch. The wife, known as "Tía Martina," was preparing the midday comida for her family right there in the field. She had cooked stacks of fresh tortillas on a comal—a clay disk she had propped up on three stones with a fire lit beneath. She was also grilling nopales that she had picked from a cactus in her garden. She invited me to try a taco of nopal with salt, lime, and some homemade salsa. The flavor from the grilling was fabulous! A light went on in my head: I would make my nopales salad like that! My dressing is made with star anise, not the aniseed that is commonly used. Whenever I need to buy some, I go to the farmacia, where the pharmacist, Virginia, always asks me if the baby has colic because star anise is considered a medicinal cure in this area.

MAKES 16 FIVE-INCH TOSTADAS

1 pound fresh nopales, with thorns removed; in a pinch you can use bottled, but rinse them well in cold water (see page 327)

9 garlic cloves

¾ pound tomatoes (1½ medium–large round or 6–7 plum), cut into small chunks

5 cebollitas or green onions (scallions), thinly sliced (see page 326)

2 medium ripe avocados, peeled and cut into small chunks (Haas or native type)

½ cup cilantro leaves, finely chopped

1 star anise

On a 10-inch dry *comal*, griddle, or in a cast-iron frying pan, roast the *nopales* until they are brown in color, turning them to cook evenly on both sides, about 5 minutes. Set aside to cool. Roast the garlic on the same dry griddle for about 3 minutes, until translucent. Finely chop. When the *nopales* are cool enough to handle, cut them into ½-inch strips and then cut them crosswise into 1-inch-long diagonals. Put them in a bowl and add the chopped garlic, tomatoes, *cebollitas*, avocados, and cilantro.

Grind the star anise in a *molcajete* or spice grinder, then add the vinegar, lime juice, salt, and pepper. (If you use a spice grinder, place the ground star anise in a small bowl, then whisk in the vinegar, lime juice, salt, and pepper.) Whisk in the olive oil. Pour the dressing over the salad and toss lightly, coating the vegetables well.

To serve, spread spoonfuls of the salad on the tostadas,

⅓ cup red wine vinegar or apple cider vinegar

2 tablespoons lime juice

Salt and pepper to taste

⅓ cup olive oil

2 packages small tostadas, about 5 inches in diameter, oven-toasted until crisp, or fried corn tortillas

¼ pound queso fresco (see page 346) or queso añejo, crumbled

then sprinkle with the fresh cheese. If you want the salad to be *picante*, top with a bit of *salsa de chile pasilla* (page 151).

Hints: I use small taco-size tortillas and bake them until crisp on cookie sheets at 400°F for 10 to 15 minutes, turning once.

Fresh blanched green beans would be a suitable substitute for the *nopales*, with a very different flavor.

ARROZ CON CHEPIL
Rice Flavored with Chepil

Chepil *is a pre-Hispanic herb that grows wild in the rainy season. You often see the women and their children gathering it in the cornfields a few days after a big rain, their arms laden with their findings. It is so popular in Oaxaca that some people grow it year-round to sell in the markets, although it can be dried to use out of season.* Chepil *is used in soups, stews, tamales, and, of course, rice. Serve this rice with* Estofado de Pollo *(page 33).*

MAKES 8 SERVINGS

1 cup chepil *leaves (see page 336), or salad burnet, parsley, water-cress leaves, chives, or fenugreek*

2 tablespoons butter, sunflower oil, or vegetable oil

1 medium white onion, finely chopped

7 garlic cloves, finely chopped

4 cups chicken stock (page 343)

2 cups white rice

Salt to taste

In a deep, heavy 8-inch frying pan with a lid, heat the butter and sauté the onion over medium heat until clear, about 5 minutes. Add the garlic and sauté 2 minutes longer. Add the *chepil* and sauté about 2 minutes more. Add the chicken stock and bring to a boil. Add the rice, stir well, and add salt.

Return rice to a boil, lower the heat to a simmer, and cook for 15 to 20 minutes, covered, until all the water is absorbed and the rice is dry. Do not peek at or stir the rice during the cooking process.

ARROZ BLANCO CON PLÁTANOS FRITOS
White Rice with Fried Plantains

This is one of the classic Oaxacan rice dishes usually served before the main course in the four-course lunch called comida corrida. *The components of the* comida corrida *(literally meaning "food on the run") are* sopa aguada *(a "wet" soup),* sopa seca *(a "dry" soup),* plato fuerte *(the main course), and the* postre *(dessert); served like a blue plate special each day. I usually order this sampling of typical Oaxacan fare when offered in a restaurant, because it's bound to be the freshest food on the menu and the dishes change daily.*

MAKES 8 SERVINGS

For the rice:

3 tablespoons sunflower or vege-
    table oil
½ cup chopped white onion
1½ tablespoons finely chopped
    garlic
2 cups white rice
4 cups chicken stock, heated
    (page 343)
2 sprigs hierbabuena (see
    page 336), or 2 tablespoons
    mint leaves
Salt and pepper

For the plantains:

1 pound ripe plantains, peeled
1 cup sunflower or vegetable oil

FOR THE RICE:

In a heavy 4-quart stockpot, heat the oil over low heat. Add the onion and fry until soft and clear, about 5 minutes. Add the garlic and continue to fry for another 3 to 5 minutes. Add the rice and stir well. Fry slowly without moving the rice too much, about 10 minutes. Stir in the hot chicken stock and the *hierbabuena* or mint. Add salt and pepper to taste. Cover and let cook for 15 to 20 minutes, or until all the stock is absorbed. Do not peek at or stir the rice during the cooking process.

Mound the rice on a plate or a platter and serve with the fried plantains on top.

FOR THE PLANTAINS:

Cut the plantains in half. Cut each half lengthwise into ¼-inch-thick slices (4–5 slices). In an 8-inch cast-iron frying pan, heat the oil until smoking. Add the plantains and fry 3 to 5 minutes on each side or until brown. Remove them from the oil and drain on paper towels.

TACOS DE NOPALES
CON CHILE MANZANO
Prickly Pear Cactus Tacos with Yellow Chile Sauce

A simple and spicy way to start your day is to eat these tacos for breakfast. This treat came to me as I was on the train to Cuicatlán to buy mangoes one year, and I've looked for them every year since. If you can't find the very hot, canary-yellow chiles in your Mexican market, you could substitute habaneros, *(probably more readily available in the United States than they are in Oaxaca), or any other hot, fresh chile. We eat these tacos on the ranch in the summer when the* manzanos *come in season and the* nopales *are abundant.*

MAKES 6 SERVINGS

4 cups julienned nopales
(1 pound; see page 327)
½ pound tomatoes (1 medium–
large round or 4–5 plum)
1–2 chiles manzanos *or*
1–2 chiles habaneros, *or*
7 fresh chiles jalapeños *(see
page 329), depending on taste*
3 garlic cloves
1 teaspoon salt
1 tablespoon minced cilantro leaves
6 corn tortillas, 8 inches in
diameter

In a 2-quart saucepan, bring about 1 quart of water to a boil. Add the *nopales* and cook, covered, until they change color and are cooked through, 15 to 20 minutes. Drain off all the water (it should be gelatinous) and rinse the *nopales* with cool water.

In another 2-quart saucepan, bring about 3 cups of water to a boil. Make an x in the bottom of each tomato and place in the boiling water. Boil 3 minutes or so, until the skins can be removed easily. Peel the tomatoes and discard the skins. Reserve the cooking water.

On a 10-inch dry *comal*, griddle, or in a cast-iron frying pan, grill the chiles until blistered and giving off their scent. Place them in a plastic bag to "sweat" for about 5 minutes. When the chiles are cool enough to handle, remove the skins with a small paring knife.

In a blender or *molcajete*, blend the chiles, garlic, and tomatoes, using about half of the tomato water to blend. Add salt and stir in the cilantro. Return the sauce to the pot, add the *nopales*, and reheat.

Over a direct flame or on the *comal*, heat the corn tortillas quickly on both sides until pliable. Fill each tortilla with a sixth of the *nopal* mixture and serve, or serve the *nopales* on the plate and the heated tortillas stacked up in a cloth in the center of the table.

Hint: Serve the tacos with eggs, beans, and potatoes of your choice for a hearty breakfast.

RAJAS DE CHILE POBLANO CON HUEVO
Scrambled Eggs with Roasted Chile Poblano Strips

Rajas de chile poblano, or chile strips with onions, are presented in many forms at a meal. This is one of the popular ways to eat them for mid-morning brunch, or almuerzo. They are sold in the markets as take-out fillings for tacos and on the early-morning train to Puebla. Serve with Frijoles Charros *(page 237).*

MAKES 4 TO 6 SERVINGS

3 chiles poblanos *(see page 329)*

4 tablespoons sunflower or
   vegetable oil

2 tablespoons finely chopped white
   onion

1 tablespoon finely chopped garlic

1 pound potatoes, cooked in their
   jackets, peeled, and cut into
   ½-inch pieces

¾ teaspoon salt, or to taste

9 eggs

2 tablespoons milk or water

1 teaspoon pepper

¼ cup parsley leaves, epazote
   (see page 336), or cilantro,
   finely chopped

In a 10-inch dry *comal*, griddle, or in a cast-iron frying pan or over an open flame, roast the chiles until they blister, turning to roast all sides. Place in a plastic bag to "sweat," about 10 minutes. Peel and remove the stems and seeds. Cut the clean flesh into strips ½ inch wide—these are called *rajas.*

In an 8-inch cast-iron frying pan, heat the oil and fry the onion until transparent, about 5 minutes. Add the garlic and fry for 5 minutes more. Add the potatoes and chiles and fry 10 minutes more. Add ¼ teaspoon salt.

Whip the eggs in a bowl with the milk or water. Add the remaining ½ teaspoon salt and the pepper. Add the egg mixture to the vegetable mixture. Cook over low heat for 10 minutes, gently moving clumps of eggs at a time as they cook, *not* stirring. Add the parsley. Serve immediately with corn or flour tortillas, *bolillos* (see page 347), or beans and cheese.

EMPANADAS DE NANACATES
Baked Wild Mushroom Turnovers

Nanacates are one of the joys of the rainy season. These wild mushrooms are found in the Sierra Mountains surrounding the Central Valleys and are brought down to market loosely packed in reed baskets. They are very similar to the portobello mushrooms available in the United States and Europe. These empanadas are so good you may want to make them with commercially raised mushrooms if you can't get the wild or portobello varieties. They are best eaten right off the comal.

MAKES 10 EMPANADAS

2 tablespoons butter or oil

1 medium white onion, finely chopped

½ pound nanacates (see page 327) or portobello mushrooms, finely chopped

7 garlic cloves, finely chopped

1 tablespoon finely chopped epazote leaves (see page 336)

Salt

½ teaspoon finely ground black pepper

1½ pounds prepared masa for tortillas, or 3 cups masa harina for tortillas

10 ounces quesillo, manchego, Gouda, or Muenster cheese, shredded or grated (see pages 345 and 346)

In an 8-inch cast-iron frying pan, heat the butter or oil over medium heat and fry the onion until transparent, about 5 minutes. Add the *nanacates* and garlic and continue to fry 10 to 15 minutes over low heat. If you need to, add a bit more butter or oil to the pan to keep the mushrooms from sticking. Add the *epazote*, ½ teaspoon salt, and the pepper and stir well. When the mixture is dry, remove from the heat and allow to cool.

Preheat a 10-inch clay *comal*, griddle, or cast-iron frying pan over medium heat.

If using prepared *masa*, place in a mixing bowl, add 1 tablespoon salt and a few sprinkles of water, and knead to a soft dough. If using *masa harina*, place in a large mixing bowl and add 1 tablespoon salt and 2¾ cups water. Knead until the dough is soft, about 1 minute. Allow dough to rest for 15 minutes. Divide the *masa* into 10 balls. Roll into a ball, then shape into a log 5 inches long and 1½ inches wide.

Place a log between two sheets of plastic placed inside a tortilla press and press down. An oval shape will appear. Rotate the oval and press again. Remove the plastic from the top and place 3 to 4 tablespoons of cheese in the middle. Top with 2 tablespoons of the filling. Place a little bit of water around the edge of the tortilla with your finger, fold the empanada over, and press to seal it closed.

Lift the empanada from the plastic and place in the middle of the heated *comal*, griddle, or cast-iron frying pan. Cook about 3 to 5 minutes on each side, or until it starts to brown and removes easily from the *comal* without breaking. Turn it over and cook on the second side. Serve at once or continue with all the balls until all the *masa* is gone. If you must, keep the empanadas warm, wrapped well in a cloth napkin, until serving time.

Hint: You can fry these empanadas if you like in hot sunflower or blended vegetable oil. Turn once to cook all the way through, then drain well (see page 58).

QUESADILLAS DE FLOR DE CALABAZA
Fresh Cheese and Squash Blossom Turnovers

The first time I ever made quesadillas was in the kitchen of a Spanish flamenco dancer in New York City. I arrived to cater her party with Diana Kennedy's The Cuisines of Mexico *under my arm. I had no idea how hard it would be to actually make quesadillas and that it takes time to get the hang of it! It took so long to make them that the dinner was late and the hostess was a bit miffed, but after it was all over we both agreed that the food was very special indeed. Now in Oaxaca, I have made a lot of quesadillas, and it took some serious eating to understand the local twists, the various salsas, and the garnishes. This is one of my favorite market/street foods, and I adore them either cooked on the comal or fried, so I have included both methods in the recipe.*

MAKES 8 *QUESADILLAS*

For the salsa de guacamole:
1 ripe Haas avocado
1–2 chiles jalapeños, *seeded and stemmed (see page 329)*
¼ cup cilantro leaves
1 garlic clove
Salt to taste

FOR THE *SALSA DE GUACAMOLE*:
Put all the ingredients in a blender or food processor and blend until smooth. You can add up to 1 cup of water to make the salsa more liquid. It should be fairly runny.

FOR THE *SALSA DE CHILE DE ÁRBOL*:
Bring 2 cups of water to a boil. Remove from heat. Toast the chiles on a dry *comal*, in a cast-iron frying pan, or on a griddle over medium heat. The chiles cook quickly, so watch them carefully. When the skins are blistered, remove them from the heat, place in a bowl, and add the boiled

For the salsa de chile de árbol:

6 chiles de árbol, *or chiles
    japonés, stemmed and seeded
    (see pages 330 and 331)*

¾ *pound* tomatillos *(7 medium),
    husks removed (see page 327)*

Salt to taste

3 garlic cloves

For the masa:

1 *pound prepared* masa *for tor-
    tillas or 1¾ cups* masa harina
    for tortillas

1 *teaspoon salt, or more to taste*

For the filling:

½ *pound* quesillo *or* queso fresco
    *(see pages 345 and 346) or
    Muenster, Monterey Jack, or
    Armenian string cheese,
    shredded or grated*

2 *bunches* flor de calabaza *(about
    16), stems and pistils removed
    (see page 326)*

24 *fresh* epazote *leaves (see
    page 336) or 8 tablespoons
    cilantro leaves*

To finish:

1½ *cups peanut, sunflower, or
    vegetable oil, for frying
    (optional)*

2 *cups thinly sliced green cabbage*

water. Allow to soak 5 minutes. Roast the *tomatillos* on the *comal* until they are soft and cooked throughout, about 10 minutes. Remove them from the *comal* and set aside.

Grind the chiles in a *molcajete* or mortar and pestle, blender, or food processor with the salt. Add the garlic to make a paste. Continue to grind, adding in the *tomatillos* one at a time. The sauce should have a rough texture. Add ¼ cup of water and season with salt.

FOR THE *MASA*:

If using fresh *masa*, break up the *masa* in a large mixing bowl with your fingers. Knead the *masa* with the salt and add 4 tablespoons warm water if needed to make a soft, even dough. If using *masa harina*, mix with 1 cup plus 2 tablespoons warm water to make a soft but not dry dough. Cover with a damp cloth and allow the dough to rest 15 minutes. Add the salt and knead for 1 minute. Add 2 tablespoons warm water and knead.

Divide the dough into 8 balls that are 2 inches in diameter and cover with a damp cloth.

FRYING METHOD:

Press the *masa* balls out on a tortilla press between two sheets of plastic. If you do not have a tortilla press, you can flatten the dough as thin as you can between the two sheets of plastic by using the heel of your hand. Remove the top piece of plastic and place 3 to 4 tablespoons of cheese, 2 squash blossoms, and 3 *epazote* leaves on the bottom half of each tortilla toward the center. Fold the top half of the tortilla over the filling to make a half-moon. Dab a little water on the edge to seal it shut. If the dough breaks, moisten the dough to patch and seal it. Lift the quesadilla with the bottom sheet of plastic and invert it onto a baking sheet covered with waxed paper. Pull the plastic away from the dough, place it back on the tortilla press, and repeat the procedure with the remaining balls of dough.

Heat the oil in a deep, heavy 8-inch frying pan, over high heat. When the oil is hot, place the *quesadillas* in the pan, lower to medium heat, and fry on one side for approximately 2 minutes. Do not crowd them in the pan. When the *quesadillas* are golden brown, turn them over and fry on the other side about 2 minutes more. Drain the *quesadillas* on paper towels. Keep them hot until ready to serve.

COMAL OR "BAKING" METHOD:
Make each quesadilla as you are cooking it on the hot *comal*. Press the *masa* balls out on a tortilla press between two sheets of plastic. Remove the top sheet of plastic from the tortilla. Lay it gently on top of the tortilla and invert the tortilla, leaving the plastic on both sides. Peel off the plastic on top and invert the tortilla onto your hand. Remove the remaining already loosened piece of plastic. Lay the tortilla on a 10-inch dry *comal*, griddle, or in a cast-iron frying pan, and cook it for 1 minute. Then turn it over, fill it, fold it, and seal it, as described above. Cook 2 to 4 minutes on each side, until cooked through and the cheese is melted.

TO SERVE:
Top each *quesadilla* with ¼ cup shredded cabbage, 2 tablespoons *salsa de guacamole*, and 1 tablespoon *salsa de chile de árbol*. Serve immediately.

Hints: The salsas can also be used for *tlayudas* (see page 19), or served as table sauces.

For the *salsa de chile de árbol*, you can substitute tomatoes for the *tomatillos*, if you like.

CHILAQUILES ROJOS
Fried Tortillas Smothered in Chile Sauce

I've heard this dish being called "old broken up sombreros" from Diana Kennedy, which I think is a Mexican way of describing this dish. It is what every household makes with its old blandas *(soft corn tortillas) after a few days so they don't go bad. Irene Sánchez Santiago, our friend and left-hand assistant to the family (Jose being the right!), makes this version of* Chilaquiles Rojos *at least once a week. The method is the stovetop version, where you simmer the sauce, place the fried tortillas in it, and after the sauce is absorbed a little, add the toppings.*

MAKES 6 SERVINGS

For the sauce:

1 pound tomatoes (2 medium–large
    round or 8–10 plum)

5 chiles guajillos, stemmed,
    seeded, and deveined (see
    page 331)

½ medium white onion, chunked

7 garlic cloves

1 tablespoon sunflower or vegetable
    oil

For the chilaquiles:

12–15 fresh corn tortillas, cut into
    triangles, or 9 cups tostada
    chips

1 cup sunflower or vegetable oil

1 medium white onion, halved and
    thinly sliced along the lines of
    the onion

12 ounces queso fresco, crumbled
    (see page 346)

¾–1 cup crema (see page 345),
    crème fraîche, or sour cream

FOR THE SAUCE:

In a 2-quart saucepan, bring 2 cups of water to a boil. Make an x in the bottoms of the tomatoes. Place them in the boiling water and cook for 3 to 5 minutes. Remove the tomatoes and set aside. Reserve the water. Put the chiles in a small bowl and cover with the hot tomato water. Allow to soak for 15 minutes. Remove and discard the skins of the tomatoes. Place the chiles, tomatoes, onion, and garlic in a blender and blend well. Pour through a strainer to remove the chile skins.

In a 4-quart heavy saucepan or *cazuela*, heat the oil. Add the sauce and cook until bubbling. Add 2 to 3 cups of water and simmer for 20 minutes, covered.

FOR THE *CHILAQUILES*:

In a large, heavy frying pan, fry the tortillas bit by bit in the oil until slightly brown. Drain well. (If you are using tostada chips, omit this step.) You can also do this in the oven by baking the triangles on baking sheets at 400°F for 5 minutes. Turn them over and bake for an additional 5 minutes. Add the tortilla triangles or chips to the sauce. Cover and continue to cook for 5 minutes.

Spoon out the *chilaquiles* onto each plate or onto a large platter if you are going to serve it family style. Top with the sliced onion, crumbled *queso fresco*, and *crema* drizzled liberally over the top. Serve with any type of *frijoles* on the side.

Hint: Sometimes I mash avocado with the cream, thin it with milk to make it runny, and add salt and pepper.

ENFRIJOLADAS
Stuffed Tortillas Bathed in Bean Sauce

Enfrijoladas *is one of the dishes in the Oaxacan kitchen that I call a comfort food. The rich, dense bean sauce is almost sweet, and it's one of the first foods served to children when they are young. This version of* enfrijoladas *is stuffed with* quesillo, *then bathed with the sauce and topped with the traditional garnishes. Serve with Ensalada de Botana (page 235) for a satisfying lunch.*

MAKES 8 SERVINGS

4 *cups* Frijoles Negros de Olla (page 146), *cooked and drained, water reserved*

3 *chiles pasillas oaxaqueños, stemmed (see page 331)*

2 *chiles de árbol, stemmed (see page 330)*

7 *avocado leaves* (hoja de aguacate; *see page 338)*

2 *cups reserved bean broth or chicken stock (page 343) or water*

2 *teaspoons plus ½ cup sunflower or vegetable oil*

16 *fresh corn tortillas, 8 inches in diameter*

8 *ounces* quesillo *(see page 345)*

1 *small white onion, cut in half and thinly sliced lengthwise*

8 *ounces* queso fresco, *crumbled (see page 346)*

½ *cup parsley leaves, finely chopped*

In a small saucepan, bring 1 cup of water to a boil. On a 10-inch dry *comal*, griddle, or in a cast-iron frying pan, toast the chiles until they give off their scent. Place the chiles in a bowl and pour the hot water over them. Soak for 5 minutes. On the same *comal*, toast the avocado leaves. Hold the main leaf stem of each leaf and crumble both sides of the leaf into the blender jar. Discard the stems. Continue until all the leaves are added. Add the *frijoles*, bean broth, and chiles to the blender and puree until smooth.

Heat the 2 teaspoons oil in an 8-inch cast-iron frying pan. Pour the mixture into the frying pan to heat. As it heats, don't let it dry out, as the sauce needs to be soupy.

In another 8-inch cast-iron frying pan, heat the ½ cup oil over high heat. Place a tortilla in the frying pan and fry quickly on each side, turning once. Remove to a plate to drain. The tortillas should be pliable. Continue with the remaining tortillas.

Fill one quarter of each tortilla with 2 tablespoons of *quesillo*, fold it in half, and then fold in half again. This should make a triangle stuffed with cheese. Place four of the stuffed tortillas in the black bean sauce, being sure to cover them with sauce. Cover the pan, lower the heat, and cook over low heat until the cheese melts, about 5 minutes. If the sauce starts to dry out, add more water. It should be soupy. Repeat with all of the tortillas.

Place a coated tortilla on a plate and lay a second tortilla on top of the first with the points going in the same direction. Spoon more sauce on top. Repeat with the other tortillas, two per plate. Garnish with the onion slices, *queso fresco*, and parsley. Serve immediately.

Hints: If you get fresh, hot corn tortillas made with *nixtamal* (see page 320), you can place them directly into the sauce and omit frying them.

This recipe works very well with flour tortillas, only stuff them and lightly fry them first, then bathe them in the bean sauce.

TESMOLE DE PAVO
Light Turkey Mole

These light moles made in clay pots or ollas are characteristic of the area of the Cañada. Señora Silvia Carrera Gamboa, of Restaurant Silvia in Teotitlán de Flores Magón, makes this tesmole with turkey for banquets—the everyday tesmole she would serve at the restaurant would have chicken. She insists that the turkey be a female and the egg-laying type to really make the tesmole taste as good as it can be. Tamales can be made from the leftovers by cooking frijoles bayos (brown beans), mixing them with the tesmole, and enveloping them with a coarse masa made with lard. These are wrapped up like little packages in banana leaves (page 339). Serve with Arroz con Chepil (page 52) or white rice and hot corn tortillas.

MAKES 8 SERVINGS

Seasoning ingredients for chicken stock (page 343)
3½ pounds turkey legs (approximately 2 legs)
About 20 chiles guajillos (see page 331)
½ cup chiles chiltepecs (see page 330)
1 medium white onion, chunked

Put the seasoning ingredients and 5 cups water in a 6-quart stockpot and bring to a boil. Add the turkey legs and cook as per the directions on page 343 for about 45 minutes covered over low heat or until done. Remove the turkey from the stock. Separate the meat from the bones and cut into 8 big pieces. Set aside. Strain the stock and reserve.

Boil the chiles, onion, and garlic for 10 minutes in 3 cups of water, covered, over low heat. Drain. Place the chiles, onion, garlic, and tomatoes in a blender with 1 cup of the reserved stock. Blend well. Strain through a colander or food mill to remove tomato and chile skins.

Cleaning chiles for tesmole *(Barbara Lawton)*

½ head of garlic, cloves separated

½ pound tomatoes (1 medium–large round or 4–5 plum)

2 tablespoons sunflower or vegetable oil

For the masa:

½ pound prepared masa *for tortillas or 1 cup* masa harina *for tortillas mixed with ¾ cup water to make a soft dough*

1 teaspoon lard or sunflower oil

1 teaspoon salt

In an *olla* or clay pot, fry the turkey pieces in the oil until browned, about 3 minutes. Remove the turkey meat and set aside. Add the chile mixture to the pot and fry for about 5 minutes, stirring. Add the remaining 3½ cups turkey stock and turkey meat and cook, covered, for 30 minutes over low heat.

FOR THE *MASA*:

In a 2-quart saucepan, heat 1 quart of water with a pinch of salt.

Mix the *masa* with the lard or oil and salt. Roll the dough into small balls the size of a walnut. Make an indentation in the center of each one with your finger. When the water is simmering, slip the dumplings into the pot. Cook until firm, about 5 minutes. Remove from the water and place in the *tesmole*. Adjust the salt and serve immediately.

BISTECES ENTOMATADOS
Spicy Beefsteaks with Tomatoes

When you take the train to Puebla, it goes through an area of Oaxaca called La Cañada Chica, or Little Canyon. My favorite place to stop and jump off is Cuicatlán, home of varieties of mangoes and other luscious fruits. Right off the train station is La Abuelita restaurant, where the abuelita, Señora Avendaño, is over 100 years old. Her granddaughter still runs the restaurant, using her recipes.

MAKES 6 TO 8 SERVINGS

Salt and pepper

1½ pounds boneless round steak, slightly pounded

5 tablespoons sunflower or vege-table oil

1½ medium white onions, halved and thinly sliced

1½ pounds tomatoes (3 medium–large round or 12–15 plum), sliced

3–4 chiles jalapeños, seeded and cut into strips (see page 329)

2 tablespoons finely chopped garlic

1 teaspoon dried Oaxacan oregano (see page 336)

1½ pounds red potatoes, sliced in ¼-inch slices

2 cups chicken stock (page 343)

½ cup parsley leaves, finely chopped

Salt and pepper the steaks lightly. In a 6-quart heavy braising pot with a lid, fry the meat in 3 tablespoons of the oil over high heat for 1½ minutes on each side or until brown. Do not crowd the meat in the pan. When done, remove from the pot and set aside.

Add the remaining 2 tablespoons of oil to the pot and sauté the onions until translucent, stirring constantly, about 3 to 5 minutes. Add the tomatoes and caramelize them until their juices come out (about 4 minutes), stirring as needed, but don't break up the tomatoes entirely. Lower the heat to medium, add the chiles and garlic, and continue to cook. Add the oregano and 1 teaspoon each salt and black pepper, and stir. Lay the potato slices on top of the mixture, then the steaks with any juices. Pour the chicken stock in slowly. It should just come to the level of the meat, no more. Sprinkle the parsley leaves on top. Cover, lower the heat to a simmer, and cook for 1 hour.

Serve with tortillas, steamed green beans or *Frijoles Negros de Olla* (page 146), or fried eggs on the side for a hearty breakfast.

Hint: The tomatoes really need to caramelize or they won't have the sweetness needed to make this its best.

QUESILLO FUNDIDO CON VERDOLAGAS
Fondue of Quesillo with Purslane

Verdolagas *(purslane)* is a succulent herb that is good for the heart and blood, as it helps to make red corpuscles. It is eaten in soups, stews, and quesadillas, but my favorite way is with pork, salsa verde, and quesillo. This is an appetizer that should be served with soft hot corn tortillas. For a hearty main course, cut the pork into big chunks and serve it without the cheese topping, with rice or potatoes.

MAKES 8 TO 10 SERVINGS

Seasoning ingredients for pork stock (page 344)

1 pound boneless pork shoulder, cut into ½-inch cubes

Salt to taste

For the salsa verde:

1 pound fresh tomatillos *(10–12 medium), husked*

3 chiles jalapeños, stemmed (see page 329)

½ medium white onion, quartered

3 garlic cloves

For the verdolagas:

2 tablespoons sunflower or vegetable oil or lard

1 bunch verdolagas *(purslane) leaves (2–3 cups tightly packed), stems removed (see page 327)*

½ pound of quesillo, manchego, Muenster, or Gouda, shredded (see pages 345 and 346)

Salt to taste

In a 4-quart saucepan with a lid, bring 2 quarts of water to a boil. Add the seasoning ingredients for the pork stock, bring to a boil, add pork cubes, then follow instructions on page 344, simmering the stock for 45 minutes to 1 hour, until pork is tender. Add salt. Remove the pork from the stock; strain and reserve the stock.

FOR THE *SALSA VERDE*:
In a 2-quart saucepan, boil the *tomatillos* and chiles in 2 cups of water until the *tomatillos* just change color, about 10 minutes. Put the *tomatillos*, chiles, onion, garlic, and cooking water from the *tomatillos* in a blender. Blend until smooth.

TO PREPARE THE *VERDOLAGAS*:
Preheat the oven to 350°F.

In a deep, heavy 8-inch frying pan, heat the oil or lard over high heat until smoking, and fry the cooked pork pieces, a few at a time, until well browned, about 10 minutes. Add the *salsa verde*, stir, and then add the *verdolagas* leaves. Add 1½ cups of the reserved stock. Cook for 20 minutes over low heat, covered. Add salt to taste.

Spoon the mixture into 4-ounce *cazuelitas* or ramekins and top with shredded cheese. Place in preheated oven and bake until brown and bubbly, about 20 to 25 minutes. Serve with fresh corn tortillas.

TESMOLE DE PIPIÁN DE GALLINA
Pumpkin Seed Mole with Chicken

This pipián-*type* tesmole *is from Santa María Chilchotla, a high-altitude area very north in Oaxaca, near the Puebla border. This area is the largest zone producing Pergamino coffee. Here in this village the* tesmole *is not as thin as in other parts of the Cañada because of the pumpkin seeds. It also has the red* achiote *to color and season it. The señoras also insist on egg-laying hens for better flavor, which is a real sacrifice. I tried the recipe with a market-bought chicken (sex unknown) and it worked just fine—you can also use turkey if preferred. Serve this with* Arroz Blanco con Plátanos Fritos *(page 53) or* Arroz a la Jardinera del Restaurante Yalile *(page 174).*

MAKES 6 SERVINGS

1 medium white onion, chunked

½ head of garlic

1 tablespoon chile chiltepec *seeds or* chile de árbol *seeds (see page 330)*

1½ cup pepitas *(see page 338)*

4½ cups chicken stock *(page 343), or more if needed*

2½–3 pounds chicken, cut into 6 pieces

2 tablespoons sunflower or blended oil

1½ teaspoons achiote *paste (see page 337)*

2 hierba santa *leaves (see page 336)*

2 teaspoons salt, or to taste

On a 10-inch dry *comal*, griddle, or in a cast-iron frying pan, roast the onion and garlic until clear, about 8 to 10 minutes over medium heat. You have to really watch the garlic so it doesn't burn. Set aside. Add the chile seeds to the *comal* and toast, stirring with a wooden spatula or a brush, so they don't burn. Set aside. Add the *pepitas* and toast them until they puff up and are browned, stirring constantly for about 5 minutes over medium heat. Set aside.

In a blender, combine the onion, garlic, chile seeds, and *pepitas* with 1 cup of the chicken stock.

Fry the chicken in the oil in a 4-quart heavy braiser or *cazuela* until nicely browned, about 10 minutes, turning once. Remove the chicken pieces from the pot and set aside. Fry the *pepita* paste in the remaining oil for 5 minutes, stirring constantly. Add 3 cups of chicken stock and stir in.

In a *molcajete* or a blender, dissolve the *achiote* in the remaining ½ cup chicken stock. You may need to blend this a few times and strain it each time to dissolve it well, depending on the hardness of the *achiote* paste. Add to the *pipián*.

Return the chicken to the pot, then add the *hierba santa* leaves and salt. Cover and cook 45 minutes over low heat, until the flavors have time to meld.

Hint: You can substitute boneless, skinless chicken breast, browning it first. Add to the sauce during the last 15 minutes.

PÍLTE DE POLLO MAZATECO
Chilled Chicken Wrapped in Herbs and Banana Leaves

This dish is from the upper part of the Cañada, called the Sierra Mazateca, and is made in the village of Huautla de Jiménez. This village is built on a mountainside, and you can see for miles when clouds don't block the view. It's a special dish made for fiestas, or you can have someone make it especially for you. The chicken can be substituted with pork ribs or backstrap. Serve with Arroz con Chepil (page 52) or Arroz Blanco con Plátanos Fritos (page 53).

MAKES 8 SERVINGS

8 large banana leaves (see
     page 339)
1 chicken (about 3 pounds),
     cut into 8 pieces
Salt
2 cups chiles chiltepecs
     (about 400 chiles; see page 330)
½ medium white onion
½ head of garlic, cloves separated
1 teaspoon salt, or to taste
16 hierba santa leaves (see
     page 336)

Soften the banana leaves by boiling them for 30 to 40 minutes in 1 quart of water.

Salt the chicken pieces and allow to sit while you make the chile mixture.

Boil the chiles, onion, and garlic in 1½ cups water until soft, about 10 minutes. Grind the chiles, onion, and garlic on the *metate* or in a blender until completely smooth. Strain through a food mill or a strainer into a bowl. Add salt to taste.

Put the chicken pieces into the *pílte* mixture to coat them evenly. Lay a banana leaf down horizontally on a counter. Place 2 *hierba santa* leaves in the middle of the banana leaves with the wide ends together and the tips pointing outward. Put a piece of chicken on top and fold the leaves around to enclose it. Fold up the banana leaves to enclose the package of chicken in the *hierba santa*. Repeat with the remaining pieces of chicken.

Place water and salt in the bottom of a large stockpot or steamer pot with a rack. Place the packets of *pílte* on the rack. Cover and steam over high heat until cooked through, about 1½ hours. Serve.

CECINA ENCHILADA
Grilled Thinly Sliced Pork Marinated in Chile Paste

I remember Sunday afternoons when our friends Lulú and Benjamín, their six sons, and various in-laws would come to our ranch for a day in the campo. They would bring piles of thinly sliced tasajo, cecina, and links of chorizo sausages to cook on our parrilla (grill). I would make the beans, salads, and dessert and supply the onions from the garden. Benjamín was a master of the grill, and he cooked the meats and onions to perfection. We always made our own enchilada paste for the cecina, so we could be sure of the quality of the pork and have some unseasoned meat for the toddlers of the group. By the time they were two or three years old, they were eating the spicy meat with the rest of us!

MAKES 4 SERVINGS

For the enchilada paste:

6–7 chiles guajillos, *stemmed, seeded, and deveined (see page 331)*

3 black peppercorns

1 whole allspice

1 whole clove

1 piece of Mexican cinnamon, *about 1 inch long (see page 337)*

¼ teaspoon dried Oaxacan oregano *(see page 336)*

½ cup fruit or cider vinegar

7 garlic cloves

½ teaspoon salt, *or to taste*

1 pound boneless cecina *or pork loin, thinly sliced*

FOR THE ENCHILADA PASTE:
Heat 2 cups of water in a medium saucepan. Soak the chiles in the hot water for 10 minutes. Reserve the water. On a 10-inch dry *comal*, griddle, or in a cast-iron frying pan, toast the peppercorns, allspice, clove, cinnamon, and oregano.

Put the cleaned chiles, spices, garlic, vinegar, salt, and ½ cup chile water in a blender and blend well. Spread the paste over the pieces of meat and let sit for 1 to 2 hours. (If you want, this can be done overnight.) Grill the *cecina* over hot coals or sear on a cast-iron griddle.

FOR THE GARNISH:
Make an x in the top of each onion about a third of the way into the onion. Place directly on the coals and allow to roast about 15 minutes or until the onion is transparent inside. Peel off the outer skin of each onion, squeeze a lime over the top, and serve with avocado slices, radish flowers, lime wedges, and hot corn or flour tortillas. Any of the hot sauces would work with this, but generally the *Cecina Enchilada* is spicy enough as it is. I prefer the freshness of *salsa cruda* (page 197) or *salsa de chile pasilla* (page 15).

For the garnish:

8 green onions or 4 medium or
large white onions, skins on

2 avocados, peeled and cut into
wedges

8 radishes, cut into flowers

4 limes, cut in half

1 dozen corn or flour tortillas

Hint: The chile paste can be put on *nanacates* (portobello mushrooms; see page 327) and grilled. The paste is also good as a seasoning for ribs or chops that can be grilled, then slowly baked in the oven with some beer.

DULCE DE MANGO
Mangoes in Sweet Syrup

One morning, on my way to Cuicatlán on the train, I sat with a local woman from that village. It was high mango season and I was excited to go to her village and buy cases of mangoes to bring back home. We started a conversation and, as often happens, the discussion included exchanging recipes. I talked about Indian mango chutney, and she told me about this dessert dish that is a specialty of Cuicatlán. Serve one whole mango per person with the syrup spooned over top.

MAKES 8 SERVINGS

5 pounds mangoes (approximately
8 large Petacón), peeled

½ cup cal (slaked lime; see
page 320)

2½ pounds piloncillo or brown
sugar (see page 348)

2 pieces of Mexican cinnamon,
1 inch long (see page 337)

Place mangoes and *cal* in a large saucepan with 1 quart water. Soak for ½ hour. Drain and discard the water. Cover the mangoes with 5 cups water. Bring to a boil and cook for 15 minutes. Drain and discard the water.

Refill the pan with 5 cups water. Make 3 cuts lengthwise in each mango and place in the water. Add the *piloncillo* and cinnamon. Bring to boil, then lower the heat and cook for 1 hour. Serve chilled or at room temperature.

ANTE DE MANGO
Layered Mango Pudding or Charlotte

There are many variations of antes, *using different dry breads or cakes layered with seasonal fruits and pastry cream. This version was shared by my friend Luz Elena, the mother of my son Kaelin's classmate Pedro, during mango season this year. Although it seemed too easy to be true, it's delicious. You can use any fruit you have on hand and any type of dry, airy bread or cake. You should make this dessert at least a day or two in advance for all the flavors and textures to combine. It's great after a big dinner because it's so light and fruity.*

MAKES 8 TO 10 SERVINGS

½ cup raisins
⅔ cup sweet sherry
7 cups cubed pan de yema
   (page 347) or challah or other egg
   bread, fresh or a few days old; or
   dry anise sponge cookies, biscuits, panettone, or ladyfingers
3 large ripe mangoes, peeled and
   pit removed, cubed (5½–7 cups)
1 cup evaporated milk
¾ cup sweetened condensed milk
1½ teaspoons vanilla extract

In a small saucepan, plump the raisins in the sherry for 15 minutes over low heat, covered. If you are using fresh bread, dry the bread in the oven for 10 minutes. (If using dry bread, anise sponge cookies, panettone, or ladyfingers, omit this step.)

Place half of the mango and all the evaporated milk in a blender. Puree until smooth. Empty this mixture into a bowl and repeat with the remaining mango and condensed milk. Add to the first mixture and mix well. Strain the raisins and reserve the sherry and raisins.

In a clear serving bowl with straight sides, make a layer of half the bread cubes. Sprinkle half of the reserved sherry over the bread, followed by half of the raisins. Add half of the mango mixture. Add another layer of bread, sherry, and raisins, saving about 5 raisins for the top. Add the remaining mango mixture and the raisins to decorate the top. Cover well with plastic wrap and refrigerate for 1 to 2 days. (You can make this in the morning and serve at night, but it really is better if you leave this a day or two.) Serve in wineglasses with a dollop of whipped cream, if you wish.

PLATANADA
Banana and Cinnamon Milkshake

This is one of the Mexican preparadas *(fruit drinks made with milk) that I've made for years. You can combine papaya or mango with the bananas and also add wheat germ, almonds, or lecithin for extra* fuerza *(strength), if you wish. There are so many types of bananas in the Cañada region, but I particularly enjoy the plátanos morados (a red variety), which make a great* platanada.

MAKES 4 SERVINGS

2–3 ripe bananas, peeled
4 cups milk
1 teaspoon ground Mexican cin-
    namon (see page 337)
1 teaspoon vanilla extract
½ cup sugar

Place all the ingredients in a blender with 8 ice cubes. Blend until smooth. Serve with a sprinkle of cinnamon on top.

AGUA DE LIMÓN
Limeade

Along the Cañada region there are groves and groves of lime trees. These are the small Key lime variety that have lots of juice and an intense flavor. Agua de Limón, or limonada, is probably the most refreshing and popular flavored water that is offered in everyone's home. It can quench your thirst like nothing else, and its astringent qualities are good for you. I always say that if you eat a raw garlic clove and half a lime every day, you will never get sick.

MAKES 2 QUARTS

1 cup fresh lime juice
1½ cups sugar
2 lime peels, minced or grated

Put the lime juice, sugar, lime peels, and 2 quarts of water in a large pitcher. Mix well. Serve well chilled.

CHAPTER FOUR

The Coastal Region
(Región de la Costa)

Juana Ramírez and Susana with Camarones al Mojo de Ajo, Chacahua (Barbara Lawton)

Overleaf: Tina Coaché Chacón and Susana eating tamarind candies at Danni Baan, Zipolite, Puerto Angel (Barbara Lawton)

The first time I came to Oaxaca, in 1983, I drove south down the Pacific coast from Acapulco toward the Isthmus with my friends Roger and Justin. On approaching Puerto Angel, I was so sick from turista, I thought I'd be arriving just to die. I had heard about the Costa Chica for years, and I felt it was a triumph just to be there, let alone die there. Maybe I could be buried in the beautiful graveyard in Puerto Angel with its magnificent view of the bay. But to my delight and good fortune, my time had not come.

It didn't seem my style to die from *bad* food or drink, anyway!

The first person I met in Puerto Angel was also named Susana. She owned a beautiful *posada* (inn) that she and her husband had built in a canyon just off the beach. He was a Mexican and a true artist, as his building reflected, using natural materials, pieces of old boats, and tropical woods. She was an ex-restaurateur from Greenwich Village, who had given up the fast life for the creativity and challenge of raising two kids in a small fishing village, while gradually building up their inn. Their slogan was "This is a place to escape from the world," which it truly was. Susana took one look at me doubled over in agony from *turista,* and said, "Garlic!" After fixing me garlic tea, she served me garlic soup, and slowly I began to mend. The healing powers of the medicinal plant began to work and, after a while, I was able to rise, feeling reborn and ready to take in the beauty of Oaxaca and its people. It was love at first sight.

My friends and I had made this trip to volunteer at a home for disabled children, called the Centro de Atención Infantil Piña Palmera (the Palm Grove Children's Center), on nearby Zipolite Beach. Panchito, an ex–Wall Street stockbroker who had changed his life to help children, founded the home. He was a great healer who could look into people's souls and guide them on their own paths. So, we had come to get away from our hectic businesses and jobs in New York City and to do something totally different. We worked with the children during the day and partied under the stars at night. What a great way to spend a vacation, I thought. Little did I know that this trip would change my world forever.

I was totally impressed with the fabulous tastes of the *costeña* food I got to know at that time, and I continue to be excited by the region and its bounty. The fish was as fresh as you could imagine—we got up before dawn to go on *lanchas* (small boats) to catch them. The ocean was loaded with fish, and it seemed as though there was an endless supply. We ate fresh fish and seafood in more ways than you can conceive: *al mojo de ajo* (soaked in garlic), *a la parrilla* (on the grill), *caldo de mariscos* (seafood soup), *pescadillas* (hot fish tacos), and more. We used heaps of salsa made from fiery *chiles costeños* and drank *atoles* (hot gruel drinks) of corn and sesame seeds and high-altitude Pluma Hidalgo coffee. At the children's home, the young cook made *mole amarillo de iguana* (yellow iguana *mole*) for us. We helped her make tortillas over the open fire on her *comal* and had the best black beans I'd ever eaten. The experience bonded me to the Oaxacan universe and was the stimulus to make Oaxaca my home. To this day we are connected to the Piña Palmera by doing fund-raisers for the school. We adopted two of their boys (who are now young men) to share our home, and they have enriched our lives as we have theirs.

There is a new road connecting Oaxaca city to the coast via the Sierra Madre del Sur that passes through the village of Sola de Vega, where a famous fiesta dish, *pastel de sola de vega,* a layered garbanzo pie, originated. Farther down the mountain is the turnoff at El Vidrio that goes to the sacred site of the Virgen de Juquila, one of the most popular saints of the Oaxacans. Year after year, in December, hundreds of people make a pilgrimage here to ask for good health and other special favors. Everyone returns home with medallions and *jamoncillo*, a sweet that is made from *piloncillo* and coconut.

As we drive on the winding road that is virtually all curves, we pass hillside after hillside terraced with corn and bean crops. As we get closer to the coast, we see coconut and banana groves, papaya orchards, fields of peanuts, sesame, *chile serrano,* and the colorful *chile tuxta*. Not long ago these crops were transported to the city on muleback, entailing days of travel. Now the trip is about seven hours from Oaxaca through the mountains, ending right on the coastline at Puerto Escondido.

The variation in altitude in the coastal regions is as striking as the mosaic of cultures, the people, and their food specialties. Chilean sailors and African slave ships that were shipwrecked on the shores led to a blending of cultures unique to the coast. The indigenous groups are the Mixteco, the Chatino, the Tacuate, and the Amuzgo, in addition to Negroes and mestizos. One of the most exciting examples of this fusion is evident during the November festival Costeño, when the different groups come together to perform their dances, many wearing masks through which the dancers are totally transformed. The costumes and the performances are magnificent.

One of the most remarkable women I've met on my trips to Puerto Escondido is Mamá Goya. Orphaned as a young girl, she was adopted by her aunt, who taught her how to cook. They were one of the three families who first settled Puerto Escondido, which is now a thriving beach community. Her daughter, Carmen Herrera Silva, now runs the popular restaurant Junto del Mar, which her mother started more than fifty years ago to feed the men who brought the first electrical (power) lines to Puerto Escondido. Another wonderful getaway on the Pacific coast is the Laguna de Chacahua. Our favorite spot is Los Delfines de Chacahua, a *palapa* restaurant on the beach. It is here that Juana Ramírez cooks specialties of the house, including *Pescado Empapelado al Diablo* (page 92), a whole fish layered with other ingredients and a special "devil" sauce, then cooked on the *plancha* or griddle.

Traveling down the coast road from Zapotalito toward the east, we pass various lime plantations, coconut groves, and fields of sweet potato and *chile jalapeño*. Then we pass through the small towns right on the beach, such as Mazunte, where Hurricane Paulina caused her terrible destruction in October 1997. The turtle museum here was created to benefit the village after the turtle factory was closed. Not only was the turtle meat popular, the eggs were a delicacy and skin creams and lotions were made from the rich turtle oil. Environmentalists had campaigned for years to close the slaughterhouse, since this beach was a nesting ground for an endangered species. A museum was founded as a source of income for villagers who had lost their livelihoods.

Farther down the coast is Zipolite, home of the Piña Palmera as well as the bed-and-breakfast Danni Baan, which means "Sacred Mountain" in Zapotec. Perched on a hill overlooking the ocean is a lovely home built by Jim Clouse and Tina Coaché Chacón. Tina is a dressmaker and an incredible cook who makes delicious *Cazuelitas de Tamarindo* (page 101) from the tamarind pods hanging from the trees in her yard, as well as other regional favorites from the coast and her hometown of Zaachila in the Central Valleys of Oaxaca. She has one of the nicest gardens I have ever seen, very green and lush. Jim runs the carpentry workshop at Piña Palmera, teaching the children to make toys for therapy and profit.

Over the years Piña Palmera has grown from a home for orphans and handicapped children to a center for disabled people of all ages. A family member of the special-needs person comes with him or her to learn the care each person requires. In addition, the center has started an outreach program whereby the staff goes to pueblos all over the coastal region, uniting people with similar problems and teaching group classes. In this way they have more contact with the people who need their services. All this is made possible through donations from people the world over.

One of the outings I particularly enjoy is going to the coffee *finca* (plantation) near Santa María Xandani, Finca de la Gloria. A beautiful plantation with a spring-fed waterfall, the *finca* is owned by Señor Gustavo Scherenberg Noyola, a retired senator of Oaxaca, and his wife, Señora María Isabel, who is in charge of their large kitchen. Daily she prepares a huge buffet to feed the plantation workers, visitors, and family. The couple also has a bed-and-breakfast where people can learn about growing coffee while enjoying a relaxing holiday. The old farmhouse is exquisite, decorated in antiques.

Since it was my introduction to Oaxaca and its people, the Costeña region has forever remained close to my heart—with its wonderful food from the sea and its warm, sensual people. As the coastal group Trio Fantasia sings their song from Pinotepa, *¡Viva la Costa!*

Señora Isabel Scherenberg making **Sopa de Almendras** *at Finca de La Gloria (Barbara Lawton)*

IN THIS CHAPTER

CALDO DE MARISCOS A LA COSTA
Seafood Soup

Wherever I look at a seafood menu I want to try the caldo de mariscos. *Seafood soup is one of my biggest weaknesses. I've even eaten it for breakfast (if I'm traveling along the coast) just to satisfy my quest to find the best. This recipe is inspired by Carmen Vásquez, Irma Hernández, Oresta Serefino, and every other* cocinera *who has blessed me with her rendition of this satisfying stew. It appears to have its roots in Veracruz.*

MAKES 8 BIG SERVINGS

For the seafood stock:

1 pound fish heads and tails (see caldo ingredients below)

Heads and shells from 1 pound of medium shrimp (see caldo ingredients)

1 medium white onion, chunked

2 celery ribs with leaves

½ head of garlic

2 bay leaves

5 black peppercorns

2 tablespoons fresh lime or lemon juice

Salt to taste

For the guisado:

5 carrots, peeled and cut into big chunks

2 pounds tomatoes (4 medium–large round or 16–20 plum), halved

1 medium white onion, chunked

13 garlic cloves

4 chiles guajillos, *stemmed, seeded, and deveined (see page 331)*

4 chiles chipotles, *stemmed, seeded, and deveined (see page 330) or chiles*

FOR SEAFOOD STOCK:

In a 5-quart stockpot, place 4 quarts water with the fish heads and tails and shrimp shells. Bring to a boil, skim the foam that rises to the top, and add the onion, celery, garlic, bay leaves, peppercorns, lime juice, and salt. Lower the heat and simmer for 30 to 45 minutes. Strain and reserve the stock.

FOR THE *GUISADO:*

In a 2-quart saucepan, heat 1 quart of water. Add the carrots, tomatoes, onion, garlic, chiles, cinnamon stick, allspice, and bay leaves and bring to a boil. Cover, lower the heat, and simmer for 15 to 20 minutes or until the carrots are soft. Remove from the heat and place in a blender. Puree the mixture until smooth, then strain through a food mill or wire-mesh strainer to remove seeds and skins.

FOR THE *CALDO:*

In a heavy 6-quart stockpot with a lid, heat the butter until it sizzles over high heat. Add the *guisado* and fry for 10 to 15 minutes or until it is bubbling and well seasoned. Add 6 cups of the reserved stock and simmer about 15 minutes more.

Add the clams, crabs, and large shrimp to the pot and simmer 10 minutes. Add the fish steaks, oysters, and medium shrimp and cook 5 minutes more. Stir in the octopus, conch, and *epazote* and simmer 5 minutes more. Season with salt.

(continued)

chipotles en adobo *(page 332)*

1 piece of Mexican cinnamon stick,
1 inch long *(see page 337)*

2 whole allspice

2 bay leaves

For the caldo:

2 tablespoons butter

2 dozen littleneck clams, scrubbed
well

8 blue crabs, boiled in their shells
and split in half

2 dozen oysters, shucked, with
their liquor

16 large shrimp (about
1½ pounds), heads and shells
on, or peeled if desired

1½ pounds whole red snapper,
bass, or other firm fish, cut into
8 steaks, skins on (save head
and tail for stock)

1 pound medium shrimp, peeled
and deveined (save the shells
and heads for the stock)

1 pound octopus or squid, simmered in water and salt for
1 hour, covered, cut into
16 pieces

½ pound conch meat, simmered in
water and salt for 1 hour, covered, cut into 8 pieces

¼ cup fresh epazote leaves *(see
page 336)*

Salt to taste

For the garnish:

4 limes, cut into wedges

½ medium white onion, finely
chopped

2 chiles jalapeños, finely chopped
(see page 329; optional)

Serve immediately, dividing the seafood among large bowls and ladling the broth over the top. Serve with lime wedges, chopped white onion, and fresh *chiles jalapeños* on the table to add as you wish. Tostadas or *totopos* usually accompany this satisfying dish.

Hints: You can use any combination of seafood available, so if you can't get all the ingredients don't worry. I've also made this with just fish steaks and shrimp and been quite happy with the results, although the other seafood flavors round out the dish.

Be sure to simmer the octopus separately, as it will turn the conch and crab purple if it's cooked with them.

SOPA DE ALMENDRAS
Almond and Chicken Soup

The charming Finca de la Gloria is located in the mountains above the coastal resort of Bahías de Huatulco. The Scherenberg Noyola family has owned it for years. Señora Isabel Scherenberg makes a huge buffet daily on her old wood-burning stove to feed her guests, workers, and family. This soup is always on the menu, and I can see why. It's easy, simple, and delicious.

MAKES 8 SERVINGS

8 cups chicken stock (page 343)

½ pound boneless, skinless chicken breast

4 carrots, peeled and cut into julienne strips

5 garlic cloves, finely chopped

3 eggs, hard boiled, whites and yolks separated

½ cup almonds, blanched and skins removed

Salt and white pepper to taste

5 sprigs parsley, leaves finely chopped

In a heavy 4-quart stockpot, bring the chicken stock to a boil and add the chicken. Cover and simmer for 25 minutes, or until just done. Remove the chicken and set aside to cool. Strain the chicken stock.

Return the stock to a stockpot and place over medium heat. Add the carrots and garlic. Cover and cook 10 minutes.

Put the cooked egg yolks and almonds in a blender with 1 cup of the stock. Blend well.

Shred the chicken into ½-inch pieces.

Add the almond mixture to the soup and allow it to thicken slightly, stirring occasionally. Coarsely chop the egg whites and add them, along with the chicken meat, to the soup. Add salt and white pepper. Stir in the parsley.

Ladle the soup into bowls and serve hot with an extra pinch of parsley on top and a side of tostadas or hot *bolillos* (see page 347).

Hint: To remove skins from almonds, blanch almonds until the skins loosen. Place almonds in a towel, fold the towel over them, and rub.

Opposite: Boiling shrimp to be salted and dried, Chacahua (Alfredo Díaz Mora)

CALDO DE CAMARÓN
Clear Shrimp Soup

The aroma of Caldo de Camarón is heavenly after a morning of swimming and walking on the beach. You return totally relaxed and hungry, and a bowl brimming with shrimp in a clear, flavorful consommé is welcome. Serve this with beer or white wine, or a tall glass of Agua de Limón (page 71).

MAKES 6 TO 8 SERVINGS

9 garlic cloves

¾ pound tomatoes
   (1½ medium–large round
   or 6–7 plum), chunked

¾ medium white onion, chunked

6 small chiles chipotles en
   adobo, stemmed (page 332)

1½ tablespoons sunflower or vegetable oil

2 pounds shrimp, heads and shells
   on (see Hint)

¼ cup epazote leaves (see
   page 336)

Salt to taste

For the garnish:

1 cup finely chopped white onion

½ cup chopped chile jalapeño (see
   page 329)

4 limes, wedged or halved

Put the garlic, tomatoes, onion, and chiles in a blender and blend well. Pour through a strainer or food mill to remove the skins.

In a 2-quart saucepan, fry the tomato mixture in the oil for 5 minutes over high heat. Add 2 quarts of water and bring to a boil. Add the shrimp, *epazote*, and salt. Cover and lower the heat, then simmer for 20 minutes.

Serve with onion, fresh *chile jalapeño* pieces, and wedges or halves of lime on a plate on the table to use *al gusto*.

Hint: If you object to serving shrimp with heads at the table, clean the heads and shells from the shrimp and cook them in the water for 20 minutes to make a shrimp stock. Strain and add to the soup instead of the water. Add the peeled and deveined shrimp to the soup and cook over low heat for 10 minutes only.

Tomato lunch in the tomato field. Clockwise from left: Ensalada de Botanas, sangrita *(orange and tomato juice),* totopos, Coctel de Camarón *(Mexican shrimp cocktail),* Capirotada *(Mexican bread pudding),* Entomatadas *(tortillas dipped in spicy tomato sauce with fresh cheese) (Marcela Taboada)*

Above: Sopa de Guías de Calabaza con Chochoyones *(fresh squash vine soup with young squash and its flowers, corn, chepil, and dumplings) (Marcela Taboada)*

Opposite, top left: Selecting and packing the harvest; Eric Ulrich (center) and Salvador "Chava" Arelleanos, with assorted family and workers during the harvest, San Sebastian Etla, Central Valleys (Marcela Taboada)
Opposite, top right: Fruits at Mercado de Salina Cruz, Isthmus, Oaxaca (Alfredo Díaz Moreno)
Opposite, bottom: Vegetables at Mercado de Salina Cruz, Isthmus, Oaxaca (Barbara Lawton)

Opposite, clockwise from top left: Eating Ma'ach (center) the traditional way with Tasajo (grilled meat) and guías de calabaza (simmered squash vines), Tamazulapan, Sierra Mixe (Alfredo Díaz Mora); Woman selling tostadas (fried corn tortillas) in San Blas Atempa, Isthmus (Barbara Lawton); Susana with Chica Mon's daughter, Margarita, making iguana tamales with yellow mole, San Blas Atempa, Isthmus (Barbara Lawton); Susana tasting botanas with a Mexican telenovela star at the Lavada de Olla, Juchitán, Isthmus (Barbara Lawton)

Left: Admiring the village of Teotitlán del Valle from the sacred mountain, Gie Betz, Día de Santa Cruz, May 3, Central Valleys (Marcela Taboada)

Above: Traditional blessing before wedding feast of José Luis Gutierréz and his bride, Guillermina, Teotitlán del Valle, Central Valleys (Marcela Taboada)
Above, right: Cocineras grinding for the mole, Teotitlán del Valle, Central Valleys (Marcela Taboada)
Right: Female elders mounding plates of bread that will be served with hot chocolate, Teotitlán del Valle (Marcela Taboada)

Above: Virgen de Guadalupe with dishes for religious holidays; back row, left to right: Rosca de Reyes, ponche, Frijol Blanco con Camarón Seco, *syrup and* buñuelos; *front row, left to right:* Sopa de Vigilia, Bacalao Navideño, Ensalada de Betabel Bendito, *and* Calabazas y Tejocotes en Dulce *(Marcela Taboada) (Talavera dishes courtesy of La Mano Mágica, Oaxaca City)*

Opposite, clockwise from top left: Offering to San Antonino, Blessing of the Fruits and Vegetables, Palm Sunday, San Antonino Castillo Velasco, Central Valleys (Marcela Taboada); Woman offering tejate drink, Ash Wednesday, San Andres Huayapam, Central Valleys (Marcela Taboada); Curandera with her Día de Muertos altar, San Sebastian Tutla, Central Valleys (Marcela Taboada); Zapotec women with fruits and palm fronds, Palm Sunday, San Antonino Castillo Velasco, Central Valleys (Marcela Taboada)

Panuchos. Masa *on the* metate *(far back) is pressed into tortillas that are filled with black bean paste (center back); the tortillas are then fried in hot oil and drained (left), then layered with chicken, shredded cabbage (far right), cheese, and cream (right center); topped with salsa hand ground in the stone* molcajete, *they are then served hot (right front) (Marcela Taboada)*

CHILAQUILES VERDES
Fried Tortillas Smothered in an Herb Sauce

This dish has been a specialty of Señora Isabel Scherenberg of the Finca de la Gloria for over twenty years. One of the plants that grows prolifically in the moist tropical heat is the hoja *or* hierba santa, *which is the flavoring in this dish.*

MAKES 6 SERVINGS

½ cup plus 1 teaspoon sunflower or vegetable oil

½ pound corn tortillas, cut into triangles

10 hierba santa *leaves, torn into big pieces, center ribs removed (see page 336)*

7 garlic cloves

5 chiles jalapeños, *stemmed (see page 329)*

½ large white onion, chunked

3 cups chicken stock (page 343)

Salt and pepper to taste

For the garnish:

1 medium white onion, halved and thinly sliced

½ pound queso fresco, queso cotijo, *or* queso ranchero, crumbled or finely grated (see page 346)

½ cup parsley leaves

In an 8-inch cast-iron frying pan, heat the ½ cup oil. Fry the tortilla triangles for 3 to 5 minutes over medium heat, until toasted and crisp. Drain well.

Place the *hierba santa* leaves, garlic, chiles, and onion in a blender with 2 cups of the chicken stock. Blend well until smooth and aromatic.

In a deep frying pan, heat the 1 teaspoon oil until smoking. Add the blended herb mixture and cook over high heat, stirring constantly, about 8 minutes. Add the remaining 1 cup chicken stock to give it a soupy consistency and simmer about 15 minutes. Add salt and pepper.

Add the tortilla triangles and stir in well. Lower the heat, cover, and simmer gently about 10 minutes, or until all the sauce has been absorbed. Remove to a serving platter and top with a layer of onion slices, cheese, and parsley. Serve with simple grilled meats, chicken, or black beans on the side.

TORTA DE CAMARÓN OAXAQUEÑA
Oaxacan Baked Eggs with Fresh Shrimp

This is Mamá Goya's recipe, given to me by her daughter Carmen, who, with her children, runs the restaurant Junto del Mar in Puerto Escondido. It's not on her menu, but it is one of her longtime favorites to serve at home. I made it into a fritada-style cooked egg dish by setting the eggs in the butter and oil and then cooking the whole thing in the oven and topping it with a sauce. A great breakfast includes the torta with Frijoles Negros de Olla (page 146), Café de Olla (page 103), and tortillas or toasted bread.

MAKES 6 SERVINGS

For the shrimp:
½ pound shrimp with heads
½ small white onion
1 tablespoon fresh chopped epazote, or substitute 2 tablespoons dry (see page 336)
7 garlic cloves
½ teaspoon salt

For the sauce:
1 pound tomatoes (2 medium–large round or 8–10 plum)
3 chiles jalapeños or 5 chiles serranos, *stemmed (see page 329)*
2 teaspoons sunflower or blended oil

For the torta:
9 eggs
½ teaspoon salt
½ teaspoon ground black pepper
2 teaspoons butter
1 tablespoon sunflower or olive oil

TO COOK THE SHRIMP:
Remove the heads from the shrimp and reserve them. Remove the shells and devein the shrimp.

In a 2-quart saucepan, heat 1 quart water. Add the onion, *epazote*, garlic, and salt. Boil for 5 minutes. Add the shrimp, lower the heat, cover, and cook for 10 minutes. Remove the shrimp and drain well. Reserve the onion and garlic, and chop the shrimp finely. Set aside.

FOR THE SAUCE:
In a blender, combine the shrimp heads and 1 cup water. Blend well. Remove and set aside.

On a 10-inch dry *comal*, griddle, or in a cast-iron frying pan, roast the tomatoes and chiles over medium heat. When they are well roasted, about 10 to 15 minutes, and the skins are blistered, remove them from the heat. Place the *jalapeños* in a plastic bag to "sweat." After 5 minutes, remove the skins and seeds and discard. Remove the tomato skins and discard.

In a blender, combine the tomatoes, chiles, and reserved onion and garlic. Blend well. Pour through a strainer.

In an 8-inch cast-iron frying pan, heat the oil, add the tomato mixture, and fry at least 5 minutes. Add the shrimp head liquid. Cook, uncovered, for 10 minutes.

FOR THE *TORTA*:
Preheat the oven to 400°F.

In a mixing bowl, beat the eggs. Add the shrimp meat, ¼ cup water, and the salt and pepper. Mix well.

In an 8-inch cast-iron frying pan, heat the butter and oil, then add the egg mixture. With a wooden spatula, move the egg mixture from the sides of the pan as it sets. Let it cook rapidly, about 2 minutes. Place the pan in the oven for 15 minutes or until it rises. Remove from the oven and place under the broiler for 1 to 2 minutes to brown the top.

Serve the *torta* with the sauce spooned over the top.

COCTEL DE CAMARÓN
Mexican Shrimp Cocktail

This is a Mexican-style shrimp cocktail that has all sorts of variations on every coast of Mexico. Typically very small shrimp are bought precooked, but I like to buy the shrimp fresh and make a stock with the shells to use in the sauce. Another very popular seafood cocktail using the same sauce is called vuelve a la vida, or "return to life"; it has not only shrimp but also oysters, octopus, crab, clams, and any other seafood that may be fresh that day. This recipe is inspired by Carmen Herrera of Puerto Escondido, Oaxaca.

MAKES 4 TO 6 SERVINGS

1 pound small shrimp, peeled and deveined (save shells for shrimp stock)

For the shrimp stock:
½ small white onion
3 garlic cloves
¼ teaspoon salt

For the sauce:
1 cup ketchup
4 tablespoons orange soda

FOR THE SHRIMP STOCK:
In a 2-quart saucepan, heat 1 quart water. Boil the shrimp shells with the onion, garlic, and salt for 20 minutes. Strain the stock. Discard the shells, onion, and garlic.

Return the stock to the 2-quart saucepan and add the shrimp. Cook over medium heat for 10 minutes. Remove the shrimp and cool them rapidly by pouring ice over them. Reduce the stock for 10 more minutes.

FOR THE SAUCE:
Mix the ketchup, orange soda, Worcestershire sauce, *Bufalo* sauce, *Salsa Valentina,* Tabasco sauce, salt, pepper, and ½ cup shrimp stock in a small bowl. Mix well and add the tomato, onion, and cilantro. Stir in the shrimp.

(continued)

2 tablespoons Worcestershire sauce

2 tablespoons Bufalo *sauce (see page 331) or Lea & Perrins Hot Pepper Sauce*

2 tablespoons Salsa Valentina *(page 331)*

4 teaspoons *Tabasco sauce*

½ teaspoon salt, or more to taste

½ teaspoon ground black pepper

4 tablespoons chopped tomato

2 tablespoons chopped onion

2 teaspoons chopped cilantro leaves

For the garnish:
2–3 limes, halved

6 cilantro sprigs

2 avocados, sliced

To serve, place the shrimp in a cocktail glass. Garnish with lime halves, cilantro sprigs, and the avocado slices draped over the edge of the glass.

Hint: Use the remaining shrimp stock for *Caldo de Mariscos a la Costa* (page 79) or *Caldo de Camarón* (page 82).

TORTITAS DE CAMARÓN SECO
Shrimp and Potato Cakes

This is adapted from a recipe given to me by Mamá Goya, of the restaurant Junto del Mar in Puerto Escondido. It is one of her older, more traditional recipes, using the tiny ¼-inch shrimp called camaroncitos secos *that are taken from the rivers close by. All day long women walk up and down the beach selling bags of these dried shrimp.*

MAKES 4 SERVINGS
(12 *TORTITAS*)

For the sauce:
1 pound tomatoes (2 medium–large round or 8–10 plum)

3 chiles jalapeños, *stemmed and left whole (see page 329)*

FOR THE SAUCE:
On a 10-inch dry *comal*, griddle, or in a cast-iron frying pan, roast the tomatoes until soft and blistered, about 4 minutes. Set aside. On the same *comal*, roast the chiles until they blister and give off their scent, about 12 minutes. Set aside.

Put the tomatoes, chiles, garlic, and onion in a blender and blend well.

7 garlic cloves

2 tablespoons chopped white onion

1 tablespoon sunflower or vegetable oil

1 sprig epazote or 3 sprigs cilantro (see page 336)

For the tortitas:

12 ounces new potatoes, skins left on

1 cup camaroncitos secos or ¾ cup ground dried shrimp

2 tablespoons finely chopped onion

5 garlic cloves, finely chopped

1 egg

2 tablespoons flour

½ cup bread crumbs

2 teaspoons lime juice

¼ teaspoon ground white pepper

2 tablespoons finely chopped cilantro (see page 336)

2 tablespoons sunflower or vegetable oil

¼ pound queso fresco, cut into 12 strips (see page 346)

4 sprigs cilantro or epazote (see page 336) (for garnish)

In a deep frying pan, heat the oil and add the tomato mixture. Cook for 10 minutes, until bubbling.

Add the *epazote* and ¾ cup water. Cook for 10 minutes.

FOR THE *TORTITAS*:
Preheat the oven to 250°F.

In a 2-quart saucepan, bring 3 cups of water to a boil. Add the potatoes and cook for 20 minutes or until done. Remove from the water; allow to cool a little and then peel.

Soak the shrimp or ground shrimp in 2 cups water for 10 minutes. Drain the shrimp in a wire mesh strainer. Soak a second time for 10 minutes. Drain. In a medium mixing bowl, mash the potatoes, then add the shrimp, onion, and garlic. In a small bowl, beat the egg. Add the flour and mix well. Add to the potato mixture, along with the bread crumbs, lime juice, pepper, and cilantro, and blend well. Make 12 balls from the mixture and flatten them to make thick little patties, each about 2 inches around.

In a medium frying pan, heat the oil until hot, over medium heat. Place the patties into the oil and fry 2 to 4 minutes or until golden. Turn the cakes over to brown on the other side for 2 to 4 minutes. Remove from pan and drain well. You can place the cakes in the oven to keep warm.

TO ASSEMBLE:
Cover each plate with a little of the sauce. Place three *tortitas* and three pieces of *queso fresco* alternately on each plate. Place a nice sprig of cilantro or *epazote* in the center of each and serve immediately with tostadas or *totopos*.

Hint: These must be eaten fresh and do not keep well.

PESCADILLA DE CAZÓN

Warm, Spicy Shark Salad

Playa Cangrejo is a jewel of a spot along the Pacific coast near Salina Cruz. There are only about eight families in this little fishing village, where the pelicans still feast daily offshore and the crabs come out to dance at night. Our favorite spot with the best food is La Perla, run by Angel and Oresta, who will take great care of you and even bring out a bed with a mosquito net if you're having too much fun and want to spend the night. This spicy fish salad can be eaten hot or at room temperature, and served with totopos *or* tostadas, *as Oresta does. Enjoy this dish with a beer and you'll swear you hear the gulls calling.*

MAKES 4 SERVINGS

For the fish:

¾ pound shark steak or other firm
    fish
¼ teaspoon salt
1 lime, halved

For the sauce:

¾ pound tomatoes (1½ medium–
    large round or 6–7 plum)
2 chiles chipotles en adobo
    (page 332)
½ medium white onion, chunked
3 garlic cloves
2 black peppercorns
1 whole clove
1 tablespoon sunflower or vegetable
    oil
¼ medium white onion, finely
    chopped
½ pound tomatoes
    (1 medium–large round or
    4–5 plum), finely chopped

FOR THE FISH:

In a medium saucepan, simmer the fish over low heat in 1 quart water, salt, and lime for 1 hour, covered.

FOR THE SAUCE:

In another medium saucepan, bring 2 cups water to a boil. Cut an x in the bottoms of the tomatoes. Place the tomatoes in the boiling water and leave for 5 minutes. Remove them from the water. Peel them and discard the skins. Reserve the water.

Remove the stems from the chiles and place in a blender with the tomatoes, onion, garlic, peppercorns, and clove. Blend well with ½ cup of the reserved tomato cooking water.

In a medium frying pan, heat the oil and sauté the chopped onion until transparent. Add the chopped tomatoes, garlic, and parsley and cook for 5 minutes over high heat.

Add the chile mixture and cook for 15 minutes over low heat. Add the bay leaf and thyme. Crumble the oregano in your hands and add to the mixture. Continue to cook for 10 minutes.

Drain the fish in a colander. Place the fish in a cheese-cloth or towel and wring out the water. Flake the fish. Add

3 garlic cloves, finely chopped

½ cup finely chopped parsley leaves

1 bay leaf

½ sprig thyme, or a pinch of dried

½ teaspoon fresh Oaxacan
    oregano, or ¼ teaspoon dried
    (see page 336)

Salt to taste

For salad garnish (optional):

½ pound tomatoes
    (1 medium–large round or
    4–5 plum), thinly sliced

¼ medium red onion, thinly sliced

1–2 carrots, thinly sliced on the
    diagonal

1 cucumber, thinly sliced on the
    diagonal

1–2 mangoes, thinly sliced

¼ jicama, peeled and cut into
    strips

Pinch of salt

2 tablespoons fresh lime or lemon
    juice

2 avocados, peeled and cut into
    wedges

2 chiles jalapeños en escabeche,
    cut into strips (page 333)

6 sprigs parsley

2 limes, quartered

Pinch of Salsa Valentina (see
    page 331)

the fish to the tomato mixture and cook for 15 minutes or until the mixture is dry. Add salt.

TO GARNISH:

On a serving platter, lay the tomatoes, red onion, carrots, cucumber, mangoes, and jicama in concentric circles, leaving a space in the middle for the *pescadilla*. Sprinkle the vegetables with salt and lime juice. Pile the *pescadilla* in the middle and top with wedges of avocado and strips of pickled *chiles jalapeños*. Garnish with the parsley and lime quarters. Sprinkle the *salsa valentina* or other bottled chile sauce on top of the vegetables. Serve with tostados, *totopos*, or soft tortillas.

Hint: You can substitute any fish for the shark, but it should be firm, such as tuna, halibut, or redfish.

Doña Meche delivering tortillas and fish, Chacahua (Barbara Lawton)

ENSALADA DE PULPO
Octopus Salad

Octopus is one of the popular seafood items offered at most coastal restaurants. The octopus must cook slowly over low heat so the meat becomes soft. But you can substitute any cooked fish or seafood here, such as shrimp, crab, oysters, mussels, or clams. Accompany this dish with beer or white wine as a first course or serve after Guisado de Garbanza Istmeño *(page 203), alongside the vegetable salad from the* Pescadilla de Cazón *(page 88), as the main course after.*

MAKES 4 TO 6 SERVINGS

1 pound octopus, cleaned

½ teaspoon salt

½ pound tomatoes (1 medium–large round or 4–5 plum), chopped

½ medium white onion, chopped

1½ chiles jalapeños, finely chopped (see page 329)

7 garlic cloves, finely chopped

¼ cup cilantro leaves, chopped

2 tablespoons fresh lime or lemon juice

Salt and pepper to taste

For the garnish:
Lettuce leaves to line the platter

2 avocados, sliced

2 limes, quartered

Salsa de guacamole (page 57)

In a medium saucepan, bring 1½ quarts water to a boil. Add the octopus, along with the salt. Simmer over low heat, covered, for 1 hour or until tender. Allow to cool. Cut the octopus into 1-inch chunks.

In a medium bowl, mix the tomatoes, onion, chiles, garlic, and cilantro. Add the octopus and mix well. Add the lime juice, salt, and pepper. Chill well.

Line a platter with lettuce leaves. Mound the salad in the middle. Garnish with the avocado slices and lime.

Serve with tostadas or *totopos* and *salsa de guacamole*.

FRIJOLES BLANCOS CON CAMARÓN SECO
Dried Shrimp Simmered with White Beans

The first time I tried this recipe was after market day in Zaachila. I had met a few women selling beans whom I knew from another market. They had beautiful black-eyed peas from Miahuatlán, a town on the way to the coast. Seeing them I immediately thought about making hoppin' John for my next New Year's Day celebration. I asked them what they would do with the beans, and one of the women gave me this recipe. Being a big fan of dried shrimp and hierba santa, I needed no more convincing. We eat this a lot, especially during Lent, when there are tons of dried shrimp in the market.

MAKES 8 TO 10 SERVINGS

½ pound whole dried shrimp, deheaded and peeled if large, whole if using the very small camaroncitos (see page 345); reserve heads

1 pound black-eyed peas or small white beans (about 2½ cups) or 6 cups canned, drained and rinsed, 1 cup water added to beans

1 small white onion

1 small head of garlic

2 tablespoons sunflower or vegetable oil

1 medium white onion, finely chopped

2 tablespoons finely chopped garlic

1 pound tomatoes (2 medium–large round or 8–10 plum), boiled, peeled, and finely chopped

2 fresh or dried hierba santa leaves (see page 336) or anise sprigs or

Rinse the shrimp well. Soak them for 15 minutes in 2 cups of water. Discard the water and rinse again. Place the heads in a blender with 1 cup water and blend well. Strain through a fine-mesh strainer and reserve the liquid.

Place the beans in a heavy 6-quart stockpot and add 7 cups of water. Bring to a boil and, after 5 minutes, discard the water. Replace with 10 cups of hot water and add the whole onion and garlic head. Return to a boil, lower the heat, cover, and simmer for 1 to 1¼ hours or until soft. Omit this step if using canned beans.

In a heavy 4-quart stockpot, heat the oil over medium-high heat and add the chopped onion. When it becomes transparent, add the chopped garlic. When starting to brown, add the tomatoes. Fry until well cooked, about 10 minutes, stirring. Add the shrimp and the shrimp-head mixture. Lower the heat and simmer about 20 minutes. Add the beans, broth, *hierba santa,* and pepper and simmer 30 minutes more, covered. At the very end of the cooking time, taste for salt and add if needed.

Hints: You can make this same dish with lima or fava beans, but instead of *hierba santa,* use cilantro for the flavoring. Serve with *salsa de chilito verde* (see page 175) made with any of the three chiles mentioned.

(continued)

anise leaves or a large shot of
    Pernod
1 teaspoon black pepper
Salt to taste

You must wash the shrimp well to release the salty flavor, and taste before adding salt. Remember, the shrimp are salted heavily before they are dried, so there should be enough salt in the dish without adding much at all.

PESCADO EMPAPELADO AL DIABLO
Fish Cooked in Paper with Devil's Sauce

One of the most relaxing places on Oaxaca's coast is the picturesque Lagunas de Chacahua. At the restaurant Los Delfines de Chacahua, owner Juana Ramírez says that this is by far the most popular dish she serves. The "paper" used in this dish is actually foil, but it creates a steamed fish effect as the foil fills with steam. She uses this technique to cook two styles of fish. The "natural" version cooks the fish with tomatoes, onions, and epazote, but my favorite by far is with the spicier devil's sauce. Serve with Arroz Blanco con Plátanos Fritos (page 53) or Arroz con Cilantro (page 120).

MAKES 4 SERVINGS

For the salsa del diablo:
¼ pound tomatoes (½ medium–
    large round or 2–3 plum)
5 chiles guajillos, *stemmed and
    seeded (see page 331)*
3 chiles costeños rojos, *stemmed
    and seeded, or 3 chiles de árbol
    (see page 330)*
¼ medium white onion, thickly
    sliced
5 garlic cloves

FOR THE *SALSA DEL DIABLO:*
In a small saucepan, bring 2 cups of water to a boil. Cut an x in the bottoms of the tomatoes. Place the tomatoes in the boiling water and boil for 5 minutes. Remove the tomatoes from the pot and reserve the water. When tomatoes are cool enough to handle, remove and discard the skins.

On a dry *comal*, griddle, or in a cast-iron frying pan, toast the chiles until they give off their aroma. Place in a bowl and cover with the reserved tomato water. Soak for 20 minutes. Remove chiles from the water. Reserve the water.

On the same *comal*, roast the onion and garlic for 8 to 10 minutes over medium heat or until transparent.

1 teaspoon fresh Oaxacan oregano
  or ½ teaspoon dried (see
  page 336)
2 whole allspice
3 black peppercorns
2 tablespoons white vinegar
1½ teaspoons Worcestershire sauce
1 teaspoon butter
1 teaspoon sunflower or
  vegetable oil
1 bay leaf
½ teaspoon salt, or more to taste

For the fish:
2½ pounds whole sea bass, red
  snapper, or striped bass,
  butterflied
4 tablespoons (½ stick) soft butter,
  to coat the foil and fish
Salt and pepper mixed, to sprinkle
  on fish
3 tablespoons Worcestershire
  sauce
3 tablespoons Maggi sauce
½ pound tomatoes (1 medium–
  large round or 4–5 plum), thinly
  sliced
½ medium white onion, thinly
  sliced
5 bay leaves
2 tablespoons finely chopped
  parsley leaves

Place the chiles, tomatoes, onion, garlic, oregano, all-spice, peppercorns, vinegar, and Worcestershire sauce in a blender. Blend well with ½ cup chile soaking water. Pour through a strainer to remove the skins.

In a medium frying pan, heat the butter and oil. Pour in the chile mixture and add the bay leaf. Fry for 5 minutes. Add salt.

TO PREPARE FISH:
Heat a long griddle that covers two burners until very hot. Open the fish so it is lying flat, skin side down.

Cut a piece of heavy-duty aluminum foil twice the size of the fish. Totally butter one half of the foil. Place the fish on the buttered portion of the foil. Sprinkle salt and pepper over the fish. Sprinkle the Worcestershire and Maggi sauces over the fish, including the head. Dot butter over the fish. Spoon ¼ cup of the *salsa del diablo* over the fish. Add the tomato and onion slices. Add the bay leaves and parsley. Pull the foil over the top of the fish and seal by folding over the edges. It is important to have a good seal on all three edges, so the steam does not escape during the cooking process. Carefully move the fish to the griddle and cook for 10 minutes. The foil should fully puff up in the process. Watch the foil to make sure that the steam is not escaping. If it is, reseal the fish.

Serve immediately with tostadas or *totopos*.

Hint: You can use the extra *salsa del diablo* to cook beef-steaks, as in *Bisteces Entomatados* (page 64), or to season chicken for grilling or roasting.

CALDILLO DE NOPALES
CON CAMARÓN DULCE
Clear Nopal and Sweet Shrimp Soup

This soup was inspired by Flor, a housekeeper at Posada Cañón Devata in Puerto Angel. Every day, when she would come to clean my room, I would talk with her about coastal food. This is one of her mother's recipes and, to Flor, comfort food. After eating it, I can see why.

MAKES 4 TO 6 SERVINGS

½ pound fresh small shrimp, cleaned (save the shells for stock)

For the shrimp stock:
¼ medium white onion
3 garlic cloves
1 lime, cut in half
A few black peppercorns
2 bay leaves
1 chile de árbol *(see page 330)*
Pinch of salt

For the nopales:
1 pound fresh nopales, *julienned* (see page 327)
2 tablespoons sunflower or vege-table oil
½ cup finely chopped white onion
5 garlic cloves, finely chopped
1 pound tomatoes (2 medium–large round or 8–10 plum), boiled, peeled, and finely chopped
1 cup fresh peas

FOR THE SHRIMP STOCK:
In a heavy 4-quart stockpot, put the shrimp shells in 2 quarts of water with the onion, garlic, lime, peppercorns, bay leaves, *chile de árbol*, and salt. Cover and simmer over low heat for 30 minutes. Strain the stock and reserve.

FOR THE *NOPALES*:
In a small saucepan, heat 2 cups of water and a pinch of salt. Add the *nopales* and cook for 10 minutes, covered, over high heat. Drain in a colander for 10 minutes.

In a heavy 4-quart stockpot, heat the oil over medium heat. Add the onion, garlic, and tomato. Fry for 10 minutes, stirring occasionally. Add 1½ quarts of the reserved shrimp stock and the peas. Add the shrimp, *epazote*, and parsley. Cover and cook over medium heat for 15 minutes. Add salt.

Raise the heat, and when the soup comes to a boil, add the beaten eggs by pouring them around the perimeter of the pan in concentric circles so the liquid egg doesn't touch the egg already cooking. Simmer 5 minutes and turn off the heat. Serve immediately, with lime quarters.

1½ tablespoons fresh epazote
    leaves or 2 tablespoons dried (see
    page 336)
1 tablespoon finely chopped parsley
    leaves
Salt to taste
4 eggs, beaten
1–2 limes, quartered

CAMARONES AL MOJO DE AJO
Sautéed Shrimp Soaked in Garlic

This coastal classic is especially liked by everyone who loves garlic. You can use any seafood or the more commonly used whole fish as the vehicle for the garlic. I found more ways of making this garlic mixture than I thought possible, from preserving the garlic in vinegar or lime to blending compound butters with some other ingredients in this recipe. The one thing the coastal cooks did have in common was using Knorr Suiza (a commercial chicken bouillon powder) as a seasoning. Because it contains MSG, however, I prefer to leave it out of my version.

MAKES 4 SERVINGS

1 pound large shrimp, heads and
    shells on
3 whole allspice
½ cup garlic cloves
⅓ cup parsley leaves
1 tablespoon sunflower or
    vegetable oil
1 tablespoon Worcestershire sauce
½ teaspoon ground black pepper
1 teaspoon salt
½ cup (1 stick) butter

Butterfly the shrimp by cutting the rounded end from the head to the tail with a sharp knife. Clean the shrimp well.

In a *molcajete*, grind the allspice, garlic, parsley, oil, Worcestershire sauce, pepper, and salt. You can do this in a blender or food processor, but you must pulse or grind.

Put 1 teaspoon of the garlic mixture inside each shrimp and fold the shrimp together.

In an 8-inch cast-iron frying pan, heat the butter over medium heat. Add the shrimp and the remaining garlic mixture and cook over low heat, covered, for 10 minutes.

CAMARONES AL AJILLO
Shrimp Sautéed with Garlic and Chile Guajillo

*Playa Panteón, in Puerto Angel, is named for the beautiful graveyard
perched on the hill overlooking the sea. It is here that our friend Panchito,
who started Piña Palmera, is buried. Always a lucky person, his final resting
place is lulled by the sounds of waves at the beach. On the beach, there are a few
places to eat with the fishermen's families who over the years have grown to
be professional restaurateurs. This recipe was inspired by Señora Torres of
Restaurant Susi, where you can eat great seafood while you wiggle your toes in the
sand. Serve this with Arroz Blanco con Plátanos Fritos (page 53).*

MAKES 4 SERVINGS

For the chiles guajillos:
3–4 chiles guajillos, *stemmed,
    seeded, and deveined (see
    page 331)*
2 tablespoons sunflower or vege-
    table oil

For the shrimp:
2 tablespoons butter
1 tablespoon sunflower or olive oil
1 pound shrimp, shelled and
    deveined, with the tails left on
2 tablespoons finely chopped garlic
2 tablespoons finely chopped
    parsley leaves
2 tablespoons lime juice
Salt and pepper to taste

FOR THE *CHILES GUAJILLOS:*
Wash the chiles well and cut them into ¼–½-inch strips.
Place them in a glass jar with the oil.

FOR THE SHRIMP:
Heat a medium frying pan with the butter and oil. Add the
shrimp and garlic and sauté 3 to 4 minutes. When they start
to brown, add the chile strips, reserving the oil in the jar to
soak more *guajillos.* Cook over medium to low heat, covered, for 8 to 10 minutes. Add the parsley and the lime juice,
and salt and pepper.

Mound hot cooked rice on a platter in the middle and
spoon the shrimp all around the perimeter. Serve with hot
tostadas and a salad.

TOSTADAS DE COCO
Coconut Tostadas

I've been eating the tostadas de coco for years at the Monday market in Pochutla, the largest municipality near Puerto Angel and Zipolite. The best maker of these tostadas is a señora named "Tía Valy," or Valentina Gopar Vásquez. She has been known for years as the one-legged tortilla woman in Zipolite. The last time I went to order some tostadas, she proudly showed me her new leg, which is just as shapely as her other one. Serve these with Café de Olla (page 103) or Atole de Maíz (page 160).

MAKES IO TOSTADAS

1¼ cup grated fresh coconut

1 piece of Mexican cinnamon,
 3 inches long (see page 337)

1 pound prepared masa for tortillas or 2 cups masa harina for
 tortillas mixed with 1¼ cups
 warm water

½ cup sugar

Grind the coconut and cinnamon in a hand grain mill or grinder. Add to the prepared *masa* with the sugar. Mix them to make a dough. Grind it a second time. Lay the dough on a tray and extend it in two directions to form a rectangle. Let the dough dry out somewhat for 20 minutes.

Preheat *comal* over medium heat. Mix the dough together and form 10 balls. Press each ball in a tortilla press, between two sheets of plastic (a plastic bag cut in half is best). If you do not have a tortilla press, use the heel of your hand to flatten the dough. Press the ball first on one side, then turn it over and, giving it a half turn, press out the other side, making a flat tortilla. Peel the plastic off one side and lay it on top of the tortilla. Turn it over and peel off the other piece of plastic.

Lay the tortilla on your hand and then on a preheated clay *comal* or a cast-iron frying pan over very low heat. Cook for about 10 minutes on each side. If the tortilla starts to bubble up, lay a stone or a weight in the middle and it will remain flat. Allow it to really dry out and be crispy; the heat must be low for this to happen. When done, place the tostada between the layers of a cloth napkin or tortilla cloth. Continue until all the tortillas are cooked. Serve hot.

Hint: Eating the tostadas while hot is heavenly, but once cooled off, they harden and can last for weeks, stored in plastic.

FLAN DE COCO
Coconut Ginger Flan

The first time I made this recipe using creamed coconut milk was for Carol Brock, then food editor of the New York Daily News, for an article she was writing about my catering company, Seasons of My Heart. In 1987 I traveled to Thailand, and upon my return, I began cooking an exotic Thai-Mexican blend of foods. The crystallized ginger in this recipe is definitely a Thai influence. When I moved to Oaxaca in 1988, I began using fresh coconut milk, since fresh coconuts are so plentiful here, and sweetened condensed milk as a thickener.

MAKES 12 SERVINGS

¾ cup sugar, or enough to coat bottom of the pan

1½ cups milk and 2 cans (12 ounces each) sweetened coconut milk; or 2 cups milk, 1 cup unsweetened fresh or canned coconut milk, and 1 can (12 ounces) sweetened condensed milk

5 egg yolks

6 whole eggs

1 teaspoon vanilla extract

3 pieces crystallized ginger (1½–2 inches long), finely chopped

1 cup sliced almonds, toasted

Preheat the oven to 350°F.

Bring 1 quart of water to a boil.

In a thin sauté pan, cook the sugar over medium heat until it is brown and bubbly. (Do not stir while it is cooking, or you will get spun sugar and a big mess.) Watch the pan closely and lift the pan off the burner if the sugar is cooking quickly or unevenly. Shake the pan to distribute the melting sugar. When the sugar is completely caramelized, pour the hot mixture into the bottom of a 3-quart flan mold, Bundt pan, loaf pan, or individual molds. Rotate the mold in your hands, using pot holders, so that the sugar syrup covers the entire bottom of the pan. Set aside. Please be careful, because the sugar is extremely hot and it can burn your skin.

In a medium mixing bowl, combine the milk, sweetened coconut milk (or unsweetened coconut milk and sweetened condensed milk), egg yolks, eggs, vanilla, and ginger and whisk well. Pour the batter over the caramelized sugar in the mold, making sure to evenly distribute the crystallized ginger. Top with the sliced almonds.

Place the flan into another pan a bit larger. Add the hot water to the large pan around the flan mold. Cover with a lid or thin foil so that both pans are covered completely (bain-marie). Bake the flan for 1 hour or until a knife inserted in the middle comes out clean. Remove the flan from the water bath and chill it in the refrigerator for at least 3 hours. To serve, loosen the sides with a knife and flip the flan mold over onto a platter. Garnish with flowers or fresh fruit and serve.

Hint: It is better to make this a day ahead and chill it until it is as icy cold as possible, so that the flavors have time to blend. The oven and water in the bain-marie must be very hot to cook the flan correctly. Be careful not to overcook it; the flan should be creamy. If there are small holes throughout, it is overcooked.

EMPANADAS DE COCO O PIÑA
Coconut or Pineapple Turnovers

Aldolfa Cortéz Vásquez was born in San Pedro Mixtepec, Juquila, in the 1920s. In 1973, she moved to Zipolite, then a small beach community on a wild stretch of the Pacific coast. There she built an adobe oven and started a bakery. Her reputation as the best empanada baker in town quickly developed, primarily because her turnovers were baked, not fried. Her fillings were delicious: coconut, pineapple, mango, and tamala squash (pumpkin). The volunteers at Piña Palmera would go there and pour their hearts out to her, and she always doled out great advice along with her empanadas. She died in 1995, and her recipe went with her. I make these in her honor.

MAKES 12 EMPANADAS

For the dough (or substitute 1 pound frozen pastry dough):
1¾ cups all-purpose flour
¾ teaspoon salt
1½ teaspoons sugar
1 tablespoon vegetable shortening
1 egg
½ tablespoon fresh lime or lemon juice, for flavoring
½ cup (1 stick) butter, cold

FOR THE DOUGH:
In a medium bowl, mix the flour, salt, and sugar with your fingers. Cut in the vegetable shortening with your fingers and thumbs until you have pieces about the size of small peas. Mix in the egg, ⅓ cup water, and the lime juice to make a soft dough. Knead the dough about 3 minutes.

Place the dough on a floured board. Cut a cross in the dough three-fourths of the way down and roll or extend the dough out with your hand to make the four sections of the cross. Put the butter in the middle and fold up the four ends to completely enclose the butter. Roll out the dough in one direction. Then make a quarter turn and roll out again

For the coconut filling:
2 cups grated fresh coconut, toasted
1 cup sugar

For the pineapple filling:
½ pound pineapple, peel and core
   removed, chopped (1 cup)
¼ cup sugar
1 piece of Mexican cinnamon,
   1 inch long (see page 337)
1 tablespoon cornstarch
1 tablespoon grated lime rind

For the assembly:
1 egg, beaten
½ cup sugar, for coating

gently. Fold the dough in thirds two times. Put the dough in a plastic bag to rise, about 20 minutes.

Flour the board and roll out the dough lengthwise. Fold the dough in thirds again. Add more flour to the board, make a quarter turn with the dough, and roll out again. Fold the dough in thirds again and return the dough to the plastic bag. Wait 20 minutes. Repeat this two more times, folding the dough in thirds and letting it sit for 10 minutes. The fifth time, roll out the dough until it is 18 inches long by 6 inches wide. Cut the dough into 12 squares, 3 inches by 3 inches.

FOR PREPARED PASTRY DOUGH:
Allow the frozen dough to thaw at room temperature. On a floured board, roll out the dough, 18 inches long by 6 inches wide. Cut the dough into 12 squares, 3 inches by 3 inches.

FOR THE COCONUT FILLING:
In a medium bowl, mix the grated coconut with the sugar.

FOR THE PINEAPPLE FILLING:
In a 2-quart saucepan, combine the pineapple, sugar, cinnamon, and ½ cup water. Bring to a boil, then lower the heat and simmer for 20 minutes. In a small mixing bowl, mix the cornstarch with 3 tablespoons of cold water. Add the mixture to the pineapple and mix well. Cook for another 10 minutes or until thick, stirring constantly, over medium heat. Allow to cool before using.

FOR THE ASSEMBLY:
Preheat the oven to 425°F. Fill each square with 1 to 1½ tablespoons of the filling of your choice. Beat the egg and paint the edges of the squares. Fold each dough square over to make a triangle, and seal shut with your fingers. Place them on a baking sheet and place in the freezer for 15 minutes. Bake for 10 to 15 minutes or until well browned. Roll in sugar. Allow to cool, then serve.

Hint: You can also try pumpkin squash filling. Cook 1 pound of pumpkin squash pieces with a 3-inch stick of Mexican cinnamon and ½ cup sugar in 2 to 3 cups water. Bring to a boil and cook 25 minutes. Remove the skin and mash. Use as directed for filling.

CAZUELITAS DE TAMARINDO
Ramekins of Tamarind Candy

This is one of the tamarind sweets I learned from my friend Tina, on the coast. This tamarind candy is slightly soft and must be eaten with a spoon. These are also favorites at children's fiestas, when the tamarind is served in tiny clay pots and has bright cellophane wrappers. We've served this over ice cream and it was quite a success, or it could be a topping for sweet crepes.

MAKES 4 TO 6 SMALL
CAZUELITAS

15 tamarind pods (4 ounces),
peeled (see page 338), or
2 ounces tamarind pulp

2 cups sugar

1 teaspoon ground chile piquín
(see page 331)

1 teaspoon salt

Soak the tamarind pods or pulp in 1 cup water for 20 minutes. Strain to remove the seeds. If the fruit sticks to the seeds, rub the seeds with the back of a spoon against a strainer. Discard the seeds.

Put the tamarind liquid in a small saucepan over medium heat. When it comes to a boil, add the sugar, chile, and salt. Lower the heat and simmer, uncovered, for 25 minutes. Pour the liquid into *cazuelitas* (see page 352).

AGUA DE JAMAICA
Hibiscus Flower Cooler

One of the most refreshing drinks made in Oaxaca is actually an infusion of hibiscus flowers. Grown on the coast, the plant is a thorny bush that boasts flowers as red as its branches. It is loaded with vitamin C and has astringent qualities. San Pedro Amuzgos during the harvest season in December is beautiful. On both sides of the narrow road, the jamaica flowers dry on palm mats called petates. Walking down the center of the street, you feel like royalty.

MAKES 8 CUPS

¾ cup honey, or to taste
1½ cups dried jamaica flowers (see page 336)

In a 2-quart saucepan, bring 2 cups of water to a boil. Add the honey and mix well to dissolve.

Put the jamaica flowers in a pitcher. Pour the boiling water over the flowers and let steep for 10 minutes.

Strain the mixture to remove the flowers. Add 6 cups water. Serve well chilled.

AGUA DE TAMARINDO
Tamarind Water

When I worked at Piña Palmera, one of the kids' favorite activities was to pick tamarind pods off the trees and give them to Juana, the cook, to make aguas. They are also made into candies (see page 101) and ices, as well as sauces and moles in other parts of Mexico. This sweet-and-sour pod is used extensively in Asian countries as well.

MAKES 8 CUPS

8 ounces tamarind pods, shells removed, or 4 ounces pulp (see page 338)
½ cup sugar, or to taste

Bring 2 cups of water to a boil. Soak the tamarind pods or pulp in the water for ½ hour. Stir often to dissolve the pulp.

Put the water through a sieve into a large pitcher to remove the seeds and pulp remains. Add 6 cups water and the sugar. Mix well.

Serve well chilled.

CAFÉ DE OLLA
Cinnamon-Flavored Coffee Cooked in a Clay Pot

One of my best memories of our car trips back from the States was driving south through Mexico and finally crossing the border into Oaxaca, usually at dawn. We always looked for the first place to stop and order mugs full of aromatic café de olla and pan dulce. Nowhere else had we tasted the rich "cinnamony" flavor of café de olla equal to Oaxaca's. I think it has something to do with the leña (wood) that is used for cooking fuel, but you can still achieve good results on a home stove. Make sure you have your coffee ground extra fine to get the most flavor. Serve it in clay mugs, if you have them, with some sweet bread or Panqué de Tía Elena (page 37).

MAKES I QUART

¼ cup sugar, or to taste
1 piece of Mexican cinnamon,
   1 inch long (see page 337)
5 tablespoons finely ground coffee

In a medium earthenware pot or saucepan, heat 1 quart of water. Add the sugar and cinnamon. Just before the water starts to boil, add the coffee, stir well, and simmer for 2 minutes. Pour the coffee through a sieve and serve hot in clay mugs.

CHAPTER FIVE
The Mixteca Region
(La Mixteca)

Guelaguetza dancers, Huajuapan de León (Marcela Taboada)

Overleaf: A panoramic view (Stephen Honeybill)

The northwest region of the state of Oaxaca is a large area known as the Mixteco. It is made up of the Mixteca Alta (High), Mixteca Baja (Low), and Mixteca de la Costa (Coastal). The region is as varied in landscapes and micro-climates as it is in dialects and indigenous peoples. The land ranges from very dry, desolate, and eroded to high-altitude pine forests to low, lush, fertile, tropical coast.

Oaxaca's second-largest indigenous group, the Mixtecs, have a rich pre-Hispanic history as precious-metal workers, musicians, and herbal healers. Mixtec historians were trained to keep records using complex pictograms that are called codices. The mythical story of the Archer of the Sun depicted the Spanish conquest in picture form well before it happened. The Spanish sent a few codices to Europe, but they destroyed thousands of these valuable records done on *amatl* (tree bark), paper, or stone. The records showed many aspects of typical life, such as the founding of villages and the birth of people through a calendar system; important fiestas and weddings; the use of cacao as money (for a dowry) and as a drink to ritually seal a pact. Also shown were lifestyle details, elaborate forms of dress, and customs such as hair cutting every eleventh year, sophisticated braids, and hairstyles.

Another indigenous group living in the Mixteca are the Triqui. They live high and low in the remote area near the Guerrero border. The women are easily recognized by their heavy, long *huipiles* of red, white, or black worn over a black woolen skirt, which is held up by a red belt. Living in the mountains, they are traditional agriculturists who produce corn, beans, and *chilacayota*, a large squash; on the coast, they grow coffee, bananas, pineapple, avocados, mamey, mangoes, and other tropical fruits. They supplement their diet with insects, wild plants, roots, sweet potatoes, and, during the rainy season, various wild mushrooms.

The road to the coast runs south through San Pedro Amuzgos, where beautiful *huipiles* are brocaded on backstrap looms. During the *jamaica* harvest, burgundy-red hibiscus flowers dry on *petate* mats lining both sides of the road. Arriving in the area known as Mixteca de la Costa, we enter the sultry town of Pinotepa Nacional, immortalized in song by Alvaro Carrillo, my favorite Oaxacan composer.

Recently, I journeyed with some *amigas* through these wild mountains and attended two village fiestas. Our first stop was Santa María Tindú, in the middle of the mountain range some 6,000 feet high. It was the celebration of Padre Jesús, as he is known in the Mixteca. After arriving, we went to look for my friend Norma's mother, Doña Sofía, who was born and raised here. She had sewn new clothes to dress the saint as her *gueza*—her offering.

Watching the villagers who had gathered for the *jaripeo* (bareback bull riding), I tried to put my finger on what was strange: there were a lot of older folks and children, but not many were present from the middle generation. That's because many of them had gone to work in California and Oregon on agricultural estates. This trend is evident throughout the Mixteca, and has become a huge regional problem. In some areas there are virtually no men to govern the towns and serve on the tribunals that hear problems and help solve them as a group.

In the fiesta kitchen, the *mayordomía* (each year village fiestas are hosted by different families, the *mayordomía*) was organizing the cooks and serving food to all the villagers. The women in the cookhouse were part of the *mayordomía's* extended family: twenty to thirty women who were also contributing, also giving their *gueza* in offering their help to her. The women in this village were so friendly and they all wore embroidered blouses, voluminous gathered skirts, and long aprons. Everyone wore her *rebozo* (black shawl) as she cooked. Everyone else was seated on palm *petates*, except the women stirring the giant *ollas* (clay kettles) of soup set up on large stones on the floor, with wood fires burning underneath. They were filling clay dishes with *caldo de res*, a spicy *mole* or soup made from beef that has been butchered, salted, and dried for this occasion. They also offered us some "white *caldo*," a soup without the hot *chile costeño* that contains a variety of vegetables and lots of cilantro and oregano. The *rojo* variety was pure fire in the throat. Doña Sofía had warned me about the piquancy of the food. Thinking it would be no problem, I dug in and wow!! Smoke came out my ears and the coughing started. It was then that I began my study of the *chile costeño*. I had used it before, but for the next few days I would taste it in many forms and learn to enjoy its piquancy. It's truly *the* chile of the Mixteca.

The next day we attended the village fiesta in Tecomaxtlahuaca near Juxtlahuaca. Hundreds of people were selling their wares. Located in the center of the *feria* (fair) were the food stalls. *Pozole Mixteco* was the favorite here, the big hominy corn cooked with *hierba santa* leaves and garnished with a separate pork *mole* ladled over the top. The *mole*, of course, was made from the *chile costeño*, to which *chile guajillo* had been added. We tried the *amarillo de res* (yellow *mole*) and Juxtlahuaca's triangular *Tetelas* (page 112), which are tortillas filled with a spicy bean paste. There were big vats of *barbacoa de borrego*, served with cracked corn *masa*, rich with lamb fat that dripped into it as it cooked. Also here were good sweets—bread made with *pulque* and soaked pecans and empanadas and little tarts called *tecuta*, both filled with *chilacayota* paste.

Our next destination really captured my heart. The tiny town of Yucunama, where people have lived since 2000 B.C. and almost the entire village and its streets are stone. In the community museum we saw an original *lienzo* (fragment of a codex) that describes the founding of the village in pictograph form. We also saw many artifacts and old tools that had been unearthed nearby. But the real treasure of Yucunama for me was Cafetería del Danzante, a tiny colorful restaurant owned by a folkloric dance teacher and regional historian, Antonio Martínez, and his mother. We ate the *Mole Verde de Yucunama*, made with greens and *pepitas* and served with chicken. Then we sat for hours and talked to *El Maestro* about his village, the history, the food, and the customs of the Mixteca. He spoke at length about the tradition of *Guelaguetza*.

In a village, when a young couple decides to marry, the scenario can go like this: Our friend José Cruz decides to marry Yolanda Martínez. The family agrees to have a *fandango*, or big fiesta, for their friends and extended family. Almost everyone in the village is invited to José's home. About two weeks before the fiesta begins, Jaime Pérez arrives at the Cruz homestead with a burro laden with sixty kilos (one hundred thirty pounds) of *maíz* for the tortillas. Juan Pinto comes with twenty kilos (forty-four pounds) of cacao to make the chocolate, for no wedding would be complete without it. María comes with a live turkey weighing twelve kilos (twenty-six pounds). All of these gifts are recorded by weight and logged into a big book. Later, when Jaime Pérez's daughter turns fifteen, he will return to José's father and ask him for the sixty kilos (one hundred thirty pounds) of *maíz*. Juan Pinto and María can later ask for reimbursement of their gifts. This spontaneous gift giving is called *gueza*. The reciprocal giving and taking is *Guelaguetza*.

Nowadays, *Guelaguetza* has also become known as the biggest tourist event of the year in Oaxaca, when dancers from all seven regions come to dance and share their offerings and the spiritual traditions of their region. It is a celebration of the exchange of culture, of gifts, of dance and music that spreads the magic of Oaxaca throughout the audience. These are the very dances that a *Maestro* such as Don Antonio teaches to his young students. We were invited to spend the night in Yucunama in the apartment above the restaurant. In the hallway, there was a huge closet that held all the regional dance costumes and native garments. That night, unbeknownst to *El Maestro*, we tried on the beautiful costumes, some tattered and worn, but each handmade and filled with the inspiring energy of past dancers. We danced around the room, each of us in our own fantasy and remembrances.

Jarabe Mixteco en la Mixteca
(Marcela Taboada)

IN THIS CHAPTER

TACOS DORADOS DE POLLO CON GUACAMOLE Y QUESO

Fried Chicken Tacos with Guacamole and Cheese

Every night throughout Oaxaca state, street vendors arrive with portable stands to sell their edibles. In Tlaxiaco, among the offerings one night were these rolled and fried chicken tacos. These are wonderful with beer or margaritas and served as part of a botanas *platter. You can use any meat or fish instead of the chicken for the filling.*

MAKES 6 SERVINGS

½ teaspoon salt

2 cups shredded cooked chicken

12 soft corn tortillas (blandas; see page 321)

¾ cup sunflower or vegetable oil or lard, to fry the tacos

Salsa de guacamole *(page 57)*

2 cups thinly shredded lettuce or cabbage

¼ pound queso fresco, *crumbled (see page 346)*

Salsa de chile de árbol *(page 57)*

Add salt to the chicken. Mix well.

Place a corn tortilla on a dry *comal* or frying pan to heat it and make it pliable. Heat it on both sides. Remove to a plate. Continue with all the tortillas.

Put a strip of chicken down the center of each tortilla and roll it up. Either secure with a toothpick or line them up side by side in a baking pan.

Heat the oil in a large, heavy frying pan until smoking. Grab each tortilla with a pair of tongs and place it in the hot oil. Fry the tacos until crispy, about 6 minutes, and drain well.

Top with *salsa de guacamole*, lettuce, crumbled cheese, and *salsa de chile de árbol*. Serve immediately.

TETELAS DE JUXTLAHUACA
Triangular Corn Turnovers Stuffed with Red Beans

At the village fiesta in Tecomaxtlahuaca, cooks from all over the Mixteca make special dishes to feed the hundreds of people who come to pay homage to Padre Jesús. *Outside the church are food stands, and this is where I first encountered* tetelas, *or triangular* memelas. *Later that night and early the next day, Señora Esther Cervantes, who, among others, makes this town's specialty dish, sold them in the Juxtlahuaca's* zócalo.

MAKES 6 SERVINGS

For the bean paste:

6 ounces dried red beans (¾ cup) or pinto beans, or 2 cups cooked beans

½ medium white onion, finely chopped

5 garlic cloves, finely chopped

Salt to taste

7 chiles costeños, *stemmed, or* chile de árbol *(see page 330)*

½ small white onion, chunked

3 garlic cloves

Salt to taste

1½ teaspoons sunflower or vegetable oil

For the masa:

1 pound masa *for tortillas, or* 1¾ cups masa harina *for tortillas*

FOR THE BEAN PASTE:

In a heavy 4-quart stockpot, cook the dried beans, finely chopped onion, and chopped garlic in 1 quart water over medium heat for 2½ hours or until tender. Add salt to taste. (If using cooked beans, skip this step.)

In a small saucepan, bring 1 cup of water to a boil. Toast the chiles on a 10-inch dry *comal*, griddle, or in a cast-iron frying pan until they blister and give off their scent. Soak the chiles in the hot water for 15 minutes.

In a blender, puree the chunked onion, whole garlic, chiles, and salt with enough bean broth to move the blades. Remove the beans from the water and add to the blender. (Add cooked beans, if using.) Reserve the broth. Add enough bean broth to the beans to make a thick puree.

In a medium, heavy frying pan over medium-high heat, heat the oil and add the bean paste. Cook until the paste is thick and dry, about 20 minutes. Stir constantly. Add salt to taste.

FOR THE *MASA*:

If using prepared *masa*, mix the *masa* with ¼ cup warm water in a medium mixing bowl to make a soft, pliable dough (it shouldn't crack when it's rolled into balls or pressed out). Cover with a damp towel and allow to rest, about 15 minutes. If using dry *masa harina*, mix the *harina* with 1 cup plus 2 tablespoons warm water in a medium

6 tablespoons Mexican crema *(see page 345), heavy cream, or crème fraîche*

Salsa de chilito verde *(page 175)*

mixing bowl until you have a slightly dry dough. Cover with a damp towel and allow to rest for 15 minutes. Add ¼ cup warm water to the *masa* to make a soft, pliable dough (it shouldn't crack when it's rolled into balls or pressed out).

Divide the *masa* into 6 balls. Cover with a damp cloth.

Press the *masa* balls out on a tortilla press between two sheets of plastic. (If you do not have a tortilla press, you can flatten the dough between two sheets of plastic by using the heel of your hand.) Remove the top piece of plastic. Spread ¼ cup of the bean paste in a triangle in the middle of the tortilla. Fold in the three sides of the tortilla, using the plastic underneath to help you, to form a triangle. A little of the bean paste should show in the middle of the triangle. Press the corners of the triangle to seal shut. Invert the triangle onto your palm and peel off the plastic.

On a 10-inch dry *comal*, griddle, or in a cast-iron frying pan over medium heat, invert the triangle (solid side down) onto the center of the *comal* and cook until toasted, 3 to 5 minutes, on each side. Repeat the procedure with the remaining balls of *masa*.

Serve the *tetelas* with 1 tablespoon cream on top of each and *salsa de chilito verde* on the side.

CHAYOTES RELLENOS
Stuffed Chayotes

The idea for this recipe is from Diana Kennedy's Recipes from the Regional Cooks of Mexico, *a great cookbook with wonderful stories and recipes, including some excellent dishes and adventures from Oaxaca. While teaching in New York City, I combined the* pipián *in her recipe with dried shrimp and vegetables and piled it on steamed chayote for an appetizer. I have also served it as a main course and even over pasta for dinner.*

6 ounces dried shrimp, deheaded
   and peeled if large, whole if
   using the very small
   camaroncitos (see page 345)

3 chayote squash (see page 326),
   peeled, seed removed, and
   quartered

2 calabacitas criollas (see
   page 325) or zucchini, thickly
   sliced and quartered

½ pound shiitake mushrooms,
   quartered

½ pound (1½ cups) plus 2 tablespoons hulled pepitas (see
   page 338), unsalted

1 chile ancho, stemmed, seeded,
   and deveined (see page 330)

5 chiles costeños or 3 chiles guajillos, stemmed, seeded, and
   deveined (see pages 330 and
   331)

1 teaspoon cumin seeds

5 garlic cloves

2 tablespoons lard, sunflower oil or
   vegetable oil

Salt to taste

¼ cup fresh epazote (see page 336)
   or cilantro leaves

To garnish:
1 tablespoon finely chopped
   cilantro leaves

Soak the shrimp in water for ½ hour. Drain. Cover with
fresh water and let them sit for 5 minutes, then drain.

Steam the chayotes in 3 cups of water for 20 to 30 minutes, or until you can pierce with a fork. In the same water,
steam the *calabacitas* or zucchini and mushrooms for
10 minutes.

On a 10-inch dry *comal*, griddle, or in a cast-iron frying
pan over medium heat, toast the *pepitas*, stirring all the time
until nicely browned, about 5 minutes. Cool completely and
grind in a *molcajete* or food processor until powdery. Measure 1½ cups for the sauce and 2 tablespoons for the garnish.

Bring 2 cups of water to a boil. On the same 10-inch dry
comal, griddle, or cast-iron frying pan, toast the chiles until
they brown and give off their scent. Put them in a bowl and
cover with the hot water and soak for 15 minutes.

On the *comal*, toast the cumin seeds quickly and put in a
blender. Remove the chiles from the water with tongs.
Reserve the chile water. Add the chiles, garlic cloves, and
shrimp to the blender and puree to a smooth paste, using as
much chile water as needed to make it smooth (about
1 cup). Strain the mixture through a food mill or strainer.

Drain the remaining chile water into a bowl with the
1½ cups ground *pepitas*. Add enough water to cover and stir
well to incorporate. It should be a loose mixture.

In a deep, heavy 8-inch frying pan, heat the oil and add
the chile puree, stirring with a wooden spoon for about
5 minutes. Add the soaked ground *pepitas* and more water
to make a smooth sauce. Add to the *pipián*. Lower the heat
and simmer for 10 minutes. Add salt. Add the mushrooms
and *calabacitas* or zucchini to the *pipián*. Stir in the chopped
epazote or cilantro leaves.

On a serving platter, arrange the steamed chayote quarters in a spiral pattern. Spoon the *pipián* over the top of each
slice and garnish with a pinch of cilantro mixed with the
reserved toasted ground *pepitas*.

Hint: If you have only dried shiitake mushrooms, soak
them in warm water for 15 minutes. The soaking water
should be added to the sauce to give it added flavor.

HUAUZÓNTLES DE JOSE
Jose's Pre-Hispanic Broccoli Fritters

Josefina Avendaño Cruz has worked for me for many years and we've cooked countless meals together. One year during Lent she taught me how to cook the pre-Hispanic vegetable known as huauzóntle *that looks somewhat like an early species of broccoli. I have also been served the* huauzóntle *batter-fried and still attached to the stem, which is a dramatic presentation, but I prefer the cheese filling inside.*

MAKES 5 TO 6 SERVINGS OF
2 FRITTERS EACH

2 bunches (2–3 large stalks)
    huauzóntle *flowers (see*
    page 326) or 1 head of broccoli
Salt
5–6 ounces queso fresco *(see*
    page 346), cut into 10–12 strips
    lengthwise
½ cup sunflower or vegetable oil
6 eggs, at room temperature for
    1 hour
½ teaspoon salt
1 cup flour
1 teaspoon salt
½ teaspoon ground black pepper
2 cups tomato sauce (page 154)

Preheat the oven to 400°F.

Peel the little branches off the thick stalks of *huauzóntle* or broccoli.

In a medium saucepan, bring 1½ quarts of water to a boil. Add a pinch of salt. Blanch the *huauzóntle*, covered, for 5 minutes. Drain well and plunge into cold water to stop the cooking. Drain again and dry on cloth towels.

Make a little "patty" of branches in your hand. Place a strip of cheese down the middle and cover with more *huauzóntle* branches. Repeat with the remaining *huauzóntle* and cheese.

In an 8-inch cast-iron frying pan, heat the oil until smoking.

Separate the eggs and whip the whites with ½ teaspoon salt until stiff and dry. Add the yolks and incorporate well, whipping just until they are mixed.

Mix the flour, salt, and pepper in a medium mixing bowl. Dredge the *huauzóntle* bundles in the flour and press between your hands. Shake off any excess flour. Hold on to the end of the branches and pass through the batter, twirling them to coat the whole bundle. (If you can't hold on to the branches, place a large spoon in the egg batter and scoop up a generous amount. Place the mound of *huauzóntle* with cheese inside on top of the batter and cover with more batter so the *huauzóntle* is completely covered.) Place this bundle in the hot oil. Fry for a couple of seconds and flick the oil, with the back of a spatula, over the top of the mound of batter. Turn slowly, using two spatulas, and fry on all sides to make a rounded form. Remove from the oil and drain on paper towels. Continue until all the bundles are fried. Keep the *huauzóntles* warm in the oven and serve them hot, over the tomato sauce.

Hint: You can substitute whole tender *nopal* paddles (see page 327), with the cheese inserted between two paddles or cauliflower flowerets that are blanched, stuffed with cheese and batter fried. (You will need a few more whipped eggs for the broccoli and cauliflower batters.) Serve with the same sauce.

SOPA DE GUÍAS DE CALABAZA
Summer Squash Vine and Flower Soup

This pre-Hispanic soup is a favorite in Oaxaca during the rainy season, when the corn, chepil *(a wild herb), and* guías *(tender young vines and leaves of the güiche squash plant) are fresh and producing baby squash and lots of brilliant yellow flowers. In the* campo, *you see women carrying huge bunches of squash vine tips on their heads, and in the markets they are laid out on straw* petates *to be sold. After the Spanish brought domesticated pigs to the New World from which lard was rendered, the women added* chochoyones *(dumplings made from ground corn and lard) to the soup. The accompanying sauce is the* chile bravo, *named for the fierce bite of chile it uses. The women who sell the fresh vegetables for this soup always sell tiny bunches of the red and very dark green, almost black,* chiles bravos. *They are small, pointed, and very hot. In some villages they are also called* chiles parados, *which means "standing up" because this is the way they grow—standing up right on the bush.*

For the guías:

1 medium white onion, roughly chopped

1 small head of garlic, finely chopped

4 fresh ears of corn, cleaned and sliced in rounds 1½ inches thick (about 6 cups)

4 bunches guías (about 6 cups; see page 326)

3 cups chepil leaves (see page 336)

5 small round güiche squash (1¼ pounds; see page 325) or zucchini

4 bunches güiche squash flowers (16 or 2½ cups), sepals and pistil removed and flowers torn into halves, well cleaned in water

Salt to taste

For salsa de chile bravo:

3 fresh chiles bravos, destemmed (see page 328), or fresh Thai chiles or the hottest chiles jalapeños you can find

3 large ripe plum tomatoes

5 garlic cloves

½ lime, juiced, or a splash of fruit vinegar

Salt to taste

For the chochoyones:

½ pound prepared masa for tortillas or 1 cup masa harina for tortillas

1 tablespoon lard

½ teaspoon salt

4 limes, halved

FOR THE GUÍAS:

In a large stockpot, bring 4½ quarts of water with the onion and garlic to a boil. Lower the heat and add the corn rounds and cook, covered, for ½ hour.

Clean the stems and tendrils of the guías, using the youngest part of the plant and the softest leaves. Strip the larger stems of the fibers and cut into small pieces.

Clean the chepil leaves thoroughly. Cut the squash into wedges 1 inch thick.

Add the squash vine greens, chepil leaves, young squash, and flowers to the soup. Allow to cook, covered, at least 30 minutes or until the vegetables are cooked. Season with salt.

FOR SALSA DE CHILE BRAVO:

Make a slit in each chile before you toast it so it doesn't jump off the comal or explode in your face. Roast the tomatoes, chiles, and garlic on a dry comal, griddle, or in a cast-iron frying pan. Allow them to cool. Remove the tomato skins and discard.

In a molcajete or blender, grind the chiles and garlic until smooth. Add the peeled tomatoes one by one, slowly, so they don't spurt up into your eyes. Add the lime juice and salt.

FOR THE CHOCHOYONES:

If using prepared masa, mix the masa with the lard and salt in a mixing bowl. If using masa harina, mix the harina with 1 cup plus 2 tablespoons water in a mixing bowl until you have a soft dough. Cover with a towel and allow to rest for 15 minutes. Add the lard and salt. Mix in well.

Roll the dough into 50 small balls. Make an indentation in the center of each one with your finger and continue until all chochoyones are made. While the soup is simmering, slip the chochoyones into the soup. Cook until firm, about 5 minutes. Adjust seasoning.

Ladle the soup into bowls and serve with salsa de chile bravo and the limes.

CREMA DE CHAMPIÑÓNES
Cream of Mushroom Soup

In Oaxaca, and probably throughout Mexico, soups are an important part of the meal. At times they are served as the first part of a comida *or for the main course for a* cena *(light dinner).* Cremas *are pureed soups, like bisques, that have a mellow flavor from the addition of milk, cream, or cheese to thicken them. This soup is a classic, European-inspired one that can be made with wild mushrooms as well. You can substitute chicken or vegetable stock for the beef stock.*

MAKES 6 SERVINGS

1 quart beef stock (page 344)

1¼ pounds mushrooms, cleaned, and 1 pound left whole, ¼ pound sliced

1 small white onion, ½ quartered and ½ finely chopped

1 head of garlic, cloves separated, ½ finely chopped, ½ left whole

2 tablespoons butter

1 tablespoon olive oil

½ cup pecan pieces

2 tablespoons finely chopped fresh garlic chives

1 tablespoon Worcestershire sauce

2 cups milk or light cream

½ teaspoon salt, or to taste

2 teaspoons freshly ground black pepper

3 tablespoons brandy

½ teaspoon freshly ground nutmeg

To serve:

1 tablespoon finely chopped pecans

1 tablespoon finely chopped parsley

In a heavy 2-quart saucepan, bring the stock to a boil. Add the whole mushrooms, quartered onion, and whole garlic cloves. Cover and simmer for 35 minutes.

In a medium frying pan, heat the butter and olive oil. Add the chopped onion and sauté until clear. Add the sliced mushrooms and continue to cook. Add the chopped garlic and the pecan pieces. Add the chives and the Worcestershire sauce and continue to sauté for 5 minutes.

In a blender, puree the stock mixture until smooth. Return to the stockpot and add the sautéed mushroom mixture. When it returns to a boil, lower the heat and add the milk, salt, pepper, brandy, and nutmeg and heat through.

TO SERVE:
Mix the pecans and parsley. Ladle the soup into bowls and put a pinch of the pecan-parsley mixture in the middle of each serving.

EJOTES CON HUEVOS
Green Beans with Eggs

This breakfast dish is a staple here in Oaxaca. In the markets, vendors bring it ready-made to sell with salsa and tortillas. I became enamored of this dish at Carlota's little fonda in San Lorenzo Cacaotepec, and we make it at home when green beans are abundant. The amount of butter or oil might seem excessive, but it's needed to cook the eggs properly. Serve with salsa de chile bravo (page 117) or salsa de chile pasilla (page 151).

MAKES 6 SERVINGS

¾ pound green beans, cleaned and cut into 1½-inch pieces

½ cup (1 stick) butter or sunflower oil, or ¼ cup butter and ¼ cup sunflower oil

1 medium white onion, finely chopped

1¼ pounds tomatoes (2½ medium–large round or 10–13 plum), finely chopped

9 garlic cloves, finely chopped

Salt and ground black pepper

7 eggs, beaten

7 sprigs cilantro, finely chopped

3 dashes of Tabasco sauce or other hot sauce

In a 2-quart saucepan, bring 2 cups of salted water to a boil. Blanch the beans for 5 minutes and drain. Cover with cold water to stop the cooking and drain again.

In an 8-inch cast-iron frying pan, heat the butter or oil until it sizzles. Add the onion and sauté until transparent. Add the tomatoes, garlic, ½ teaspoon salt, and ½ teaspoon pepper and continue to cook over medium-high heat for 10 to 15 minutes or until browned nicely. The tomatoes should start to caramelize and thicken.

In a medium bowl, whip the eggs and add ¼ cup water, ¼ teaspoon salt, ¼ teaspoon pepper, cilantro, and Tabasco sauce. Add the blanched beans to the tomato mixture. Adjust salt and pepper to taste. Pour the eggs into the vegetable mixture and stir lightly. Allow to set in the pan and cook slowly, stirring occasionally for 5 to 8 minutes.

Serve immediately with *frijoles*, tortillas, and chunks of fresh cheese.

ARROZ CON CILANTRO
Cilantro Rice

I've been making cilantro rice for more than twenty years. I learned how to make it while cooking at Fonda San Miguel in Austin, Texas. Patty, the wild tortilla lady from Reynosa, taught me this and I still use it. Although not really Oaxacan in nature, it goes well with many of the dishes, so I thought to include it here. You can use any herb or fresh chile you like; the varieties are endless.

MAKES 8 SERVINGS

½ *medium white onion, cut into chunks*

1 *bell pepper, cut into chunks*

1 *chile poblano or 2 chiles jalapeños, roasted, peeled, and seeded (see page 329)*

5 *garlic cloves*

1 *cup cilantro leaves*

4 *cups chicken stock (page 343) or water*

1 *tablespoon butter or chicken fat*

2 *cups white rice*

Salt and pepper to taste

2 *limes, cut into quarters*

Put the onion, bell pepper, chile, garlic, cilantro, and 1 cup chicken stock or water in a blender. Blend for 2 minutes. Put the liquid plus the remaining 3 cups stock and the butter in a 4-quart heavy stockpot and bring to a boil. Add the rice and stir well. Season with salt and pepper. Return to a boil, then lower the heat and cover the pot tightly. Simmer for 15 to 20 minutes or until the liquid is totally absorbed.

Serve with lime wedges.

Hint: Make sure you add enough salt after the rice is added to the stock. The rice absorbs the salt flavor and you can't add it once the rice is cooked. And remember the years-old adage "Don't peek at the rice!"

MOLITO DE FRIJOL COLORADO
Red Bean Mole

This recipe for red beans cooked with chiles and corn masa was given to me by the enthusiastic Gónzalo Cruz Ramírez, of Restaurante Rincón de Gon in Tlaxiaco, a town in the heart of the Mixteca with a great Saturday market. Chiles costeños are very popular in this region and give these beans a unique flavor. Thickening with the corn masa and the addition of nopales make this a hearty side dish or a satisfying main course after a soup and salad. Serve with Arroz con Chepil (page 52) or Arroz Blanco con Plátanos Fritos (page 53).

MAKES 6 TO 8 SERVINGS

1 pound frijol colorado (see page 324) or pinto beans

1 medium white onion, ½ chunked, ½ left whole

1 small head of garlic, cut in half, plus 7 garlic cloves

1 teaspoon salt, or to taste

5 chiles costeños, *stemmed, seeded, and deveined (see page 330)*

½ pound nopales (see page 327), cut into ½-inch pieces

½ cup prepared masa *for tortillas* or 6 tablespoons masa harina *for tortillas mixed with 6 tablespoons water*

5 avocado leaves (hoja de aguacate; see page 338)

1 teaspoon salt, or to taste

In an *olla* (clay pot), combine the beans, ½ whole onion, and head of garlic with 8 cups water and cook for 2½ hours or until beans are soft. Add salt.

In a saucepan, bring 2 cups of water to a boil. On a 10-inch dry *comal*, griddle, or in a cast-iron frying pan, toast the chiles until they blister and give off their scent. Place the chiles in a small bowl and pour the hot water over them to cover. Soak for 10 to 15 minutes.

Place the chiles in a blender with the chunked onion and garlic cloves. Blend well, adding 1 cup bean juice. Add the chile mixture to the beans and allow to cook, covered, for 30 minutes.

In a medium saucepan, boil the *nopales* in 2 cups salted water for 20 minutes. Drain well.

In a small bowl, mix some of the bean juice with the *masa* and mix well to dissolve. Add the mixture to the beans. Add the avocado leaves and cook over low heat for about 15 minutes or until thick. Add the *nopales* and salt. Heat through, then serve.

TAMALES DE FRIJOL
Black Bean Tamales

This tamal is a sophisticated example of pre-Hispanic cooking using fine corn masa *and a seasoned bean paste. In the* Florentine Codices, *the tamal sellers are described in great detail and Sahagún writes of various bean-paste tamales. He also described special ceremonial tamales filled with beans, with a conch shell design on top used only for fiestas. Although these tamales are eaten as everyday fare, they are special in the flavor from the beans, the "mintiness" of the* poleo, *the picanteness of the chiles, and the anise suggestion of the* hierba santa.

MAKES 12 *TAMALES*

For the masa:

1 pound prepared masa *for tamales* or 1¾ cups masa harina *for tamales*

½ teaspoon salt, or more to taste

For the filling:

7 chiles de árbol *(see page 330)*

¼ cup poleo *leaves (see page 337),* or 9 avocado leaves (hoja de aguacate; *see page 338), or* 1 tablespoon ground anise

2½ cups cooked Frijoles Negros de Olla *(page 146)*

Salt to taste

To make the tamales:

2 packages cornhusks, soaked in warm water for ½ hour *(see page 321)*

6 fresh hierba santa *leaves (see page 336), ripped into quarters, or 6 large pieces dried*

FOR THE *MASA*:

If using prepared *masa*, break up the *masa* in a mixing bowl. Add the salt and mix well. Add 3 to 4 tablespoons warm water to make a soft dough. If using *masa harina*, put the *masa harina* in a mixing bowl and add 1 cup plus 2 tablespoons warm water to make a soft dough. Allow it to rest for 15 minutes. Add the salt and 3 to 4 tablespoons warm water if needed to make a spreadable dough.

FOR THE FILLING:

Toast the chiles and *poleo* leaves on a hot *comal*, griddle, or in a cast-iron frying pan over medium heat, turning constantly, about 3 minutes, or until the chiles and herbs give off their scents and start to brown. Remove from the *comal* and allow to cool.

Puree the herbs in a blender with the cooked black beans. Add salt.

TO MAKE THE *TAMALES*:

Dry 12 cornhusks in a tea towel. Make 4 balls of *masa* and flatten them in your hands to make thick patties. Using a large rectangular tortilla press or your hands, flatten the *masa* between two sheets of plastic. Give the plastic a quarter turn and press out the *masa* again so it is thin. Carefully peel the plastic off the top layer.

Spread the bean paste on the flattened *masa*. Fold in thirds lengthwise. Cut into three equal pieces. You will have three *tamales* per ball of *masa*.

Spread 1 tablespoon bean paste onto the wide half of a dried cornhusk. Place a piece of *hierba santa* on top of the bean paste. Add one piece of the folded *tamal*, more bean paste, and another piece of *hierba santa* on top. Fold the cornhusk in thirds horizontally, enclosing the *tamal*. Then fold the empty end over the *tamal*. Place *tamales* in a steamer on a rack lined with cornhusks over salted water. Steam 1 hour.

Although these *tamales* were inspired by Bertha Galvan and her mother, Juana, my assistant Jose makes these in an old-fashioned way by putting a thin clean towel or cheesecloth on the top surface of the *metate*. She then smears the *masa* down the towel, the same size as the *metate*. When it is completely covered, she spreads a layer of the bean paste on top. Using the towel as leverage, she folds the *masa* over itself three to four times vertically. She cuts them into thirds and fills the husks in the same manner. These are called *tamales de servilleta*.

Man with the barbacoa on maguey leaves (Stephen Honeybill)

TAMALES DE ELOTE
Fresh Corn Tamales

Every summer during the rainy season we look forward to the fresh corn harvest and elotes. We make Esquites *(page 231),* Chileatole *(page 217), and the best of all,* Tamales de Elote. *My friend María Taboada says you must make them on the* metate *and, having done that exhausting task, I tried making them in the hand grinder and blender with good results. Margarita Vásquez Nuñez, who taught me this recipe, said you cannot let the blended corn sit around at all or it becomes bitter. The best way is to blend and assemble them immediately. This is one of the joys of summer in Oaxaca. Serve with* Café de Olla *(page 103),* Chocolate de Agua *(page 349), or tea.*

MAKES 15 TO 20 SMALL *TAMALES*

13 ears of corn

1 cone piloncillo *(6 ounces; see page 348), or 1 cup brown sugar*

3 tablespoons Mexican cinnamon (see page 337)

1¼ cups sunflower or vegetable oil

1¼ cups granulated sugar

¼ cup (½ stick) butter, cut into chunks

2 packages cornhusks (optional; see page 321)

Husk the corn by cutting with a knife around the stem and peeling off each layer. This way you don't break the cornhusks and they can be used for the *tamal* wrappers. If you feel you can't do this, soak 2 packages of dried cornhusks in warm water for 20 minutes.

Remove the kernels from the ears by holding the cob upright on a cutting board and cutting down the sides; you should have 8 cups of kernels. With a knife or grater, chop or grate the *piloncillo* bit by bit into the corn and add the cinnamon. Mix well. In a blender, puree this mixture until smooth. Add the oil, granulated sugar, and butter.

Fill a *tamalera* with water (no salt) and lay the rack in. Bring to a boil over high heat.

Fill the husks immediately with 2 to 3 large spoonfuls of filling. Fold the husk by one-third over to cover the filling and fold down the husk on top. Fold over the remaining side to close the *tamal*. Place each *tamal* on the rack. You may tie them if you want to, but they are very runny so it's best just to lay them side by side. Steam the *tamales* for 35 minutes or until cooked through. These will look very soft until they cool off, then they will firm up. Serve.

MOLE VERDE DE YUCUNAMA

Green Mole from Yucunama

We arrived off the hot dusty road from Teposcolula in the enchanting village of Yucunama around three in the afternoon, a perfect time for comida. Walking through the door of the Cafetería de Danzantes was a delight to the eyes as well as the nose, and I knew I was in for a treat. The whole meal was delicious, but the best course was this mole, or pipián verde, served by the friendly Vicenta. She smugly laid each plate in front of me and said, "Let's see what you think of this!" and went back to the kitchen to listen for the oohs and aahs from our table.

MAKES 8 SERVINGS

Seasoning ingredients for chicken stock (page 343)

2 chickens (3 pounds each) cut into 8 pieces, skin removed (save back and neck for stock)

1 cup sesame seeds

1 cup pepitas (see page 338)

8 ounces tomatillos, husked (see page 327)

5–7 chiles jalapeños, stemmed (see page 329)

1 medium white onion

7 garlic cloves

1 tablespoon sunflower or vegetable oil

1 cup cilantro leaves and stems

1 cup radish leaves

1 cup fresh epazote leaves (see page 336)

1 cup torn lettuce leaves

½ cup hierba santa leaves (see page 336), fresh or dried

1 cup flat-leaf parsley leaves

½–1 teaspoon salt, or to taste

In a heavy 6-quart stockpot, combine the seasoning ingredients, chicken backs and necks, and 4 quarts water. Bring to a boil, then add the chicken and poach as instructed on page 343, covered, for 35 to 45 minutes or until cooked through and juices run clear when pierced with a fork. Remove the chicken from the stock. Strain and reserve the stock.

On a 10-inch dry *comal*, griddle, or in a cast-iron frying pan, toast the sesame seeds until light brown, stirring constantly. Remove from the pan and follow with the *pepitas*, stirring also, until they puff and are a nutty brown. Allow them to cool.

Place the *tomatillos*, *chiles jalapeños*, onion, garlic, and 1 cup reserved stock in a blender and blend until smooth.

In a heavy 4-quart stockpot or *cazuela*, heat the oil and fry the *tomatillo* mixture, stirring occasionally. Grind the *pepitas* and sesame seeds in a *molcajete* or blender. If using a blender, add 2½ cups reserved stock and grind to a textured paste. Add the mixture to the *tomatillo* sauce.

Blend the cilantro, radish leaves, *epazote*, lettuce, *hierba santa*, and parsley in the blender with 1½ cups stock. Add to the *tomatillo* sauce and heat through. Do not overcook or the sauce becomes somewhat brownish green. Add salt.

Reheat the chicken in some of the reserved stock. Place a piece of cooked chicken on a plate. Cover with the *mole* and serve with fresh corn tortillas.

CHILEAJO DE PUERCO
Pork with Chile Garlic Sauce

This Mixtecan dish is from Huajuapan de León, but was taught to me by Doña Sofía Hernández Cervántes from Santa María Tindú. I love cooking with Doña Sofía and her daughters when she teaches her native dishes. Most of her days she spends at her food booth at the University of Benito Juárez, making snacks and dishes for the lucky students who go there. If you can't find the chiles costeños needed for this dish, substitute chiles guajillos or chiles de árbol to get the proper heat for this rico, but picoso dish. Serve with Frijoles Negros de Olla (page 146) and rice made with the leftover pork stock.

MAKES 6 SERVINGS

For the meat:

Seasoning ingredients for pork stock (page 344)

1 pound pork ribs, cut into 2-inch pieces

1½ pounds boneless pork shoulder, cubed

For the sauce:

28 chiles costeños (see page 330), stemmed and broken in half

1 pound tomatoes (2 medium–large round or 8–10 plum), boiled, peeled, and finely chopped

½ cup sesame seeds

3 tablespoons lard or sunflower or vegetable oil

3 garlic cloves

½ teaspoon cumin seeds

¼ teaspoon fresh thyme, or ⅛ teaspoon dried

In a large 6-quart stockpot, bring 3 quarts of water and the seasoning ingredients for the stock to a boil. Once it is boiling, add the meat and return to a boil. Skim off the foam that appears on the top of the surface, and discard. Cook the meat until tender, covered, about 1 hour, following the directions on page 344. Remove the meat from the pot and set aside. Reduce the stock by simmering, uncovered, for 10 minutes. Strain the stock to remove the vegetables; reserve the stock.

In a small saucepan, bring 3 cups of water to a boil. Place the chiles in a bowl, pour the boiling water over them, and soak for 15 minutes.

In a large saucepan, heat 1 quart water. Cut an x in the bottoms of the tomatoes. Add the tomatoes and boil for 5 minutes. Drain and allow to cool. Remove and discard the skins.

On a 10-inch dry *comal*, griddle, or in a cast-iron frying pan, toast the sesame seeds. Add a pinch of salt to keep the seeds from jumping around, and stir them constantly until they brown. Set aside.

In a heavy 6-quart stockpot, heat the lard until it smokes. Add the cooked pork pieces and ribs and fry until brown.

In a blender, grind the garlic, cumin, thyme, oregano, and 2 tea-

spoons fresh Oaxacan oregano or 1 teaspoon dried (see page 336)

½ teaspoon salt

⅓ pound tomatillos (3–4 medium; see page 327)

chiles with ¼ cup stock. Pour through a food mill or strainer into the pork mixture. Stir well and add the salt.

Blend the sesame seeds with ¼ cup plus 1 tablespoon water until smooth. Pass the sesame seeds through a strainer and add to the pork mixture. Add 2 cups of the reserved pork stock. It should be the consistency of a textured, but not thick, sauce.

Blend the peeled tomatoes and raw *tomatillos*. Strain and add to the pork sauce and cook 10 minutes. Adjust the salt if needed. Serve.

CHILATE DE POLLO
Chicken with a Chile Corn Sauce

The name of this dish literally means "chile with masa" in Mixteco. It's a light, delicate sauce that uses the ever-popular chile costeño, which abounds in this region. Doña Sofía uses noniodized salt mined from the area, which tastes a lot like baking soda to me, but it does cut the acidity of the tomatillos. You can use salt and a pinch of baking soda if you like, but I make this without it, with good results.

MAKES 8 SERVINGS

Seasoning ingredients for chicken stock (page 343)

2 chickens (3 pounds each), cut into 8 pieces

23 chiles costeños, stemmed (see page 330)

¾ pound tomatillos (about 15, see page 327)

1 large plum tomato (5 ounces)

3 garlic cloves

¼ cup lard or sunflower or vegetable oil

In a 6-quart stockpot, bring 4 quarts of water and the seasoning ingredients to a boil as instructed on page 343. Boil for 15 minutes, then add the chicken. Cover the pot and poach the chicken for 30 minutes over medium-low heat. Remove the chicken from the pot and allow to cool. Strain and reserve the stock.

Toast the chile whole and set aside. On a 10-inch dry *comal*, griddle, or in a cast-iron frying pan, roast the *tomatillos* and tomato over medium-high heat until they change color and are soft. When the tomato is cool enough to handle, remove and discard the skin. In a blender, puree the chile with the garlic and ½ cup water.

In a heavy 4-quart stockpot, heat the lard. Strain the chile mixture through a food mill or strainer into the hot lard and fry for about 5 minutes, stirring well.

(continued)

½ cup prepared masa *for tortillas,
or 6 tablespoons* masa harina
*for tortillas, mixed with 6 table-
spoons warm water*

¼ cup fresh epazote *leaves (see
page 336), loosely packed*

2½ teaspoons salt, *or small pinch
of baking soda*

½ medium white onion, *finely
chopped*

4 limes, *quartered or halved
depending on size*

In a blender, puree the *tomatillos* and tomato. Strain them into the chile mixture and cook for 10 minutes. Add 1 quart of the reserved chicken stock.

Blend the prepared *masa* with ¼ cup of the reserved stock. When the sauce is boiling, add the *masa*, stirring constantly. Allow the sauce to thicken, about 10 minutes. Add the *epazote* and return the chicken pieces to the pot. Add salt or a pinch of baking soda.

Serve with fresh corn tortillas, and chopped onion and lime on the table.

POZOLE DE CALABAZA BATIDA
Pozole with Sweet Pumpkin Squash

This is a refreshing way to eat pozole—*vegetarian style and rather filling. It's usually served cold or at room temperature as a kind of thick drink, or as more of a
snack or dessert. I've added the* chile de árbol *to give it a little more heat and to open
up the sinuses. We make it every year for* Día de Muertos, *when we make* Calabaza
en Dulce *(page 348). If you can't find the dried* pozole *or hominy, use packaged
prepared* pozole *and omit the beginning directions.*

MAKES 6 SERVINGS

To cook the pozole:
½ pound dried pozole *(1½ cups;
see page 320), or 1 quart canned
hominy*
1 ounce cal *(see page 320), soaked
in 2 cups water for 40 minutes*
Salt

FOR THE *POZOLE:*
In a 4-quart saucepan, boil the *pozole* in 6 cups of water and 1½ cups of the lime water. Do not use the thick lime that has settled to the bottom. Cook until the *pozole* is soft and peels easily, about 1 hour. Remove from the heat and allow to cool. When it cools, wash it several times. Peel off the skins and pick off the head of each kernel. The *pozole* should be white.

In a 4-quart stockpot, cook the *pozole* with 2 quarts of water, covered, over medium to low heat for 3 hours. It should burst open or start to "flower," as it's called. Add salt to taste. The *pozole* should be soft. Drain excess water.

For the calabaza:

1½ cones (9 ounces) piloncillo (see page 348), or 1½ cups light brown sugar

2 pieces of Mexican cinnamon, 2 inches long (see page 337)

2 chiles de árbol (see page 330)

2 pounds calabaza tamala (see page 325) or pumpkin, peeled

FOR THE CALABAZA:

In a clay *olla* or a heavy 4-quart stockpot, combine the *piloncillo*, cinnamon, and *chiles de árbol* with 3 cups of water. Heat until the *piloncillo* dissolves, then add the *calabaza*. Cover and simmer for 1 hour over low heat or until soft.

Mash the *calabaza* with a potato masher until smooth, keeping in the liquid to make a loose puree. Add the mashed *calabaza* to the *pozole* and mix well. Serve chilled or at room temperature.

CAPIROTADA
Mexican Bread Pudding

This dessert recipe draws its inspiration from The Book of Latin American Cooking, *a wonderful book by Elisabeth Lambert Ortiz originally published by Alfred A. Knopf in 1985. The sauce is one of the most interesting I have seen for a sweet bread pudding, an aromatic sweet-and-savory mixture. I replaced the bell pepper that was in the original recipe with* chile poblano, *which is more readily available in Oaxaca. I added guavas, which are aromatic and grow all around our ranch, and raisins plumped in mezcal, which is our local spirit made from the maguey plant.*

MAKES 12 SERVINGS

For the sauce:

2 cones (12 ounces) piloncillo (see page 348), or 2 cups dark brown sugar

2 pieces of Mexican cinnamon, 1 inch long each (see page 337)

1 small white onion, studded with 5 whole cloves

1 medium chile poblano (see page 329), halved and seeded

FOR THE SAUCE:

In a 2-quart stockpot, bring 4 cups of water, the *piloncillo*, cinnamon sticks, onion, *chile poblano*, orange peel, cilantro, and tomato to a boil and immediately lower the heat. Simmer over low heat, partially covered, for 30 minutes. Strain the mixture and let cool.

FOR THE PUDDING:

Preheat the oven to 350°F.

In a small saucepan, heat the mezcal and 2 tablespoons of water. Add the raisins. Simmer, covered, for 5 to 10 minutes, until soft. Drain the raisins and add the liquid to the simmering sauce. Let the raisins cool.

(continued)

Peel from 1 orange

½ cup cilantro leaves

1 medium round tomato (about 3 ounces), halved

ℱor the pudding:

2 tablespoons mezcal (see page 350) or any liquor of your choice

1 cup raisins

2 tart apples, unpeeled, cut into ½-inch cubes

1 cup fresh guavas, unpeeled, seeded and cut into ½-inch cubes, or canned guavas or other dried fruit

½ pound manchego or Muenster cheese (about 1½ cups), cut into ½-inch cubes

1 cup almonds, blanched, skinned, and toasted, thinly sliced

6 cups crustless 1-inch bread cubes, toasted

2 tablespoons butter, in pieces

Pinch of ground cinnamon

2 cups heavy cream

1 teaspoon vanilla extract

¼ cup confectioners' sugar, sifted

Mix the apples, guavas, cheese, and almonds in a medium bowl. Add the raisins to this mixture and toss well.

Generously butter a round, deep 10-inch cake pan, mold, or deep cast-iron frying pan. Put one layer of toasted bread cubes in the bottom of the pan, using half of the bread. Add a layer of half of the fruit, cheese, and nut mixture over the bread. Add another layer of bread and top with the remaining fruit and cheese mixture. Pour the sauce slowly over the top and dot with the butter. Sprinkle the top with the cinnamon. Cover and bake for 45 minutes.

Whip the cream with the vanilla until soft peaks form. Add the confectioners' sugar and whip until stiff. Serve hot, topped with the whipped cream.

ALEGRÍAS
Amaranth Candy

This amaranth bar is a healthy snack for children. It can be made in loaf pans or cans, then sliced. Amaranto is a pre-Hispanic grain that has enjoyed a big comeback as a nutritious addition to the diet. Luz Elena, my neighbor, grew amaranth one summer. We walked through the giant plants with bright red flowers right before she harvested. She gave me this recipe from Y la comida se hizo de dulces y postres, *a Mexican cookbook on desserts and candies. Serve these with* Café de Olla *(page 103), any flavored* atole, *or tea.*

1 cone (6 ounces) piloncillo *(see page 348), broken in small pieces, or 1 cup brown sugar*
4 cups amaranth

In a saucepan, combine 1 cup of water and the *piloncillo.* Cook over medium heat until it becomes a light syrup, 13 to 15 minutes. Remove from the heat. Let cool a little, then add the amaranth. Mix well.

Pour the sugar mixture into a 1-quart mold lined with waxed paper. Let dry for a couple of hours, then take out of the mold and cut into pieces.

Hint: Keep this candy in an airtight plastic container.

AGUA FRESCA DE TUNA
Cactus Fruit Water

During the summer months, the round fruits that grow on the cactus, called tunas, *are collected and eaten. One of the biggest delights my children have is to knock the fruits off with a piece of* carrizo *(bamboo) to have an instant feast. If they gather enough fruits, we make them into water or ice cream, but it's a real temptation to eat them whole with chile powder sprinkled on top. If you can't get* tunas, *substitute kiwis to make this refreshing drink.*

6 large red prickly pear fruits
   (1 pound; see page 340) or
   kiwifruit
⅔ cup sugar, or to taste

Peel the fruit (see Hint). In a blender, blend the fruit with 2 quarts water and the sugar. You will have to do this in two batches. Strain the mixture through a strainer. Serve well chilled.

Hint: The peel of a prickly pear fruit is very thick but peels easily. Cut the top and bottom off, then cut an incision down the side and pull the peel off in one piece.

ATOLE DE TRIGO
Hot Wheat Drink

When the Spanish arrived in the Mixteca in the 1500s, they began to build monumental churches and convents. In the fields surrounding the churches they planted lots of wheat, which is still cultivated today. The wheat is sold as wheat berries, from which this atole is made. This recipe, taught to me by Margarita Vásquez Nuñez, is a nourishing breakfast or evening drink.

MAKES 2 QUARTS

½ cone (3 ounces) piloncillo
   (see page 348), or ½ cup dark
   brown sugar
1 piece of Mexican cinnamon,
   1 inch long (see page 337)
1½ cups wheat berries, soaked in
   2 cups water for 5 minutes
3 tablespoons sugar

In a 4-quart saucepan, bring 1½ quarts of water to a boil. Add the *piloncillo* and cinnamon.

In a blender, puree the wheat berries and soaking water until fairly smooth. Add the blended wheat to the boiling cinnamon water. Bring again to a boil, stirring constantly with a wooden spoon. Add the sugar and stir well to dissolve. Allow to thicken and serve immediately.

Hint: This stays extremely hot, so be careful when you drink it.

Opposite: Spinning coyuche, *a natural brown cotton, Jamiltepec, Mixteca de la Costa (Barbara Lawton)*

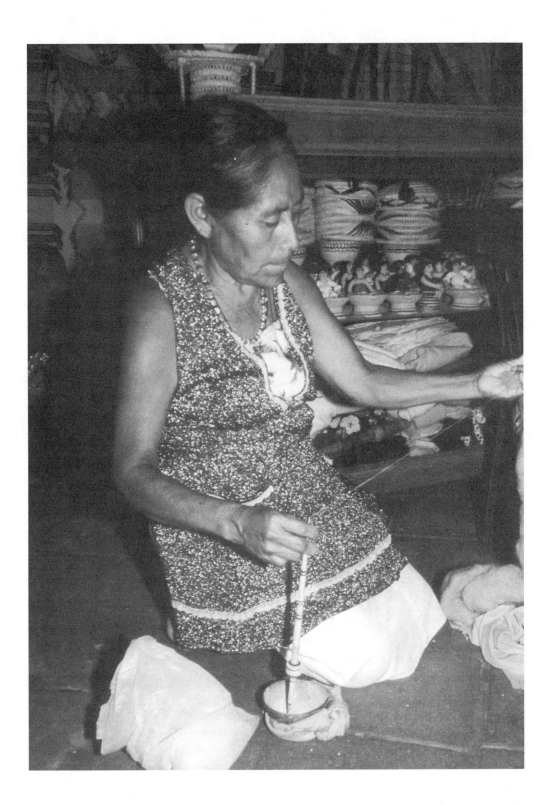

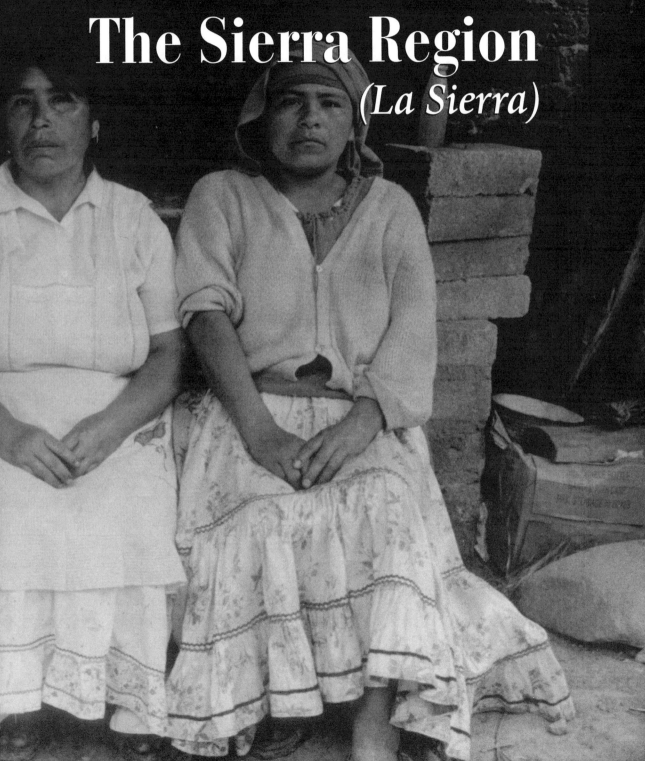

CHAPTER SIX

The Sierra Region
(La Sierra)

One-hundred-year-old woman with Serrano corn, Totontopec, Mixe (Marcela Taboada)

Overleaf: Village cocineras, Santa María Tlahuitoltepec, Mixe (Marcela Taboada)

The Sierra Madre is made up of a crescent-shaped chain of mountains that surround the Central Valleys of Oaxaca. The people who inhabit the eastern part of the Sierra Madre Norte are the Mixe (MEE-hay). The climate, the height of the mountain range, and its remoteness are factors that have preserved many indigenous customs, including culinary practices, in the Mixe villages.

The Sierra Mixe is centered on a sacred mountain of twenty peaks called Zempoaltépetl, which reaches 11,037 feet above sea level, the highest in Oaxaca state. Although the name "the cloud people" has been given to the Mixtecos and the Zapotecos, this name seems to fit the Mixe also because so many of the villages are immersed in clouds most of the year. The Mixe are a proud and fascinating tribe said to be descendants of the Olmec people and also said to have originated in Peru. Spending time with these people has given me a wonderful glimpse into their past—so much of how they live is the way their ancestors lived.

In Tamazulapan Mixe, *Ma'ach* (page 152) is a ceremonial dish that must be eaten, by village law, on August 1 every year. This celebration occurs one month before harvest time and is said to help ward off starvation later on, when food supplies are at their lowest. One variation of *ma'ach* contains corn, beans, and squash—the holy trinity of Mexican cooking—and is still prepared in the ancient way.

A fire is built on the ground and three stones are set around it, supporting a large pottery *comal*. Like spokes on a wheel, boot-shaped clay *ollas* (pots) are laid under the *comal* in between the stones, utilizing the same heat. One-handled *cazuelas* are filled with hot rocks and thick burning embers so that the pots become white-hot. *Nixtamal* corn is ground on a *metate* and shaped into large *memelas* (oval patties). Sauces, such as black bean, tomato and green chile, and *chilacayota* seeds (mature squash seeds) are made in the boot-shaped clay pots. In other *ollas*, chicken broth flavored with *chile pasilla* (regional smoked chiles) and *guías* (the tender, young leaves and stems of squash vines) are cooked. The *memelas* are cooked on the *comal* and then placed on the *metate*, to be kneaded and reshaped again into patties, then baked again on the *comal*. Meanwhile, the hot rocks and wood are removed from the *cazuelas*, which are then carried on long sticks to groupings of three rocks set on the ground. Low chairs are arranged in circles around the *cazuelas*. The *memelas* are removed from the *comal* and returned to the *metate*, and the mixture is mashed together to make a giant mass. The women carry the corn mixture over to the *cazuelas* and place it inside the pots. One of the sauces is poured over the top. The heat of the pot causes the sauce to spatter and bubble. The villagers, in groups of ten, gather around a *cazuela* and eat the *ma'ach* with their hands, pinching off a mouthful at a time. The *guías* and broth are served in little clay bowls on the side.

It is an extraordinary procedure and tradition that is also celebrated at the birth of a child. The mother is honored with a nourishing bowl of chicken broth flavored with avocado leaves while the rest of the family gathers to eat the *ma'ach* and dream about the qualities this child will bring to the village. The sharing of the *ma'ach* reinforces the bonds within the family and, as my friend Hermenegildo Rojas Ramírez explained, the communal sharing, celebrated since the Mixe beginning of time, has broken down any familial hard feelings that have arisen.

Nestled deeper in the mountains, a few hours past Tamazulapan, is the lovely village of Totontepec. Its ten natural springs, abundant rainfall, and frequent cloud cover make it a fertile growing environment for greens, vegetables, and flowers.

Here I encountered the world's largest corn plants and a corn expert, Juan Areli Bernal. Confined to a wheelchair because of an accident when he was young, Juan Areli is a most respected person in the village because of his knowledge of corn and because of his book, *El camino de añukojm-totontepec y los salesianos,* about the history of the village. He told me that not only is corn the most important food in their diet but it also provides security for the family, security for the village, and personal respect from the villagers if one harvests a good crop of corn. He also indicated that if you planned to be a government official in the village, the first question would be about your ability to grow corn. Corn is also the offering given most often as a donation to the church.

Walking through Juan's *milpa* (plantation) of corn, beans, and squash, I was amazed to see the corn stalks growing over fifteen feet high. Doña María, his mother, gave me an ear of corn that was at least fifteen inches long. The corn grows so tall, Juan Areli explained, because *serrano* (mountain-type) corn is "looking for the sun through the clouds." The growing season, which is stretched to eight months, produces this very long corn, which contains an enormous amount of oil in the kernels and is almost translucent when held up to the light.

Staying in Juan Areli's home for a few days, I began to realize that these people subsist almost totally on what they grow. His family walks an hour and a half to the lowlands where their ranch is located in a different microclimate. Coffee, sugarcane, sweet potatoes, bananas, and other fruits are grown and harvested. Juan Areli's sister, Elda, taught me many dishes cooked over a wood fire hearth plus various other fires on the earthen floor. While we cooked, she told me of the customs surrounding the planting of corn. Usually before the planting begins, a chicken is sacrificed in the field and the blood put in the four corners of the land. Sometimes mezcal or *aguardiente* is also sprinkled on the edges of the field to keep animals out while the crop is growing. I later discovered many variations on these rituals, including some using a mixture of pagan and Catholic rites. Also important is the thanksgiving ritual of the harvest, which includes sharing the fruits with workers.

Previous to my visit, a family member had called Rancho Aurora with instructions to bring with me a live egg-laying turkey from Oaxaca, which I did, in my Volkswagen bug! The turkey sacrifice is the most valuable offering one can give God, Mother Earth, or the Holy Trinity to ask for a good corn crop, good health, or any other important request.

We used the turkey meat to make *Caldo Mixe* (page 143), a rich fiesta dish of the area. We needed two other meats for the recipe, but though we strolled through the entire village, we were unable to purchase the necessary chicken, so we went to their *comadre* to buy salted and dried beef. The *señora* explained that she kills a cow every twenty days and salts and dries whatever part of the animal she cannot sell fresh within two days of the butchering.

We cooked for hours on the wood fire, making *Caldo Mixe*, to be served with the *Tamales de Pata de Burro* (page 150) and giant *Tamales de Frijol* (page 122). Elda and I were struggling to grind the beans for this dish on the *metate* when her mother walked in and looked at our results in disgust. Taking the *mano* from our hands, she assumed the job even though she was twice our age. While the *mano* glided over the *metate*, they explained that in Totontepec this is another dish they make for the celebration of the birth of a child. If a boy child is born a rooster is put in the pot, and if it's a girl, a hen.

Once the *tamales* were steamed and the *caldo* pronounced ready to serve, we gathered everyone to eat. The *tamales* were used as the "edible spoon" for the soup and, when they were eaten, the remainder of the soup was drunk out of wide-mouthed bowls. Juan Areli, eloquent as ever, made a wonderful speech thanking us for coming and bringing the opportunity for the family to eat the ceremonial *caldo* together, and he toasted us with *aguardiente*, made from sugarcane from their ranch.

On our way out of the Sierra Mixe we stopped at Santa María Tlahuitoltepec, home of the most famous Mixe orchestra and music school in the area. This enchanting village, hung on a mountainside, is picturesque for the strains of music that carry in the air and partly because of the dress of the indigenous women who wear full skirts, embroidered blouses, and leather *huaraches*. It is here that we filmed the village *cocineras* grinding a chile paste out of *chile pasilla Oaxaqueño*, called *chintestle*. The chiles are smoked in nearby villages, only a five-hour burro ride away! As a result of the constant cloud cover, the farmers are unable to dry the chiles successfully in the sun. Necessity being the mother of invention, the people build a wooden rack in an enclosed room, on which the chiles are laid and smoked. The smell of the local *encino* smoke (a kind of oak wood) permeates the chiles, giving them their unique flavor. These chiles are used whole elsewhere, but mostly ground into *chintestle* paste here. Because transportation in these villages is so difficult, people walk to their fields, or wherever they are going, often not returning home for meals. They take this paste with them to spread on their tortillas, making a nutritious and instant meal. The paste is also used as a seasoning for soups and salsas, and is the main product of this area. The chiles themselves are made into *chiles rellenos*, *pasillas en vinagre,* and the popular table sauce *salsa de chile pasilla*, which I feel is one of the main tastes of the Oaxacan kitchen.

Descending from the cloud forest and driving on the curvy roads toward the Central Valleys of Oaxaca, I reflected on how fortunate we were to have this glimpse into the past. Having visited these *pueblos* and cooked the most ancient of dishes with people who still grow, harvest, and prepare their own food, I have seen time stand still. What I love most of all is their respect and appreciation of God, the land, and the way even the most humble foods are received as an offering or gift to nourish the heart, body, and soul.

IN THIS CHAPTER

PAPAS EN ESCABECHE
Pickled Potatoes with Chile Pasilla

These pickled potatoes are delicious to serve as an appetizer on a botanas *platter or as an accompaniment to grilled meats. They are served on the streets in Oaxaca as a dish called* piedrazos, *in which hard, twice-cooked bread is placed in a bag with pickled potatoes, mangoes, quince, or other fruits and the chiles are spooned on top. Salty cheese and bottled hot sauce complete this dish that is a shocker to your mouth and is reputed to be a hit with college students. You can substitute dried* chipotles *if the chiles pasillas oaxaqueños are unavailable.*
Allow to sit at least 1 week before serving.

MAKES 2 QUARTS

2 pounds small new potatoes

3 carrots, peeled and sliced diago-
    nally into ½-inch rounds

6 cups cider vinegar

6 large chiles pasillas oaxa-
    queños (see page 331), toasted,
    stemmed, seeded, and cut into
    thin strips

5 heads of garlic

1½ medium white onions, thinly
    sliced

1 teaspoon black peppercorns

1 teaspoon whole allspice

1 teaspoon whole cloves

2 teaspoons salt

½ teaspoon sugar

3 tablespoons fresh Oaxacan
    oregano, or 2 tablespoons dried

1 sprig fresh thyme or ¼ teaspoon
    dried

In a heavy 4-quart stockpot, bring 2 quarts of water to a boil. Add the potatoes and boil for 15 minutes. Remove the potatoes with a slotted spoon, then rinse them with cold water and drain well. Add the carrots to the water and cook for 5 minutes. Drain in a colander and rinse with cold water. When the potatoes are cool, remove the skins.

In a large saucepan, warm the vinegar over low heat. Add the potatoes, carrots, and all the other ingredients and mix well.

Put the potatoes in sterilized glass jars or large plastic containers with cheesecloth placed over the mouth of the container to allow the vegetables to breathe. Refrigerate. Will keep indefinitely.

SOPA FLORENTINA
Spinach and Chard Soup

This soup is full of greens, with a base of garbanzo beans that are grown here in Oaxaca. You can use mustard greens or any other type of green instead of the Swiss chard, and use bacon instead of beef. In other words, be creative. My friend Gudelia Garrido taught me this soup by using garbanzo bean flour, but I prefer the blended cooked beans myself.

MAKES 12 SERVINGS

For the garbanzo broth:

1 pound dried garbanzo beans, soaked overnight, or 7 cups canned beans

Pinch of baking soda

½ medium white onion, finely chopped

3 garlic cloves, finely chopped

For the soup:

½ head of garlic, cloves separated

½ small onion, chunked

½ pound tomatoes (1 medium–large round or 4–5 plum), boiled and peeled, finely chopped

1½ teaspoons fresh Oaxacan oregano (see page 336) or 1 teaspoon dried

Pinch of cumin seeds

3 tablespoons sunflower or vegetable oil

¾ pound boneless top round, cut into small pieces, or smoked bacon or pork

1 pound acelga leaves (Swiss chard), torn into bite-size pieces, stems cut into ¼-inch slices

FOR GARBANZO BROTH:

In a medium stockpot, cook dried garbanzo beans with baking soda in 1 quart of water for 20 minutes. Drain and place some of the garbanzos on one half of a terry-cloth towel. Fold the towel over the beans and rub vigorously. The skins will separate from the beans. Remove the skins and discard. Repeat with the remaining beans. Rinse the beans. If you are using canned garbanzos, omit this step, but wash the garbanzos well to remove the metal flavor from the beans.

In a medium stockpot, combine the beans, onion, garlic, and 2 quarts of water. Bring to a boil, then lower the heat to a simmer. Cover and cook for 1 hour or until beans are soft.

FOR THE SOUP:

In a blender, put the garlic, onion, tomatoes, oregano, and cumin with 1 cup water and blend well. Pass through a food mill or sieve. Add another ½ cup water to rinse the mill.

In a 6-quart Dutch oven or heavy stockpot, heat the oil until smoking. Add the meat pieces and brown for about 5 minutes. Add the stalks of the chard and sauté until clear, about 7 minutes. Add the tomato puree and fry 10 minutes more.

Puree the beans in a blender using all of the cooking water plus an additional 1 cup if needed. Add to the meat mixture with the milk. Cook for 10 minutes. Add the salt. Add the chard and spinach leaves, cover, and cook for 40 minutes. Add the parsley and cook for 5 minutes more. Adjust the salt if needed.

Serve with the hard-boiled egg pieces on top.

½ cup milk

1–1½ tablespoons salt, or to taste

½ pound spinach leaves, torn into
bite-size pieces

½ cup chopped parsley leaves

For the garnish:

2 hard-boiled eggs, peeled and cut
into 12 pieces each

CALDO MIXE
Mixe Fiesta Soup

Señora María Alcántara Gómez de Bernal and her daughter Elda taught me this special fiesta soup as described on page 138. I've adapted the recipe to be smaller than the original version, but it's still a large quantity. Make it for a fiesta or freeze the leftovers. Serve with Tamales de Pata de Burro (page 150) and Tamales de Frijol (page 122).

MAKES APPROXIMATELY 18
SERVINGS

1½ pounds dried and salted beef
shortribs, or fresh meat, cut into
2-inch pieces

1 pound dried and salted beef
shoulder or boneless lean chuck
(fresh), cut into 2-inch pieces

2 medium white onions, 1 finely
chopped and 1 chunked

2 large heads of garlic, 1 finely
chopped and 1 separated and
left whole

3½–4 pounds turkey legs

¾ pound tomatoes (1½ medium–
large round or 6–8 plum)

In a large stockpot, bring 7½ quarts of water to a boil. Add the beef ribs and shoulder or lean chuck, the chopped onion, and the chopped garlic. Return to the boil and skim off any foam that comes to the surface, lower the heat to medium, and cook 1 hour covered or until the meat is almost soft. Add the turkey legs to the soup. Cook over medium to low heat for 1 hour.

On a 10-inch dry *comal*, griddle, or in a cast-iron frying pan, roast the tomatoes, chiles, whole garlic, and chunked onion slowly until cooked. Put these ingredients into a blender with 1 cup of the broth. Blend until smooth. Pass the mixture through a food mill or strainer and add to the soup.

Add the chicken pieces, vegetables, *hierbabuena*, cilantro, and salt. Continue to cook 30 to 45 minutes more or until everything is just tender. If you want, skim off the fat

2 chiles guajillos, *stemmed, seeded, and deveined (see page 331)*

1 chicken (3½–4 pounds), *cut into serving pieces, or 3 whole breasts, cut into 6 pieces, skin removed*

½ pound green beans, *cut into 2-inch pieces*

3 carrots, *peeled and cut into long, thick slices*

2¼ pounds chayotes (2–3) *(see page 326), peeled and cut into wedges about 1 inch thick*

¾ pound green cabbage, *sliced thickly or cut in wedges*

½ cup hierbabuena leaves *(see page 336)*

½ cup cilantro leaves

1 tablespoon salt

For the garnish:

3 chiles jalapeños, *stemmed, seeded, and finely chopped (see page 329)*

1 medium white onion, *finely chopped*

4–5 limes, *cut into quarters*

that rises to the surface. (In the Mixe this is not done because the fat is considered rich and gives it a wonderful flavor. Their diet is mainly vegetables, so this soup is a luxury.)

Place the jalapeños and onion on a plate with the limes on another and serve as a garnish with the soup.

Cocinera *spreading* **chintestle paste on a tortilla, Santa María Tlahuitoltepec, Mixe (Marcela Taboada)**

NOPALES CON HUEVOS
Cactus with Eggs

This egg dish is one of the standard Mexican breakfasts of all time. It is particularly popular during Lent, when nopales *are used as a main ingredient in many dishes. In my interviews with older people one woman told me, "In Oaxaca one can never starve. There is always a tree that is bearing fruit, and there are always* nopales.*" Serve these with* Frijoles Negros de Olla *(page 146).*

MAKES 6 SERVINGS

1 pound nopales, *cut into ½-inch cubes (see page 327)*

Salt

¼ cup sunflower or vegetable oil

1 small white onion, finely chopped

5 garlic cloves, finely chopped

¾ pound tomatoes (1½ medium–large round or 6–7 plum), finely chopped

½ teaspoon plus a good pinch of salt

2 sprigs fresh epazote *(see page 336) or 4 sprigs cilantro, finely chopped*

6–7 eggs

½ teaspoon ground black pepper

In a saucepan, bring 3 cups of water to a boil with a pinch of salt. Add the *nopales* and cook for 10 minutes. Drain well and rinse with cold water.

In a 10-inch frying pan, heat the oil over medium heat. Add the onion and cook until transparent. Add the garlic and tomatoes and fry until golden brown and the tomatoes start to caramelize, about 10 to 15 minutes. Add the *nopales* and fry well. Add ½ teaspoon salt or to taste. Add the *epazote* or cilantro and stir well.

In a separate bowl, beat the eggs with a pinch of salt and the black pepper. Add the eggs to the *nopales* mixture. Allow the eggs to set, then slowly stir them to expose more eggs to the surface of the frying pan, cooking them until cooked through, but soft and fluffy.

Serve at once with soft corn tortillas and beans or fried potatoes.

FRIJOLES NEGROS DE OLLA
Black Beans

We always make our black beans in a clay olla, *or bean pot, cooking them slowly on the stove or somewhat faster over the open fire in the outdoor kitchen. The wood smoke improves the flavor, and some of the best beans I've eaten are in the campesinos' (farmers') homes in the hills surrounding Oaxaca. This recipe is a good base from which to make the many dishes that call for* frijoles negros. *Black beans should always be soupy, but not watery. The best beans to use are the small, native* delgado *types.*

MAKES APPROXIMATELY 7 CUPS

1 pound dried black beans
 (2½ cups)
1 medium white onion, quartered
1 head of garlic, whole
1 chile de árbol (optional; see
 page 330)
2–3 sprigs epazote (9 large leaves),
 or 2 teaspoons dried (see
 page 336)
1 bay leaf
¼ teaspoon ground black pepper,
 optional
1 teaspoon salt, or more to taste

Clean the beans, picking through them carefully to remove any stones and dirt. Wash well in cold water until the water is clear. Fill a clay pot (with a lid) or a 6-quart soup pot with 12 cups of water, and add the onions, garlic, chile de árbol, epazote, bay leaf, and pepper. Bring to a boil, add the beans, then cover and simmer over low heat for 3 to 3½ hours, adding water (see Hints) as needed until the beans are soft. Add the salt only after the beans are almost cooked. Remove the bay leaf.

Hints: For a thicker broth, you can mash ½ cup of cooked beans and a little cooking liquid with a bean masher or with the back of a spoon, or puree in a blender, and then return them to the pot.

If you are using the beans as a side dish, you can substitute leftover water from soaking *chile ancho* or *chile guajillo* for part of the water in this recipe, and it will add a rich flavor.

For refried beans: In a heavy frying pan heat 2 tablespoons oil or lard until it is smoking. Sauté ½ white onion, finely chopped, over medium heat until clear. Add 7 cups cooked beans and 1 cup of their liquid to the pan and fry them, for 20 to 30 minutes, mashing all the while with a bean or potato masher, over medium heat, adding more bean liquid as they dry out. Salt to taste.

TORTILLAS DE PLÁTANO
Green Banana and Corn Tortillas

I've eaten these green banana tortillas each time I've visited my friend Juan Areli Bernal in Totontepec, Mixe. The family ranch is a beautiful 1½-hour walk to the lowlands, where bananas, coffee, and fruit trees are abundant. Usually Areli's sister, Elda, makes their homegrown zatope beans to go with them and toasted corn coffee to wash it all down. We made dumplings out of the same dough and added them to the beans in a soupy, satisfying dish called bodoke *in Mixe.*

MAKES 8 TORTILLAS

1½ pounds green plantains or green bananas

1 pound prepared masa *for tortillas or* 2 cups masa harina *for tortillas mixed with 1½ cups warm water*

Heat a 10-inch dry *comal*, griddle, or cast-iron frying pan over medium-high heat.

Peel the plantains and cut them into 2-inch chunks. (They might give off a black tinge to your hands. Do not be alarmed; it will come off after washing your hands a few times.) Place the bananas in a hand grinder or grinder attachment for a mixer and grind to a puree. (In the Sierra Mixe this is done on a *metate*, and it took me hours to do!)

If you are using prepared *masa*, break the *masa* up in a large mixing bowl and mix with a little water to soften it.

Add the banana puree to either *masa* and mix well. The *masa* to banana puree should be a ratio of half banana to half *masa*.

Divide the dough into eighths. Place one eighth on a cloth napkin or in between 2 layers of a large plastic bag cut in half. Using the heel of your palm, pat it out to make a large tortilla. Lift the cloth napkin, fold the ends under the tortilla so they won't burn, and invert the tortilla on to the *comal*. Peel off the napkin and let the tortilla cook on the first side. If you are using the plastic bag, peel off the top layer of plastic and lay it on top of the tortilla, invert it, and peel the other piece of plastic from the tortilla. Lay the tortilla on your hand and flip it onto the *comal*. When the tortilla doesn't stick on the *comal* (in about 1 minute), carefully lift it up and flip it over, cooking it on the other side for 2 minutes. Turn it over again and cook 2 minutes more. Continue with the remaining dough. Keep the tortillas warm in a cloth napkin.

(continued)

Hint: You must use very green plantains for this dish. The hand grinder works almost as well as the *metate*, and is a lot faster.

TAMALES DE CALABAZA Y FRIJOLES
Squash and Bean Tamales

This recipe comes from the Sierra Sur (the southern chain of the Sierra Madre), from a small village in the mountains above Miahuatlán called San Pablo Coatlán. Esther Mora Villar taught me these tamales at the home of her sister, Olga. The sweetness of the tamal dough is offset by the "spiciness" of the beans (the filling mixture is hot). That day, the tamales were perfect washed down with a good cup of Oaxacan Pluma coffee made by Olga's husband, Jaime; see Café de Olla (page 103).

MAKES 36 TO 40 MEDIUM TAMALES

For the calabaza:

2½ piloncillo *cones (6 ounces each; see page 348),* or 2½ *cups dark brown sugar*

2 *pieces of Mexican cinnamon, each 2 inches long (see page 337)*

5 pounds calabaza tamala *(see page 326) or pumpkin squash unpeeled and cut into chunks, or 5 cups squash puree*

For the frijoles:

20 avocado leaves (hoja de agua-cate; *see page 338)*

16 *small* chiles pasillas oa-xaqueños *(see page 331) or* 10 chipotles en adobo *(see page 332)*

FOR THE *CALABAZA*:

In a heavy 4-quart clay *olla* or stockpot, combine the *piloncillo*, cinnamon, and 3 cups of water. Heat over high heat until the *piloncillo* melts, then add the *calabaza* pieces. Cover and cook for 1 hour or until soft. Spoon the sauce over the *calabaza* pieces to moisten well, then remove from the pot with a slotted spoon to a plate to cool.

FOR THE *FRIJOLES*:

In a small saucepan, bring 2 cups of water to a boil.

On a 10-inch dry *comal*, griddle, or in a cast-iron frying pan, toast the avocado leaves, chiles, and garlic. Place the chiles in a small bowl and cover with the hot water. Allow to soak for 10 minutes. When the chiles have cooled, remove the stems, seeds, and veins.

Remove the inner ribs from the avocado leaves and discard. Put the leaves in a blender and grind well. Remove any long pieces of avocado leaf fiber from the ground mixture. Add the chiles and garlic. Blend well. Add the beans with their liquid and blend until smooth. Do this in batches, if you need to.

9 garlic cloves

6 cups Frijoles Negros de Olla
(page 146)

*2 tablespoons sunflower or vege-
table oil*

For the masa:

2 pounds prepared masa *for
tamales or 3½ cups* masa
harina *for tamales, firmly
packed*

1⅓ cups lard, melted

3 teaspoons salt, or more to taste

To make the tamales:

*4 packages cornhusks (see page
321), soaked in water for ½
hour to soften*

In a 10-inch cast-iron frying pan, heat the oil and add the bean mixture. Fry the mixture over medium to high heat, stirring constantly, until dry, about 10 minutes.

FOR THE *MASA*:

Remove the peel from the cooled *calabaza* and discard. Place the *calabaza* in a bowl and mash until smooth. This should yield 5 cups. If using prepared *masa*, break up the *masa* in a large bowl. If using *masa harina*, put it in a mixing bowl and add 2¼ cups of water. Mix it well and allow the dough to sit 15 minutes. Add the salt to the *masa* and mix in well. Add the mashed *calabaza* and mix well. Add the lard a little at a time and mix well. Whip the *masa* until light and fluffy, by hand or by mixer, for about 20 minutes.

TO MAKE THE *TAMALES*:

Pat dry a soaked, softened cornhusk. Hold the cornhusk with the wide end on the palm of your hand. Spread 4 table-spoons of *masa* in the husk toward the wider end, leaving a 1-inch border on the sides and about half the husk empty on top. Spoon 3 tablespoons of the bean paste in the middle of the *masa*, extending it as long as the *masa* is long. Lay the *tamal* on the table horizontally, and join the two long edges of the husk together and roll them up until firm. The filling should be enclosed. Fold the thin side over the fat filled end to double it. Secure it with ties made of shredded husks or put the folded side down into another husk. Repeat with the rest of the *masa*.

Fill a *tamalera* (or steamer) with salted water to the level of the rack. Place the rack in the pot. Cover it with extra cornhusks, and fill the steamer with the *tamales*. Cover and weight the lid with a heavy object to keep it snugly closed. Steam over a slow rolling boil for 1 to 1½ hours, or when the *tamal* separates easily from the husk and it "smells like tamales."

You can substitute pumpkin or sweet potatoes for the *calabaza*. Any leftover bean puree can be used for *Tlayudas con Frijoles* (page 19) or tostadas.

TAMALES DE PATA DE BURRO
Burro's Foot Tamales

In tamal-*making A to Z,* Tamales de Pata de Burro *ranks about A. This simple and delicious* tamal *got its name from its shape. In Totontepec, the leaves that the* tamal *are wrapped in are called* hoja de tamal *and are the same as I saw in the Chinantantla region called* hoja de pozole; *the latter were used to make "dog's head"* tamales. *In either case, you won't be able to find those leaves, so use banana leaves instead. Serve with* Caldo Mixe *(page 143).*

MAKES 8 *TAMALES*

1 package or enough fresh banana
    leaves for 8 tamales, or
    1 package frozen Thai banana
    leaves
2 pounds prepared masa for tor-
    tillas, or 3½ cups masa harina
    for tortillas
Salt to taste (optional)

Cut the banana leaves into 12-inch pieces and parboil them in 1 quart of water until soft, about 45 minutes. Cool and drain the leaves. (If using frozen Thai style, defrost them slowly, and then boil for 25 minutes.)

If using prepared *masa*, break up the *masa* in a large bowl. Add 10 to 12 tablespoons warm water, 2 tablespoons at a time, to the dough. If using *masa harina*, put it in a large mixing bowl and add 2¼ cups warm water. Mix it well and allow the dough to sit for 15 minutes. Then add 10 to 12 tablespoons warm water, 2 tablespoons at a time. By hand, whip the *masa* until light and fluffy for about 10 minutes. The dough should be soft and a little sticky. If you want to add salt, do it here. We make these without salt, as we make corn tortillas.

Divide the *masa* in eighths and roll each one into a ball. Take the first ball and flatten it into a disk. Lay the disk on the corner of the banana leaf. Fold up the banana leaf around the *tamal,* completely enclosing it like a neat package. Repeat with all the remaining dough.

Fill a *tamalera* or steamer with salted water to the level of the rack. Place the rack in the pot and cover the rack with cornhusks for flavor. Lay the *tamales* in the steamer and cover with a cloth. Cover with the lid and steam the *tamales* over a rolling boil for 1 hour or until the *masa* falls away from the banana leaf when opened.

TAMALES DE CHEPIL
CON SALSA DE CHILE PASILLA
Herbal Tamales with Smoked Chile Sauce

I always joke that this is a vegetarian tamal, *except for the large amount of lard in the* masa! *If you cannot locate* chepil, *you can substitute* epazote, parsley, cilantro, *or any other green leafy herb. The chiles used in the salsa are smoked or "baked" in the Mixe area of Oaxaca. The men of the Mixe group cultivate and harvest these chiles, then smoke them in adobe ovens over aromatic wood to give them their unique flavor. The salsa is by far the most popular table sauce in Oaxaca City. To me, it represents the real Oaxacan flavor. If you don't have* chiles pasillas oaxaqueños *for the salsa, substitute* chiles chipotles.

MAKES 12 *TAMALES*

For the masa:
1 pound prepared masa *for* tamales *or* 1¾ cups *masa* harina *for* tamales, *firmly packed*
1½ teaspoons baking powder
7 tablespoons lard
1–1½ teaspoons salt, or to taste
½ cup plus 2 tablespoons warm *chicken stock (page 343)*
1 cup chepil *leaves, washed and drained (see page 336)*

For the salsa de chile pasilla:
2–3 small chiles pasillas oaxaqueños, chiles chipotles, *or other smoked chile (see pages 330 and 331)*
7 large tomatillos (5½ ounces)
2 garlic cloves
Salt to taste

FOR THE *MASA:*
If using prepared *masa,* break up the *masa* in a large bowl. If you are using *masa harina,* place it in a mixing bowl and add 1 cup plus 2 tablespoons warm water, to make a soft dough. Allow it to sit 15 minutes. Add the baking powder to the *masa* and mix it in well. Add the lard if it is fresh (soft); if the lard is the block type, whip it as much as possible to get it light, then add it to *masa.* Mix the *masa* well by hand or mixer. Dissolve the salt in the stock and add to the *masa,* stirring well. Whip well until light and fluffy, about 20 minutes. Add the drained *chepiles,* stir, and taste for salt.

FOR THE *SALSA DE CHILE PASILLA:*
On a hot *comal* or griddle, toast all the ingredients, making sure not to burn the chiles and garlic—they will toast fast. When the chiles are cool, remove the stems, seeds, and veins. Grind the chiles and garlic in the *molcajete* or a blender. Add the grilled *tomatillos* one at a time and the salt. (Add at least ¼ to ½ cup of water bit by bit to make more liquid.) This should be chunky!

(continued)

To make the tamales:
2 packages dried cornhusks, soaked
½ hour in water to soften

TO MAKE TAMALES:

Blot dry soaked cornhusks in a tea towel. Take a dried husk and place 2 spoonfuls of *masa* in the lower third toward the wider end of the cornhusk. Join the two sides of the husk together, roll it up until firm, and then fold the thin side over the fat, filled end. Fit the *tamal* folded side down into another husk. Repeat with the rest of the *masa*.

Fill a *tamalera* (steamer) with salted water up to the level of the rack. Place the rack inside, cover it with extra cornhusks, and fill the steamer with the *tamales*. Cover and weigh the lid down with a heavy object to keep it snugly closed. Steam over a slow rolling boil for about 1 hour, or until the *tamal* separates easily from the husk and it "smells like *tamales*." Serve with the *salsa de chile pasilla* or other hot sauce. Many people serve them with *atole*, coffee, or chocolate.

MA'ACH
(Mashed Corn and Potatoes with Tomato Sauce

I first learned about Ma'ach by tracking down a young, handsome Mixe filmmaker nicknamed Gordo, who showed me a documentary he had made on this antiquated dish. I was fascinated because there are versions of Ma'ach that contain corn, beans, and squash in the same dish. Later, he took me to his Godmother Josefina, who owns Artesanias El Tlacoyal (a pottery store), who had her daughter Swilma Pérez García and Isabel Aguilar María make another version of this ceremonial dish for me. Serve with thin strips of grilled beef (Tasajo y Cebollitas a la Parrilla, page 244).

MAKES 8–10 APPETIZER
SERVINGS

For the sauce:

1 pound tomatoes (2 medium–large
    round or 8–10 plum)
2 chiles pasillas oaxaqueños,
    stemmed, seeded, and deveined
    (see page 331)
3 garlic cloves
¼ medium white onion, chopped
½ teaspoon salt

To assemble:

1 pound guías (see page 326) or
    young spinach leaves, cleaned
    and ripped into large pieces
Pinch of salt
1½ pounds prepared masa for tor-
    tillas or 2⅔ cups masa harina
    for tortillas mixed with 1½ cups
    plus 3 tablespoons water
½ pound potatoes, peeled
1½ teaspoons salt

FOR THE SAUCE:

In a 2-quart clay *olla* or stockpot, bring 1 quart of water to a boil. Add the tomatoes and cook over medium heat for 6 to 8 minutes or until soft. Remove from heat, then add the chiles to the water and soak for 10 minutes.

In a blender, combine the tomatoes, chiles, garlic, onion, and 3 cups of the soaking water and blend until smooth. Pass through a food mill or sieve and put in a clay *olla* or saucepan and heat over low heat for 5 minutes. Add salt. Keep warm.

TO ASSEMBLE:

Preheat a 3-quart clay bowl or heavy pot over medium heat, and allow to get white hot.

In a 4-quart clay pot or saucepan, bring 1 quart of water to a boil. Add the salt and *guías* or spinach. Cook for 15 minutes, covered, over low heat. Keep warm.

Heat a large 10-inch dry *comal*, griddle, or cast-iron frying pan over high heat.

Mix the *masa* with a little water to make a soft dough and place in a bowl. Blend the raw potato in a blender until smooth. Add to the *masa* mixture with the salt and mix well.

Make 6 large balls and flatten to ½-inch-thick round *memelas* or thick patties. Place them on the *comal* and cook them for 4 minutes on each side until they are browned. Remove from the *comal*, place on a board, and mash with a bean masher. When the mixture is cooled, knead well. Make more *memelas* of the same size and bake them again on the *comal* for 4 minutes on each side. Remove from the *comal* and mash together again.

Mound the mixture in the white-hot clay bowl or pot and pour the hot sauce over the top. Be careful, as the sauce will splatter about.

Serve immediately with the greens. (Traditionally, diners sit in a circle around the bowl and pinch bits of *ma'ach* off with their fingertips. You can also put the bowl in the center of a table and scoop bits of *ma'ach* onto a small plate. Try it!)

CHILES RELLENOS OAXAQUEÑOS
Smoked Chiles Stuffed with Cheese

This is another version of chiles rellenos *that is quite popular in Oaxaca, served as part of the hot* botanas *platter with* bocadillos, tamalitos, *rolled and fried tacos,* empanadas, *and* quesadillas, *just to name a few. We often eat these as an* almuerzo *or hearty midmorning brunch. The smoky flavor of the chiles offsets the cheese quite nicely, and the tomato sauce helps to cut the heat of the chiles somewhat. These chiles are not for the fainthearted or those with sensitive stomachs. Always serve them with soft tortillas, rice, or beans to balance them.*

MAKES 8 SERVINGS

For the tomato sauce:

2 pounds tomatoes (4–5 medium–large round or 16–20 plum)

¼ medium white onion, chunked

3 garlic cloves

1 tablespoon sunflower or vegetable oil

Salt to taste

1 tablespoon fresh epazote leaves or 1 teaspoon dried (see page 336)

For the chiles:

16 large chiles pasillas oaxaqueños (about 4–4½ inches long; see page 331)

¾ pound queso fresco *or* manchego, Muenster, *or* Gouda cheese (see page 346)

16 large or 32 medium epazote leaves (see page 336), depending on size

½ cup flour mixed with salt and pepper, to dredge chiles

FOR THE TOMATO SAUCE:

On a 10-inch dry *comal*, griddle, or in a cast-iron frying pan, grill the tomatoes, onion, and garlic until they blacken slightly. Remove the tomato skins and discard. Blend the tomatoes, onion, and garlic together until smooth, and pass through a food mill or a sieve.

In a heavy saucepan or wok over medium-high heat, heat the oil until smoking. Fry the tomato mixture in the oil, stirring with a wooden spoon. Lower the heat, stir once more, and simmer 15 minutes, covered. Add the salt and *epazote* and cook a few minutes more. Keep warm.

FOR THE CHILES:

Heat 1 quart water in a medium saucepan to boil. Remove from heat.

Toast the chiles on both sides on a dry *comal* or griddle until they blister and puff up. Remove from the *comal* and soak in hot water until the chiles are soft, about 10 minutes. Remove chiles from water, and make a slit down the side of each chile with a small paring knife to remove the seeds, leaving the stems intact.

Cut the cheese into ¼-inch strips that can fit into the chiles, or crumble or grate it on the large side of a grater.

Stuff the cleaned chiles with the cheese, being careful not to fill them too much so that they can close well without

For the batter:

4 large eggs, at room temperature at least 30 minutes

Pinch of salt

2 cups peanut, sunflower, or vegetable oil

bulging open. Line the inside seam with *epazote* leaves to hold the filling in and close the chiles. Dredge the chiles in the flour and shake off excess flour. Mold each chile with your hands to seal it shut.

FOR THE BATTER:

Separate the egg yolks and whites into two bowls. Whip the whites with the salt until stiff peaks form. Add the yolks, all at once, and whip for 30 seconds more. You want the yolks to be incorporated into the whites, but try not to lose any of the air that you've whipped into them.

Heat the oil in a large frying pan until smoky. Pass the chiles through the batter holding them by the stems, rotating to cover the chiles completely. Place the chiles directly into the pan and fry. With the back of a metal spatula, flick oil over the top of the chiles to form their shape. Using two spatulas, turn carefully to cook all sides. By holding the chiles up on their sides with the spatula, they will come out rounded, not flat. Continue to cook the remaining chiles, one or two at a time. Remove them from the pan and drain them on paper towels. You can keep them warm in a 300°F oven.

Ladle the tomato sauce into flat bowls. Place 2 chiles over the sauce and serve with hot tortillas, rice, and beans as a main course, or pile the chiles on a *botanas* platter and serve the sauce on the side.

Hints: You can substitute the filling for *Chiles Rellenos de Picadillo* (page 27) and vice versa.

Don't cook too many chiles at once or the oil will cool down too much.

If your chile is broken and you can't twirl it in the egg batter, spoon a good amount of batter onto a spoon and place the chile on top. Cover it with batter and lower the whole thing into the hot oil. Flick oil over the top to form its shape and slip it off the spoon.

TORTITAS DE POLLO CON NOPAL EN SALSA DE CHIPOTLE

Chicken Croquettes with Cactus in Chipotle Sauce

About halfway from the Isthmus to Oaxaca, driving through the Sierra Madre del Sur, one comes upon a spectacular view of the fertile valley of Nejapa and El Camarón. We always stop here to eat and stretch our legs. On a recent trip, I ate this lovely dish at a restaurant called El Puente in El Camarón. I liked it so much I came home and made it the next day for lunch, and everyone enjoyed the results. This salsa is very hot, so reduce the amount of chiles if you do not want it picante. Serve these with Arroz Blanco con Plátanos Fritos (page 53) with or without the plantains or Arroz con Chepil (page 52).

MAKES 6 TO 8 SERVINGS

Seasoning ingredients for chicken stock (page 343)

1 chicken (3 pounds), including the feet and neck, skin removed

For the salsa:

1 pound tomatoes (2 medium–large round or 8–10 plum)

1 cup chiles chipotles en adobo *(page 332), stems removed*

1 medium white onion, chunked

1 tablespoon chopped garlic

1 tablespoon sunflower or vegetable oil

2 sprigs epazote, *leaves only (see page 336)*

¼ teaspoon salt

Place the seasoning ingredients and chicken feet and neck in a 6-quart stockpot with water to cover, about 3 quarts. Prepare stock following directions on page 343, replacing the whole chicken for the chicken pieces. Cover the pot and poach the chicken for 30 minutes over medium-low heat. Remove the chicken from the pot and allow to cool. Remove the chicken meat from the bones and shred finely. Reserve the stock.

FOR THE SALSA:

In a medium saucepan, bring 2 cups of water to a boil. Add the tomatoes and boil for 3 minutes, then remove from the heat. Remove and discard the skins. Blend the tomatoes, chiles, onion, and garlic until smooth.

In a deep, heavy 8-inch frying pan, heat the tablespoon of oil. Add the tomato puree and fry for 5 minutes, stirring constantly. Add 1 to 2 cups of the reserved chicken stock to make a thin sauce. Cook 10 minutes, then add the *epazote* and salt.

For the nopales:

½ teaspoon salt

1 pound nopales *or string beans, julienned (see page 327)*

For the croquettes:

1 tablespoon butter

½ small white onion, finely chopped

7 garlic cloves, finely chopped

¾ large plum tomato, finely chopped

2 teaspoons fresh Oaxacan oregano leaves *(see page 336)*

1 teaspoon salt

½ teaspoon ground white pepper

1¼ cups bread crumbs

5 eggs, *left at room temperature for at least 1 hour, separated*

½ cup peanut oil, *or more for frying*

FOR THE *NOPALES*:

In a medium saucepan, heat 3 cups water with the salt. Add the *nopales*, cover, and cook 10 minutes over medium-high heat. Drain the *nopales* and set aside.

FOR THE CROQUETTES:

In a small frying pan, heat the butter until it sizzles. Add the onion and sauté for 2 minutes over medium heat. Add the garlic and sauté for 1 minute longer. Allow to cool.

In a medium mixing bowl, mix the shredded chicken, onion, garlic, tomato, oregano, salt, white pepper, and bread crumbs. In a separate mixing bowl, beat the egg whites with a wire whisk or a mixer until stiff peaks form. Add the egg yolks and beat 30 seconds more. Fold the chicken mixture into the eggs until well incorporated. Form into 8 large croquettes or 12 to 14 small ones, if you prefer.

In a large frying pan, heat the oil until very hot. Add the croquettes and fry until golden brown on each side, about 2 to 3 minutes on each side. Remove from the oil and drain well. Place the croquettes and the *nopales* in the salsa and reheat.

Divide the cooked *nopales* into 8 portions. Place 2 croquettes on each plate with 1 portion of *nopales* between the croquettes. Spoon sauce over each croquette.

PAN AMARILLO
Yeasty White Bread

This is a yeasty sandwich bread made all over the state of Oaxaca. In the Sierra Juárez in Ixtlán, there is a wonderful eighty-year-old woman who makes this with a starter she has had going for fifty years. Most people, however, bake with fresh or dried yeast, and they are traditionally baked in wood-fired adobe ovens.

MAKES 12 ROLLS

For the sponge:
2 tablespoons active dry yeast
Pinch of sugar
1 cup all-purpose flour

For the bread:
1½ teaspoons salt
5 cups all-purpose flour
2 teaspoons vegetable shortening
2 teaspoons sesame seeds

FOR THE SPONGE:
In a medium bowl, whisk together the yeast, sugar, flour, and 1 cup warm water. Let sit in a warm place for 15 minutes to proof.

FOR THE BREAD:
In another medium bowl, mix the salt, sugar, and 4 cups of flour. Make a well in the flour and add the sponge mixture. Mix well, adding 1 cup more water. Knead the dough for 10 to 15 minutes, working in up to 1 additional cup of flour. Put the dough in a greased bowl, turn dough over to grease top, and cover the bowl with a towel or plastic wrap. Let dough rise for 20 to 30 minutes, or until double in size, or until a dent remains when the dough is poked with your finger.

Knead dough 8 times. Cut into 8 pieces and roll into balls. Rub each ball with oil. Sprinkle sesame seeds on the counter. Invert each ball onto the seeds. Cover. Let rise for 20 to 30 minutes.

Invert balls onto greased cookie sheets (6 per sheet) and flatten with the palm of your hand. Make a slice in the top of each ball with a knife or razor blade.

Place in a cold oven.

Heat oven to 400°F. Bake for 30 minutes or until lightly browned and when the bottom crust makes a hollow sound when tapped.

Remove from oven. Cool on rack.

PALANQUETAS DE AJONJOLÍ Y PEPITAS
Sesame and Pumpkin Seed Brittle

In the streets of Oaxaca, it is not unusual to see women carrying baskets on their heads with a range of things to sell. This type of brittle usually comes as either pepitas, *peanuts, or squash seeds. We adapted this recipe from the Mexican sweets and pastry book* Y la comida se hizo de dulces y postres, *but combined the sesame seeds and* pepitas *for a more interesting texture and flavor.*

1 cup sesame seeds, toasted
1 cup pepitas *(see page 338)*
1 cup sugar
½ cup (1 stick) butter

In a dry medium cast-iron or heavy frying pan, toast the sesame seeds for 5 minutes, stirring constantly. Remove them from the pan and allow them to cool completely on a plate.

In the same frying pan, toast the *pepitas* for 10 minutes. Remove them from the pan and allow them to cool completely on a plate. When both the seeds and the *pepitas* are cool, mix them well.

In a 10-inch cast-iron frying pan, melt the sugar over low heat until it is a light brown color, about 8 to 10 minutes. Do not stir the sugar. Tilt the pan to evenly distribute the sugar as it melts. Be careful not to touch the sugar as it is very hot.

Remove the pan from the stove. Add the butter and the seed mixture and stir constantly. Mix quickly and pour onto a plain greased surface. With the back of a wooden spoon, mash down the mixture until it is ½ to 1 inch thick (about 9″ × 11″). When it is completely dry, crack it into pieces.

Hint: Store in an airtight plastic container.

ATOLE DE MAÍZ
Hot Corn Drink

Atole *is one of the most ancient drinks in Mexico. It can be made with many variations, based on corn, wheat, sesame seed, rice, or amaranth. Here, it is made from dried corn that is boiled (without* cal) *and ground, either at the* molino, *in the hand grinder, or in a blender. Milk, coconut, strawberries, pecans, or* piloncillo *sugar can be added to this recipe.*

MAKES 4 CUPS

1 cup dried corn, or ¼ cup
  maizena (cornstarch)
1 piece of Mexican cinnamon,
  2 inches long (see page 337)
¼ cup sugar

FOR DRIED CORN:
In a saucepan, bring 4 cups of water to a boil. Add the corn and cook, covered, over medium-high heat for about 1 hour or until the corn is medium soft. Remove the corn from the water and reserve the water. Grind the corn in a hand grinder or blender with 2 cups of the cooking water until smooth. Strain the ground corn through cheesecloth into the saucepan and return it to a boil. Add the cinnamon and sugar. Cook for 30 minutes. Lower the heat and continue to stir as it thickens. Serve warm.

FOR THE *MAIZENA*:
Put 4 cups of water and the cinnamon in a medium saucepan over high heat. When the water is warm, take ¼ cup of the warm water and mix it with the *maizena*, allowing the remaining water to come almost to a boil. Stir in the *maizena* mixture just before the water boils. Stir well and add the sugar. Lower the heat to a simmer, and let simmer for 10 minutes, stirring until it thickens. Serve at once.

Hint: You can make many variations on *atole*.

Atole de granillo: If using dried corn, keep some apart and lightly mill it so it is a little chunky. Add this to the cooked *atole* and cook some more to give texture.

Atole de fresa: For strawberry-flavored *atole*, blend 2 cups hulled strawberries with 1 cup of the cooked *atole* and 6 tablespoons sugar. Add the mixture to the pot and let simmer for 1 minute.

AGUA DE NOPAL Y PIÑA
Cactus Pineapple Cooler

Every time we drive to the home of Gudelia and Tino Garrido, Gudelia greets us with a pitcher of cool water flavored with the fruit or vegetable of the day. Because it gets so hot in the Sierra Sur, nopales are abundant and Gudelia has many recipes that include this nutritious plant. It is believed that this drink works to lower cholesterol and add fiber to your diet. This one is refreshing after a long, hot drive through the mountains—or anywhere else, for that matter.

MAKES 2 QUARTS

¼ pound fresh nopales *(see page 327), chopped*
½ pineapple *(1¾ pounds), peeled, cored, and cut into small cubes*
½–¾ cup sugar

In a blender, combine the *nopales*, pineapple, and 1¾ quarts of water. Blend well. Strain through a food mill or a sieve. You will have to make this in batches. Add the sugar and stir well. Serve well chilled.

Cloud forest, Sierra Mixe (Barbara Lawton)

CHAPTER SEVEN

The Tuxtepec Region
(Región de Tuxtepec)

Cleaning
achiote *seeds in*
Nuevo Arroyo
Camarón
(Barbara
Lawton)

Overleaf:
Unloading caña
at the trapiche,
Tuxtepec
(Barbara
Lawton)

Of all the regions of Oaxaca my favorite is Tuxtepec.
Descending from the winding roads of the Sierra Juárez
into Valle Nacional has always been inspirational to me.
I remember my earliest travels in Oaxaca, as I posed for
pictures next to giant elephant ear plants and collected
bromeliads near the Río Papaloapam, never ceasing to be
in awe of the fertility surrounding me. It's the home of the
Chinantecan and Mazatecan peoples, some of the most
friendly and gracious people I have ever met.

In the areas surrounding the city of Tuxtepec, there are many crops planted, primarily sugarcane for the production of *piloncillo* (raw sugar cones) in the rustic colonial *trapiches* (sugar mills) and for refined sugar at the city factory begun fifty years ago. Other crops include rice, corn, coffee, cacao, tobacco, and the aromatic *chile seco*. Wild and cultivated herbs and greens are abundant on the hillsides rising out of the reservoir behind the Cerro de Oro Dam. Vanilla beans are cultivated in the hills below Cerro Rabán, an immense mesa rising up from the rich valley of the Río Santo Domingo. The area is rich with banana and mango trees and pineapple plantations, which are the inspiration for the regional dance La Flor de Piña.

My view of Tuxtepec was changed radically by my friendship with Bartola Morales. Bartola is the founder of the Human Rights Organization of Chinantecan Women. She and her husband Fidel Pereda are making great strides in helping women to deal with the financial and judicial land-rights problems that occurred after construction of the Cerro de Oro Dam in 1972, which flooded 65,134 acres of Chinanteca land. Many families were relocated, and the ones that remained had to find alternative ways to live. The Human Rights Organization helped these women realize the enormous potential of their region, including the possibility of utilizing the soil and lake for productive economic activities. All of the participants in the organization are indigenous women who produce and sell fruit, vegetables, meat, fish, and handicraft products. All the women Bartola introduced me to were extraordinary, but no one was quite as amazing as Bartola herself. She is an expert on the foods, customs, and handicrafts of the Chinanteca. On my various visits to Tuxtepec to study the foods of the region, she and Fidel took me on whirlwind tours to meet regional cooks and food producers.

Tuxtepec is a small city, with great food and fun people. Bartola and I visited many cooks and restaurants, trying exotic dishes such as *tepescuintle* (agouti—a wild rodent), armadillo, deer, and wild rabbit. The influence of nearby Veracruz was evident in both the abundance of seafood and the warm and friendly manner of the people. We sampled all kinds of snacks at the restaurant Antojitos Yoli after I struck up a conversation (which is easy to do in Tuxtepec) with the owner, Señora Tomasa, in a banana store one morning. She invited me into her restaurant's kitchen and taught me many dishes, as well as let me work for free to get some practice. We also met Elida Silva Nuñez, a cake maker with a large list of clients and friends. Her bubbly personality and nonstop energy were a perfect qualification for the cake baking and decorating she does for the fancy weddings and *quinceaños* fiestas that are so popular in this country. She was Miss Tuxtepec in 1963, during the years when they still had the spring carnival; she reigns today as "queen of the *pasteles*."

Down the highway, through miles of sugarcane fields, is a wonderful and unique spot called Restaurante Carmelita. The chef is María del Carmen Vásquez.

The restaurant is renowned in this region for the pre-Hispanic dishes it serves. Animals are hunted in the nearby mountains and brought to her by local campesinos. Here, I found dishes made from *tepescuintle, jabalí* (wild boar), *liebre* (hare), and deer. She also serves armadillo and iguana inspired by her homeland of Juchitán, and makes one of the best *caldo de mariscos* I've ever eaten. People come from all over to eat her exciting dishes and drink the *piña Chinanteca*, a beautiful pineapple hollowed out and filled with juices and liquor. Outside the restaurant is an odd assortment of pets to amuse the children, all very exotic in these parts, but they definitely wouldn't end up on the dinner table.

One of the best places Bartola took me was Ojitlán, a jungle village near where she was born. It was there I learned to make *popo*, an ancient Chinantecan drink traditionally served at weddings, baptisms, and (she would say with a wink) to welcome only the most special guests. We were at the home of María Cabrera Miguel, one of three midwives and herbal healers in the village. It was a simple and rustic hut with thatched roof, hard mud floor, wood slat walls, hammocks, and *huipiles* hung on the walls. Young granddaughters with calf-length *huipiles* and plastic bead necklaces were helping María and her daughter-in-law to prepare the drink. The ingredients were *criollo* (wild) cacao, *colcameca* vine, yellow corn, sugar, and water.

We walked the paths outside her home and found an amazing array of cacao trees. Her charming daughter-in-law showed me how the fresh cacao pod was opened and the soft beans removed. The fiber inside was soft and gelatinous. Later the beans were to be washed, fermented, and dried.

They were working at a waist-high firebench filled with sand, where the fire was placed. An iron ring on legs supported a new clay *comal* (only new greaseless *comales* are used in the making of *popo*, or the drink will never foam). Above the fire, *chicales* (large gourds) were hanging among handmade baskets made of tree vines and twine. Previously dried, irregular-shaped cacao beans were laboriously toasted over an open fire, while a wooden sword-shaped implement was used to stir. The toasted cacao beans were cracked on a little rock, peeled to reveal the whitish inner nib of the *criollo* cacao, and put in the *chicales*.

Dried corn was ground into *nixtamal masa*. The *colcameca* vine, which grows wild among the corn, was toasted over an open flame; if this step is omitted, the raw stem will scratch your throat. The roasted vine was then rammed into the hand grinder piece and milled—no greasy hands can touch it or it will ruin the foamy froth. All the ingredients were ground for a second time; the mixture looked like black mud, but the smell was nutty and aromatic. The cleaned cacao was ground and kneaded with the corn and *colcameca* mixture. Part of this paste was made into little balls mixed with sugar and toasted directly on the coals for a snack. By this time we were all very hungry and these morsels tasted incredibly good.

María added sugar to the remaining paste, then she filled a large tub halfway with water and submerged a woven sack that contained the *masa*. She squeezed the *masa* to release its flavor into the water, turning it milk-chocolate brown. She repeated this many times. The bag served as a strainer for the *masa*, which was later discarded and fed to the pigs. She pulled out a giant *molinillo* (Mexican whisk) from an embroidered cloth and began to whip up a froth. She whipped for an hour, serving froth off the top and filling *jícaras*, or gourds, full of foam for each guest. One has to inhale the *popo*, which is aromatic and exotic—the original chocolate mousse!

Another woman I met in my travels with Bartola Morales was Judith Hernández Sánchez, who lived in the heart of the jungle with her beautiful children and husband. She is one of the major cooks of the village and she prepares food for the village fiestas. She explained that the family giving the fiesta hired her in exchange for a portion of the food. She taught me many dishes; one of them was *Caldo Ranchero de Paisano* (page 170), which is a traditional wedding soup and by far the most popular dish in Ojitlán.

Bartola also took me to her village of Nuevo Arroyo Camarón, which had been relocated to higher ground because of the dam. We piled into dugout canoes for a half-hour ride to the island in the lake. Children ran to the shore to greet us in Chinanteca, where we walked around with Esteban Morales, the young *presidente* (mayor) of this village of twenty-four families. I was excited to see the *achiote* tree (annatto) that bears the bright red pods with seeds inside. *Achiote* had been used by the early Mayans, Zapotecs, and Chinantecs as paint and as flavoring in food, and is still a popular flavoring. The pods were bright red when I saw them and needed to dry more. When harvested, the bright red seeds are removed from the pods and put into water to release their flavor and color. The red mixture is cooked in a special pot stirred continuously for three days until dry. The paste is then molded into logs that are pure *achiote*, with no additives.

The island-village was even more tropical and lush than Ojitlán, and the smell from the drying aromatic *chiles secos* in the school yard permeated the area. As we walked down the path, a little boy ran by with a load of wiggling fish on a string, just out of the reservoir. When we returned to meet the families, we were served an incredibly delicious fish soup flavored with *achiote*. That night, as we toasted each other, laughed, sang songs, and conversed in three languages, I knew that this was one of the best days of our journey.

IN THIS CHAPTER

SOPA DE LENTEJAS

Savory Lentil Soup with Pineapple and Plantains

When our friends Michelle and Alejandro invited us for lunch to meet their new son Miguel, they had a marvelous cook who served typical Oaxacan food. The lunch was elaborate, with many courses, but nothing outshone the soup course. Tiny pieces of pork gave this soup a wonderfully sweet flavor. It is also an especially good main course, with the meat cut into 2-inch cubes, served with rice and greens.

MAKES 6 SERVINGS

1½ medium white onions, 1 left whole and the half finely chopped

9 garlic cloves, 2 left whole and 7 finely chopped

2 bay leaves

½ pound boneless pork shoulder or dark chicken meat, cut into 1-inch cubes

½ pound small brown lentils, picked through and washed

¾ pound tomatoes (1½ medium–large round or 4–5 plum)

3 black peppercorns

¼ teaspoon cumin seeds

1 whole clove

1 whole allspice

1 piece of Mexican cinnamon, 1 inch long (see page 337)

2 tablespoons sunflower or vegetable oil

Pinch of sugar

1 sprig thyme, or pinch of dried

1½ sprigs Oaxacan oregano, or ½ teaspoon dried (see page 336)

1 chile de árbol or chile japonés (see pages 330 and 331)

In a heavy 4-quart stockpot, bring 2 quarts of water to a boil. Add the whole onion, whole garlic, and 1 bay leaf. When the water is boiling, add the pork or chicken and cook over medium to low heat, covered, until soft, about 45 minutes.

Remove the stockpot from the heat and discard the onion, garlic, and bay leaf, reserving the stock. Leave the pork meat in the stock. Add the lentils to the pot, cover, and lower the heat to a simmer.

Grill the tomatoes on a 10-inch dry *comal*, griddle, or in a cast-iron frying pan over medium heat until the skins are black and the tomatoes have softened, about 10 minutes. Immediately remove the tomatoes to a plate and let them cool.

Toast the peppercorns, cumin seeds, clove, allspice, and the cinnamon stick on the *comal* or griddle until they are browned a bit and a scent is released, about 3 minutes. Remove the spices from the *comal* and cool.

When the tomatoes are cool enough to handle, skin them, discarding the skins, and puree the tomatoes with the toasted spices in a blender until smooth. Strain into a bowl to remove the seeds. Set aside.

In an 8-inch cast-iron frying pan, heat the oil and fry the chopped half-onion over medium heat until it is limp and clear, about 5 minutes. Add the chopped garlic and continue to fry for a few more minutes until the garlic is clear. Add the tomato and spice mixture and stir well. Cook, stirring over medium heat, for about 10 minutes, then stir the puree into the pot with the lentils and pork. Add the sugar, thyme,

1 cup peeled and chunked fresh
   pineapple, in 1-inch pieces
1 ripe plantain, peeled and sliced
   into ¾-inch pieces, then quartered (about 1 cup)
Salt to taste
4 sprigs parsley, leaves finely
   chopped

oregano, remaining bay leaf, and chile. Continue to cook,
covered, over low heat until the lentils are almost done,
about 25 minutes. Add the pineapple chunks and plantain
slices to the pot and cook for ½ hour more. Season with salt
and add the parsley. Serve immediately.

Hints: You can grill the onion and garlic with the tomatoes,
then puree them together before frying and adding them to
the lentil and pork stock.

   You can make this soup meatless by using vegetable
stock instead of the pork or chicken and water.

CALDO RANCHERO DE PAISANO
Countrymen's Soup

---

*In the jungle village of Ojitlán, near Tuxtepec, when a young couple gets married
the women of the village join together to make this special wedding soup. The
flavoring comes from the dark liquid made from achiote seeds (annatto). Pure
achiote is hard to find, but you can use the Yucatecan variety, which has other
spices and sometimes* masa harina *added. Serve this with* Arroz a la Jardinera
del Restaurante Yalile *(page 174) or other type of rice. Sometimes I ladle the
soup directly over a large spoonful of rice. Fresh corn tortillas are always
served with this soup at the fiestas where it is usually eaten.*

MAKES 8 SERVINGS

1½ pounds pork ribs
1¼ pounds boneless pork shoulder
3 tablespoons chiles secos
   (see page 331)
1 head of garlic, cloves separated
1 pound tomatoes (2 medium–large
   round or 8–10 plum), peeled
3 sprigs mint

In a heavy 6-quart stockpot, bring 3 quarts of water to a boil.
Add the pork, cover, lower the heat to a simmer, and cook
about 45 minutes. Keep warm.

   Remove ¼ cup liquid from the stockpot and soak the
chiles for 5 minutes. Grind them in a *molcajete* or a blender
with the garlic until the mixture is a paste. Add the tomatoes
and blend well, then add the mixture to the stockpot. Stir in
the mint and chives.

   Remove ½ cup of broth from the stockpot and put it in a
molcajete or small bowl. Dissolve the *achiote* by rubbing it

12 chives, cut into 2-inch pieces
1 tablespoon achiote *paste*
½ *small bunch cilantro, leaves only*
Salt to taste

with the *tejolote* (pestle) or the back of a spoon. As the *achiote* dissolves, add the liquid to the stock, then add more broth and continue to dissolve the remaining *achiote*. It may take a few tries to soften the *achiote* paste if it is the pure product. If using commercial *achiote*, you can do this in the blender. Add the cilantro and simmer meat for 5 minutes more. Add salt.

PLÁTANOS RELLENOS CON QUESO
Plantains Stuffed with Cheese

One morning, while walking in downtown Tuxtepec, I passed by a little molino *that had whole branches of plantains hanging from hooks on the wall. I asked the señora what she did with all of them. She rattled off the names of six different plantain dishes. She then showed me what she was feeding her husband for his midmorning meal. I went back at 7 o'clock that night to learn this recipe from Señora Tomasa, owner of the nearby Antojitos Yoli Restaurant. Thus began one of my most endearing friendships in Tuxtepec.*

MAKES 8 SERVINGS

For the plantains:
2½ *pounds plantains, peeled and cut into 3-inch pieces (see Hint)*
½ *teaspoon salt*
8 *ounces* queso fresco *(see page 346; see Hints)*
1½ *cups sunflower or vegetable oil*

For the topping:
4 *tablespoons* crema *(see page 345), crème fraîche, or sour cream mixed with a little water*
½ *cup* queso cotija, *finely grated (see page 346)*

Bring 4 cups of water to a boil in a 2-quart saucepan. Add the plantain pieces and salt. Cook over medium heat, covered, for 20 minutes or until soft. Remove the plantains and transfer to a colander to drain.

Mash the drained plantains with a potato masher. Divide and roll the mashed plantains into 16 balls. With a tortilla press or rolling pin, press the balls into 3- or 4-inch circles between two sheets of plastic. Place a small wedge of *queso fresco* in the center of each circle. Fold the top of the circle down over the cheese and the bottom part up to enclose the cheese in the plantain—it should look like a fat cigar. Place each plantain "cigar" lengthwise in your hands between the palms and your fingertips and roll, putting a little pressure on the ends to completely enclose the cheese. They should look like torpedoes.

In a deep 8-inch frying pan or a wok for frying, heat the

oil over high heat. Fry the stuffed plantains in small batches until they are browned, about 1 to 2 minutes on each side. Drain well, keeping the cooked ones warm in a cloth napkin while you finish the frying (see Hints).

FOR THE TOPPING:
Spoon or drizzle the *crema* on the plantains. Sprinkle the cheese on top. Serve immediately, with Mexican beer.

Hints: The secret of this dish is to use plantains that are not too ripe. They must be just turning from green to yellow. Riper plantains have lost their starch content, which is important for keeping the dough together when frying.

You can substitute *picadillo* (page 342) made with chicken or beef for the cheese filling.

Reheat cooled plantains in a hot 400°F oven.

PANUCHOS
Stuffed Fried Cortillas with Spicy Chicken Topping

A trip to Tuxtepec wouldn't be complete without a visit to the restaurant Antojitos Yoli. Every day Señora Tomasa and her extended family feed botanas or various corn masa snacks to their faithful following. The little two-room restaurant is usually packed, with more folks coming to the open window next to the huge deep-fryer and calling out orders to go. One of the most popular dishes is Panuchos. You can use leftover chicken, beef, or pork for the topping or omit it and use cheese for a vegetarian version.

MAKES 6 APPETIZER
SERVINGS, 3 *PANUCHOS* PER
SERVING

For the chicken topping:
1 tablespoon coarsely chopped
   white onion
2 garlic cloves
1 bay leaf

FOR THE CHICKEN TOPPING:
Put onion, garlic, bay leaf, tomato, chile, and ½ cup water in a blender and blend well.

In a medium frying pan, heat the oil and fry the chicken until it starts to brown, about 5 minutes. Pour the tomato mixture through a sieve or food mill into the chicken and fry until the mixture is dry, about 10 minutes. Add salt. Set aside.

¼ cup coarsely chopped tomato

1 small chile jalapeño, seeded (see page 329)

1 tablespoon lard, sunflower oil, or vegetable oil

1½ cups shredded cooked chicken

Salt to taste

For the bean filling:

2 chiles jalapeños, stemmed (see page 329)

7 avocado leaves (hoja de aguacate; see page 338)

2 cups Frijoles Negros de Olla (page 146)

2 tablespoons sunflower or vegetable oil

Salt to taste

For the cabbage mixture:

2 cups thinly sliced green cabbage

1 carrot, peeled and grated

For the masa:

1 pound prepared masa for tortillas or 1¾ cups masa harina for tortillas

Salt to taste

To assemble:

½ cup peanut or vegetable oil, for frying

2 tablespoons and 2 teaspoons mayonnaise (page 232)

½ pound queso fresco or fresh Mexican cheese, crumbled (see page 346)

¼ cup Mexican crema (see page 345), crème fraîche, or sour cream mixed with salt and pepper and a little milk

Salsa de chilito verde (page 175)

FOR THE BEAN FILLING:

On a dry 10-inch *comal* or griddle or in a cast-iron frying pan, roast the *chiles jalapeños* until their skins start to blister. Remove them from the *comal* and place them in a plastic bag a few minutes to "sweat."

On the same *comal*, toast the avocado leaves on both sides until they give off their aroma. Hold the stem of each leaf and crumble both sides of the leaf into a blender. Discard the stems and grind the leaves into a powder.

Remove the skins from the chiles and seed them. Place the chiles in the blender with the cooked beans and a little of their juice. Blend until smooth.

In an 8-inch cast-iron frying pan, heat the oil until smoking. Add the bean puree and cook until thickened, about 10 minutes. Add salt. Set aside.

FOR THE CABBAGE MIXTURE:

In a small bowl, mix the cabbage and carrot. Set aside.

FOR THE *MASA*:

If using prepared *masa*, knead with the salt and a little water to make a soft dough. It shouldn't "crack" if you roll it into a ball. If using *masa harina*, mix it with 1 cup plus 2 tablespoons warm water. Cover with a damp towel and let sit for 15 minutes.

Make 18 balls of *masa* and press them out in a tortilla press between two sheets of plastic (a plastic bag, cut in half works best). If you don't have a tortilla press, spread the balls out with your fingertips or the heel of your hand. Don't press them too thin or they will be too hard to work with. Peel the plastic sheet from the top and place it on the tortilla again. Turn over the tortilla to your other hand and peel off the other piece of plastic. You should have the tortilla dough lying on a piece of plastic.

TO ASSEMBLE:

Spread 1½ tablespoons of the bean filling in the center of a tortilla, leaving a ¼-inch border around the edge. Make another ball of dough. In two more sheets of plastic, press out another tortilla the same size and thickness. Peel off the top plastic, lay it back on, turn over the tortilla, and peel off the remaining plastic. Place the tortilla in your hand and lay it on top of the first tortilla, then press the edges together to seal the bean filling inside.

In a wok or deep frying pan, heat the oil until it shimmers and splatters if you put a drop of water in it. Slide the *panucho* into the oil; it will puff up as it fries. When it is brown and floats to the top (after about 8 to 10 minutes), remove it from the heat and drain on paper towels. Continue to make the *panuchos*, frying them and draining well on paper towels. Cover them with a cloth napkin. Keep them in a warm oven until ready to serve. Spread 1 teaspoon mayonnaise on top of each *panucho*, top with 2 tablespoons of the chicken filling, ¼ cup of the cabbage mixture, and a tablespoon of the crumbled cheese, then drizzle a little cream on top. Serve at once with *salsa de chilito verde*.

Hint: If this preparation seems too greasy a concept for you, omit the mayonnaise.

ARROZ A LA JARDINERA DEL RESTAURANTE YALILE
Gardener's Rice from Restaurant Yalile

I learned this rice dish from Irma Hernández, owner of the Fonda Restaurante Yalile, in the Central Market in Tuxtepec. It is a variety of typical "Mexican rice," but the addition of many vegetables gives it an added dimension. Here in Mexico you can buy a bag of cut-up vegetables to give your rice instant nutrition and color. Use any variety of vegetables you want, as long as you put in the potatoes and carrots for the sweetness.

MAKES 8 SERVINGS

2 cups long-grain white rice
¼ cup sunflower or vegetable oil
7 garlic cloves
¾ pound tomatoes (1½ medium–
large round or 6–7 plum), peeled

Wash the rice thoroughly and soak it in warm water for 10 minutes. Drain in a colander for 5 minutes.

In a deep, heavy 8-inch frying pan, heat the oil over medium heat until smoking. Add the rice and fry until golden brown, about 5 minutes.

Put the garlic, tomatoes, onion, pepper, and 2 cups of water in a blender. Blend well and strain through a sieve

1 slice of white onion

¼ teaspoon ground black pepper

3 cups chicken stock (page 343)

1½ teaspoons salt, or to taste

2 cups prepared mixed vegetables (about ½ pound)—cubed potatoes and chayote; sliced carrots; peas; thickly sliced Swiss chard or spinach; thinly sliced cabbage; sliced green beans

3 sprigs hierbabuena (see page 336)

into the rice mixture. Fry the mixture for 5 to 8 minutes, stirring constantly. Add the stock and bring to a boil, stirring constantly. Add salt. Stir in the vegetables and *hierbabuena*, cover with a tight-fitting lid. lower the heat to a simmer, and cook until the rice is done and all the water is absorbed, 20 to 30 minutes. Do not stir the rice while it is cooking.

Hint: This makes a very light rice. For firmer rice, omit the frying stage, bring the stock and tomato mixture to a boil, and add the rice (2 cups of liquid to 1 cup rice), *hierbabuena*, salt, and vegetables. Simmer for 15 minutes, covered.

YERBA MORA CON SALSA DE CHILITO VERDE
Wild Greens with Sauce of Little Green Chiles

Yerba mora is a wild herb growing all over the state of Oaxaca, but very popular in Tuxtepec. The tasty green is boiled or steamed rather simply with onion and garlic and served with a fresh green chile sauce. There is always a stack of fresh tortillas, an egg, or beans served with the yerba mora for a great breakfast. You can substitute young spinach, Swiss chard, or quelites (wild amaranth leaves). Serve these greens with one of the popular basic fresh chile sauces that accompany any dish that needs a little lift. The chiles can change with the season or by what is available in your garden or grocery. The chile serrano is on the milder side, while the chile jalapeño is hotter and the chile bravo has a real bite.

MAKES EIGHT ½-CUP
SERVINGS

For the salsa de chilito verde:

¾ pound tomatoes (1 medium–large round or 7 plum)

FOR THE *SALSA DE CHILITO VERDE*:

Bring 1 cup of water to a boil in a small saucepan. Cut an x in the bottom of each tomato. Place the tomatoes in the boiling water and blanch to loosen their skins, 3 to 5 minutes. Remove the tomatoes from the water and reserve the water. When tomatoes are cool enough to handle, remove and discard the skins.

(continued)

20 chiles serranos, *or 4 chiles jalapeños, or 3 chiles bravos, stemmed (see pages 328 and 329)*

2 tablespoons chopped white onion

3 garlic cloves

¾ cup cilantro leaves, finely chopped

Salt to taste

For the yerba mora:

5 bunches yerba mora *(8 cups), whole leaves, or spinach or Swiss chard, leaves cut into 5-inch pieces*

½ cup finely chopped white onion

7 garlic cloves

½–1 tablespoon salt, or to taste

On a 10-inch dry *comal*, griddle, or in a cast-iron frying pan over high heat, toast the chiles until they blister on all sides, moving constantly with a wooden spoon. Place them in a plastic bag to "sweat." After they are cool enough to handle, scrape the skins off with a small paring knife.

Remove the chiles to a *molcajete* or blender. If using a *molcajete*, grind the chiles first with salt, then add the onion and garlic, and follow with the tomatoes, one by one. When it is all ground together, add half of the reserved tomato water and the cilantro. Adjust the salt and serve out of the *molcajete*. If using a blender, add the chiles, onion, garlic, peeled tomatoes, and half of the tomato water. Grind coarsely so the sauce has some texture. Add the cilantro and salt.

FOR THE *YERBA MORA*:
Heat 1 quart of water in a 2-quart saucepan. Add the *yerba mora*, onion, and garlic. Simmer for 10 minutes, covered. Add salt.

Serve the *yerba mora* in bowls with the liquid and *salsa de chilito verde*.

Hint: You can make any leftovers into an omelet filling with manchego cheese and the salsa on top.

LIEBRE EN ADOBO
Stewed Hare in Chile Sauce

Hares and rabbits have been sacrificed for food since the earliest peoples inhabited Mexico. They are abundant and offer good healthy eating. I learned this style of stewing a hare from María del Carmen Vásquez in her Restaurante Carmelita outside of Tuxtepec, but it's actually the cooking style of the Isthmus, where Carmen comes from. Make sure to cook the rabbit until it is soft before you marinate it in the garlic.
Serve this with Arroz con Chepil *(page 52),* Calabazas Horneadas *(page 17), and fresh corn tortillas.*

MAKES 6 TO 8 SERVINGS

To stew the hare:

1 hare or rabbit (3–3¾ pounds),
  cut into 6–8 pieces (see Hint)

5 bay leaves

3 guava (guayaba) leaves
  (optional, see page 338)

1 head of garlic

1 medium white onion, cut into
  chunks

1 bottle of beer

Salt to taste

To marinate the hare:

½ head of garlic, cloves separated

3 tablespoons fresh lime or lemon
  juice

½ teaspoon salt

For the adobo sauce:

6 chiles guajillos, stemmed,
  seeded, and deveined (see
  page 331)

5 chiles anchos rojos, stemmed,
  seeded, and deveined (see
  page 330)

20 chiles secos (see page 331)

1 tablespoon black peppercorns

2 tablespoons cumin seeds

1 small head of garlic, cloves
  separated

1 medium white onion, cut into
  chunks

To cook the hare:

2 tablespoons sunflower or vegetable oil

1 bottle of beer

2 teaspoons salt, or to taste

TO STEW THE HARE:

In a heavy 6-quart stockpot over medium heat, stew the hare in 2½ quarts water, covered, with the bay leaves, guava leaves, garlic, onion, and beer for about 1½ hours or until soft. Remove the hare from the pot and dry. Strain the stock and set aside.

TO MARINATE THE HARE:

In a *molcajete* or blender, blend the garlic, lime juice, and salt to a paste. Marinate the cooked hare pieces in the garlic paste for 15 to 30 minutes.

FOR THE *ADOBO* SAUCE:

In a small saucepan, bring 3 cups of water to a boil. On a 10-inch dry *comal*, griddle, or in a cast-iron frying pan, toast the chiles until they give off their scent. Place the chiles in a bowl and pour the boiling water over them. Soak for about 20 minutes, then remove chiles to a blender. Reserve the water. Add the remaining ingredients to the blender and as much of the chile water as needed to move the blender blades. Strain through a food mill or strainer to remove the chile skins.

TO COOK THE HARE:

In a heavy 6-quart stockpot or *cazuela*, heat the oil. Fry the hare until it browns nicely, then remove from the pan. Add the *adobo* sauce and 2 cups reserved stock and cook down until it thickens, about 20 minutes. Return the hare to the sauce and simmer at least 15 minutes more. The *adobo* should be fairly thick, but not dry. Serve at once.

Hint: The hare should be divided into 2 breasts, 2 legs, and the saddle (the back and the sides) cut into 2 or 4 pieces, depending on the size. The head, if you have it, can be used for stock. If using farm-raised rabbit, stew the meat for about 45 minutes or until soft, then cook in the *adobo* sauce as directed.

ASADO DE VENADO ENCHILADO

Grilled Venison Smeared with Chile Paste

Oaxaqueños *have been eating venison since pre-Hispanic times. Although it is less available now, it's still used in* moles *and stews. I learned how to make this tasty dish from Carmen of the Restaurante Carmelita, located outside of Tuxtepec. After marinating the venison in chile paste, it is grilled over a wood fire. Beef can be substituted if venison is not readily available.*

MAKES 6 SERVINGS

For the salsa de chile seco tuxte-
pecano:

2 tablespoons plus ½ cup sunflower
  or vegetable oil
1½ tablespoons sliced garlic
1 cup chiles secos, *stemmed (see*
  page 331)
Salt to taste

For the venado:

4 chiles anchos, *stemmed, seeded,*
  and deveined (see page 330)
8 chiles guajillos, *stemmed,*
  seeded, and deveined (see
  page 331)
½ small white onion
5 garlic cloves
½ teaspoon black peppercorns
½ teaspoon cumin seeds
1 tablespoon lard, sunflower oil, or
  vegetable oil
Salt to taste
A splash of beer
2 pounds boneless venison (backstrap or from chops), cut in
  5-ounce servings

FOR THE *SALSA DE CHILE SECO TUXTEPECANO*:
In an 8-inch cast-iron frying pan, heat 2 tablespoons oil over medium heat. Add the garlic and chiles. Cook slowly, stirring constantly, until the chiles turn slightly brown, about 5 minutes. Transfer mixture to a *molcajete* and grind, adding 2 tablespoons of the remaining oil at a time, using up the ½ cup of oil. When the mixture is ground uniformly, remove from the *molcajete*. The sauce will be oily, but this will preserve it for weeks. Add salt to taste. This salsa is very hot, so be careful; a tiny speck will give you the flavor to adjust the salt.

FOR THE *VENADO*:
In a small saucepan, bring 2 cups of water to a boil. On a 10-inch dry *comal*, griddle, or in a cast-iron frying pan over medium to high heat, toast the chiles on both sides until they blister and give off their scent. Keep turning them with tongs to keep them from burning. Place them in a medium bowl with the boiling water and allow them to soak about 15 minutes.

On the same *comal*, grill the onion and garlic cloves, turning them so they will not burn, but turn clear and soft. Remove them and place them in a blender. Add the peppercorns and cumin seeds to the *comal*, stirring constantly until they brown and give off their scent, about 2 minutes. Add them to the blender. When the chiles are soft, place them with tongs in the blender and add ½ to ¾ cup of the chile soaking water. Blend until smooth.

2 tablespoons vegetable oil

For the topping:
1 tablespoon olive oil
1 tablespoon butter
1½ medium white onions, halved
  and thickly sliced
½ pound tomatoes (1 medium–
  large round or 6–7 plum)
1 tablespoon capers

For the garnish:
Lettuce leaves
Tomato slices
Avocado slices
Onion slices
Lime wedges

In an 8-inch cast-iron frying pan, heat lard or oil until smoking hot over medium to high heat.

Pour the chile mixture through a food mill or strainer into the pan and fry, stirring constantly for 5 to 7 minutes or until it thickens. Add the salt and beer, and continue to cook 5 minutes longer. Remove from the heat and allow to cool.

In a medium bowl, combine the meat and chile mixture. Marinate the meat ½ hour or more. It's better if you do this overnight.

Prepare a wood or charcoal fire or preheat the broiler.

Grill the meat over a wood or charcoal fire, or place under the broiler to brown, about 4 to 7 minutes.

FOR THE TOPPING:
Heat oil and butter in a 9- or 10-inch cast-iron frying pan over high heat. Add the onions and sauté until transparent, about 2 minutes. Add the tomatoes and capers and cook until caramelized, about 8 to 10 minutes. Keep warm.

FOR THE GARNISH:
Spoon the meat onto half a large serving platter. Garnish with lettuce, tomato, avocado, and onion slices attractively laid out on the side of the meat. Add the topping. Serve with lime wedges, soft corn tortillas, and the salsa.

PÍLTE DE BARBACOA DE POLLO
(Marinated Chicken Wrapped in Banana Leaves

This is a wonderful dish that is served when a family is all together on Christmas Day, a quinceaños celebration, or a baptism. The chicken packets can be assembled a day ahead and steamed on the day of serving. I prepared a version of this dish with my friend Judith Hernández Sánchez and her wonderful family on one of my visits to the jungle village of Ojitlán. In place of banana leaves, we used the large tropical leaves growing along the path outside her house. Serve with Arroz con Chepil (page 52) or Arroz Criollo Mexicano (page 299).

MAKES 8 SERVINGS

8 fresh banana leaves (12 inches by
8 inches), washed in warm
water, or substitute frozen
banana leaves, completely
defrosted

For the chicken:

5 tablespoons sunflower or vegetable oil

5 chiles guajillos, stemmed,
seeded, and deveined (see
page 331)

3 chiles anchos, stemmed, seeded,
and deveined (see page 330)

½ medium white onion, thickly
sliced

15 garlic cloves

2 bay leaves

1 cup chicken stock (page 343)

Salt and pepper

1½ chickens (about 4 pounds), cut
into 8 pieces

For the topping:

2 medium white onions, thinly
sliced

1¼ pounds tomatoes (2½ medium–
large round or 10–13 plum),
sliced

Salt to taste

To assemble the dish:

8 pieces of aluminum foil, 12 inches
by 8 inches

8 avocado leaves, fresh or dried
(hoja de aguacate; see
page 338)

Cover the banana leaves with water. Boil for 20 to 30 minutes, covered, or until soft. Older, thicker leaves will take
longer. Drain and cool.

FOR THE CHICKEN:
Bring 1 cup of water to a boil.

Heat 3 tablespoons of the oil in a medium frying pan. Fry
the chiles until they are browned on both sides, then
remove from the oil and place in a small bowl. Cover with
the boiling water and allow to soak 10 minutes.

In the same oil, fry the onion slices until soft. When they
become transparent, add the garlic and fry until clear. Remove from the oil and place onion and garlic in a blender.
Add the soaked chiles and just enough of their soaking water
to be able to blend mixture well. Reserve the pan and the oil.

In a heavy medium saucepan, heat the remaining 2 tablespoons of oil until smoking hot. Pour the chile mixture
through a sieve or food mill, add the bay leaves, and fry the
sauce 10 minutes. Add the stock and season with salt. Allow
to cool.

Place the cut-up chicken in a medium bowl and season
with salt and black pepper. Pour on the sauce and marinate
the chicken for ½ hour.

FOR THE TOPPING:
In the same oil as you fried the chiles, fry the sliced onions
over medium to high heat until they are clear. Then add
the tomato slices and fry until they brown and dry, about
10 minutes. Add salt. Set aside.

TO ASSEMBLE THE DISH:
On a clean work space, lay a piece of foil horizontally on the
table. Cover with a banana leaf in the same direction. In
the center, place 1 avocado leaf and a chicken piece on top.
Place 2 tablespoons of the marinade over the chicken. Add
2 tablespoons of the onion and tomato topping. Fold the top
third of the leaf down over the chicken piece; fold the
remaining third to cover it. Fold the right side in by a third to
cover the chicken and the left side over to create a package.
Fold the aluminum foil in the same fashion so you have a
rectangular package. Repeat with the remaining pieces.

Meanwhile, put salted water in the bottom of a steamer pan or wok with a steamer tray inside. Bring the water to a boil and place the chicken packages on the steamer rack. Cover well and steam over high heat for 1 hour. Serve immediately in the packages.

LOMO CON PIÑA
Pork Loin with Pineapple

Irma Hernández Zárate, a great cook whose butcher husband provides her with an ongoing supply of meat, inspired this pork dish. She cooked a whole loin with big pieces of the stuffing laid on top and baked in her horno magico *(magic oven), similar to a bain-marie that cooks on the stove top. With the help of my butcher Socorro and friends Cheryl and Roger, I came up with this rolled pork dish that's great at a dinner party. The leftovers are also very nice served at room temperature. Serve this with* Chayotes Asados *(page 236) or Arroz Blanco con Plátanos Fritos (see page 53).*

MAKES 6 SERVINGS

For the stuffing:
2 chiles pasillas oaxaqueños or pasillas mexicanos, stemmed, seeded, and deveined (see page 331)
2 tablespoons butter or oil
1 medium white onion, finely chopped
6 ounces thickly sliced smoked ham, diced
1½ tablespoons sliced garlic
1 cup pitted prunes, chopped
2 cups diced fresh pineapple
1 tablespoon finely chopped chives
1 tablespoon finely chopped parsley

Preheat the oven to 400°F.

FOR THE STUFFING:
In a small saucepan, bring 2 cups of water to a boil.

On a 10-inch dry *comal*, griddle, or in a cast-iron frying pan, toast the chiles until they give off their scent. Place the chiles in a bowl and pour boiling water over them. After 10 minutes, remove the chiles from the water and slice thinly.

In a medium frying pan with cover, heat 1 tablespoon of the butter and fry the onion until clear, about 1 minute. Add the ham and garlic, and continue to fry about 3 minutes. Add the prunes, pineapple, chile, herbs, spices, Maggi sauce, and salt. Continue to cook over low heat, covered, for 5 minutes. If mixture dries out, add some pineapple juice. Transfer the mixture to a medium bowl.

½ teaspoon coarsely ground
  allspice

½ teaspoon coarsely ground black
  pepper

¼ teaspoon Maggi sauce (optional)

¼ teaspoon salt, or to taste

For the meat:

2 pounds boneless pork loin, prepared for stuffing in a roll (have
  butcher do it)

Salt and pepper

2 cups finely chopped pineapple

2 slices bacon, chopped

2 tablespoons finely chopped
  parsley

2 tablespoons butter

2 cups pineapple juice

Salt and pepper to taste

FOR THE MEAT:

Lay the pork out horizontally on a board and salt and pepper it. Spread the inside with the filling, keeping a ½-inch border around all sides. Fold in the two shorter side edges about 1 inch to enclose the filling. Roll up the pork firmly from the bottom to top and tie with butcher twine to secure it. It should be a long roll.

In a mixing bowl, combine the pineapple, bacon, and parsley.

In a flameproof roasting pan, melt the butter and brown the pork roll on all sides. Add 1 cup of the pineapple juice, cover roll with foil or lid, place in the oven, and roast for 10 minutes. Remove the meat from the oven and cut away the strings. Place the pineapple mixture on top of the pork. Cover again and return to the oven to roast for 15 to 20 minutes more, until meat reaches 170°F on a meat thermometer.

Remove the meat from the pan and allow to rest, covered, for 5 minutes.

Add the remaining 1 cup pineapple juice to the drippings and cook the sauce over high heat on the stove top for 10 to 15 minutes to reduce. Adjust the seasoning and strain. Slice the pork roll. Pour some sauce onto each plate and place a slice of pork on top. Serve immediately.

Hint: It's easy for pork to dry out, so if you feel you can't watch it closely enough or you need to hold it over before serving, brown the rolled and tied pork in a sauté pan, then place the pork roll in buttered foil and seal well. Heat 1 cup of the pineapple juice and an additional cup of water with a dash of salt in a Dutch oven with a tight-fitting lid and place the roll in the liquid. Roast the meat about 10 minutes. Remove strings from the pork and add the pineapple mixture. Rewrap in the foil and continue to cook for 20 minutes more or until it reaches 170°F on a meat thermometer. Remove the pork to a platter and add the juice remaining in the foil to the juices in the pan. Reduce the sauce over high heat for 10 to 15 minutes, then serve under slices of the meat.

ROBALO A LA VERACRUZANA
Veracruz-Style Sea Bass

This fish dish is a classic in Mexican cooking, originating in the state of Veracruz, which shows a lot of Spanish influence. You can find it on any menu that features mariscos (seafood). Any fish (whole or fillet) or seafood can be served with the sauce, so be creative. You can sauté the fish right in the sauce if you are cooking for one or two, but I find, in feeding my family of six, it is easier to partially cook the fish in the oven and finish it with the sauce on top. Serve with hot tostadas or Arroz con Cilantro (page 120).

MAKES 6 SERVINGS

For the stock:
1½ pounds fish heads
1 medium white onion, cut in half
1 celery rib with leaves
2 bay leaves
½ head of garlic
1 chile de árbol *(see page 330)*
5 black peppercorns
1 lime or lemon, cut in half
½ teaspoon salt, or to taste

For the sauce:
¼ cup (½ stick) butter
1 medium white onion, finely
    chopped
1 pound tomatoes (2 medium–large
    round or 8–10 plum), finely
    chopped
13 garlic cloves, finely chopped
¼ cup green olives (about
    16 whole), pitted and sliced
1 tablespoon capers (about 20),
    roughly chopped if they are big,
    left whole if they are little

FOR THE STOCK:
In a heavy 4-quart stockpot, place the fish heads and 6 cups water. Add the onion, celery, bay leaves, garlic, chile, peppercorns, and lime, and bring to a boil. Lower the heat to a simmer and cook for ½ hour. Add salt. Strain and set aside.

FOR THE SAUCE:
In an 8-inch cast-iron frying pan, melt the butter over medium-high heat and sauté the onion until transparent and soft, about 5 minutes. Add the tomatoes and garlic and sauté for 5 to 10 minutes more. Stir in the olives, capers, cinnamon, and raisins. Add 1 cup of the reserved stock and simmer 5 minutes. Add the *chiles jalapeños* and salt. Keep warm.

FOR THE FISH:
Preheat the oven to 375°F. Place the fish fillets in a baking dish and dot with the butter. Sprinkle with lime juice. Season with salt and pepper. Bake the fish for 10 minutes, then remove from oven. Spoon the sauce over the fillets, and sprinkle the parsley over the top. Return the fish to the oven for 8 to 10 minutes more, or until flesh flakes apart when pierced with a knife. Serve immediately.

(continued)

1 teaspoon cinnamon bits

1 tablespoon raisins

4 *pickled* chiles jalapeños, *sliced (see page 329)*

1 teaspoon salt, or to taste

For the fish:

6 robalo *or sea bass fillets (about 2 pounds)*

2 teaspoons butter

1 tablespoon lime or lemon juice

¼ cup parsley leaves, chopped

Salt and pepper to taste

Hint: You can substitute *rajas de chile poblano* (page 329) for *chiles jalapeños*; just add them with the tomatoes and garlic.

SALSA DE COSTILLA DE PUERCO
Pork Ribs in a Spicy Tomato Sauce

One of the joys of living with a tomato farmer is the amount of tomatoes always on hand. This is an easy way to prepare pork ribs with a sweet and somewhat spicy tomato sauce. The pork stock is essential for the sweetness of the dish. Serve it with Frijoles Negros de Olla (page 146), either whole or mashed and fried, and Arroz con Cilantro (page 120), or try Relleno de Papas del Istmo (page 207). Of course, the ever-present corn tortillas usually serve as edible spoons for the sauce.

MAKES 6 TO 8 SERVINGS

For the meat:

Seasoning ingredients for pork stock (page 344)

3 pounds baby-back pork ribs, cut into 2-inch sections

2 teaspoons salt, or to taste

FOR THE MEAT:

In a heavy 4-quart stockpot, bring 7 cups of water and the seasoning ingredients to a boil as instructed on page 344. Then add the pork ribs and return to a boil. Skim off foam, cover, lower the heat, and simmer 45 minutes. Add the salt. Remove the pork ribs and set aside. Reduce the stock over high heat for about 30 minutes. Set aside.

FOR THE SALSA:

On a 10-inch dry *comal*, griddle, or in a cast-iron frying pan, roast the tomatoes over medium to high heat until soft, 10 to 12 minutes. Set aside. Roast the chiles until soft and

For the salsa:

4 pounds tomatoes (8 medium–
    large round or 32–40 plum)
8–10 chiles jalapeños (see
    page 329)
7 garlic cloves
3 tablespoons sunflower or vege-
    table oil
1 cup cilantro leaves
Salt and pepper

lightly charred on the outside. Scrape off the charred skin from the chiles. Place the tomatoes, chiles, and garlic in a blender with 1 cup of the reserved stock. Blend until smooth. Pass the mixture through a food mill or sieve to remove the tomato skins.

Heat the oil in a heavy 6-quart stockpot or *cazuela*, and brown the pork ribs for about 10 minutes over medium-high heat. Remove the ribs and set aside. Spoon out the extra grease, leaving about 1 tablespoon in the pot. Add the tomato mixture and fry for 5 to 10 minutes, stirring constantly. Add 2 to 3 cups of stock and cover, letting the sauce simmer for ½ hour. Return the ribs to the sauce for 10 minutes longer. Add the cilantro and adjust the seasoning.

Inspired by Judith Hernández Sánchez

PASTEL DE TRES LECHES CON MOCA
Three-Milk Cake with Mocha

On one of my visits to study with Elida Silva Ñeco, I arrived at her house and this cake was in her parlor waiting to be picked up by some lucky customer. It smelled so good in the hot, sticky heat of Tuxtepec that we changed our plans and made this chocolate variation of the traditional favorite. She made the mocha with instant cocoa, but I prefer to use Mexican chocolate. This cake should be made a day ahead, so it really absorbs the soaking liquid.

MAKES 8 TO 12 SERVINGS

For the cake:

1½ cups all-purpose flour
2 teaspoons baking powder
5 eggs, separated and at room tem-
    perature for ½ hour
1 cup plus 2 tablespoons sugar

FOR THE CAKE:
Preheat the oven to 350°F. Oil and flour or line with waxed paper two 8-inch square baking pans.

Sift the flour and baking powder together.

Beat the yolks until light and lemon colored, about 20 minutes. Add the sugar and beat well. Mix the evaporated milk with ¾ cup water in a small bowl and slowly add to the egg yolks. Beat for 3 minutes more. Add the melted butter and

(continued)

¼ cup evaporated milk
¼ cup (½ stick) butter, melted

For the soaking liquid:
1 can evaporated milk
¼ cup sweetened condensed milk
½ cup milk
1 tablespoon vanilla extract

For the mocha:
¼ cup sweetened condensed milk
¼ teaspoon instant coffee
¼ cup Rompope (page 350) or
   evaporated milk
¼ cup rum or other liquor
1 egg yolk
1 cup grated Mexican chocolate
   (5 ounces), or ½ cup Dutch cocoa
   mixed with ½ cup sugar, plus
   ¼ teaspoon ground cinnamon

To assemble the cake:
½ cup pecan pieces, toasted

mix well. Beat in the flour mixture and incorporate well.

In a separate bowl, beat the egg whites until stiff, but not dry. Fold the egg whites into the batter, one third at a time.

Pour the batter into the cake pans and bake for 20 to 30 minutes, or until lightly brown on top and the cake sides come away from the pan. Allow to cool in the pan for 10 minutes. Remove from the pans and cool.

FOR THE SOAKING LIQUID:
Mix the three milks and vanilla with a whisk. Set aside.

FOR THE MOCHA:
Combine all the ingredients in a small saucepan over low heat. Whisk the mixture constantly until smooth and thick, about 8 to 10 minutes. Allow to cool slightly, about 3 minutes.

TO ASSEMBLE THE CAKE:
Place one cake layer on a large platter. Prick the cake all over with a fork to allow for greater absorption, then ladle half of the soaking liquid over it slowly and allow to soak in. Spread half the mocha mixture over the top of the cake and sprinkle half the pecans over the top. Place the other layer of the cake on top, and repeat the above procedure. Serve at room temperature. The cake keeps for about three days in the refrigerator.

PASTEL DE PIÑA REAL
Royal Pineapple Cake

Elida Silva Ñeco is a baker with an amazing bundle of energy and love. She has the ability to bake dozens of cakes in a short amount of time and make them all look beautiful. After filming her for our television show about Tuxtepec, the soundman came to me and said of her boundless enthusiasm, "What's she on and where can I get some?" Although she uses a cooked meringue icing that I find too sweet, this cake is one of her classics.

For the cake:

1½ cups all-purpose flour

2 teaspoons baking powder

1 cup (2 sticks) butter (see page 345)

¾ cup piloncillo or light brown sugar

3 egg yolks

2 eggs

½ cup milk

For the filling and topping:

3 cups diced fresh pineapple (about 1 medium)

1 cup fresh coconut, grated and toasted, or grated dried (see Hint)

½ cup granulated sugar

1 tablespoon grated lime rind

For the buttercream frosting:

¾ cup (1½ sticks) butter

1 cup confectioners' sugar, sifted

2 teaspoons vanilla extract

1 tablespoon dark rum

¼ cup milk, if necessary

To assemble the cake:

½ cup pecan pieces, toasted and ground (optional)

FOR THE CAKE:

Preheat the oven to 325°F. Grease two 8-inch square cake pans, and line them with waxed paper.

In a small mixing bowl, sift the flour and baking powder together.

In a medium mixing bowl or the bowl of your mixer, beat the butter until light and creamy. Add the sugar, egg yolks, and eggs, beating well after each addition. Add the flour and mix well. Slowly add the milk.

Pour the batter into the prepared baking pans and bake for 35 minutes, or until cake is lightly browned and the sides come away from the edge. Allow to cool. After 10 to 15 minutes, loosen the cake from the pan with a knife. Turn the cake onto a baking rack and continue to cool.

FOR THE FILLING AND TOPPING:

Put the pineapple pieces in a blender or food processor with the coconut, sugar, and 1 cup water. Pulse the mixture so that it remains chunky. Pour the mixture into a medium saucepan, set over high heat, cover, and boil for ½ hour. The mixture should be the consistency of marmalade, but not totally dry.

FOR THE BUTTERCREAM FROSTING:

In a medium bowl, cream the butter until light and fluffy. Add the confectioners' sugar, ¼ cup at a time, until mixture is light and creamy. Add the vanilla and rum. If the frosting is too thick, add a little milk to thin it out.

TO ASSEMBLE THE CAKE:

Dust the crumbs from the tops of the cakes. Frost the top of the first layer with buttercream frosting. Add a layer of the pineapple filling. Lay the second cake on top of the first. Frost the sides with the buttercream frosting. Lay the ground pecans on a plate. Place one hand on the top of the cake and one on the bottom. Lift it up, turn it sideways, and roll it in the nuts. The sides of the cake should be evenly coated with nuts.

Put the cake on a serving platter and frost the top. Spoon the remaining pineapple filling over the top. You can decorate the edges with extra icing to make a pretty border. This cake will keep for at least a week in the refrigerator.

Hint: To remove the meat from a coconut, make a hole in one of the eyes. Drain the coconut water and reserve. Halve the coconut with a *machete* or cleaver, or drop it on the floor to break it open. Scoop out the white meat with a rounded knife and grate coarsely.

CREPAS RELLENAS CON SALSA DE CAMOTE Y PIÑA
Stuffed Crepes with Sweet Potato and Pineapple Sauce

I have always loved the smoky-flavored farmer cheese of Etla. These crepes filled with it make a nice combination with the Salsa de Camote y Piña (page 188) for a healthy dessert. The sauce is a typical cooked fruit in dulce that's so popular here in Mexico. The region of Tuxtepec, where the pineapples grow abundantly, inspires this recipe, while the sweet potatoes give it depth of flavor. You could also serve this sauce alone with a nice cup of coffee or tea.

MAKES 10 TO 12 CREPES

For the crepes:
4 eggs
1⅓ cups milk
2 tablespoons melted butter or oil
1 cup all-purpose flour
½ teaspoon salt
2 teaspoons sugar

For the sauce:
1 cone piloncillo (6 ounces; see page 348), or 1 cup dark brown sugar
1 piece of Mexican cinnamon, 1 inch long (see page 337)
3 cups peeled and cubed orange sweet potato
2 cups cubed pineapple, in ¾-inch pieces

FOR THE CREPES:
In a medium mixing bowl, beat the egg. Add the milk and melted butter. Add the flour, salt, and sugar, then beat until smooth. Leave for 30 minutes. (The batter is better if it sits before being used.)

FOR THE SAUCE:
Bring 3 cups of water to a boil. Add the *piloncillo* and cinnamon. Cover and bring to a boil over medium heat. When the *piloncillo* is melted, add the sweet potatoes and pineapple, lower the heat to a simmer, and continue to cook, uncovered, for 40 minutes. Keep warm.

FOR THE FILLING:
Heat the raisins, rum, and 2 tablespoons water in a small saucepan, covered, over medium heat until they plump up and are soft, about 10 minutes. Drain, then add the honey.

In a medium mixing bowl, beat the egg. Add the cheese and mix well. Stir in the raisins, grated lime, and orange peel.

For the filling:

¼ cup raisins

1 tablespoon rum or other liquor

¼ cup honey

1 egg

¾ pound requesón (see page 346), or farmer cheese, or ricotta

1 tablespoon finely grated lime

1 tablespoon orange peel

To assemble:

½ tablespoon sunflower or vegetable oil

TO ASSEMBLE:

Heat ½ tablespoon oil in an 8-inch crepe pan. Wipe out the pan with a paper towel, making sure that the entire surface is coated with oil. Pour ¼ cup crepe batter into the pan and roll the pan around to coat the surface. When the edges of the crepe start to turn up, flip over the crepe. Leave for 1 minute. Remove from pan and place on a plate. Continue to make crepes until batter is used up. Stack the crepes on top of each other. Fill each crepe with 3½ tablespoons of the filling and roll up. Spoon the sauce over the top and serve.

Hint: The sauce keeps well in an airtight container. It can also be eaten alone or over ice cream.

HORCHATA
Rice Water Drink

This is one of the typical aguas de sabor, or flavored waters, served at children's fiestas. We made it for my son Kaelin's third birthday party, where we had barbacoa de chivo and tons of horchata. I did not realize how much rice water 10 pounds of rice would make, and we had it for days afterward. Without the fruit and nuts, and at room temperature, it is a great drink when you have a stomachache.

MAKES 2 QUARTS

1½ cups white or brown rice, soaked in 3 cups water for ½ hour

2 tablespoons Mexican cinnamon pieces (see page 337)

¼ cup cantaloupe seeds

½ cup sugar

1 cup diced cantaloupe

¼ cup chopped pecans

Drain the rice and put in a blender with the cinnamon and 1 cup water. Blend until the rice is dissolved. Strain the mixture through a piece of cheesecloth placed in a colander. Use a spoon to push the water through the cloth. Wring the cloth to get all the liquid out.

Put the cantaloupe seeds in a blender with some of the rice water. Blend well.

Mix the sugar with 2 quarts of water. Mix the rice water and blended seeds with the sugar water. Add the cantaloupe and pecans. Serve well chilled.

Hint: Honeydew melon can be substituted for the cantaloupe.

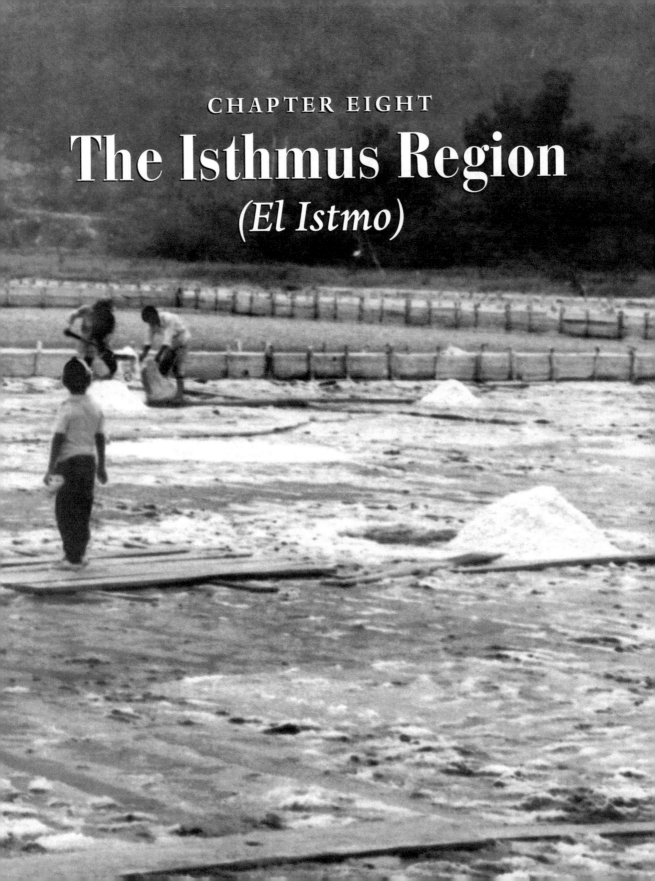

CHAPTER EIGHT

The Isthmus Region
(El Istmo)

Juchiteca woman selling achiote paste, Juchitán (Barbara Lawton)

Overleaf: Salt diggers from La Colorada, Salina Cruz (Barbara Lawton)

(Mexico's narrowest point and the only coast-to-coast low-land stretch is the 124-mile-wide Isthmus of Tehuantepec. Lying between the Gulf of Mexico and the Pacific Ocean, it connects the state of Oaxaca with the states of Veracruz and Chiapas. Descending from the Oaxacan mountains into the heat and high winds of the Isthmus gives just a pre-view of the warmth and intensity of the people from this region. Roads from Oaxaca city, the Oaxacan coast, Chiapas, and the northern part of the Isthmus converge on the three Isthmus towns of Tehuantepec, Juchitán, and Salina Cruz.

Originally the Huave Indians were the inhabitants of the area of Tehuantepec and Juchitán. By the mid-1300s, the Zapotecs had conquered the Huaves and had relocated them to seaside lagoons. Around the 1500s, the Zapotec king Cosijoeza held off the Aztec invaders on the sacred mountain of Guiengola (Big Rock), near Jalapa del Marqués. The powerful Aztec merchants fought to conquer and maintain their commercial trade routes to Guatemala and Central America, so as to obtain the valuable products from the south. But seeing that they couldn't conquer the Zapotecs, the Aztec emperor gave his daughter's hand in marriage to Cosijoeza and united both groups. During the Spanish invasion in the 1520s, some of the strongest resistance took place in the Isthmus. Spending time there and observing the will and unity of the people, I find it easy to understand their force and determination.

Out of all the culinary traditions in the state, I find the Isthmenian cuisine one of the most complex. Their foods, both in the ingredients and the way they're prepared, are unique. In the markets of the Isthmus, I found wild animals like iguanas, armadillos, rabbits, and doves either freshly butchered or prepared into *guisados* and flavorful *tamales*. Chickens are displayed freshly killed with their eggs inside (a real selling point because an egg-laying hen has the best flavor) or covered with a *guajillo* and *achiote* marinade. At times venison or turtle are offered discreetly, indicating the remnants of an ancient cuisine. Large *lisa* fish (mullet) and the smaller *charalitas* fish are salted, dried, and piled high in baskets, but most impressive are the mounds of salted dried shrimp, heads on, in all sizes. In the smaller market at San Mateo del Mar these were virtually all anyone had to sell besides a few small *lisa* from the nearby lagoons and a couple of iguanas on a string.

In the prepared-food sections of the region's markets, whole pigs and chickens are lathered with marinades and chile pastes (*Pollo Enchilado Estilo Tehuantepec*, page 208) and baked in adobe ovens along with mashed potatoes (*Relleno de Papas del Istmo*, page 207), a sweet bread called *pan guapa*, and a bread made from fresh corn (*Pan de Elote*, page 214). The pork, chicken, and potatoes are served with a red *mole* sauce, sweetly seasoned with pork fat. Virtually everything is fried in lard and liquid *chicharrón* drippings (*sorrapa*), and when it comes to flavor, nothing is spared. Prepared biscuits called *Gueta Bi'ngui'* (page 198) are croquettes that are baked, not fried, and made of *nixtamal* corn seasoned with chile, *pepitas*, and lard. These most popular morsels are stuffed with dried shrimp or fish and are traced back to their Huave roots in the dish called *mengui*, although the ancient dish is made without the pork fat. One of the signature dishes of the Isthmus is *Garnachas* (page 199), and I found them in morning and evening street stalls in villages large and small. Better still than these fried open-face beef tostadas were the chicken, onions, and tomatoes fried in the meat grease. Compared to other regions of the state, these are some of the richest and most exotic flavor combinations I've tasted.

The cheeses are different and superb. The *queso fresco* is made with or without minced fresh red or green *chiles jalapeños* mixed into the curds before being molded. One of my favorite market snacks is the sweet *pan guapa*, or the thick biscuit-like tortillas from San Mateo del Mar that are stuffed with this hot, spicy cheese. Drier, saltier cheeses are cut in diamond forms and the double-cream cheeses from nearby Chiapas are sold in chunks or wrapped in red or gold foil.

Spices, such as pure *achiote* pastes shaped into brick-red disks, are mounded and sold with pickled fruits such as plums, figs, and tiny cherries (called *nanches*) that are displayed in glass jars. Cabbage and other vegetables are also pickled and served to brighten up many of the meat dishes. Cracked corn for *molito de maíz tostado* or *guiñado xuba*, garbanzo flour for *cremas*, and ground *pepitas* for *pipianes* and *molitos* are sold at stalls that also sell freshly ground corn *masa*. Drinks such as a chilled *pozole* and the *jalapeño*-infused *Chileatole* (page 217) are made with the local *criolla* corn that is a very short variety, owing to the area's high winds. These winds are actually important in the production of sea salt in Salina Cruz. On several trips to the different cooperatives, I came to admire and respect the salt workers. Men and women dig with picks and shovels on blinding white salt flats to harvest the salt. Holding freshly dug salt crystals in my hands was such an inspiration.

Nearby, tiny beach villages such as Playa de Cangrejo thrive as weekend recreational spots for Oaxacans. At Restaurante La Perla, the owners, Oresta and Angel, have been cooking seafood specialties for twenty years, and I have been going there for nine years. While the pelicans fished along the beach in front of us, Oresta told me of the *molitos* (little *mole* sauces, as they are affectionately called) of green plantains, cactus, and venison her mother used to make. She lamented that the food now is not as pure and natural as the food of the past. Drinking fresh *coco* milk out of a hole in the top of the coconut, and waiting to see what the fishing boats would bring to decide the day's menu to be cooked over her wood fire, I couldn't imagine getting much more natural!

The first time I went to the Isthmus (other than passing through to go to Guatemala), I was visiting my friend Guadalupe Rodríguez and her family. It was she who introduced me to Juchitán de las Flores and the ways of the Juchitecan women. In this matriarchal society, the women play a dominant role in the marketplace, and in society in general, because of their frankness, their social and economic independence, and their position of equality that is unique in Mexico.

Lupe comes from a line of strong businesswomen, and she herself is a beautiful talented artist who makes flower designs from cornhusks (*totomoxtle*) and other artistic decorations. Following her dream to become a clothing designer, she explained that clothing styles in the Isthmus go back to the turn of the century, when long dresses were the fashion in Europe and fabrics from China became available. The costume of the Isthmenian woman is something to be admired. The satin or velvet flowered *huipil* and matching hand-embroidered long skirts have an intricate white lace trim at the hem with equally beautiful petticoats worn underneath. Casual wear is machine-stitched *huipiles* and billowing skirts. Hair is braided and decorated with ribbons, ornaments, and always flowers, both for fiestas and every day. They also drape themselves in gold jewelry, which is a sign of wealth, and much time and effort is spent on their beauty.

Using the local means of transport, on a whim I boarded a *moto* in the market at Tehuantepec and headed toward San Blas Atempa. In the local fashion of the women, I stood on the flatbed trailer being pulled by a motorcycle. I hung on as we ascended a hill with an awesome view of Tehuantepec below. I asked my driver if he knew anyone who could make *totopos*, the thin, flat, baked corn tostadas that come from this region. He laughed and set off on the dirt roads that make up the town. By the graveyard we turned into an alleyway. The largest pig I've ever seen was lying in a pool of mud, having the time of her life. He pulled up to a house and a dozen children ran out. Inside the house was a hubbub of activity. His wife, Margarita Molino de la Rosa, was in her hammock and several women were busily leaning into a circular round oven called a *comiscal*, pulling out *totopos*. One was pressing out the corn *masa* disks while her daughter made holes in each one with her little finger. Another one wet her hand and slapped the circle of dough inside the oven with bright coals burning below. Later, I had my first lesson and found slapping them into the oven was no easy feat. We laughed at my attempts until tears streamed down my face. I don't know if it was tears or sweat—it must have been well over 100°F in there.

I have had many wonderful visits to the towns of the Isthmus, but nothing was quite as magical as attending the Vela Zandunga last May. We were visiting our friend Julin Contreras, who invited us to go to the celebration. Upstairs in the bedroom, women were dressing with a flurry of anticipation. One pulled out incredible costumes and doled them out to me and my *amigas* to wear. Another woman did our hair and lent us heavy gold necklaces and jewels. In the Isthmus of Tehuantepec, the whole month of May is dedicated to the ritual dance of the *vela*. A *vela* is a ceremonial gathering where the women come together to show off their beauty and grace. Elaborate costumes inspired by the fashion of the early 1900s are created months in advance. At each *vela*, a young woman is chosen to be the princess. In Tehuantepec, the final and most important event of the season is the Vela Zandunga. It is at this dance that a young woman is chosen for the highest honor of Queen. That night I felt like Cinderella at the ball, and dancing with the other *zandungas*, young and old, I felt the unity, sisterhood, and sense of belonging that a woman has in the Isthmus. The meaning of a true *zandunga* is a woman who radiates beauty, enthusiasm, and pride—and these women truly bear that honor.

IN THIS CHAPTER

BOTANA DE CHICHARRÓN O CAMARÓN
Pork Rind or Shrimp Appetizer

I first had this appetizer made with dried shrimp and another bowl made with chicharrón at the wedding of Lupe Rodríguez and Jonathan Barbieri in Juchitán, years ago. The two ingredients can easily be interchanged. The salsa must be prepared on the spot and chicharrón added at the last minute, so it won't get soggy.

MAKES 6 TO 8 APPETIZER
SERVINGS

For the salsa cruda:

1 pound tomatoes (2 medium–large round or 8–10 plum), chopped

1½ medium white onions, chopped

1–2 tablespoons finely chopped chiles jalapeños (*see page 329*)

2 tablespoons finely chopped cilantro leaves

1 tablespoon lime juice

1 teaspoon salt

For the assembly:

3 ounces chicharrón, broken in bite-size pieces (*see page 342*); or 4 ounces fresh shrimp, peeled, deveined, and boiled (*see Hint*)

Avocado wedges

FOR THE *SALSA CRUDA*:
Mix the tomatoes, onions, *chiles jalapeños*, cilantro, lime juice, and salt.

FOR THE ASSEMBLY:
Add the *chicharrón* pieces or shrimp to the *salsa cruda* and stir well. Serve immediately, with *totopos* or tostadas and avocado wedges on the side.

Hint: Dried shrimp can be substituted if they are soaked twice in cold water for 20 minutes and drained. Peel them and add to the vegetables.

GUETA BI'NGUI'
Baked Spicy Shrimp Croquettes

Every morning Geralda Matus Jímenez and her daughter Teresa Morales Matus make
Gueta Bi'ngui' in Teresa's home in San Blas Atempa. These baked biscuit-like
croquettes are spicy, chock-full of lard, and stuffed with dried shrimp,
which gives them their wonderful flavor.

MAKES 16 CROQUETTES

1 pound dried shrimp, heads
removed and saved, tails saved
separately

⅓ cup cal or slaked lime (see
page 320)

1 quart dried corn for tamales, or
1⅓ pounds prepared masa for
tamales, or 2½ cups masa
harina for tamales

2 cups pepitas, toasted (see
page 338)

10 chiles guajillos, soaked in hot
water for 15 minutes; reserve
the water (see page 331)

2 chiles de árbol, soaked in hot
water for 15 minutes; reserve
the water (see page 330)

1 teaspoon pure achiote paste or
the commercial variety from the
Yucatán (see page 337)

2 cups lard

2 teaspoons salt

Soak the shrimp tails in cold water for at least 15 minutes. Strain the liquid and soak the tails again in fresh water for 15 minutes. Strain the liquid.

If using dried corn, put the *cal* in 6 cups water and stir well. Allow the *cal* solids to settle to the bottom. Put the corn and the top of the *cal* water in a clay *olla* or pot and cook over low heat for 1 hour or until the corn absorbs the water and is soft. Drain the corn and rinse well to remove all of the *cal*. In a hand grinder, grind the corn twice. The texture should be coarse. If using prepared *masa*, place the *masa* in a large mixing bowl and break up with your fingers. If using *masa harina*, combine the *masa harina* in a large bowl with 2 cups plus 1 tablespoon warm water. Mix well, cover the dough with a damp towel, and allow to rest for 15 minutes.

Preheat the oven to 400°F.

Put the *pepitas*, shrimp heads and tails, soaked chiles, and *achiote* through the grinder or in a blender with ¼ cup of the chile water—just enough to move the blades. Blend until well incorporated.

Melt the lard and add it to the *masa*, mixing in well by hand or electric mixer, 5 to 10 minutes. Add the salt. Taste the *masa* to check the salt; it should not be too salty as the shrimp can be salty.

Make 16 balls from the *masa*. Put 4 or 5 pieces of shrimp (depending on the size of the shrimp) in the middle of each and roll *masa* into oval-shaped croquettes. Lay them out on a jellyroll pan and bake for 30 to 35 minutes or until done.

Hint: Do use lard in these for the texture, taste, and success of the dish. Take a walk after dinner!

GARNACHAS CON REPOLLO EN VINAGRE
Garnachas with Pickled Cabbage

Garnachas are a wonderful dish that is typically Isthmenian. I've eaten them in the markets in Salina Cruz and also in Tehuantepec, either early in the morning or late at night at a stand in the main square owned by Reyna. One night, Lupe Barbieri and her aunt took me to eat "the best ever" in Juchitán, but what really sparked my appetite was the fried chicken, onions, and tomatoes that were cooked in the garnacha grease and served as the other offering on the menu. I suggest you make the pickled cabbage and the fat tortillas a day ahead.

MAKES 8 SERVINGS

For the cabbage:

2 chiles jalapeños, *seeded (see page 329)*

4 *cups shredded green cabbage*

½ *pound carrots, peeled and thinly sliced*

1 *tablespoon dried Oaxacan oregano (see page 336)*

1 *quart fruit vinegar or white vinegar, or 1 pint cider vinegar mixed with 2 cups water*

1 *heaping tablespoon salt, or to taste*

2 *teaspoons sugar*

For the masa:

1½ *pounds prepared* masa *for tortillas, or 2⅔ cups masa harina for tortillas mixed with 2¼ cups water*

For the filling:

1 *teaspoon sunflower or vegetable oil*

1½ *pounds ground sirloin*

FOR THE CABBAGE:

Cut the chiles in half lengthwise and place in 1 cup water mixed with 1 teaspoon salt. Soak for ½ hour.

Mix the cabbage, carrots, and oregano in a medium bowl.

In a 2-quart saucepan, heat the vinegar and add the salt and sugar, stirring well to dissolve.

Drain the chiles and slice into lengthwise strips, then add to the cabbage mixture. Pour the vinegar over the cabbage and mix well. Pack the mixture in glass jars and refrigerate for at least 1 hour (see Hints).

FOR THE *MASA*:

Divide the fresh *masa* or the mixed *masa harina* into 16 balls. Pat out the balls between two sheets of plastic to make 2½-inch rounds. Remove the plastic and place on a hot *comal* or griddle. Cook the small fat tortillas on both sides for 4 to 5 minutes or until browned. Set aside to cool.

FOR THE FILLING:

In a large frying pan, heat the oil over medium heat and add the meat. When half cooked, about 1 minute, add two-thirds of the onion and the garlic and cook 2 to 3 minutes longer. Add about 1½ teaspoons salt and allow to cool. When cool, transfer meat to a medium bowl. Add the remaining onion and mix well. Add salt to taste.

(continued)

1½ medium white onions, finely
   chopped
7 garlic cloves, finely chopped
Salt

For the garnachas:
¼ cup Mexican crema (see
   page 345), heavy cream, or
   crème fraîche
½ cup sunflower or vegetable oil
2 ounces queso cotija or queso
   fresco, finely grated (see
   page 346)
1 cup salsa de chilito verde made
   with jalapeños (see page 175),
   or another hot sauce

FOR THE GARNACHAS:
Mix the cream with a little milk to make a watery sauce to
drizzle on top of the *garnachas*.

   After the tortillas are cool, split them down the middle
with a knife to make two thin tortillas, and hollow out the
soft interiors. Lay the tortilla halves on a cookie sheet and
cover each tortilla with some filling, using all of the mixture.

   In a large frying pan, heat the oil until smoking. Place 4 to
8 *garnachas* in the pan and cook for 2 minutes, flicking oil
over the *garnachas* with a spatula to cook them thoroughly.
Remove, drain well, and keep warm. Repeat the process
with all the remaining *garnachas*.

   Place 4 *garnachas* on each plate and sprinkle on a little
cheese. Put a dab of salsa on each *garnacha* and drizzle
the cream on top of each. Mound the pickled cabbage in
the center of the plate. You can serve the
remaining salsa on the table.

Hints: The pickled cabbage lasts for about
a month in the refrigerator or even longer
if you seal it in sterilized jars. It improves
with age.

   Garnachas can be made with finely
shredded cooked chuck roast, but the ground
beef seems more popular and stays on the tortilla better.

*Juchiteca woman with
dried shrimp, Juchitán
(Barbara Lawton)*

CALDO DE VIGILIA
Lenten Soup of Cactus and Smoked Fish

Fresh seafood and fish from the Gulf of Tehuantepec are abundant in the Isthmus. These "fruits of the sea" are salted, sun-dried, or smoked to preserve them for later use. Smoking gives the food a richer flavor, especially lisa *fish (mullet) and small tuna varieties such as* barrilete. *Both preserved and fresh fish reach the height of popularity during Lent, when many Catholic Oaxacans observe the forty days of* Vigilia *by not eating meat on Fridays and during Holy Week.*

MAKES 6 TO 8 SERVINGS

1 pound ripe tomatoes (2 medium–large round or 8–10 plum)

1 medium white onion, chunked

3 garlic cloves

3 tablespoons sunflower or vegetable oil

2 quarts chicken stock (page 343) or water

½ pound smoked fish, skinned, cleaned from bones, and broken into 1-inch chunks (see Hint)

¼ pound tiny potatoes, whole with skin on

¼ pound green beans, trimmed and cut into 1-inch pieces

¼ pound shelled fresh peas or frozen

½ teaspoon salt, or more to taste

¼ pound nopales, cut into ½-inch to ¼-inch slices (see page 327)

2 large sprigs epazote, leaves only (see page 336)

2 large eggs

Salt and black pepper to taste

On a dry *comal* or frying pan, roast the tomatoes until they are soft, about 8 to 10 minutes, then peel and discard the skins. Grind them with the onion and garlic in a blender or *metate*, and strain through a food mill or a sieve.

In a heavy 6-quart stockpot, heat the oil until it is smoking. Fry the tomato mixture well, about 5 minutes, stirring all the while. Add the stock or water and bring to a boil. Add the smoked fish, potatoes, beans, and peas. (If you are using early peas, add them later with the *nopales*.) Cover and simmer until just done, about 15 minutes.

In a saucepan, bring 2 cups of water with the salt to a boil. Add the *nopales*, lower the heat to medium-high, and cook for 10 minutes. When the *nopales* are cooked, drain well. Rinse them with cold water and drain again. Add the *nopales* and the *epazote*, and continue to cook 5 minutes more.

Beat the eggs in a small mixing bowl with a whisk and add to the soup in a very fine stream. When the eggs are done, in about 2 minutes, take the soup off the heat, adjust the seasonings, and serve.

Hint: You can use the readily available smoked sable or whitefish which have a delicate flesh and smoky flavor. The soup also can be made with dried shrimp instead of the smoked fish.

SOPA DE FRIJOL NEGRO CON CHOCHOYONES
Black Bean Soup with Dumplings

This soup is a classic here in Oaxaca, and I've eaten it in all regions of the state. In Ocotlán de Morelos, it was made with pickled pigs' feet (a real Oaxacan delicacy), which made the beans even more gelatinous and sweet. In Totontepec, in the Sierra Mixe, it was made with local zatope beans that were incredibly delicious and served with dumplings of corn and plantains called bodoke. In the Isthmus, the dumplings are seasoned with epazote and jalapeños for an exciting twist. Try them any way you wish and serve them with nopales asados (page 327) and fresh cheese for a home-style lunch.

MAKES 8 SERVINGS

1 tablespoon lard or sunflower oil

1 medium white onion, finely chopped

7 garlic cloves, finely chopped

6 cups chicken stock (page 343)

1½ cups (10 ounces) harina de frijol (see page 325; see Hint)

1 teaspoon salt, or to taste

For the chochoyones:

1 pound prepared masa for tortillas, or 2 cups masa harina for tortillas

2 tablespoons lard

1 teaspoon salt

3 large chiles jalapeños, seeded (see page 329)

4 tablespoons epazote (see page 336) or cilantro leaves

In a heavy 6-quart stockpot, heat the lard or oil over medium heat. Add the onion and fry until clear. Add the garlic and fry a few minutes longer. Stir in 2 cups of the chicken stock.

In a large mixing bowl, combine the *harina de frijol* and 3 cups water to make a smooth paste. Add to the onion mixture and stir constantly. As the puree starts to thicken, add the rest of the stock. Cook for 15 to 20 minutes, stirring occasionally so it won't stick. Add salt. Set aside.

FOR THE *CHOCHOYONES*:

If using prepared *masa*, mix the *masa* with the lard and salt in a medium mixing bowl. Cover with a towel and allow to rest. If using *masa harina*, mix the *masa harina* with 1 cup plus 2 tablespoons warm water in a medium mixing bowl until you have a slightly dry dough. Cover with a towel and allow to rest for 15 minutes. Add the lard and salt.

Put the chiles and *epazote* leaves in a blender with 1½ tablespoons of water and blend until smooth. Add this mixture to the *masa* and knead well. Roll the seasoned *masa* into 24 balls and make an indentation in the top of each ball. When all are made, bring the soup back to a boil and add the *chochoyones*, a few at a time, so they won't stick. (If the soup is getting too thick, add 3 or 4 cups of hot water and stir carefully as not to break up the *chochoyones*; don't allow the puree to stick.) Cover and cook over low heat for 15 minutes, stirring occasionally. Add more salt if necessary and serve hot.

Hint: To make this dish with *Frijoles Negros de Olla*, blend 4 cups beans with 2 cups stock until smooth. Add to the onion mixture, and add an additional cup of stock. Cook as directed.

GUISADO DE GARBANZO ISTMEÑO
Lupe's Stewed Garbanzo Beans

Guadalupe Barbieri was the first Oaxaqueña *I became a friend with when I arrived in Oaxaca city. She is a raven-haired beauty from the city of Juchitán on the Isthmus of Tehuantepec. We recently went back to her grandmother's house, where she had taken me eleven years ago to meet her family. Under the watchful eye of her Tía Candida we made several Isthmenian dishes. This stew is one of Lupe's favorites, using the large garbanzas instead of the smaller garbanzos. You can use whichever variety you have on hand.*

MAKES 12 SERVINGS

For the broth:
1 pound dried garbanzo beans, soaked overnight, or 5 cups canned
Pinch of baking soda
½ medium white onion, finely chopped
3 garlic cloves, finely chopped

For the guisado:
½ pound tomatoes (1 medium–large round or 4–5 plum)

FOR THE BROTH:
In a medium stockpot, bring the dried beans to a boil with the baking soda in 1½ quarts of water. Lower heat to medium and cook for 20 minutes. Drain and place some beans on one half of a terry-cloth towel. Fold the towel over the beans and rub vigorously. The skins will separate from the beans. Remove the skins and discard. Repeat with the remaining beans. Rinse the beans. (If using canned beans, omit this step, but wash the beans well to remove the tin flavor from the beans.) Put the beans back in the stockpot and add the onion, garlic, and 2 quarts of water. Bring to a boil, then lower the heat to a simmer. Cover and cook for 1 hour.

(continued)

½ pound *chorizo (see page 342)*

1 *medium white onion, chunked*

7 *garlic cloves*

½ *teaspoon pure* achiote *paste or the commercial variety from Yucatán (see page 337)*

1 *just-ripe plantain (½ pound), sliced in ½-inch rounds, then cut in half-moons*

1–2 *tablespoons strips of pickled chile jalapeño (see page 329)*

3 *tablespoons finely chopped parsley*

2 *teaspoons salt, or to taste*

FOR THE *GUISADO*:

In a 2-quart saucepan, bring 2 cups of water to a boil. Make an x on the bottoms of the tomatoes. Drop the tomatoes in the boiling water and cook for 3 to 5 minutes. Remove them from the water, allow them to cool, and then skin the tomatoes.

Remove the meat from the chorizo casings. In a medium frying pan over high heat, fry the chorizo meat for 6 to 10 minutes, stirring constantly. When the meat is dry, add to the stockpot, leaving the extra grease in the frying pan.

Place the tomatoes, onion, garlic, *achiote,* and 1 cup of the bean broth in a blender and puree well. Add the mixture to the broth in the stockpot.

Fry the plantains in the remaining chorizo oil, adding more oil if needed, until well browned. Add to the broth along with the chile and parsley. Cook, covered, over medium to low heat for an additional hour or until the beans are soft. Add more water if needed. Add salt. Serve with *bolillos* (or French rolls) and salad for a wonderful lunch or as a first course for a dinner.

TAMALES DE CAMBRAY
Thin Rolled Tamales in Banana Leaves

My friend Lupe's aunt, Candida Blas Aguilar, sold tamales in the market for decades until she lost her arm from complications resulting from diabetes. Her specialty was Tamales de Cambray. *One day, Lupe and I, along with other women in her family, went to Tía Candida's house to learn how to make these wonderful treats. We were all amused by the constant arguments that ensued between Tía and her assistant, who had worked for her for years and had been trained how to make the tamales.*

MAKES 28 *TAMALES*

For the tamales:

28 banana leaves

5 eggs

Seasoning ingredients for chicken
   stock (page 343)

1½ pounds chicken backs and necks

1½ pounds chicken parts

For the mole:

5 chiles anchos, *stemmed, seeded,
   and deveined (see page 330)*

1 chile chipotle, *stemmed, seeded,
   and deveined (see page 330),
   dried not canned*

4 tablespoons sunflower oil, vegetable oil, or lard

1 large white onion, coarsely
   chopped

1 piece of Mexican cinnamon,
   about 1 inch long (see page 337)

½ teaspoon dried Oaxacan oregano
   (see page 336)

Pinch of cumin seeds

½ teaspoon ground black pepper

1½ tablespoons minced garlic

1 sprig thyme, leaves only

1 tablespoon sugar

1 small piece (1 ounce) Oaxacan
   chocolate

½ ripe plantain (¼ pound), finely
   chopped

1 medium boiling potato, peeled
   and finely chopped (about 1 cup)

½ pound tomatoes (1 medium–
   large round or 4–5 plum), finely
   chopped

¼ cup green Spanish olives, pitted
   and finely chopped

2 tablespoons capers, finely
   chopped if large, whole if small

FOR THE *TAMALES*:

Cut the banana leaves into 12-inch pieces and parboil in
1 quart of water until soft and pliable, about 30 minutes.
Cool and drain the leaves. (If using frozen Thai style, just
defrost slowly, then parboil for 10 minutes.)

In a small saucepan, hard-boil the eggs. When the eggs
are cool, peel and cut each into 12 pieces.

In a 6-quart stockpot, combine the seasoning ingredients
and 3 quarts water. Bring to a boil, then add the chicken and
cook as directed on page 343. Remove the chicken, discard
the bones, and shred the meat. Set aside. Reserve the stock
for the *mole*.

FOR THE *MOLE*:

In a small saucepan, bring 2 cups of water to a boil. In a
small bowl, cover the cleaned chiles with the boiling water
and allow to soak for 15 minutes. Remove from the water
and discard water.

In a 9- or 10-inch cast-iron frying pan, heat 2 tablespoons
of the oil over medium heat. Add the onion, cinnamon,
oregano, cumin, pepper, garlic, and thyme and cook for
5 minutes, stirring continuously.

In a blender, combine 1½ cups of the reserved broth, the
chiles, and the onion mixture and blend well. Strain the mixture through a food mill or strainer. In a heavy 4-quart
stockpot, heat 2 more tablespoons of oil over high heat until
smoking. Add the chile puree, lower the heat to medium,
and fry the puree for 10 minutes, stirring with a wooden
spoon. Add the sugar and chocolate and stir to dissolve well.
Keep chile mixture on low heat, stirring occasionally.

In the cleaned cast-iron frying pan, add 2 more tablespoons of the oil and fry the plantains for 2 to 4 minutes or
until golden brown over moderately high heat. Remove
them from the pan with a slotted spoon and add to the chile
mixture. Add 1 tablespoon oil to the pan, if necessary, and
fry the potato over medium-high heat for 8 minutes or until
browned. Remove from the pan and add to the chile mixture. Add the remaining tablespoon of oil to the pan and fry
the tomatoes, olives, capers, and raisins, stirring slightly until
thick and dry. Add to the chile mixture.

(continued)

The Isthmus Region (El Istmo) • 205

2½ tablespoons raisins

2 cups coarsely chopped pan de
   yema *(see page 347)* or challah,
   soaked in 1 cup chicken stock

2 teaspoons salt, or to taste

For the masa:

2 pounds prepared masa *for
   tamales, or 3½ cups* masa
   harina *for tamales*

1½ cups lard (¾ pound)

¾ cup chicken stock *(page 343)*

2 teaspoons salt

To assemble:

1–2 packages cornhusks to line the
   tamalera *and to make ties*

Puree the soaked bread in a blender and add it to the *mole*. Add the salt and more, if needed, to taste. Cook the *mole* over low heat for 10 minutes more, allowing the flavors to blend. The consistency should be thick but not dry. Add a bit more chicken stock, if needed. Let the *mole* cool.

FOR THE MASA:

If using prepared *masa*, break up the *masa* in a large bowl. If using dry *masa harina*, place it in a mixing bowl and add 1½ cups plus 3 tablespoons warm water to make a soft dough. Allow the dough to rest for 15 minutes. Add the lard if it is soft. If hard, whip as much as possible to get it light, then add to the *masa*. Mix in well by hand or with a mixer. Dissolve the salt in the chicken stock and add to the *masa*. Whip the *masa* for about 20 minutes by hand or with your mixer. The *masa* should look light and fluffy.

TO ASSEMBLE:

Shred 6 cornhusks into thin strips or "ties."

Lay a single banana leaf on a tray. Place 2 level tablespoons of *masa* on the center of the leaf. Put a sheet of plastic (a plastic bag cut in half works best) on top of the mass of dough. Distend the *masa* to 4 inches wide and 3 inches high in the center of the leaf. Remove the plastic wrap and set aside for the next *tamal*.

Place 2 tablespoons of *mole* in the center of the *masa*. Add two pieces of shredded chicken and two pieces of egg on top of the chicken. Fold the top edge of the banana leaf down to cover the *masa* (this should just enclose the filling). Starting from the top of the folded banana leaf, roll the *tamal* into a tight roll. Tie each end of the *tamal* with a cornhusk tie. Use the same process to make the rest of the *tamales*.

Fill a *tamalera* (steamer) with salted water to the level of the rack. Place the rack inside, cover it with extra cornhusks, and fill the steamer with the *tamales*. Cover and weight the lid down with a heavy object to keep it snugly closed. Steam over a slow rolling boil for about an hour, or until the *tamal* separates easily from the leaf and it "smells like *tamales*."

RELLENO DE PAPAS DEL ISTMO
Baked Potatoes from the Isthmus

This is one-third of the popular trio of baked potatoes, meat, and molito *that are eaten together for holidays in Tehuantepec. Every Sunday morning women sell this in the city markets of the Isthmus for families to take home for* almuerzo *or brunch. I have eaten many different versions of this dish, so be creative when you try it. You can add cheese if you like, and omit the banana leaves if you don't have any. This recipe is inspired by Julin Contreras, Chica Mon, and the women in the markets of the Isthmus on Sunday morning.*

MAKES 8 SERVINGS

2 pounds potatoes, in their jackets

3 carrots, peeled and cut in small cubes

1 cup shelled fresh peas or frozen

13 garlic cloves, finely chopped

½ medium white onion, cut into small chunks

½ cup crema *(see page 345), crème fraîche, or sour cream*

3 eggs

½ tablespoon Dijon mustard

3 tablespoons mayonnaise (page 232)

½ teaspoon grated nutmeg

10 pitted green olives, chopped

1 tablespoon salt

1 teaspoon ground black pepper

½ cup parsley leaves, finely chopped

3 tablespoons chiles jalapeños, seeded and finely chopped (see page 329)

2–4 banana leaves, depending on size (optional; see Hint)

In a heavy 4-quart stockpot, boil the potatoes in 1 quart of water, covered, for 30 minutes or until soft. Remove the potatoes and drain well. Remove and discard the skins. Reserve the water.

In the same pot, cook the carrots for 10 minutes. Add the fresh peas and cook, covered, over medium heat for 5 to 10 minutes, depending on tenderness. Remove and drain vegetables in a colander.

Preheat the oven to 400°F.

Cut the potatoes into large pieces. In a large mixing bowl, mash the potatoes slightly with your hands, then add the carrots, peas, garlic, onion, *crema*, eggs, mustard, mayonnaise, nutmeg, and olives. Mix well to blend all the ingredients. Add salt and pepper. Stir in the parsley and chiles.

Line a deep clay *cazuela*, or casserole, with a few banana leaves and pile the potato mixture on top. Top with remaining banana leaves and cover. Bake for 1½ hours. Remove the cover and continue to bake for 20 minutes more.

Hint: If using frozen Thai banana leaves, simply defrost and use.

POLLO ENCHILADO ESTILO TEHUANTEPEC
Tehuantepec–Style Chile Chicken

The first time I ate the classic trio of Pollo Enchilado, Relleno de Papas del Istmo *(page 207), and* Molito Rojo de Tehuantepec *was in Salina Cruz at 7 A.M. on a Sunday. We had slept on the beach all night and were up at daybreak to go to the market to eat. I learned this dish from Julin Contreras, a fine painter and the recently retired director of La Casa de La Cultura in Tehuantepec. She introduced me to many of the joys of the Isthmus, but none so much fun as cooking in the kitchen with her and her friends.*

MAKES 8 SERVINGS

12 chiles guajillos, *stemmed, seeded, and deveined (see page 331)*

2 teaspoons dried Oaxacan oregano *(see page 336)*

2 teaspoons dried thyme

2 teaspoons black peppercorns

½ teaspoon Mexican cinnamon bits *(see page 337)*

1½ tablespoons salt, *or to taste*

13 garlic cloves

2 chickens (3 pounds each), *cut into 8 pieces, skin removed*

In a small saucepan, bring 2 cups water to a boil. Put the chiles in a small bowl and pour the hot water over to cover. Soak for 10 to 15 minutes.

Put all the spices, chiles, and ½ cup water in a *molcajete*, or blender, and grind. There should be bits of the chile skin in the mixture. Rub the marinade over the chicken and allow to sit for ½ hour.

Preheat the oven to 400°F.

Place the marinated chicken in a clay *cazuela*, or casserole, and bake, covered, for 1 hour. Serve hot.

PUERCO HORNEADO
Spicy Baked Pork

Every Saturday afternoon, Chica Mon's husband kills a big pig to bake in her adobe oven for her Sunday market stall in San Blas Atempa. She makes large cuts in the pig's skin and washes it with a marinade, then rubs on a chile paste and lays the pig in an oval clay pan. A fire is built in the oven and the wood burned down to the embers. The pig is then baked for hours with the Relleno de Papas del Istmo (page 207). From the pork drippings, Chica Mon fries the Molito Rojo Istmeño (page 210) that is served with the pig. She arrives at the market at 6 A.M. and sells out by 9 A.M. Now, that's business! I've adapted this recipe to use a fresh ham or center-cut pork roast, so you don't need to cook a whole pig.

MAKES 10 TO 12 SERVINGS

For the marinade:

½ head of garlic, cloves separated

1 teaspoon black pepper

4 tablespoons lime juice

1 tablespoon salt

10½ pounds fresh ham or center-cut pork roast, pierced all over with a knife to make slits

For the chile paste:

2 chiles anchos *(see page 330)*

4 chiles guajillos *(see page 331)*

1 teaspoon achiote *paste (see page 337)*

¼ teaspoon dried thyme

1 whole clove

2 whole allspice

1 teaspoon fresh Oaxacan oregano *(see page 336)* or ½ teaspoon dried

½ small white onion

FOR THE MARINADE:
In a blender, puree the garlic, pepper, lime juice, salt, and 1 cup water. Pour the marinade over the pork and leave to marinate for 1 hour.

Preheat the oven to 350°F.

FOR THE CHILE PASTE:
In a small saucepan, bring 2 cups of water to a boil. In a mixing bowl, pour the hot water over the chiles and soak for 15 minutes. Remove the chiles from the water. Reserve the water.

Dissolve the *achiote* in 1 cup of hot water.

In a blender, puree the chiles, *achiote*, plus the water, thyme, clove, allspice, oregano, onion, salt, and ½ cup of chile water. Strain the mixture through a food mill into a bowl.

Rub the chile mixture over the pork. Place the pork in a roasting pan or Dutch oven and roast, covered, for 3½ hours or until done (170°F on a meat thermometer).

MOLITO ROJO ISTMEÑO

Red Mole of the Isthmus

There are many ways to thicken a mole, *such as using bread, tortillas, nuts, plantains, or fresh* masa. *I first learned about using animal crackers for thickening in Tuxtepec, so I wasn't too surprised in Tehuantepec when my friend Julin pulled them out to thicken hers. The animal cracker takes the place of* pan guapa, *a simple bread flavored with* piloncillo, *giving a sweet molasses quality to the* mole. *One of the best cooks in San Blas Atempa, the town overlooking Tehuantepec, is Chica Mon, who taught me to make* Molito Rojo *using* pan guapa. *Take your pick and let your mouth decide. Serve with* Pollo Enchilado Estilo Tehuantepec *(page 208) and* Relleno de Papas del Istmo *(page 207).*

MAKES 8 TO 10 SERVINGS

15 chiles guajillos, *stemmed, seeded, and deveined (see page 331)*

½ *medium white onion*

½ *head of garlic*

1 *teaspoon dried Oaxacan oregano (see page 336)*

¼ *teaspoon dried thyme*

1 *teaspoon black peppercorns*

1 *tablespoon sunflower or vegetable oil, or chicken fat*

1 *teaspoon pure* achiote *paste (optional; see page 337)*

1–2 *cups chicken stock, as needed (page 343)*

1 *pound tomatoes (2 medium–large round or 8–10 plum)*

20 *animal crackers*

¼ *cup grated* piloncillo *(see page 348) or brown sugar (if animal crackers are used)*

2 *tablespoons salt*

In a small saucepan, bring 2 cups of water to a boil. Place the chiles in a small bowl and pour the hot water over them to cover. Soak for 10 to 15 minutes. Remove from water and drain well.

On a dry *comal*, griddle, or in a cast-iron frying pan, roast the onion and garlic until soft and transparent. Place them in a blender with the oregano, thyme, peppercorns, and 1 cup water. Blend well.

In a medium *cazuela* or heavy pot, heat the oil until smoking. Add the onion and garlic mixture and cook over high heat for 5 to 10 minutes.

In a small mixing bowl, mix the *achiote* paste with ¼ cup of the chicken stock. Stir well to dissolve the paste. Place the tomatoes, chiles, *achiote* mixture, animal crackers, and *piloncillo* in a blender with 1 cup stock. Blend well. Pour the mixture through a food mill or strainer to remove tomato skins, then add to the garlic and onion mixture, stirring well. Cook for 20 to 30 minutes over low heat, covered, stirring occasionally. Add the salt. If the sauce dries out too much, add more stock. The *molito* should be just thick enough to coat the back of a spoon.

Hint: If you wish to use bread, soak ⅔ cup sweet dark bread cubes in 1 cup water to soften, then squeeze lightly to release water, and blend with stock; add to the *molito*.

Late-afternoon comida *for two. Clockwise, left to right:* Loma con Piña *(pork loin with pineapple)* with Arroz con Chepil *(rice flavored with chepil),* Pastel de Tres Leches con Mocha *(three-milk cake with mocha),* mescal con sal de gusanitos con limón, Flor de Calabaza Rellena con Requesón *(squash flowers stuffed with farmer cheese)(center),* Crema de Poblano *(roasted* chile poblano bisque) (Marcela Taboada)(dinnerware courtesy of La Mano Mágica, Oaxaca City)

Breakfast at Rancho Aurora. Clockwise from upper left corner: Pan Dulce, Chocolate con Leche, canasta de frutas, Platanada, Ensalada de Piña, Jícama, y Aguacate, Chilaquiles Verdes, Ejotes con Huevos, Cecina Enchilada con Tlayudas, *and* Tamales de Dulce. *(Marcela Taboada) (dinnerware courtesy of La Mano Mágica, Oaxaca City)*

Salted shrimp drying in front of Restaurante Los Delfines, Lagunas de Chacahua (Alfredo Díaz Mora)

Chinantecan women drying chiles secos in Nuevo Arroyo Camarón, Tuxtepec (Alfredo Díaz Mora)

La Danza de Flor de Piña, Guelaguetza, Oaxaca City (Marcela Taboada)

*Pineapple dancer, Casa de la Cultura, Tuxtepec
(Barbara Lawton)*

*Chica Mon and her iguanas, San Blas Atempa,
Isthmus (Barbara Lawton)*

Noche de Rabanos *(Night of the Radishes), December 23, in the* zócalo, *Oaxaca City*
Opposite, top: At the radish harvest on December 22, El Tequio, Oaxaca City (Marcela Taboada)
Opposite, bottom: Young carver at work, Barrio La Noria, Oaxaca City (Marcela Taboada)
Right, top: Radish figures at the marketplace, Oaxaca City (Marcela Taboada)
Right, bottom: Virgen de Guadalupe sculpted out of radishes, Oaxaca City (Marcela Taboada)

Zapotec woman carrying yellow corn in jacalpextle *to be blessed,* Día de Candelaria, *February 2, Teotitlán del Valle, Central Valleys (Marcela Taboada)*

Grinding corn on the metate, *Teotitlán del Valle, Central Valleys (Marcela Taboada)*

Isabel Ruiz making tlayudas *(well-cooked large tortillas), Teotitlán del Valle, Central Valleys (Marcela Taboada)*

Above: Isabel Pérez with her Pan Amarillo *(chewy yeasty bread), Ixtlán, Sierra Juaréz (Barbara Lawton)*
Left: Susana and Samari Carrasco Sánchez frying Carnitas *(pork boiled in seasoned lard), San Agustín, Etla, Central Valleys (Barbara Lawton)*

Above: Placing maguey hearts on hot rocks to roast at Placido Hernández's La Espina Dorada, Mátatlan, Central Valleys (Alfredo Díaz Mora)
Right: Young woman grilling lisa fish, Zapotalito, La Costa (Alfredo Díaz Mora)

WMHT Public Television crew: Stephen Honeybill, producer, Gary Carter, sound man, Mike Melita, cameraman, and Cheryl Camp, Susana's assistant, at the Vela Zandunga, Tehuantepec, Isthmus (Barbara Lawton)

Ester Mora and Susana with Tamales de Calabaza y Frijoles (pumpkin squash and spicy black bean tortillas), San Agustín, Etla (Barbara Lawton)

Susana (center), Mike Melita (upper left), cameraman, and the men from La Colorado salt flats in front of the harvest, Salina Cruz, Isthmus (Barbara Lawton)

GUISADO DE RES DE SAN BLAS ATEMPA
San Blas Atempa's Fiesta Stew

I had heard about this fiesta dish from so many women in San Blas Atempa that when I went back to Oaxaca I was eager to try it. The very evening I made it, I met a woman from that village selling gold earrings in the zócalo during a fiesta. Knowing she would be at her stand for a few days, the next day I returned with a container of the stew for her approval. Her eyes widened as she opened the lid and stuck her nose in and inhaled. "How did you know," she exclaimed, "that this is the smell of my pueblo?"

MAKES 8 SERVINGS

Seasoning ingredients for beef stock (page 344)

1 pound beef ribs

2 pounds boneless stewing beef

10 chiles guajillos, stemmed, seeded, and deveined (see page 331)

2 sprigs fresh thyme or ½ teaspoon dried

10 black peppercorns

1 piece of Mexican cinnamon, 1 inch long (see page 337)

½ head of garlic, cloves separated

2 tablespoons sunflower or vegetable oil

1 pound tomatoes (2 medium–large round or 8–10 plum), halved and sliced

2 cups halved and sliced onions

1 bunch green onions, sliced with greens

1½ cups chunked pineapple

1 ripe plantain (about ¾ pound), sliced in ½-inch pieces

1 apple, cut into ½-inch chunks (about 1 cup)

¼ cup green olives, pitted and sliced

In a large 6-quart stockpot, bring 10 cups of water and the stock ingredients to a boil as directed on page 344. Once boiling, add the meat and return to a boil. Skim off the foam that appears on the surface and discard. Lower the heat to a simmer, cover, and cook 1½ hours or until the meat is tender. Remove meat and set aside. Strain and reserve the stock.

In a small saucepan, bring 2 cups of water to a boil. Soak the *chiles guajillos* for 10 minutes or until soft.

Place the chiles, thyme, peppercorns, cinnamon, and garlic in a blender and puree until smooth. Pass this mixture through a food mill or a sieve.

In the 6-quart stockpot, heat the oil until smoking and fry the chile paste until well seasoned, about 15 minutes. Add the tomatoes, onions, and green onions. Fry for about 10 minutes, stirring constantly. Add 6 cups of the reserved stock and the meat. Add the pineapple, plantain, apple, olives, capers, raisins, and *chiles jalapeños*. Simmer for another ½ hour, then add the salt or more to taste. Serve with soft corn tortillas or *totopos*.

(continued)

2 tablespoons capers, chopped if
   they are large

½ cup raisins

4 tablespoons chiles jalapeños en
   escabeche (page 333), sliced

1 teaspoon salt

PESCADO AHUMADO
Smoked Fish

This fish is typically made in clay comiscales *(ovens) that are used to cook* totopos *in San Blas Atempa. This is the kind of oven that Esteban Espinoza uses to make his wonderful smoked fish. Since not everyone has an oven like this in his or her home, my friend María Elena Mimiaga Sosa taught me this method of using an old stockpot with a tight-fitting lid. She won first prize for the smoked fish that she presented at the Pacifico Sur Competition. The corncobs give the fish their golden color. Serve this with* Ensalada de Botana *(page 235).*

MAKES 6 TO 8 SERVINGS

For smoking the fish:

3 pounds lisa *fish (mullet) or trout,
   scales left on*

1–2 teaspoons salt

20 dried corncobs (without kernels)

For the salsa:

2–3 chiles jalapeños *(see
   page 329)*

3 garlic cloves

½ medium white onion, finely
   chopped

1 lime, juiced

Salt to taste

FOR SMOKING THE FISH:
Wash fish very well and lightly salt them. Slide a long skewer lengthwise into each fish so that it will not double over. Allow them to dry in the sun for 10 minutes.

Put some charcoal inside a 5-gallon stockpot with a tight-fitting lid. Start the fire; when the coals are hot, add the corncobs and cover with pieces of clay tiles (unglazed) or pottery. Add the fish in a circle and cover the pot tightly. Cook for ½ hour.

FOR THE SALSA:
In a small saucepan, boil the *chiles jalapeños* in 1 cup water for 5 minutes. Remove from the water, peel, and discard the skins. Grind the chiles, garlic, and onion in a *molcajete* or blender. Add the lime juice and salt.

Serve the fish with soft tortillas, *totopos*, or tostadas, the salsa, and a green salad.

Hint: These fish will last a few days in the refrigerator. You can also use the fish in *Caldo de Vigilia* (page 201) or a fish salad.

LENGUADO A LA TALLA
Grilled Flounder

Grilling fish over a wood or charcoal fire makes me reminisce about living the simple life on the beach. Time seems to slow down, and hours in a hammock with only the sound of the waves nearby is the norm. The fishing boats arrive in the morning and the day's menu is selected according to what's brought in. Fillets can be used instead of whole fish here, but leave the skin on. This recipe is from Señora Oresta at Restaurante La Perla in Playa Cangrejo, and we've enjoyed it for years. Serve with Chayotes Asados *(page 236) or* Ensalada de Piña, Jícama, y Aguacate *(page 297).*

MAKES 4 SERVINGS

For chipotle mayonnaise:
1 cup mayonnaise (page 232)
¼ cup chiles chipotles en adobo (page 332)
5 cloves of garlic
5 black peppercorns
1½ teaspoons fruit vinegar of choice
¼ teaspoon salt or to taste

For the fish:
1½-pound whole flounder, butterflied (see Hints)
Salt and black pepper, to season the fish

Prepare a hardwood or charcoal fire in your barbecue grill. (If you want, you can soak some mesquite or fruitwood chips in water and place them on the coals just before cooking to give extra flavor to a charcoal fire.)

FOR *CHIPOTLE* MAYONNAISE:
In a blender, combine the mayonnaise, *chiles chipotles en adobo*, garlic, peppercorns, vinegar, and salt and blend well. Set aside.

FOR THE FISH:
Open the butterflied flounder and sprinkle with salt and pepper. Spread an even layer of the *chipotle* mayonnaise all the way to the edges of the fish. Place the flounder on an oiled fish rack for grilling skin side down and close it tight. Place the fish over the coals and grill 8 to 10 minutes or until a bit crispy. Turn the fish over and continue to grill another 8 minutes or until done. Serve immediately with *totopos*, tostadas, and lime wedges.

Hints: The *chipotle* mayonnaise can be served as a table sauce for any fried or grilled fish dishes. In Veracruz it is served in two separate bowls, one of mayonnaise and one of *chipotle* puree, each person mixing it as desired. It's also great for fish salads, fishcakes, sandwiches, or tacos. It keeps in the refrigerator for 1 month.

You can substitute red snapper for the flounder.

PAN DE ELOTE
Corn Bread

This corn bread is like a sweet corn tamal baked in pans or, using Mexican ingenuity, in the recycled sardine cans that are so popular as bread molds here. One Valentine's Day morning at the home of Teresa Morales Matus in San Blas Atempa, we baked it in her oven while she made lots of Gueta Bi'ngui' (page 198) to sell at the village festival that day. Teresa uses lots of sorrapa, liquid chicharrón drippings or lard, to make the bread, but I've adjusted this for a lighter, less greasy effect.

MAKES TWO 8-INCH SQUARE
BREADS

8 cups fresh corn kernels
1⅔ cups sugar
1 tablespoon salt
1 teaspoon baking soda
¾ cup sunflower or vegetable oil
  or lard

Preheat the oven to 350°F. Grease two 8-inch square cake pans.

Grind the corn with a hand grinder into a soft puree.

In a medium bowl, mix the corn, sugar, salt, and baking soda and stir well. Add the oil or lard and stir in. Pour the mixture in the baking pans and bake for 35 to 45 minutes.

Connia Rueda de Schuman dishing out botanas at the Lavado de Ollas, Juchitán (Barbara Lawton)

PASTEL DE COCO
Coconut Pecan Cake

This recipe is a family favorite, so I thought I'd include it in the Isthmus chapter, where so many desserts and candies are made with coconut. Do your best to get a fresh, mature coconut. Drain out the water for a refreshing cooler or make Flan de Coco (page 98). With a rounded dinner knife, scoop the flesh out of the coconut and grate and toast it. The flavor and texture of fresh coconut are far superior to those of processed coconut, but that will do in a pinch.

MAKES IO TO I2 SERVINGS

For the cake:

5 eggs, at room temperature for at
     least 1 hour

1 cup (2 sticks) plus 1 tablespoon
     butter, at room temperature

½ cup sunflower or vegetable oil

2 cups granulated sugar

1 teaspoon baking soda

1 cup milk mixed with ½ table-
     spoon lime juice

2 cups unbleached all-purpose flour

1 teaspoon vanilla extract

1 cup grated fresh coconut, toasted

½ cup pecans, chopped and toasted

For the frosting:

1 cup (2 sticks) plus 1 tablespoon
     butter, at room temperature

8 ounces cream cheese

1 teaspoon vanilla extract

2–3 cups confectioners' sugar

½ cup pecans, finely chopped and
     toasted

Rum, to taste

FOR THE CAKE:

Preheat the oven to 325°F. Oil a Bundt pan or two 8-inch square pans.

Separate the egg yolks and whites into bowls.

In a large bowl, mix the butter, oil, and sugar until creamy. Add the egg yolks one at a time, beating after each addition.

Mix the baking soda and milk.

Add the flour to the butter mixture, alternating with the milk. Add the vanilla, coconut, and nuts. Mix well. Beat the egg whites until they form stiff peaks, then fold into the batter.

Pour the batter into the greased cake pans and bake for 45 minutes or until the cake separates from the edge of the pan. Remove from oven and allow to cool for 15 minutes, then remove from pans. Cool on a rack.

FOR THE FROSTING:

Cream the butter and cream cheese with a hand or electric mixer. Add the vanilla, confectioners' sugar, nuts, and rum. Mix well.

Brush off the excess crumbs. If using a Bundt pan, frost the cake on all sides and around the center hole. Decorate with fresh flowers. If using the square cake pans, invert a layer onto a plate and cover the top of the cake with frosting. Place the second layer (inverted) on top of the first and frost the sides of the cake. Finally, frost the top and decorate with fresh flowers.

BUDÍN DE ELOTE
Corn Pudding

This pudding is a variation on the Pan de Elote *(page 214) of the Isthmus. We make it during the rainy season when the fresh corn is harvested. Originally the fresh corn was ground on the volcanic stone* metate, *but we have replaced that method with the blender. Try to make this a day ahead as it tastes much better the second day. This recipe has a sweet sauce to drizzle on top to serve it as a dessert.*

MAKES 10 TO 12 SERVINGS

For the pudding:

3 cups fresh corn kernels (from about 4 ears)

½ cup milk

½ cup sweetened condensed milk

5 tablespoons all-purpose flour

1 tablespoon baking powder

4 large eggs

¼ cup sugar

¼ cup (½ stick) butter, softened

1 tablespoon ground cinnamon

Pinch of salt

For the sauce:

1 cone piloncillo (6 ounces; see page 348) or 1 cup brown sugar

1 cup orange juice

1 piece of Mexican cinnamon, 2 inches long (see page 337)

1 shot glass (2 ounces) of mezcal or rum, or any liquor of choice

Peel of 1 orange, being careful not to include the white part

½ cup cream or ½ cup milk

FOR THE PUDDING:

Preheat the oven to 350°F. Grease a Bundt pan or 2-quart glass casserole.

Place the corn kernels, milk, and condensed milk in a blender. Blend until it is smooth.

In a small bowl, sift the flour with the baking powder and set aside.

Separate the eggs into two bowls. Beat the yolks on high speed until they are thick and lemon colored, about 15 minutes. Add the sugar slowly to the egg yolks and beat well. Add the butter to the mixture and beat until it is smooth. Add the corn mixture and the flour mixture alternately to the egg mixture. Add the cinnamon.

Beat the egg whites with the salt until they are foamy and fold them into the batter.

Pour the batter into the prepared pan and bake for 50 to 60 minutes or until a knife inserted in the center comes out clean. Allow to cool.

FOR THE SAUCE:

Place the *piloncillo* or brown sugar in a saucepan with the orange juice and ½ cup water. Heat over low heat, covered, for 10 minutes or until the sugar is melted. Add the cinnamon, mezcal, and orange peel and cook for 15 minutes longer. Add the cream or milk and simmer for 5 minutes more. Strain into a pitcher or bowl. Serve pudding with the sauce drizzled on top or over ice cream.

CHILEATOLE
Fresh Corn Drink with Chile Sauce

In the market in Tehuantepec there is a stand with a young girl selling Chileatole. The first time I tried it I was thrilled, as I usually am when I taste something new with corn, epazote, and chile. The local corn in the Isthmus is quite short, owing to the high winds, but it is delicious and the cobs are small enough to fit in the cups or bowls that this drink comes in. Señora Geralda, who taught me this, told me never to cook this drink if I was angry or the drink will curdle.

MAKES 6 SERVINGS

8 ears of white corn (5 ears a few days old so that there are indentations in the kernels and 3 tender ears)

Pinch of salt

¼ cup epazote leaves (see page 336)

½ cup sugar

2 chiles jalapeños (see page 329)

Cut the 3 tender ears of corn in 3-inch rounds. Put in a heavy 4-quart saucepan with 2 quarts of water and the salt. Bring to a boil, lower the heat, cover, and cook for 20 to 25 minutes or until done. Remove the corn rounds. Reserve the water in another container.

Remove the kernels from the 5 other ears of corn to make 4 cups of kernels. Put the kernels through a hand grinder or blender and grind them three times or until a soft puree. Mix the pureed corn and 2 cups of water, then strain the puree through cheesecloth into a medium bowl. Save the dregs in the cheesecloth. Add 1 quart of the hot water from cooking the corn to the corn puree and strain again into the pot in which the corncobs were cooked. Add ½ cup of the corncob water to the puree. Add the *epazote* and stir over medium to high heat with a wooden spoon until heated through, about 5 to 8 minutes.

Strain the rest of the cooking liquid through the corn dregs in the cheesecloth into the pot, then squeeze out the extra liquid. Discard the corn dregs. Heat over medium heat and stir constantly for 20 to 25 minutes or until thickened. Stir in ½ cup sugar.

Grill the *chiles jalapeños* over direct heat until the skins blister nicely, then place in a plastic bag to "sweat." Peel and seed them. Grind them in a *molcajete* or blender until smooth and add 3 tablespoons water.

Ladle 1 cup of *Chileatole* into a cup with corn. Add ½ tablespoon of the *jalapeño* sauce to each cup and serve.

AGUA FRESCA DE SANDIA
Watermelon Water

Every year on the fourth Friday in Lent, Oaxacans celebrate the Día de la Samaritana, which marks the story of the woman at the well who offered Christ a drink of cool water when he was very thirsty. According to my biblical advisor, the story is different from that of the Good Samaritan, but Oaxacans consider it one and the same. All the women of the churches and the businesses in Oaxaca construct a booth representing a well, decorated with reeds and bougainvillea flowers. Aguas of every description are doled out; Agua de Chilacayota (a sweet squash drink), Horchata (page 189), Agua de Jamaica (page 102), Agua de Tamarindo (page 102), and my favorite of all, Agua de Sandia. Agua de Sandia is a wonderful drink to have during pregnancy to help reduce water retention.

MAKES 8 CUPS

2½ cups cubed watermelon
  (½ pound), with seeds and rind
  removed
¼–½ cup sugar, or to taste

Put the watermelon and 1½ cups water in a blender. Mix well. Strain the mixture through a sieve into a large pitcher.

Add 6½ cups water and the sugar. Mix well. Serve well chilled.

Hint: Cantaloupe, honeydew melon, or papaya can be substituted for the watermelon.

Woman selling flan, San Blas Atempa (Alfredo Díaz Mora)

CHAPTER NINE

Oaxaca City
(La Ciudad)

Botana
platter, El
Biche Pobre II
Restaurant,
Oaxaca City
(Alfredo Díaz
Mora)

*Overleaf:
Woman frying
buñuelos,
Oaxaca City
(Marcela
Taboada)*

Oaxaca is a small city that lies in the median of the different arms of the Central Valleys. It owes its fame to its colonial architecture painted in a riot of colors, its wealth of popular traditions, and its typical but flavorful cuisine, which is a combination of foods from all over the state and the mestizo mixes that emerged after the Spanish conquest. The city was founded in 1486 as an Aztec garrison and given the name Huaxyácac, or "the place of the guajes." The town was conquered by Spanish troops under Diego

Ordaz in 1521 and renamed Antequera, but in 1529 it received the distinctive title of Villa de Antequera. The planning of the city was entrusted to Alonso García Bravo, who had already supervised the rebuilding of Mexico City and gave it a similar design, one that focused on a zócalo (main square), with streets coming out from the center in a grid fashion.

Oaxaca is magic, with its spontaneity and charm. Around any corner there could be music, a fiesta, a procession, a demonstration heading toward the governor's palace, or a crowd delighting in mimes or artists. The early-morning songs of the birds in the jacarandas, soft ballads of a lone blind guitarist, a classical piano at the Macedonio Alcalá Opera House, the spirited battle of the bands between the *marimbas* and the *mariachis* on the *zócalo*—all make Oaxaca a musical hotbed of the south. What makes Oaxaca really tick, what really fills the city dwellers with vigor and revelry, are the fiestas, which celebrate the religious holidays of the church. Village fiestas open with giant puppets dancing with young maidens carrying baskets of flowers on their heads and end with outrageous fireworks displays, celebrated for a week to ten days with special foods for each day.

Starting at the stroke of midnight on January 1, Oaxacan family members each eat twelve grapes and make twelve wishes, one for each month of the year. The New Year's Eve meal starts around 10:30 P.M., so that dinner is finished by the time the church bell starts chiming at midnight. On January 6, the Christmas season officially comes to an end with the arrival of the three kings. On this morning, the children wake to find presents left for them by the kings, and a special bread called *Rosca de Reyes* (page 245) is eaten in the evening with bowls of steaming chocolate. The *Rosca* is a ringlike bread decorated with *ates* (fruit pastes), dried fruits and *acitrón* (candied cactus pieces), sugar toppings, and sesame seeds. Inside each bread a tiny plastic doll is hidden. (These used to be made of porcelain or clay, but modern times have cheapened them.) Whoever gets the doll in his piece has to sponsor a fiesta on February 2—*Día de la Candelaria*. On that day, women dress up the baby Jesus from their family altar and parade him to the church to be blessed. The sponsor serves *tamales*, bread, and hot chocolate to all.

The Lenten season (*Vigilia*) commences with Ash Wednesday, and most people abstain from meat on Fridays during this period. Dried, salted fish and shrimp and fresh fish and seafood often take the place of meat, accompanied by special foods such as fresh peas, *nopales*, white beans, and large black bean flowers called *ayocotes*. Lenten desserts like *garbanzos en dulce*, *bocadillos de garbanzo*, or little pineapple cakes called *tortitas de piña* are served. On *Cuarto Viernes* (Fourth Friday in Lent), Oaxacans celebrate the *Día de la Samaritana*. It is a joyous holiday, when churches, schools, businesses, and homes open up their doors. Women dress in native outfits, put flowers in their hair, and dole out fruit drinks (watermelon, cantaloupe, *horchata*, pineapple, *jamaica*, and *chilacayota*) under archways of bougainvillea flowers at booths representing wells to offer each person who walks by a drink.

On the fifth Friday in Lent, in the barrio Jalatlaco, the Virgen de Dolores is honored. Sweets, ices, and ice creams are eaten, plus garbanzo treats. *Semana Santa* (Easter week) is alive with poignant traditions. Starting on Tuesday, there is a fiesta in Xochilmilco, where fruit drinks and water ices are given out, and live music is played to make a neighborhood party. By *Jueves Santos* (Holy Thursday), the feeling is much more solemn. In Xoxocotlán, there is the *Procesión de Los Cristos*. Starting with the smallest boy in the village to the oldest man, each man carries a crucifix decorated with sweet-smelling frangipani flowers. On this night, in the center of Oaxaca, locals go to seven churches in one night and look at all the special altars made for The Last Supper.

On Good Friday, there is *El Encuentro*. A person representing Jesus Christ carries a cross in a huge procession, and the crucifixion is dramatically reenacted. At *comida* time, the whole city smells like fish, mostly eaten fried with lettuce and radishes, or with white beans and dried shrimp, and *capirotada* for dessert. On Saturday night, the church is dark and everyone comes to mass carrying candles to signify the new light of Jesus, and leaves them burning until Easter Sunday.

In the summer, the important holiday in Oaxaca is *Guelaguetza*. This event falls on the two Mondays called *Lunes del Cerro* following the 16th of July, which is *la Fiesta de la Virgen del Carmen Alto*. The festival originated outside the Carmen Church, but was later transferred to the ancient fort on the Fortin Hill, where a huge amphitheater has been built. *Guelaguetza* is derived from the Zapotec, meaning "of gift or offering," and the dancers take this very seriously as they bring crafts and art from their regions. On Sunday night, dancers reenact the traditions of Oaxaca in the *Bani Stui Gulal*, and on Monday evening, the *Legend of Donají*. The *zócalo* becomes alive with food booths and offerings from all seven regions. The last day of August is important at the Church of San Ramón. This is when pets and farm animals are dressed in clothes to show their gender and brought to the church to be blessed. Dogs and cats in bonnets, cows in dresses, and donkeys in bow ties gather in front of the church. The *padre* (priest) comes out periodically and dips a gladiola in Holy Water and blesses all the animals. This is something not to be missed!

The month of September is the *mes de la patria* (patriot's month) celebrated with *mucho gusto* on the 16th, Independence Day. *El Grito* takes place at 11 P.M. the night before, when all the *paisanos* yell ¡*Viva México!* followed by a huge fireworks display. Stalls sell typical fiesta fare: *quesadillas*, empanadas, tacos, and *tlayudas*. All month long, the restaurant chefs serve *chiles en nogada*, a patriotic Poblano dish of green chiles, white nut sauce, and red pomegranate seeds to honor the colors of the flag.

On October 18, *Día de San Lucas* is celebrated. Oxen, adorned with garlands of flowers and necklaces of apples and grapefruits, are led around the tiny town of San Lucas near Zaachila. The 31st of October starts the festivities of *Día de Muertos*. At Santo Domingo Church, there is the parade of the Virgin of Rosario. In the villages and neighborhoods, parents visit the tombs of any children that have died. Candies, bread, and chocolate are left at the grave sites for the *angelitos* or placed on their home altars. November 1 celebrates the older people who have passed on, and November 2 honors all the saints. The special dishes for this holiday are *mole negro*, *mole coloradito*, *pan de muerto*, chocolate *tamales*, anise-filled candies, and *calabazas* or *tejocotes* (crab apples) *en dulce*. On subsequent Mondays in the city of Oaxaca, families eat breakfast in the cemetery with their loved ones and take them presents of food and music. On the night of November 30, locals go to San Felipé de Agua cemetery for a final vigil.

I always say that December in Oaxaca is pure fiesta. Starting on the 8th is the fiesta of the Virgen de Juquila, when Oaxaqueños petition for special favors. Literally thousands of people walk, run, or ride their bicycles to the coastal region of Juquila to pay homage to her shrine. On the 12th, the Virgen de Guadalupe is celebrated, loved by all Mexicans as the patron saint of Mexico. This holiday features the dressing up of young children in peasant costumes to represent Juan Diego and María, who were witnesses to the miracle. Outside the Guadalupe church, in the Parque del Llano, specialties such as *molotes*, *esquites*, *tacos dorados*, *tlayudas*, and empanadas are offered with candies of all sorts, including the healthy *alegrías* and *palanquetas* of sesame seeds or squash seeds. The last *Virgen*, in the holy trio of *Virgens* in Oaxaca, is *La Soledad*. She is the patron saint of the city. Incredible fireworks displays, *antojitos*, ice creams, fruit drinks, and candies are all presented on December 18—her day.

The Christmas season starts with *posadas* in the city and country alike. Every night, the celebrants go from house to house singing, reenacting Mary and Joseph's search for a room at the inn. Finally they are allowed in, a rosary is said, *tamales* are served, and *piñatas* are broken. This takes place in a different home every night, from the 16th to the 24th. On Christmas Eve, the birth of Christ is celebrated. On December 23, there is a huge festival called *Noche de Rabanos*, where local artisans carve and sculpt grotesquely overgrown radishes into art pieces that tell a story or reflect a theme. This is one of the biggest events of the year and is quite a scene in the *zócalo*, to be topped only by Christmas Eve. That night, everyone stays up to eat *buñuelos*, drink chocolate, break *piñatas*, and after midnight, eat *pavo relleno* or *pollo enchilado*, *pozole*, or whatever else strikes the fancy of the cook to celebrate the *nacimiento* (birth). The most important requirement this night is that the ingredients for the feast be the freshest and best one can afford. Each Oaxacan family has their own recipes, their own food rituals, to make the season a culinary and spiritual tradition.

IN THIS CHAPTER

MEMELAS
Corn "Boats"

One of the basic Oaxacan snacks is the memela. These can be just tortillas called picadas with asiento (chicharrón drippings) smeared on them and served with salsa. But the memelas in Oaxaca have the asiento with bean paste, cheese, and various toppings. One of my favorite stands is outside St. Agustín Church, where they offer about eight different toppings that change with the seasons. Serve with Café de Olla (page 103), Atole de Maíz (page 160) or Atole de Trigo (page 132), or an agua de sabor.

MAKES 12 *MEMELAS*

2 pounds prepared masa *for tortillas or 3½ cups* masa harina *for tortillas*

½ teaspoon salt

12 tablespoons asiento *(see page 342) or bacon drippings (optional)*

2½ cups black bean paste *(page 16)*

¾ cup queso fresco *or queso cotija, crumbled or grated (see page 346)*

¾–1 cup salsa de chilito verde *(page 175), or salsa de chile pasilla (page 151), or salsa de chile de árbol (page 57)*

1½ cups topping of your choice: nopales *(page 327),* huitlacoche *(page 320),* nanacates *(see page 327), chicken picadillo (page 27), papas con chorizo (pages 230–231), or* pescadilla *(page 88)*

FOR THE *MASA*:

If using fresh *masa*, break up the *masa* in a mixing bowl with your fingers. Knead the *masa* with the salt and add ½ cup warm water if needed to make a soft, even dough. If using *masa harina*, mix the *masa harina* with 2¼ cups warm water to make a soft but not dry dough. Cover with a damp cloth. Allow the dough to rest 15 minutes. Add ½ cup warm water and the salt and knead for 1 minute to make a soft, even dough.

Divide the dough into 12 balls and cover them with a damp cloth. Press a *masa* ball out on a press between two sheets of plastic. If you don't have a tortilla press, spread the balls out with your fingertips or the heel of your hand. Remove the top sheet of plastic from the tortilla. Lay it gently on top of the tortilla and invert the tortilla with the plastic on both sides. Peel off the plastic on top and invert the tortilla onto your hand. Remove the remaining piece of plastic. Lay the tortilla on a 10-inch dry *comal*, griddle, or in a cast-iron frying pan, and cook it for 2 to 3 minutes on each side. Remove from the *comal*, invert it, and crimp the edges of the tortilla to make a lip around the edge. You must do this while the tortilla is still hot and pliable. You can also make concentric circles, smaller inside the tortilla. Allow it to cool and continue making the remaining tortillas. Cover the finished tortillas with a cloth to keep warm.

If necessary, reheat the prepared tortillas on the *comal*.

(continued)

Spread 1 tablespoon of the *asiento* on each tortilla. Add
2 tablespoons of bean paste and spread evenly. Sprinkle the
cheese over the bean paste and spoon on the salsa of your
choice. Add the desired topping.

BOCADILLOS DE PAPA Y CHORIZO
Potato Fritters with Sausage

This is my version of bocadillos *("mouth fillers"), often found on* botana *or appetizer platters and served with mezcal or beer. I first concocted them at Pancho's Restaurant in Cabo San Lucas, to jazz up the typical Oaxacan* bocadillos. *Potato with chorizo is a typical combination for some other dishes, so I added chorizo to spike up this dish and ended up with these tasty morsels, which were the hit of the* botana *platter. Serve with Salsa de Queso de Rosa Matadamas (page 22).*

MAKES 14 TO 18 *BOCADILLOS*

*1 pound potatoes (Yukon Gold or
    other frying type)*
*½ pound Mexican chorizo sausage,
    casings removed*
*½ medium white onion, finely
    chopped*
3 garlic cloves, finely chopped
1 large egg, beaten
½ cup flour
Salt
Cracked black peppercorns to taste
Pinch of freshly grated nutmeg
*¼ cup parsley leaves, finely
    chopped*
*1 tablespoon thinly sliced fresh
    chives or garlic chives*
*½–1 cup peanut or sunflower oil,
    for frying*

In a medium pot, boil the potatoes in their skins until soft,
about 30 minutes. Drain. When they are cool enough to
handle, peel and mash the potatoes.

In a medium sauté pan, fry the chorizo over medium
heat until it is dry, about 10 minutes. Add the onion and
sauté over medium heat until clear, about 5 minutes. Add
the garlic and sauté for 5 minutes more, until soft. Drain
well and discard the fat from the pan.

In medium bowl, whisk the egg until frothy and then add
the flour all at once while continuing to whisk. When the
mass gets too thick to whisk, continue mixing with your
hands to incorporate the egg evenly with the flour until it is
a sticky, pastelike substance, about 5 minutes. Add the
mashed potatoes and chorizo mixture and mix with your
hands. Season with the salt, peppercorns, nutmeg, parsley,
and chives. Mix well, but do not overbeat or the dough will
become a sticky mass you could use as wallpaper glue!

Heat the oil in a large frying pan or wok over high heat.

Take 1½ tablespoons of the potato-chorizo mixture and roll
it into a ball. Flatten it into a 2-inch round disk. When the oil is

hot, fry the *bocadillo* for 2 to 3 minutes on each side until golden, then drain well. Always fry 1 *bocadillo* first to taste for salt before you roll the rest of the mixture into balls. If they are too sticky, dredge in flour before frying. Continue to make little cakes, frying and draining well on paper towels. Serve hot.

Hints: If you want to make the *bocadillos* ahead of time, you can reheat them in a 400°F oven before serving.

For a topping for *memelas* (page 227), use the first four ingredients and the first two steps. Mix the potato and chorizo mixtures together.

EMPANADAS DE MOLE AMARILLO
Baked Mole Amarillo Turnovers

Outside every church in Oaxaca are charcoal grills set up with a comal on top, where women make quesadillas and empanadas de pollo to order. A couple of places in particular to enjoy these are outside of the Church of Guadalupe during their fiesta, in the courtyard of the Church of Soledad, or outside of El Tule, the 2,000-year-old tree.

MAKES 10 EMPANADAS

3 hierba santa *leaves (see page 336)*

1½ pounds prepared masa *for tortillas, or 3 cups* masa harina *for tortillas*

¾ tablespoon salt

1½ cups shredded cooked chicken

2 cups mole amarillo *(page 346)*

Preheat a 10-inch clay *comal*, griddle, or cast-iron frying pan over medium heat.

If using fresh *masa*, break up the *masa* in a mixing bowl with your fingers. If using *masa harina*, mix the *masa harina* with 1¾ cups water to make a soft, but not dry, dough. Cover with a damp cloth and allow the dough to rest 15 minutes. For either dough, add ¼ cup plus two tablespoons warm water and the salt. Knead for about 1 minute to make a soft even dough.

Divide the *masa* into 10 balls. Roll into a ball, then shape into a log 5 inches long and 1½ inches wide. Place a log between two sheets of plastic placed inside a tortilla press and press down. An oval shape will appear. Rotate the oval and press again. Remove the plastic from the top. Lay it gently on top of the tortilla and invert the tortilla, leaving the plastic on both sides. Peel off the plastic on top and invert the tortilla onto your hand. Remove the remaining plastic and place the tortilla in the middle of a 10-inch clay *comal*, griddle, or in a cast-iron frying pan. Place 4 or 5 pieces of chicken on the tortilla and top with 2 heaping tablespoons of the *mole amarillo*. Place ¼ of a *hierba santa* leaf in the middle. Run a little bit of water around the edge of the tortilla with your finger, fold the empanada over, and press to seal it closed. Bake about 3 to 5 minutes on each side, until it starts to brown and removes easily from the *comal* without breaking. Serve at once. Continue making all the balls until all the *masa* is gone. If you must, keep them warm wrapped completely in a cloth napkin until serving time, but they are better hot off the *comal*.

Hint: Before you lay the *masa* balls on the press, wet your hands to moisten the dough. Don't overstuff them or they will burst and leak *mole* all over the *comal*.

TOSTADAS DE CHILEAJO
Vegetables in Garlic Chile Sauce on Tostadas

This vegetarian mixture is similar to one used as a topping for tostadas in the market stall in the Mercado de Abastos, where I go to eat serious snack food. The stall is called Sisters Marilú. When my husband left the country for a while, I was filling in and selling the tomato crop with José, my husband's partner, at 4 A.M. at the wholesale part of the market. Around 9 o'clock, he took me to eat at his favorite haunt, very popular with the farmers and locals as well. And no wonder—the food is fresh, cheap, and above all, delicious. You can also serve these tostadas with salsa de guacamole (page 57) and your favorite beer as a botana or appetizer.

MAKES 12 TOSTADAS

½ *pound potatoes, cut into ½-inch cubes*

Cook the potatoes, chayote, carrots, and cauliflower in salted water until just tender. Drain well and cover the vegetables with cold water to stop the cooking process.

Bring 2 cups of water to a boil. Toast the chiles on a dry comal, griddle, or in a cast-iron frying pan until they give off

¼ pound chayote or zucchini
  squash, cut into ½-inch cubes
¼ pound carrots, peeled and cut
  into ½-inch cubes
¼ pound cauliflower, broken into
  small florets
5 chiles guajillos, stemmed, seeded,
  and deveined (see page 331)
1 whole allspice
1 whole clove
3 black peppercorns
2 tablespoons plus ¼ teaspoon dried
  Oaxacan oregano (see page 336)
1 piece of Mexican cinnamon,
  1 inch long (see page 337)
1 head of garlic, cloves separated
1 tablespoon sunflower or vegetable
  oil
½ cup fruit vinegar
1½ teaspoons salt
12 small corn tostadas or totopos
  (see page 321)
½ pound queso fresco (see page
  345), crumbled, or feta, grated
1 medium white onion, thinly sliced

their scent. Remove from the heat and soak in the hot water until soft, 15 to 20 minutes. Remove the chiles and set aside. Reserve the chile soaking water.

On the same *comal*, toast the allspice, clove, peppercorns, 2 tablespoons oregano, and the cinnamon until they give off their scent. Place the chiles and garlic in a blender and blend well with ¾ cup of chile water. Add the toasted spices and continue to blend well. Pass the mixture through a sieve or a food mill to remove the chile skins.

Heat the oil in an 8-inch frying pan. When smoking hot, add the chile mixture, stirring constantly for about 10 minutes. Remove from the heat and allow to cool.

Add the vinegar and salt to the chile mixture. Add to the vegetables and mix well. Chill, then serve the *Chileajo* on tostadas and top with crumbled fresh cheese, white onion slices, and the remaining oregano.

ESQUITES
Oaxacan-Style Corn Soup

Esquites *is one of the best evening street foods available in Mexico. Bicycle carts sell fresh roasted* elotes *(corn on the cob) and* esquites *(corn soup) on the street corners of Oaxaca city. The soup is garnished in the same manner as the corn on the cob—with mayonnaise, salty grated cheese, ground chile pepper, and salt with lime juice squeezed over all. Served piping hot, the challenge is to let it cool down enough so that you do not burn the roof of your mouth. My patience usually runs out long before the soup has had a chance to cool off!*

For the soup:

6 fresh ears corn, husked and ker-
    nels cut from cobs (about
    4 cups), cobs reserved for stock

3 large sprigs epazote, each
    4 inches long, or 4½ teaspoons
    dried (see page 336)

1½ tablespoons butter

½ cup finely chopped white onion

7 garlic cloves, finely chopped

¼ teaspoon finely ground white
    pepper

Salt to taste

For the mayonnaise:

2 egg yolks

1 large egg

½ teaspoon white wine or apple
    vinegar

½ teaspoon Dijon mustard

Tiny pinch of sugar

¼ teaspoon ground black pepper

¼ cup olive oil

2 cups sunflower oil

1 teaspoon salt

Juice of 1½ limes (about
    1½ tablespoons)

For the garnish:

2 limes, cut into wedges

¾ cup grated aged cheese, such as
    queso cotija (see page 346), or
    Parmesan cheese

1½ teaspoons ground chile de
    árbol (see page 330) or cayenne
    pepper mixed with a pinch of
    salt

FOR THE SOUP:

In a 4-quart stainless steel stockpot, place the cleaned corn cobs and 2 quarts water. Add 1½ sprigs of *epazote* or 2¼ teaspoons dried. Cover and bring to a boil, lower the heat to a simmer, and cook for at least ½ hour. Strain and reserve the stock.

In another heavy 4-quart stockpot, heat the butter over low heat until melted, but do not let it brown. Sauté the onion over medium heat until it is transparent, about 5 minutes, stirring well. Add the corn kernels and the garlic. Cook over medium heat for 20 minutes, stirring constantly, until the corn and garlic begin to brown. (Stirring the mixture while it cooks will release the milk in the kernels and develop the corn flavor; the more you stir, the creamier your soup will be.) Add the reserved stock, remaining *epazote*, and the white pepper. Cover and bring to a boil, then lower the heat to a simmer and cook for at least 1 hour. Add salt.

FOR THE MAYONNAISE:

Have all ingredients at room temperature. Place the egg yolks, egg, vinegar, mustard, sugar, and black pepper in a food processor or blender. Whip for 10 to 15 minutes, until it becomes thick and lemon colored. With the motor running, slowly add the olive oil in a thin stream. Then continue adding the sunflower oil in the same manner and whip until all of the oil is absorbed by the eggs. Shut off the machine and add the salt and lime juice. Whip again for a moment longer to incorporate the flavorings and adjust the seasonings. Makes 2 cups.

FOR THE GARNISH:

To serve, ladle the soup into bowls. Top each bowl with a dollop of mayonnaise, a squeeze of lime juice, a sprinkle of cheese, and a pinch of chile powder. Serve immediately.

SOPA DE AGUA DE PASTOR
Shepherd's Soup

Sol Díaz Altamirano has been the owner and "soul" behind El Topil, a tiny restaurant on Labastida in Oaxaca city, for twenty-two years. We have been friends since my arrival, and she was one of my most loyal students in the first three-month course in international cuisine that I gave for the local women here. I always bring my students to eat at El Topil to taste a real Oaxacan sazón, and we all agree the soups are fantastic.

MAKES 6 SERVINGS

4 cups chicken stock (page 343), salted to taste

1 medium white onion, finely chopped

½ pound tomatoes (1 medium–large round or 4–5 plum), finely chopped

1 large chile jalapeño, finely chopped (see page 329)

1 bunch cilantro, leaves roughly chopped and stems tied together

1 celery rib, with leaves

Salt (optional)

½ pound avocados, cut into small pieces

6 ounces queso fresco, cut into small pieces (see page 346)

In a heavy 4-quart stockpot, bring the stock to a boil. Add the onion, tomatoes, and chile. Add the cilantro stems and celery, lower the heat to a simmer, and cook for 10 minutes. Add the cilantro leaves and cook for 5 minutes longer. Remove the cilantro stems and celery. Add salt, if needed.

In each bowl, put in 2 tablespoons of avocado and 2 tablespoons of *queso fresco*. Ladle the soup over the top and serve immediately.

CHILPACHOLE DE CAMARÓN LOS JORGES
Los Jorges's Spicy Shrimp Soup

Although this recipe comes from Boca del Río, Veracruz, it is a favorite of mine from a charming fish restaurant called Los Jorges in Oaxaca city. Sitting under the coffee trees in the back of the restaurant, diners can eat fish baked in an adobe oven, which is succulent and delicious, as well as everything else on the menu created by Mari and Antonio Cardenas. This soup was served at a birthday fiesta I had there, and I love the robust flavor of it. Adding the toasted corn totopos was their Oaxacan twist to this seafood classic.

MAKES 8 SERVINGS

For the shrimp stock:

1½ pounds fresh shrimp, heads on if possible

½ small white onion, chunked

3 garlic cloves

½ teaspoon salt

For the soup:

20 chiles guajillos, stemmed, seeded, and deveined (see page 331)

3 chiles anchos rojos, stemmed, seeded, and deveined (see page 330)

½ medium white onion, chunked

3 large garlic cloves

¾ pound tomatoes (1½ medium–large round or 6–8 plum), cut in half lengthwise

2 cups chicken stock (page 343)

¾ cup crumbled totopos (see Hints)

2 large sprigs epazote (see page 336)

2 teaspoons salt, or to taste

1 lemon or lime, cut in half

FOR THE SHRIMP STOCK:

Clean the heads from the shrimp and wash them well. Place in a heavy 4-quart stockpot with 2 quarts water, the onion, garlic, and salt. Bring to a boil, cover, lower the heat, and simmer 30 minutes. Strain the stock and reserve. Add the salt.

In a small saucepan, bring 2 cups of water to a boil. On a 10-inch dry *comal*, griddle, or in a cast-iron frying pan, toast the chiles well on both sides until they give off their scent and blister and brown, but don't blacken them. Soak the chiles in the hot water for 15 minutes.

On the same *comal*, roast the onion and garlic until they are translucent. Remove from the *comal*. Roast the tomato halves, first on the outside and then turn them over and roast the inside. Both sides should be blackened. Do not peel the tomatoes.

Place the chiles, garlic, and tomatoes in a blender and blend well. Strain through a food mill or strainer into a heavy 4-quart stockpot and bring to a boil. Add 6 cups of the reserved shrimp stock and all the chicken stock.

Soak the *totopos* in 1 cup water for 15 minutes, then pour the mixture into the blender and blend well. Strain it through a food mill or strainer and add to the soup. Add the *epazote* and salt. Add the shrimp and cook over low heat for 10 minutes. Add the salt.

Serve with lime wedges, *totopos*, tostadas, *bolillos*, or French bread.

Hints: Chances are you don't have *totopos*, so toast corn tortillas on a baking sheet in a 400°F oven for about 20 minutes, until dry and crispy. Then soak, blend, and strain them and add to the soup.

You can cook cleaned and deveined shrimp in the soup and add the shells to enrich the shrimp stock, but the soup is traditionally served with unshelled shrimp. You can also use whole crabs, cut in half to make *chilpachole de jaiba*.

ENSALADA DE BOTANA
Appetizer Salad

This is a great salad to serve for a group of friends or family to start a big meal. The ingredients are part of what you would be served in a botanas bar, hence the name. The first time I ate a version of this salad was at the home of my friend Juanita, who employs one of the best cooks in Oaxaca, and who is an accomplished cook herself. The salad was followed by stuffed Enfrijoladas (page 61) for a satisfying meal. The dressing is inspired by my friend Cheryl's jalapeño jelly and Dijon mustard that are part of the homemade product line she sells in Oaxaca. If you do not have jalapeño jelly, substitute apple jelly and add ½ teaspoon minced pickled jalapeños.

MAKES 8 TO 10 SERVINGS

For the dressing:
1 tablespoon finely chopped garlic
1 teaspoon Dijon mustard
2 tablespoons jalapeño jelly
¼ cup fruit vinegar
¼ cup olive oil
Salt and pepper to taste

For the salad:
1½ heads of green leaf lettuce or
  other mixed greens, torn into
  bite-size pieces

FOR THE DRESSING:
Mix the garlic, mustard, jelly, and vinegar in a bowl. Add the olive oil, whisking well. Add salt and pepper to taste. Set aside.

FOR THE SALAD:
Cover an oval serving platter with the lettuce or mixed fresh greens, mounding it in the middle. Add a layer of tomato slices around the mound, leaving a 2-inch border of lettuce. On the inside edge of the tomatoes, alternate the radish and avocado slices. Sprinkle the green onions over the vegetables and add the shredded cheese. Cover all with the cilantro leaves. Before serving, dress the salad and sprinkle the

½ pound tomatoes (1 medium–
large round or 4–5 plum), sliced

6 radishes, sliced

3 avocados, cut into ¼-inch-wide
slices

9 green onions, sliced

¼ pound quesillo (see page 345) or
Muenster, Monterey Jack, or
Armenian string cheese, cut into
1½-inch pieces, then shredded

½ bunch cilantro, leaves only

¼ pound chicharrón, broken into
1-inch pieces (see page 342)

chicharrón pieces over the top. Serve at once with hot soft tortillas (blandas) or crispy, hot totopos or tostadas.

Hint: If you don't have chicharrón, substitute bacon bits or sunflower seeds.

CHAYOTES ASADOS
Roasted Chayotes

I always love the spiny, fresh green chayotes that grow prolifically in the rainy season. Traditionally, they are boiled or steamed in their skins and sold in the market to be eaten with salsa in steaming hot tortillas, bought from the tortilleras in the aisles— healthy, instant fast food. This recipe was created by Susan Baldassano, from New York City, in one of my classes on the ranch. A great cooking teacher herself, she brings groups of students to Oaxaca and we always do one dish we've never done before.

MAKES 6 SERVINGS

4 pounds chayotes (about 6; see
page 326)

1 head of garlic, finely chopped

1 teaspoon dried Oaxacan oregano
(see page 336)

¼ cup olive oil

½ teaspoon salt, or to taste

¼ teaspoon fresh ground black pepper

Preheat the oven to 350°F.

Peel the chayotes. (It is advisable to use gloves when peeling chayotes, as a gluelike resin will coat your hands.) Cut the chayotes into eighths and place in a bowl. Use the seeds in the dish, because they are delicious. Add the garlic, oregano, olive oil, and salt. Mix well to coat the pieces.

Place the chayote pieces in a baking pan and roast for 1 to 1¼ hours covered or until tender, and then 15 minutes uncovered.

FRIJOLES CHARROS
Cowboy Beans

Frijoles Charros are often found in restaurants that specialize in grilled meats. Any kind of red bean, pinto, flor de mayo, or, in this case, frijol bayo is used. The meats mingle well with the beans to give it a hardy flavor. This dish is great to serve at a barbecue where meats are grilled on the parrilla. The recipe is based on one by my amiga Marieke Bekkers de Díaz Cruz.

MAKES 8 CUPS

1 pound dried pinto beans
(2½ cups)

2 medium white onions, finely
chopped

½ head of garlic, cloves separated
and finely chopped

1 chile de árbol (see page 330)

2 6-ounce smoked pork chops or
2 ham hocks, whole, meat cut
off the bone (add bones to the
beans)

2 bay leaves

½ teaspoon ground black pepper

2 whole allspice

½ pound tomatoes (1 medium–
large round or 4–5 plum)

4 slices smoked bacon, cut into
pieces

½ pound chorizo oaxaqueño (see
page 342)

1–2 chiles jalapeños en
escabeche (page 333), finely
chopped (optional, depending on
taste)

2½–3 tablespoons salt, or more to
taste

Clean the beans, picking through them carefully to remove any stones and dirt. Wash well in cold water until the water is clear. In a clay pot with a lid or a 6-quart soup pot, place the beans in enough water to cover (about 12 cups). Add 1½ onions, garlic, *chile de árbol*, pork meat and bones, bay leaves, pepper, and allspice. Bring to a boil, cover, and simmer over low heat for 3 to 3½ hours, adding water as needed, until the beans are almost soft.

On a 10-inch dry *comal*, griddle, or in a cast-iron frying pan, grill the tomatoes until they are blackened and soft. Let cool, then put them in a blender with a little bean broth. Strain through a wire-mesh strainer or food mill. Add the pureed tomatoes to the beans.

Put the bacon in a frying pan and fry until crisp. Add the chorizo and fry until dry. Add the remaining ½ onion and fry until soft. Add this mixture to the beans, add the *chiles jalapeños*, and cook for 1 more hour or until the beans are soft.

Add the salt when the beans are finished cooking. Remove the bay leaf.

TAMALES DE RAJAS
Chile and Tomato Tamales

This tamal is one of my favorite uses of the local chile de agua and tomato. The heat of the chiles is offset by the sweetness of the tomatoes and onions. I have found that many cooks substitute the large variety of chile jalapeño nicknamed Huachinango (because the cracks in the chile skins resemble fish scales) if the chile de agua is not available or is too expensive. Chicken or pork is an equally good filler, and sometimes I've also made them with the local requesón (farmer cheese) or mushrooms for a vegetarian version.

MAKES 14 *TAMALES*

For the masa:
1½ pounds prepared masa for tamales, or 2⅔ cups coarse masa harina for tamales
2 teaspoons baking powder
1 cup plus 2 tablespoons lard
2–2½ teaspoons salt, or to taste
7 tablespoons warm chicken stock (page 343)

For the filling:
½ tablespoon lard, sunflower oil, or vegetable oil
1½ medium white onions, halved and thinly sliced
3 chiles de agua, roasted, peeled, seeded, deveined, and cut into strips, or 4–5 large chiles jalapeños (see page 329)
1 pound tomatoes (2 medium–large round or 8–10 plum), cut into chunks
3 garlic cloves, finely chopped
Salt and pepper to taste

FOR THE *MASA*:
If using prepared *masa*, break up the *masa* in a large bowl. If using *masa harina*, put it in a mixing bowl and add 1½ cups plus 3 tablespoons warm water. Mix it well and allow the dough to sit 15 minutes. Add the baking powder to either dough and mix in well. Add the lard if it is fresh (soft). If the lard is the block type, whip it as much as possible to get it light, then add it to the *masa*. Mix in the lard well by hand or electric mixer. Add salt to the warm stock and add to the dough, stirring well. Taste for salt and add more if necessary. You should be able to taste the salt, but it should not be salty. Whip the *masa* well until light, about 20 minutes.

FOR THE FILLING:
Heat the oil in a medium sauté pan. Add the onions and sauté until clear. Add the *chiles de agua* or *chiles jalapeños*, tomatoes, garlic, salt, and pepper and cook through, about 10 minutes. Allow to cool.

FOR THE ASSEMBLY:
Tear 3 or 4 cornhusks into strips or ties for later use. Keep them in warm water. Blot the soaked cornhusks to dry them. Put a cornhusk in your hand and spread a spoonful of *masa* in a rectangle toward the wider end of the husk, leaving about ½ of husk empty on top. Spoon on 2 tablespoons of filling and then add 2 pieces of chicken or pork on

3 packages cornhusks, soaked
   ½ hour in water to soften

1½ cups shredded cooked chicken
   or pork (optional)

top. Lay the *tamal* on the table horizontally and join the two long edges of the husk together and roll them up until firm. The filling should be enclosed. Fold the thin side over the fat-filled end to double it. Secure it with the ties made of shredded husks or put folded side down into another husk. Repeat with the rest of the *masa*.

Fill a steamer with salted water to the level of the rack. Place rack in pot, cover with extra cornhusks, and fill the steamer with the *tamales*. Cover and weight the lid with a heavy object to keep it snugly closed. Steam over a slow rolling boil for about 1 hour, or when the *tamal* separates easily from the husk and it "smells like *tamales*." Serve hot.

BACALAO NAVIDEÑO
Salted Fish for Christmas Eve Day

On Christmas Eve day, this is the traditional comida *served in the afternoon, while everyone is busy preparing* tamales *or turkey for the midnight dinner celebrating the birth of the Christ child. Here in Oaxaca, salt cod from Norway is available but very expensive. Many people use the salted* cazón *(shark) meat in the exact same way. You need to soak the fish overnight for the following day's lunch. This dish is also served "religiously" on Holy Thursday or Good Friday during Lent.*

MAKES 6 SERVINGS

½ pound bacalao (see page 345),
   salted cod, or salted shark fillets

2 tablespoons olive oil

1 small white onion, finely chopped

1 pound tomatoes (2 medium–large
   round or 8–10 plum), peeled and
   finely chopped

9 garlic cloves, finely chopped

10 pitted green olives, sliced in
   rounds

Cover the salted fish with cold water in a stainless steel bowl and allow to sit overnight. The next morning, discard the soaking water and soak again. Soak for another 6 to 8 hours, then discard the soaking water.

In a 4-quart stainless steel pot, bring about 6 cups of water to a boil. Add the fish and cook over low heat 4 to 5 minutes or until the fish is soft. Remove from heat and drain. Reserve the stock. Put the fish in a piece of cheesecloth and squeeze out the water.

In a 10-inch, deep frying pan, heat the olive oil. Add the onion and fry until clear. Add the tomatoes and garlic and cook until the tomatoes give off their juices, about 10 min-

1½ tablespoons capers, finely chopped if large, whole if small

½ teaspoon ground white pepper

1 tablespoon white vinegar

4 tablespoons chiles jalapeños en escabeche (page 333), finely chopped

Salt

2 tablespoons chopped flat-leaf parsley

utes. Add the olives, capers, and white pepper. Add the vinegar, *jalapeños*, and 1½ cups of the reserved fish stock.

Break the fish into small pieces ½ to 1 inch in size and add to the mixture. Heat through. Add a pinch of salt only if needed. Add the parsley. Serve with lime wedges, *totopos*, tostadas, and fresh baked *bolillos* and a fresh green salad with radish slices.

Hint: In the Isthmus of Tehuantepec, this dish is popular, but people use *chiles chipotles* instead of *jalapeños*. Another recipe given to me by the Morales sisters in Etla calls for *chiles largos*, which are long yellow chiles in vinegar.

CAZUELA DE SOL
Sol's Savory Casserole

One afternoon when Sol Díaz Altamirano was visiting the ranch, she taught me how to prepare this simple and delicious casserole. We served it with Sopa de Agua de Pastor *(page 233) and* Arroz con Chepil *(page 52) for a satisfying meal. I don't know which was more fun, the cooking or the eating, but I always love getting together with Sol, either here or at her lively Oaxacan restaurant, El Topil.*

MAKES 6 SERVINGS

1 small white onion, chunked

5 garlic cloves

2 pounds chicken pieces

½ teaspoon salt, or to taste

½ pound potatoes (2 large)

1 pound fresh mushrooms, roughly chopped

1 large white onion, finely chopped

2½ tablespoons sunflower or vegetable oil

In a heavy 4-quart stockpot, bring 2 quarts of water with the small onion and the garlic to a boil. Add the chicken and poach, covered, for 30 to 35 minutes. Remove the chicken from the pot. Over high heat, reduce the stock for 10 minutes. Add the salt and reserve the stock.

Boil the potatoes in 2 cups water, covered, for 15 to 20 minutes. Drain and allow to cool. Peel and slice 1 potato, peel and reserve the other.

Cook the mushrooms in 3 cups of water for 10 minutes. Drain the water.

In a heavy 4-quart pot, fry the chopped onion in the oil until clear, about 3 to 5 minutes. Add the tomatoes and cook another 10 minutes. Mash the mixture with a bean

¾ pound tomatoes (1½ medium–
large round or 6–7 plum), peeled
and finely chopped

1 teaspoon salt

1 chile chipotle en adobo
(page 332), stemmed

6 ounces quesillo, manchego, or
Chihuahua cheese (see
page 345), shredded or grated

masher. Add the salt and stir in. Combine the whole potato with 1 *chile chipotle* and 1 teaspoon of the *adobo* sauce with 1 cup of the reserved stock in a blender. Blend until smooth.

Remove the chicken meat from the bones and shred finely.

In a 3½- to 4-quart oval or round Dutch oven or casserole, make a layer of the tomato mixture. Add a layer of potato slices, a layer of mushrooms, and a layer of shredded chicken. Spread the pureed potato mixture on top. Add 2 cups of reserved stock and cook over low heat, covered, for 10 minutes. Sprinkle the cheese on top, cover, and cook for 5 minutes more. Serve with rice.

CARNITAS CON SALSA DE CACAHUATE
Crispy Fried Pork with Peanut Sauce

Carnitas *are one of the favorite Oaxacan fiesta dishes, especially for* quinceaños *parties. These parties signify a young girl's becoming a woman and are her presentation to society. My first introduction to carnitas was at a fiesta for Laura González Matadamas. María and Fraulein Galvan Taboada cooked five big pigs and served them with the peanut sauce. Later, my recipe was refined with the help of Elias and Samari Carrasco Sánchez, of Restaurante Tecomate in San Agustín, Etla, where they make it every weekend.*

MAKES 6 TO 8 SERVINGS

For the salsa de cacahuate:

4 chiles guajillos, *stemmed, seeded, and deveined (see page 330)*

3 chiles moritas, *stemmed, seeded,
and deveined (see page 331)*

10 chiles de árbol, *stemmed, seeded, and deveined (see page 330)*

¼ pound tomatillos, *husked (see
page 327)*

FOR THE *SALSA DE CACAHUATE*:
In a small saucepan, bring 2 cups of water to a boil. On a 10-inch dry *comal*, griddle, or in a cast-iron frying pan, toast the chiles until they start to blister. Remove to a bowl and pour the hot water over the chiles to soak for 15 minutes.

On the same *comal*, toast the *tomatillos* about 8 to 12 minutes or until soft and they change color, turning them once.

Put the chiles, peanuts or peanut butter, and *tomatillos* in a blender with 2½ cups water. Puree to make a smooth, runny sauce. If the sauce thickens too much, add more water. Add salt.

(continued)

¼ pound (¾ cup) roasted peanuts
    or ¾ cup crunchy peanut butter
¼–½ teaspoon salt

For the carnitas:
20 sprigs thyme
2 sprigs marjoram or Oaxacan
    oregano
1 teaspoon salt
½ medium white onion, chunked
1 head of garlic
3 chiles de árbol *(see page 330)*
2 pounds boneless pork butt
2 pounds pork ribs
3 pounds lard
2 oranges, 1 juiced and 1 sliced
¼ cup sweetened condensed milk
    (optional; see Hint)

FOR THE *CARNITAS*:

In a large stockpot, heat 2½ quarts water with the thyme, marjoram, salt, onion, garlic, and chiles. When it comes to a boil, add the pork. Simmer, covered, for 1 hour or until the meat is soft. Remove the meat and drain well.

In a large wok or Dutch oven, heat the lard and add the orange juice and condensed milk. Be careful, as the oil will splatter when these liquids are added. When the lard is smoking hot, add the meat and cook until brown and crispy. Remove from the pot and drain. Serve immediately with the peanut sauce, orange slices, hot corn tortillas, avocados, and radishes.

Hint: The addition of sweetened condensed milk in the lard gives the meat a sweet taste; however, it tends to burn in the bottom of the pan. If you do not have an old deep-fryer, you can omit this ingredient.

CARNE ENROLLADA CON VERDURAS
Rolled Beef with Vegetables

I remember eating these spiral meat slices one memorable New Year's Eve in Oaxaca city. At the home of Don Paulo and Doña Irene, hot and cold botanas were served, then the main meal started: soup, rice, and meats and plenty of liquor. In front of each place were twelve grapes on a plate and everyone waited in anticipation. At the very stroke of midnight, everyone ate his or her grapes, one for each month of the New Year and made wishes with each one. We have practiced this Oaxacan tradition, brought here by the Spaniards, every year since. Serve at room temperature or chilled in a botanas selection, or serve a few pieces on a plate with Papas en Escabeche (page 141) or chipotle mayonesa (see page 213). It can also be served hot with some reduced cooking broth, mashed potatoes, and Cebollas Asadas con Crema (page 298).

MAKES 8 APPETIZER SERVINGS

3 tablespoons butter

1 pound mushrooms or portobellos,
    finely chopped

1 medium white onion, finely
    chopped

5 cloves garlic, finely chopped

Pinch of salt

1 tablespoon brandy or port

¼ teaspoon ground black pepper

2–3 carrots, peeled and cut in
    lengthwise strips

3 ounces green beans, trimmed

1 small white onion, chunked

1 head of garlic, cut in half

3 whole allspice

2 whole cloves

1 piece of Mexican cinnamon,
    1 inch long (see page 337)

2 bay leaves

1 chile de árbol (see page 330)

1 teaspoon vinegar

¼ teaspoon fresh or dried
    marjoram

¼ teaspoon fresh or dried thyme

1 pound boneless top round,
    butterflied

1 ounce (about a handful) chives or
    garlic chives

1½ teaspoons salt

1½ teaspoons pepper

3 tablespoons butter or olive oil, or
    a combination of the two

Niña María grinding corn at the
Fiesta de Virgen de Guadalupe,
Oaxaca City (Marcela Taboada)

In a medium sauté pan, heat butter until it sizzles, over medium heat. Add the onion and sauté for 3 minutes. Add the mushrooms and garlic and sauté for 15 minutes. Add salt, brandy, and black pepper and cook 1 minute longer. Set aside.

In a 2-quart saucepan, blanch the carrots and beans in salted water for 5 minutes. Rinse with cold water to stop the cooking process.

In a roasting pan on top of the stove, combine 2 quarts of water, the onion, garlic, allspice, cloves, cinnamon, bay leaves, chile, vinegar, marjoram, and thyme.

Lay the meat flat on a board. Salt and pepper the beef, then spread the mushroom mixture on the meat, leaving a 1-inch border on all sides. Lay a one-inch-wide row of chives on the bottom edge of the mushroom mixture. Then place a one-inch-wide row of carrots next to the chives. Next to the carrots, add a one-inch-wide row of string beans. Fold in the sides. Tightly roll up the beef around the vegetables and secure with butcher's string. Salt and pepper the outside of the beef. Wrap the roll in aluminum foil and put it in the roasting pan, adding more water if needed to cover the meat.

Bring to a boil, then lower the heat to a simmer. Cook about 30 minutes or until a meat thermometer in the middle indicates 160°F. Allow the meat to cool for 10 minutes. Remove the string.

In a frying pan large enough to fit the beef roll, heat the butter or oil until it sizzles. Add the meat and brown on all sides. Remove from the pan and allow to cool. Slice the meat into ½-inch-thick medallions. Serve.

TASAJO Y CEBOLLITAS A LA PARRILLA

Grilled Thinly Sliced Beef with Tiny Onions and Fresh Salsa

Thinly sliced beef called tasajo, *thinly sliced pork* (cecina), *pork ribs, and Mexican chorizo sausages are some of the many grilled meats you will receive on a* botanas *platter or are featured in the large buffet-type restaurants, which are popular with Oaxacan families on a Sunday afternoon. The tasajo is always sprinkled with lime to cut some of the salt flavor that preserves the meat. Green onions are usually grilled directly on the coals and are always served on the side with lots of lime as well. You can use a variety of salsas. This is one of my favorites from the fall, when the gusanitos de maguey are harvested and add great flavor to the sauce.*

MAKES 4 SERVINGS

For the salsa de gusanito:
14 chiles de árbol *(see page 330)*
9 gusanitos de maguey *(see page 341)*
5 garlic cloves
¼–½ teaspoon salt

For the meat and onions:
2–3 limes, juiced, depending on how salty the meat is
2 teaspoons vegetable oil, to coat the meat
1 pound tasajo, filet or sirloin tips, thinly sliced *(see page 341)*
Salt and pepper to taste

To serve:
12 green onions or 4 large white onions with skins left on
Pinch of salt
4 limes, halved
12 corn tortillas

FOR THE *SALSA DE GUSANITO*:
On a 10-inch dry *comal*, griddle, or in a cast-iron frying pan, toast the *chiles de árbol* for a few minutes until they brown and give off their scent. Remove and set aside. On the same *comal*, toast the *gusanitos* for 1 minute, stirring constantly. Remove and set aside. Toast the garlic until transparent.

In a *molcajete*, grind the chiles, *gusanitos*, and garlic. Add salt and ½ cup water. (You can do this in the blender if you wish.)

FOR THE MEAT AND ONIONS:
Mix the lime juice and oil. Portion the strips of meat into serving pieces. Coat the meat with the lime and oil mixture and allow to sit for at least ½ hour. Add salt and pepper if needed.

TO SERVE:
If using green onions, clean off the roots and keep leaves intact. If using large white onions, make an x in the tops of the onions, cutting down about ¼ deep into the onion.

Prepare a charcoal grill. When the coals are white, grill the onions directly on the coals, turning them often. Grill the meat quickly about 4 minutes on each side or according to taste. When the onions are translucent and soft, peel off the outer skins and cut the onions into quarters. Sprinkle a

2 Haas avocados or 8 aguacates
  criollos, *sliced (see page 338)*
1 bunch fresh radishes, *made into*
  flowerets, leaves intact

pinch of salt and squeeze lime juice over the onions.

Heat the tortillas and serve with the meat, salsa, onions, avocado slices, and radish flowerets.

ROSCA DE REYES
Three Kings Ring

Every year on January 6, El Día de Reyes Magos, or the day the three kings came to visit the Christ child, is celebrated. All the children receive a present, and a special cake-like bread is shared with everyone present. The ring is decorated with fruit ates *(pastes), dried fruits, and a sugar icing. A plastic baby Jesus is baked inside of the bread, and whoever receives the baby in his or her piece has to make* tamales *for the fiesta of* Día de la Candelaria *on February 2, a celebration of Jesus' first trip to the temple.*

MAKES 2 RINGS

2 tablespoons active dry yeast

2 tablespoons plus ¾ cup granulated sugar

5 cups all-purpose flour, or a mixture of 4 cups all-purpose and 1
  cup whole wheat flour

Pinch of salt

2 teaspoons toasted and finely
  ground pecans

4 tablespoons (½ stick) butter, at
  room temperature

4 tablespoons lard

6 eggs, at room temperature

½ teaspoon vanilla extract

For the decorations:
½ cup all-purpose flour
¼ cup confectioners' sugar

Mix the yeast, 2 tablespoons sugar, and ½ cup warm water. Let sit in a warm space for 15 to 20 minutes or until foamy.

In a large bowl, mix the flour, salt, remaining ¾ cup sugar, and proofed yeast. Add the nuts, crumble in the butter and lard, and mix until well incorporated.

Make a well in the center of the flour mixture and add 5 of the eggs and vanilla. Mix well. Knead dough for 5 to 10 minutes. Place in a greased bowl and coat the top of dough with oil. Cover with a damp towel or a piece of plastic, and allow to rise until doubled in size, 1½ to 2 hours.

Punch down the dough and turn over. Allow to rise another 30 minutes. Punch down and shape the dough into 2 rings, 9 inches in diameter. Place the rings on greased baking sheets.

Preheat the oven to 350°F.

In a small bowl, beat the remaining egg and lightly brush the top of the dough.

FOR THE DECORATIONS:
Mix the flour, confectioners' sugar, and shortening to make a

3 tablespoons vegetable shortening

4 ounces fruit ates, red, green, or yellow, or quince paste, julienned (see page 348)

2 ounces acitrón (crystallized cactus pieces), julienned (optional)

2 candied figs, cut into quarters

2 teaspoons sesame seeds

wet topping. Smear it on a cutting board with the palm of your hand. Cut into 6 sections and transfer to the rings with a pastry scraper or a metal spatula, to divide each *rosca* in thirds.

Decorate the sections with the *ates* and *acitrón* slices for making designs, then add the figs and sesame seeds. Extra confectioners' sugar could be placed on the sugar topping, but not on the *ates* or *acitrón*.

TO BAKE:

Bake the rings for 30 minutes, or until lightly browned. The bread should be soft.

Recipe inspired by the families of Aurelio Galvan and Galdino Lazaro

BUÑUELOS CON ANÍS
Fried Flour Tortilla Fritters with Anise

Every year during the Christmas season in Oaxaca, stands of buñuelo *sellers line the side of the zócalo, called the Alameda, beside the cathedral.* Buñuelos *are traditional holiday fare, and these flat fried tortillas can be eaten dry and dipped into their accompanied syrup, or broken up and soaked in the syrup itself. These are often served in clay bowls. When you are done eating the* buñuelos, *tradition has it that you stand with your bowl and throw it over your shoulder at the cathedral wall while making a wish. A firm believer in wishes, and opportunities to do so, I never let the chance slide by. And believer that I am, they always come true!*

MAKES 12 *BUÑUELOS*

For the buñuelos:

½ cup sugar

1 teaspoon aniseeds

4 cups all-purpose flour

½ tablespoon baking powder

Pinch of salt

In a small saucepan, place 1 cup water, the sugar, and the anise. Cover and boil for 5 minutes. Strain the liquid through a fine strainer and allow to cool.

In a medium bowl, mix the flour, baking powder, and a pinch of salt. Make a well in the center and add the eggs and anise water. Mix well with your hands until you have a soft dough. Knead for 10 to 15 minutes. Spread the top with the

2 eggs

½ tablespoon lard

3 cups sunflower or vegetable oil, to
fry the buñuelos

For the syrup:

2 cones piloncillo (6 ounces each;
light brown, if possible; see
page 348), or 2 cups light brown
sugar

1 piece of Mexican cinnamon,
about 2 inches long (see
page 337)

lard and cover the bowl with a clean cloth. Allow dough to rest about 45 minutes to 1 hour.

Make 12 balls from the dough. Roll each ball out on a floured board until very thin, about 4 inches in diameter. Add more flour to the board as needed. Lay each round out on a tablecloth or sheet (if you're making a lot) and let them air out until they become a little leathery to the touch or dry, about 1 to 1¼ hours.

In a 12-inch frying pan, heat the oil until smoking hot. Place each round in the oil and fry, using two tongs to burst the bubbles that will appear on the *buñuelo* and to submerge it into the oil. The oil should cover the *buñuelo*. Fry for 30 seconds on each side and then another 15 seconds on each side or until golden brown. Remove from the pan and drain on paper towels.

FOR THE SYRUP:
In a saucepan, heat the *piloncillo*, cinnamon, and 2½ cups water until syrupy, about 15 minutes. In clay bowls, ladle in ½ cup of syrup and place a *buñuelo* on top. Or if you want them *"remojado"* (wet), break up each *buñuelo* and place the pieces in the bowl. Ladle the syrup on top.

PASTEL DE TRES LECHES
(Three-Milk Cake)

Teresa Garcia, the talented chef who has cooked at Casa Colonial for over twenty years, makes this cake for the popular bed-and-breakfast. She always decorates the cakes with colored buttercream frostings. We catered a party together to honor the Oaxaca–Palo Alto sister city supporters. Mexico and Italy were playing each other in the World Cup Soccer game, and emotions were running high. We made the green, white, and red base for the Mexican flag, but waited for the outcome of the game before we added the eagle with the snake in its mouth. (If they didn't win, we joked, we would have to serve it upside down in honor of Italy.) Luckily, Mexico won 2 to 1. Gooooool!

For the cake:

10 eggs kept at room temperature
    for ½ hour
1 cup all-purpose flour, sifted
1 tablespoon baking powder
1 cup granulated sugar
1 tablespoon vanilla extract
Confectioners' sugar

For the filling:

2 cups heavy cream
1 teaspoon vanilla extract
½ cup confectioners' sugar, sifted
2 cups chopped strawberries,
    guayaba, or other fruit, in
    ½-inch pieces

For the soaking liquid:

¾ cup sweetened condensed milk
½ cup crema (see page 345) or
    half-and-half
1 cup evaporated milk
2 tablespoons rum, brandy, mezcal,
    or other liquor of your choice

For the frosting:

½ cup (1 stick) butter, softened
1 teaspoon vanilla extract
1½ cups confectioners' sugar, sifted
2 tablespoons milk

FOR THE CAKE:

Preheat oven to 350°F. Oil a jellyroll baking pan and line it with waxed paper oiled on both sides.

Separate the egg yolks and whites in two bowls.

Sift the flour and baking powder together.

Beat the yolks until light and lemon colored, about 20 minutes. The consistency should be very thick, and when you lift the beaters, the mixture should fall in one solid mass, known as the "ribbon stage." Add ½ cup of the sugar, 2 tablespoons at a time. Add the vanilla and beat 3 minutes more.

Whip the egg whites until soft peaks form. Add the remaining ½ cup sugar slowly until it makes a meringue. Add the whites to the yolks one-third at a time and fold in with a rubber spatula. Add the flour all at once and fold in.

Spread the batter in the pan and bake for 20 to 30 minutes or until the cake comes away from the sides of the pan. Let it rest for 5 minutes, then remove it from the pan and place on a clean tea towel that has been dusted with confectioners' sugar. Remove the waxed paper by rubbing the top of the paper with a dry cloth all over the surface and peeling off. Cover the cake with another tea towel and roll up the cake lengthwise in the towels, like a jellyroll, while still warm.

FOR THE FILLING:

Whip the cream and vanilla until soft peaks form. Add the confectioners' sugar. Add the fruit to the whipped cream and fold in.

FOR THE SOAKING LIQUID:

Mix the milks with a whisk. Add the liquor.

FOR THE FROSTING:

In a mixing bowl, beat the butter until soft and fluffy, about 10 minutes. Add the vanilla and mix for 2 minutes. Slowly add confectioners' sugar until it is well incorporated. Add the milk.

TO ASSEMBLE THE CAKE:

Unroll the cake and remove the tea towel from the top layer. Spread the fruit-soaked whipped cream on the cake and, using the bottom towel as leverage, roll it up lengthwise. Transfer the cake to a serving tray seam side down. Make holes in the cake with a skewer and add the soaking liquid, slowly, letting it absorb bit by bit. Cover the cake with the frosting.

PONCHE
Hot Punch

One of the drinks I look forward to every year at the posadas leading into Christmas is a hot, sweet drink called Ponche. Seasonal fruits are simmered together with chunks of sugarcane and dried fruits to make an aromatic warming drink. While the adults are served Ponche with tamales, the children wrestle for candy from the piñatas. If you are in (or want to get in) the holiday spirit, add a piquete (shot) of rum or mezcal.

MAKES IO CUPS

½ pound apples, cored and cut into eighths

¾ cup raisins

1 pound guava (guayaba), cut into quarters (see page 338)

3 pieces (3–4 inches each) sugar-cane, cut into julienne strips

½ pound prunes

½ pound crabapples

1 slice pineapple, cut into 1-inch pieces

1 cup sugar

4 pieces of Mexican cinnamon, each 1 inch long (see page 337)

In a heavy 4-quart stockpot, place the fruit, sugar, cinnamon, and 8 cups of water. Bring to a boil, lower the heat, and simmer for 1 hour. Serve hot in mugs or cups.

CHAPTER TEN
The Moles of Oaxaca
(Moles de Oaxaca)

Paula Cortez
toasting cacao,
Jalapa del
Valle, Oaxaca
(Alfredo Díaz
Mora)

Señor eating
an empanada
at graveyard
in San Martin
Mexicapam,
Oaxaca
(Marcela
Taboada)

It's five-thirty in the morning and the roosters of San Lorenzo Cacaotepec, a small pueblo (village) in the valley of Oaxaca, are announcing a new day. It's the magic hour in the mountains of southern Mexico, when the sun has just risen on the eastern side of the Sierra Juárez. The sun's reflection is turning the sky purple and red with a hint of orange. Indigo blue clouds drape over the Sierre Madre del Sur to the west. The air is crisp and cool.

Excitement is in the air, reminiscent of Christmas

252

mornings of my childhood. Called Día de Plaza in Oaxaca, today is the day before the celebration of *Día de Muertos* (Day of the Dead). *Muertos* is a two-day festival remembering the ancestors, celebrated on All Saints' and All Souls' Days. Today is perhaps Oaxaca's biggest shopping day of the year. Already many of the campesinos of our pueblo have joined others from the valley at the Mercado de Abastos, the nearby city of Oaxaca's central market, to sell their sugarcane, tomatoes, chiles, and jícama. With the money they earn they will buy dried chiles, spices, and nuts for their holiday meals, as well as sweets, flowers, copal incense, and sugar skulls for their home altars and the other ingredients needed to make specialties such as homemade chocolate to exchange among family and friends.

In the *pueblo* south of mine, the *tortilleras*, or tortilla makers, of San Felipe Tejalapam are returning from the *molino* (grinding mill). There they have ground a rich, spicy bean paste that will smother the tortillas used to make *Tortillas Embarradas* (page 260) for dressing their festive altars and holiday tables. These black tortillas are made especially for the celebration of *Muertos;* my tongue burns at the memory of them, well toasted and so *picante.* They will be eaten with the most revered and famous dish of *la cocina Mexicana*—mole, pronounced MO-lay.

Today, each family will make their most treasured *mole* to remember those who have come before. *Mole* is a remarkable, unique dish that joins the Old and the New Worlds in one softly bubbling pot, or *cazuela.* A complicated dish that takes hours to prepare, it seems fitting to serve it on this most special holiday, as well as at weddings, baptisms, birthdays, and the celebrations of the patron saints of each *pueblo.*

Oaxaca is known as the "Land of the Seven *Moles*," but I know of only six different *moles* here. Are there really seven *moles*? Is it just a play on words, based on the number of regions in the state of Oaxaca, the number of days in the week, or perhaps just a nod to the mystical number seven. As Ana María Guzmán de Vásquez Colmenares, author of *Tradiciones gastronómicas oaxaqueñas*, says, "There must be something magical to the number seven, for the number of Oaxacan *moles* coincides with the wonders of the world, the theological virtues, the wise men of Athens who in all their wisdom elected the number seven to represent justice." My curiosity is fired. As a professional chef with my own Mexican ancestry, and having lived in Oaxaca for many years, I am determined to explore this mystery. How could the seventh *mole* have escaped me? And what better time to search for it? For the Day of the Dead, every family in the state is making at least one *mole*, sometimes two or three, to place on the altar to please their ancestral spirits. All the women in the village—the experts—gather at the *molino* to grind their ingredients and share the latest gossip. Just the place to start my quest.

With my son Kaelin on my back I head down a dirt road toward the *pueblo* in search of the first *mole*. As I cross the river to get to the center of town, I think about the history of *mole*. There are many versions of its origin; most of them place its conception in Puebla de los Angeles, a beautiful, almost Spanish, city east of Mexico City. It is said that a group of nuns at the Convent of Santa Rosa first made the dish to please their bishop during a visit of the viceroy from Spain. In my mind, each sister wished to contribute something special to the sauce. Starting with an original native dish using dried chiles, tomatoes, and seeds, they added all the spices available from the Old World. Then they added the revered chocolate made from cacao and sugar, which, forbidden to women at that time, was served only in the royal courts. The original Nahuatl word *molli* means "mixture," which is what it truly is, and a fine one at that.

In Oaxaca, *mole* was made in the pre-Hispanic royal courts, according to my scholarly friend Maestro Rafael Ricardez. Rafael has an extensive array of archaeological books that describe fossilized *mole* ingredients found in the tombs at Monte Albán, the ruins I can see from my living room windows. *Mole* may have been served at the Zapotec palace in nearby Zaachila. I can imagine Zapotec women of the fifth century B.C. kneeling to grind chiles and tomatoes on the three-legged stone *metates* (flat grinding stones used in the home), much the same as you can see in the kitchens of *pueblo* homes around Oaxaca today.

As we approach the *pueblo*, the smell of roasting chiles permeates the air, passing through the *carrizo* (bamboo) kitchen walls of the homes we walk by. To beat the last-minute crowds, I have already purchased my ingredients at my favorite chile stall in the Mercado de Abastos. The stall is run by Eliseo, a gregarious man with a handlebar mustache, who is a wealth of information about chiles, and *moles* in general. He has stacked, from floor to ceiling, bags of dried chiles from all over Mexico. Nuts, raisins, large rolls of *canela* (cinnamon bark), seeds, and spices clutter the walls and benches and hang from the roof. All these ingredients, and more, are used to prepare the various *moles*, *guisados*, *pipianes*, and other pungent Oaxacan dishes. Face-to-face with more than twenty varieties of chiles, my heart sings and my nostrils open to embrace the pungent smells. Some chiles remind me of musty old sacks, like a fine burgundy. The smokiness of the *chipotle* and *pasilla Oaxaqueño* recall the smokehouses of the Texas Hill Country. The heat of the *árbol* and Japanese varieties of chiles take me back to Thailand, where I cried over meals that were so hot and so good!

Finally, we reach the home of the local *huesero* (village chiropractor), Chico Machine, and his wife, Paula, an excellent cook. Paula's eyesight may be failing, but her taste buds are not. She is making the king of *moles*—*Mole Negro Oaxaqueño* (page 263). This fiery black sauce is a fascinating combination of dried chiles from the region. It calls for *chilhuacle negro*, a round black chile found only in Oaxaca, plus other chiles—as many as five in all. The chiles are toasted black and soaked. The onions and garlic are roasted. The tomatoes and *tomatillos* are fried slowly until they dry out. The nuts and seeds—some are toasted and some are fried. The sesame seeds take the most care—they have to be fried slowly, carefully, with much love and attention. Hence the Mexican saying, "You are the sesame seed of my *mole!*" The spices, peppercorns, cloves, and cinnamon sticks are also toasted to bring out their flavor. The *hierbas de olor*—bundles of thyme, marjoram, and oregano—are often fried along with plantains, bread, and raisins. In some regions, ginger, tortillas, and little apples are also added. Then the whole mixture is ready for the walk to the *molino* to be ground, replacing the old custom of using the *metate* at home.

Paula's daughter, Panchita, has already returned from the *molino* and lard is smoking in a large earthenware *cazuela* over a wood fire. Paula pours the smooth black sauce into the pot, unmindful of the flames licking at her arms. She stirs it for more than an hour until it thickens, and then adds turkey broth. For the crowning touch, chocolate and toasted avocado leaves are dropped into the aromatic concoction. Then she adjusts the seasonings. *"¡Ya! ¡Hecho!"* It is ready! Of course, there are as many kinds of *mole negro* as there are families. There are hundreds if not thousands of combinations. It's like the stuff dreams are made of. In fact, I have noticed every time I eat the rich, black, silky smooth sauce that it has a great effect on me—I have fantastic dreams that night!

I find the second *mole* of Oaxaca in the *comedor*, or home restaurant, of my friend and teacher Carlota. As we enter, the aroma of *Calabaza en Dulce* (page 280) (candied squash) envelops us, and my son, who is getting heavy on my back, begins calling for food. Carlota is frying tomatoes for her mouthwatering *Mole Coloradito Oaxaqueño* (page 266) over a charcoal fire. A heavyset woman with a toothless grin, she chuckles with delight at our arrival. *Chiles anchos* and *guajillos* are soaking beside her as she fries the many ingredients needed for the brick-red *mole*. Though not as sharp as *mole negro*, it is equally tasty.

Carlota invites us to eat some of her green *mole*, called simply *"verde."* Hers is made with *espinazo* (pork backbone), boneless pork shoulder, and small white beans, though I have made it with chicken. My first encounter with *Mole Verde* (page 268) was on the Oaxacan coast, where it sauced *huachinango* (red snapper). This mild, healthy *mole* is a mixture of green herbs—*epazote*, parsley, and *hierba santa*—ground with *tomatillos* and fresh *chile huachinango*, a type of *jalapeño*. Flavored with stock and thickened with *masa*, it is heavenly aromatic. *Mole* usually tastes better on the second day, but *mole verde* tastes best as fresh as possible. When eaten right off the fire, it is exceptionally good. *Mole* is traditionally eaten with tortillas, the edible spoon, and here at Carlota's is no exception. As I dip the tortilla into the green sauce to feed Kaelin (who is a *mole verde* connoisseur), two other Oaxacan *moles* come to mind.

The fourth *mole*—*mole amarillo*—is also quite versatile. It is prepared to serve with chicken, venison, beef, or pork or made into empanadas cooked fresh to order on the street or at fiestas. *Mole amarillo* is also made vegetarian style with *chepil* (a fresh herb that grows wild in the rainy season), zucchini, chayote, and *guías* (the tender young growth of a native squash plant). For an exotic touch, a local *señora* suggested adding the bright-red flowers of the *frijolón* (scarlet runner bean) plant. *Mole amarillo* uses one or more of the following chiles—*ancho, guajillo, chilcostles, chilhuacle amarillo,* or a yellow chile from the coast called *costeño amarillo.* Thickened with *masa*, its herbal seasoning varies with the meat used.

The fifth *mole* that came to mind was *mole rojo* or *colorado*, an *ancho* and *chilhuacle rojo*–based sauce. *Mole rojo* traces back to a pre-Hispanic *clemole* sauce, according to Ana María Guzmán de Vásquez Colmenares. It is used for enchiladas, *Pozole "Mixteco"* (page 271), a layered "dry" soup of hominy cooked with aromatic leaves and pork, topped with *mole rojo* (page 347), and other dishes.

After spending the late morning in San Lorenzo Cacaotepec buying flowers, jícama, and sugarcane to make arches for our altar, I drop in at Mamá Chica's to prepare the final part of my *Calabaza en Dulce* (page 280). Dark brown *piloncillo* is added to the squash pieces that I have helped clean and cook. They are cooked once in *cal* and a second time with fig leaves. Mamá Chica is a handsome, strong, dark-skinned woman who usually wears her white braids piled on top of her head. She is one of my mentors here in the *pueblo*; she generously shares her knowledge of natural remedies and recipes. She is the mother of one of my closest friends, Yolanda, and I have spent many hours in her kitchen, which at the moment is transformed into a huge altar with pictures of saints, flowers, and fruit. I learned about the sixth *mole, Manchamanteles Oaxaqueño* (page 276) ("tablecloth stainer") from her. Though it's a recipe originally from Michoacán, Oaxacans consider it one of their seven *moles*. It uses dried *ancho, guajillo,* and the local *chiles chilcostles* in a mixture thickened with sesame seeds and simmered with pieces of fresh pineapple, ripe plantains, and tiny apples.

After promising to return to eat *mole* with Mamá Chica's family the following day, we leave for the *molino* to see what Doña Margarita, the owner, is grinding. *Molinos* are the mills where various types of ingredients are ground—for example, corn for *masa*, and cacao for chocolate. There are mills for wet ingredients, such as soaked corn or chiles, and dry mills that grind cacao for chocolate or wheat for flour. The mills also serve as meeting places where women come together to share the latest gossip. It is already eleven o'clock, two hours past normal closing time. All the corn has been ground and buckets of soaked, toasted, and fried *mole* ingredients are ready for the various families. The heat of the grinding pushes out into the air soaked with the scents of the different *moles*. What a rush for a *mole* lover like me! This is the heart and soul of Mexico! There is nothing better than seeing the many ingredients, knowing each family has ordered different measures and varieties to suit their own traditions, and imagining each family's pride in what goes into their particular sauces.

Next we stop at the chocolate *molino*, where another crowd is forming. I have already toasted and peeled my cacao beans at home to grind with long rolled cinnamon sticks and sugar. I wait with eager anticipation as the cacao mixture goes through the first grinder, coming out as a hot chocolate liquor to be hand mixed into the sugar. This mass is then poured into the second grinding mill, where it comes out a fine chocolate powder. It is put into a bag to keep warm for my trip home, where I will pound it out into tablets and pat it into tin molds made especially for this fiesta.

Once home, I begin my own preparations for the celebration of *Muertos*, the best holiday of the year for me. These two days are spent eating *moles*, black tortillas, and sweets with other families of the village. We light candles and incense and commune with our ancestors. We remember our friends and loved ones who have departed from this world by placing their pictures and their favorite treats on the altar. We drink chocolate and eat a special bread adorned with tiny painted faces, called *Pan de Muerto* (page 279), and try the heady taste of *mezcalito*. Bands of *muerteros*—men dressed as women and wearing masks—travel from house to house entertaining and making raucous jokes in exchange for food and drink.

The final morning, Israel, my husband's partner, and his Aunt Celia arrive at Rancho Aurora, our home, for a traditional breakfast. Tía Celia, a large, glamorous woman with jet-black hair, pale skin, and thick makeup, navigates our sloping driveway in her high heels. She grips the huge arm of Israel, a rotund man in his fifties, who is having a bit of a time himself. Although in her home in Oaxaca she has a cook, Tía Celia prides herself on her culinary abilities. *"Hija,"* cries Tía affectionately as she envelops me, nearly crushing me with a covered plastic bucket. She presses the bucket into my hands, which I immediately open to take a peek. It is her famous *mole chichilo*, she explains. *Chichilo Oaxaqueño* (page 274), a rare and provocative *mole*, gets its flavor from burning chile seeds on top of a tortilla. When all the seeds are blackened, they are soaked and ground. The chile seed mixture is blended with the other ingredients at the end of the cooking cycle, along with toasted avocado leaves. Chiles used include the *chilhuacle negro* from the Cañada Chica region of Oaxaca, and *chile guajillo* or *mulato*. *Chichilo* is served as a stew of well-spiced beef and pork along with potatoes, chayotes, and green beans. Usually garnished with roasted fresh chiles, onion slices, and lime wedges, it is a rich, unique, and wonderful blend. *This* must be the seventh *mole* of Oaxaca! My quest has ended where it began—in my own kitchen. After searching, tasting, and cooking *moles* for years, I have discovered that there *are* seven *moles* of Oaxaca, but hundreds of variations of each. Each cook has her own secret ingredients for this ancient magical sauce.

The recipes that follow are for the *moles* and a few other dishes made especially for *Día de Muertos*. I have included recipes on how to reconstitute the *mole* pastes with fried tomatoes and the broth of whatever meat you are going to serve. *Mole* paste is a concentration of all the prepared ingredients of a *mole*, made into a paste and fried for hours to dry. The well-fried paste will keep for months. This is an easier way to enjoy the authentic flavors of Oaxaca but spend fewer hours in the kitchen. I do encourage your getting a cooking friend to join you for an adventure in *mole* making and to make all the *moles* one by one. They are quite distinct and exciting to taste. *¡Buen provecho!*

IN THIS CHAPTER

ENCHILADAS OAXAQUEÑAS

Tortillas in Coloradito Mole or Red Mole

This Oaxacan-style dish is the perfect way to use leftover mole *sauce. In Oaxaca, enchiladas are traditionally made with* mole coloradito *or* mole rojo. *We always use* queso fresco *made by Rosa, our neighbor, but you can find many varieties of this "fresh cheese" in Mexican specialty food stores. The parsley is important to the dish, as it gives a fresh green taste as well as color. Enchiladas are red (the* mole), *white (the cheese and onions), and green (the parsley)—the colors of the Mexican flag, which makes a patriotic dish. ¡Viva México! You can stuff the triangles with chicken or cheese and fry lightly. Serve with black beans or with a fried egg for breakfast. For a heartier meal, serve with a piece of grilled* tasajo *(page 342),* cecina *(page 342), or grilled chicken. These are also nice as a light meal served with a salad. You can use* mole negro *(page 346) instead of the* mole coloradito *(page 346) to make* enmoladas *(page 321).*

MAKES 6 SERVINGS

4 cups mole coloradito oaxaqueño *or* mole rojo *sauce (pages 266 and 347)*

¼ cup chicken stock (page 343), if needed

½ cup sunflower or vegetable oil

12 corn tortillas

2 medium white onions, thinly sliced or cut into thin lengthwise wedges

¾ pound queso fresco, crumbled (see page 346)

24 sprigs (1¼ cups) flat-leaf parsley, leaves only

In an 8-inch cast-iron pan over medium heat, heat the *mole* to a boil, stirring constantly. Lower the heat and simmer 5 minutes. Add a little stock or water to thin the *mole* so that it just coats the back of a spoon, no more. Keep the *mole* hot.

In another 8-inch cast-iron frying pan, heat the oil until smoking hot. Fry each tortilla quickly on both sides until soft and then drain. Place a tortilla in the *mole* sauce and coat both sides with the sauce. Place the coated tortilla on a plate and fold it in half, then fold it again to make a triangle. Repeat with another tortilla. Lay the second tortilla on top of the first with the points going in the same direction. Spoon more sauce on top. Garnish with some onion slices, *queso fresco*, and parsley. Repeat with the other tortillas, two per plate. Serve immediately.

Hint: If you get fresh, hot tortillas made with *nixtamal*, you can place them directly into the sauce and omit frying them.

TORTILLAS EMBARRADAS
Tortillas Smeared with Bean Chile Paste

In San Felipe Tejalapan, most of the women are tortilla makers with a tradition exclusive to them. Rancho Aurora is part of this village, and we enjoy fresh handmade tortillas and tlayudas *delivered to our door five days a week. During the Day of the Dead, special tortillas are made, smeared with spicy black bean paste, and stacked on the altar to entice the spirits. After the fiesta they are given out to family and friends. They are best reheated until crispy. I look forward to receiving mine every year.*

MAKES 10 SERVINGS

6 tablespoons poleo *(see page 337), or 10 medium avocado leaves (about 5 inches each), or 1 tablespoon aniseeds*

7 chiles de árbol (see page 330) or Chinese or Thai chiles

2 cups Frijoles Negros de Olla *(page 146), broth reserved*

½ teaspoon salt, or to taste

10 tlayudas, or 10–18 tortillas 5–8 inches in diameter, left out of the package overnight to air dry

Toast the *poleo* or avocado leaves and chiles on a 10-inch dry *comal*, griddle, or in a cast-iron frying pan, until browned. Put the beans, *poleo* or avocado leaves (see Hint), salt, chiles, and reserved bean broth in a blender. Blend until smooth.

On a 10-inch dry *comal*, griddle, or in a cast-iron frying pan over medium heat, heat a *tlayuda* or tortilla on both sides, rotating it every 30 seconds so it won't burn. Spread approximately 3 tablespoons of the bean paste on a *tlayuda* or tortilla with the back of a spoon. The paste should go out to the edge of the *tlayuda* or tortilla. Continue with the remaining *tlayudas* or tortillas and place each one on top of the prior *tlayuda* or tortilla. Set aside.

Remove a *tlayuda* or tortilla from the stack and heat on both sides, turning frequently on a 10-inch dry *comal*, griddle, or in a cast-iron frying pan. Serve hot.

Hint: If using avocado leaves, toast them on both sides on a dry *comal* until they give off their aroma. Hold the stem of each leaf and crumble both sides of the leaf into the blender. Discard the stems.

TAMALES OAXAQUEÑOS
Oaxacan-Style Mole Tamales

These tamales wrapped in banana leaves are the famous tamales of Oaxaca. They are filled with chicken, turkey, or pork combined with mole negro or mole coloradito. The two moles are interchangeable according to what you may have on hand. These are labor-intensive, but quite worth the effort. I always joke that one of the reasons Mexicans have extended families is so there are always enough hands to help in making tamales. Get yourself some extra hands to help you eat them afterward, too. One of the biggest rewards is the aroma of the tamal pot in your kitchen.

MAKES 24 *TAMALES*

Seasoning ingredients for pork stock (page 344)

1¼ pounds boneless pork shoulder, cut in 2-inch cubes

Salt to taste

2 pounds prepared masa for tamales or 3½ cups masa harina for tamales

2 teaspoons baking powder

1½ cups lard (¾ pound), softened

24 banana leaves, fresh or frozen (see Hints)

4 cups mole negro (page 263) or mole coloradito (page 266)

1 package cornhusks, soaked in hot water for ½ hour

In a large 6-quart stockpot, bring 3 quarts of water and the seasoning ingredients to a boil following the instructions on page 344. Once boiling, add the pork and return to a boil. Skim off the foam that appears on the surface and discard. Lower the heat, cover, and cook the meat 1 hour or until tender. Remove the meat from the pot and set aside. Reduce the stock by simmering, uncovered, for 10 minutes more. Remove the pot from the heat and strain the stock to remove the vegetables. Reserve the stock.

If using prepared *masa*, break up the *masa* in a large bowl. If using *masa harina*, put it in a mixing bowl and add 2¼ cups warm water. Mix well and allow the dough to sit 15 minutes. Add the baking powder to either *masa* and mix in well. Add the lard if it is fresh (soft). If the lard is the block type, whip it as much as possible to get it light, then add it to the *masa*. Mix in the lard well by hand or electric mixer. Add 3 to 4 teaspoons salt to 1½ cups reserved stock and add to the dough, stirring well. Taste for salt and add more if necessary. You should be able to taste the salt, but it should not be salty. Whip the *masa* well until light, about 20 minutes.

Cut the banana leaves into 12-inch pieces and parboil in 1 quart of water until soft, about 15 minutes. Cool and drain the leaves; blot dry with a cloth.

Heat the *mole* and add more pork stock if necessary to make a sauce thick enough to coat the back of the spoon, no more. Let it cool.

Shred the cooked pork.

Shred 5 of the cornhusks into strips and tie the strips together in pairs.

Place a single banana leaf on a tray. Place 3 level tablespoons of *masa* on the center of the leaf. Place a sheet of plastic (a plastic bag cut in half works best) on top of the mass of dough. Distend the *masa* to almost cover the whole leaf, leaving a 1-inch margin on all sides. Remove the plastic wrap and set aside for the next *tamal*. In the center, place 1 tablespoon of shredded pork and 3 level tablespoons of *mole*. Fold the top edge of the banana leaf down and bottom edge up to form thirds, then fold in the sides, one by one, to make a small (or large) package. Tie with the cornhusk ties to secure. Repeat with the remaining banana leaves.

Fill a *tamalera* or steamer with salted water to the level of the rack. Place the rack in the pot and cover the rack with the extra cornhusks for flavor. Place *tamales* on rack and steam for 1 hour or until *masa* falls away from the banana leaf when opened.

Hints: You can reheat the tamales the next day on a comal or griddle by grilling them in their "wrappers," covered with a lid or steaming them, in a steamer. I prefer the slight charring of the leaves on the griddle, giving them an added smoky flavor.

In looking for banana leaves, try to get Thai leaves in the Asian markets that are frozen. I find the Filipino variety to be thick and tend to crack a lot. When you use the frozen leaves, allow them to defrost in their packages, then boil according to directions.

Minerva Méndez and her comadre with toasted chiles for Mole Negro, Fiesta de Virgen de Rosario (Alfredo Díaz Mora)

MOLE NEGRO OAXAQUEÑO
Oaxacan Black Mole

Every year families in Oaxaca get together before the Día de Muertos *to make the most celebrated dish of all—*Mole Negro Oaxaqueño. *A dish of* mole *is placed on the family altar to entice the departed loved ones to come back and join in the celebration. Days before the actual event, women's hands are busy cleaning chiles, cracking nuts, peeling cacao beans, and gathering herbs to make up the twenty-odd ingredients used in this fascinating concoction. Once the components are assembled, the fires are lit and each ingredient is either toasted, roasted, or fried to coax out the most essential flavors. For big fiestas, you need enough* mole *to serve the whole village, so the process can take days. Often there are three generations of women working on the same* mole *together, each one knowing her part in the long, complicated process.*

MAKES 12 SERVINGS

Seasoning ingredients for chicken stock (double the recipe; page 343)

2 chickens (3–3½ pounds each), cut into 12 pieces, skin removed, backs and necks saved for stock

5 chiles chilhuacles negros (about ½ ounces), stemmed, seeded, and deveined (see page 331); save the seeds

5 chiles guajillos (about 1 ounce), stemmed, seeded, and deveined (see page 331); save the seeds

4 chiles pasillas mexicanos (about 1 ounce), stemmed, seeded, and deveined (see page 331); save the seeds

4 chiles anchos negros (about 2 ounces), stemmed, seeded, and deveined (see page 330); save the seeds

In a 6-quart stockpot, heat 5 quarts water and seasoning ingredients to a boil. Add chicken pieces and poach, covered, over low heat for 35 to 45 minutes, until cooked through and juices run clear when pierced with a fork. Remove the meat from the stock. Strain and reserve the stock.

Heat 2 quarts of water in a kettle. On a 10-inch dry *comal*, griddle, or in a cast-iron frying pan, toast the chiles over medium heat until blackened, but not burnt, about 10 minutes. Place the chiles in a large bowl, cover with the hot water, and soak for ½ hour. Remove the chiles from the soaking water with tongs, placing small batches in a blender with ¼ cup of the soaking water to blend smooth. Put the chile puree through a strainer to remove the skins.

In the same dry *comal*, griddle, or frying pan, grill the onion and garlic over medium heat for 10 minutes. Set aside. Toast the almonds, peanuts, cinnamon stick, peppercorns, and cloves on the *comal*, griddle, or cast-iron frying pan for about 5 minutes. Remove them from the pan.

Over the same heat, toast the chile seeds, taking care to blacken but not burn them, about 20 minutes. Try to do this outside or in a well-ventilated place, because the seeds will

2 chiles chipotles mecos *(about ¼ ounce), stemmed, seeded, and deveined (see page 330); save the seeds*

1 medium white onion, cut into *quarters*

½ small head of garlic, cloves *separated*

2 heaping tablespoons whole *almonds*

2 tablespoons shelled and skinned *raw peanuts*

1 piece of Mexican cinnamon, *1 inch long (see page 337)*

3 black peppercorns

3 whole cloves

3 tablespoons sunflower or vege-*table oil, or more as needed (see Hints)*

1½ tablespoons raisins

1 slice of bread *(pan de yema, Pan de Muerto; see pages 279 and 347) or challah or other egg bread*

1 small ripe plantain or banana, *cut into ½-inch-thick slices (about 1 cup)*

½ cup sesame seeds *(2 ounces)*

2 pecan halves

½ pound tomatoes *(1 medium–large round or 4–5 plum), cut into chunks*

¼ pound tomatillos *(3–4 medium), cut into chunks (see page 327)*

1 sprig thyme, *or ½ teaspoon dried*

1 sprig Oaxacan oregano, *or ½ tea-spoon dried (see page 336)*

2 tablespoons lard, sunflower oil, *or vegetable oil*

1½ bars Mexican chocolate *(4½ ounces; see page 349)*

give off very strong fumes. When the seeds are completely black, light them with a match and let them burn themselves out. Remove from the heat and place in a bowl. Soak the blackened seeds in 1 cup of cold water for 10 minutes. Drain the seeds and grind them in a blender for about 2 minutes. Add the blended chile seeds to the chile mixture.

Heat 3 tablespoons of oil in an 8-inch cast-iron frying pan over medium heat until smoking. Add the raisins and fry until plump, approximately 1 minute. Remove from the pan. Fry the bread slice in the same oil until browned, about 5 minutes, over medium heat. Remove from pan. Fry the plantain in the same oil until well browned, approximately 10 minutes, over medium heat. Set aside. Fry the sesame seeds, stirring constantly over low heat, adding more if needed. When the sesame seeds start to brown, about 5 minutes, add the pecans and brown 2 minutes more. Remove all from the pan, let cool, and grind finely in a spice grinder. It takes a bit of time, but this is the only way to grind the seeds and nuts finely enough.

Wipe out the frying pan and fry the tomatoes, *tomatillos,* thyme, and oregano over medium to high heat, allowing the juices to almost evaporate, about 15 minutes. Blend well, using ½ cup of reserved stock if needed to blend, and set aside. Place the nuts, bread, plantains, raisins, onion, garlic, and spices in a blender in small batches, and blend well, adding about 1 cup of stock to make it smooth.

In a heavy 4-quart stockpot, heat 2 tablespoons of lard or oil until smoking and fry the chile paste over medium to low heat, stirring constantly so it will not burn, approximately 20 minutes. When it is "dry," add the tomato puree and fry until the liquid has evaporated, about 10 minutes. Add the ground ingredients, including the sesame seed paste, to the pot. Stir constantly with a wooden spoon until well incorporated, about 10 minutes. Add 1 cup chicken stock to the *mole,* stir well, and allow to cook 20 minutes, stirring occasionally.

Break up the chocolate and add to the pot, stirring until it is melted and incorporated into the mixture.

Toast the avocado leaf briefly over the flame if you have a gas range or in a dry frying pan and then add it to the pot. Slowly add more stock to the *mole,* as it will keep thickening

1 avocado leaf, fresh or dried (hoja de aguacate; see page 338)

Salt to taste

as it cooks. Add enough salt to bring out the flavor. Let simmer another 30 minutes, stirring occasionally so it does not stick, adding stock as needed. The *mole* should not be thick, just thick enough to coat the back of a spoon.

Place the cooked chicken pieces in the leftover stock in a saucepan and heat through.

To serve, place a piece of chicken in a shallow bowl and ladle ¾ cup of *mole* sauce over to cover it completely. Serve immediately with lots of hot corn tortillas.

Hints: Be sure to put the blended chiles through a sieve or food mill, or you will have pieces of chile skin in your *mole*, which needs to be silky smooth.

You can use oil instead of lard to fry the *mole*, but the flavor will change dramatically. In our *pueblo*, people traditionally use turkey instead of chicken, and sometimes add pieces of pork and beef to enhance the flavor. You can use any leftover *mole* and chicken meat to make *Enmoladas* (page 321) or *Tamales Oaxaqueños* (page 261) made with banana leaves.

Pan de Muerto *(Stephen Honeybill)*

Inspired by María Taboada and Paula Martínez

MOLE COLORADITO OAXAQUEÑO
Oaxacan Coloradito Mole

I learned to make this flavorful combination of chiles and spices from my friend and teacher Carlota Santos. She has a little restaurant in her home where my husband, Eric, used to eat quite often before I came to live in Oaxaca. She always joked that she lost her best customer when I started to cook here, but gained a friend in me when she taught me the dishes she knew he liked to eat! I spent hours in her kitchen learning about this mole *and the tamales and enchiladas you can make with the leftovers.*

MAKES 8 SERVINGS

Seasoning ingredients for chicken stock (double the recipe; page 343)

1½ chickens (about 4½ pounds), cut into 8 servings, reserving the back and neck for stock

18 chiles anchos (about 9 ounces), stemmed and seeded (see page 330)

21 chiles guajillos (about 4½ ounces), stemmed and seeded (see page 331)

2 black peppercorns

2 whole cloves

1 whole allspice

1 piece of Mexican cinnamon, about 1 inch long (see page 337)

½ small head of garlic, cloves separated

1 small white onion, quartered

1 pound ripe tomatoes (2 medium–large round or 8–10 plum), quartered

1 sprig marjoram or Oaxacan oregano (see page 336), or ½ teaspoon dried

In a heavy 7-quart stockpot, heat 6 quarts water and the seasoning ingredients to a boil. Add the chicken pieces and lower heat to a simmer. Cover and cook the chicken for about 35 to 45 minutes or until the meat is tender and the juices run clear when the dark meat is pierced with a fork. Remove the chicken, strain, and reserve the stock.

Bring 2 quarts of water to a boil. On a 10-inch dry *comal,* griddle, or in a cast-iron frying pan over low heat, toast the chiles on both sides for about 10 minutes, toasting the *chiles anchos* a bit slower and longer than the *chiles guajillos* because of their thicker skins. Toast them on both sides until their skins start to blister and they give off their aroma. Remove the chiles from the *comal* or pan, place them in a medium bowl, and cover with the hot water. Soak the chiles for 20 minutes, turning to soften them. Puree in a blender, using as little of the chile water as possible, about 1 cup. Pass the puree through a sieve or food mill to remove the skins.

On the *comal,* toast the peppercorns, cloves, allspice, and cinnamon stick. Quickly grill the garlic and onion, turning them often until they become translucent. Cool them, then puree the spices, onion, and garlic in a blender with ½ cup of the reserved stock. Set aside.

In an 8-inch cast-iron frying pan over medium heat, cook tomato pieces and marjoram or oregano with no oil until condensed, 10 to 15 minutes. First they will give off their juices, then they will dry out. Puree the tomato mixture in a blender, then pass the mixture through a sieve or food mill.

2 tablespoons plus 1 teaspoon sunflower or vegetable oil

½ ripe plantain, sliced

½ bolillo or French roll, sliced (see
page 347)

1 tablespoon raisins

5 whole, unpeeled almonds

3 tablespoons lard, sunflower oil,
or vegetable oil

½ cup sesame seeds

2 bars Mexican chocolate (3 ounces
each; see page 349), or to taste

Salt to taste

In a medium frying pan, heat 2 tablespoons of the oil over medium heat and fry the plantain and bread slices until brown, about 12 minutes. Remove from the pan. Add more oil (if needed) and fry the raisins until they are plump, about 3 minutes. Remove them from the pan. Fry the almonds until light brown, about 4 minutes. Remove from the pan. Place the plantain, *bolillo*, raisins, and almonds in a blender with 1½ cups of the reserved broth and blend until smooth. Wipe out the frying pan and put over low heat. Add 1 teaspoon of oil and the sesame seeds and fry until brown, about 10 minutes, stirring constantly. Cool the seeds and grind in a *molcajete* or spice grinder.

In a heavy 6-quart stockpot, heat 1 tablespoon of lard over high heat until smoking. Add the chile puree a little at a time, stirring constantly. It will splatter about a bit, but keep stirring. Lower heat to medium and after about 20 minutes, or when chile puree is thick, add the tomato mixture and continue to cook, about 15 minutes, stirring to keep the *mole* from sticking or burning. Add the onion and ground spice mixture and stir well. Add the pureed plantain mixture and ground sesame seeds, stirring constantly, about 10 minutes. Add 4½ to 5 cups of the reserved broth to thin the sauce, then add the chocolate, stirring constantly. When the chocolate dissolves, add the salt. Let it cook down for 30 minutes, stirring occasionally. The more time it has to cook, the better.

Return the chicken pieces to the broth and heat through. Add more broth to the *mole* if needed. The *mole* should be thick enough to just coat a spoon, no more. Place a piece of chicken on a serving plate and ladle a large spoonful of *mole* on top. It should completely cover the meat. Serve with corn tortillas.

Hint: You can use turkey or pork instead of chicken. If you want to make it less *picante*, use half the amount of chiles and the same amount of the other ingredients. You can use any leftover *mole* for *Tamales Oaxaqueños* (page 261) made with banana leaves or *Enchiladas Oaxaqueñas* (page 259).

MOLE VERDE
Green Mole

This is one of the seven legendary moles of Oaxaca, and the only one made with so many fresh ingredients. I have eaten this dish made with chicken and fish, but my favorite is with pork backstrap with a few pieces of boneless pork shoulder added. The white beans give the mole extra bulk and make it quite filling. Don't confuse this with the Puebla-style green mole, which is different with its pumpkin seeds and radish leaves, but equally delicious.

MAKES 8 SERVINGS

1 pound baby-back ribs, cut Chinese style

Seasoning ingredients for pork stock, made with baby-back ribs (page 344)

1 pound boneless pork shoulder, in 2-inch cubes

Salt to taste

¾ cup dried small white beans

1 pound tomatillos (13–14 large), husked (see page 327)

1 pound green tomatoes (about 6), cut into chunks

1 medium white onion, cut into chunks

1 head of garlic, cloves separated

9 large chiles jalapeños, seeded (see page 329)

1 tablespoon sunflower or vegetable oil

In a heavy 6-quart stockpot, combine 3 quarts of cold water and the ingredients for the pork stock. Bring to a boil as instructed on page 344. Add the meat and return to a boil. Skim off the foam that appears on the surface and discard. Lower the heat to a simmer and cook, covered, until tender, about 1 hour. Remove the meat from the pot and set aside. Reduce the stock by simmering, uncovered, over high heat for 10 minutes more. Remove the pot from the heat, strain the broth to remove the vegetables, and season with salt. Reserve the stock.

In a 2-quart saucepan, combine the white beans with enough water to cover, about 1 quart, and bring to a boil. Lower the heat and simmer, covered, until tender, about 1¼ hours. When the beans are soft, add salt to taste. Drain the beans and reserve.

Place the *tomatillos* in a 2-quart saucepan with enough water to cover, about 1 cup. Boil for about 10 minutes or until they just change color. Remove from the heat and drain. In a blender, place the *tomatillos*, green tomatoes, onion, garlic, *chiles jalapeños*, and 1 cup of reserved pork stock. Puree until smooth.

8 ounces prepared corn masa *for tortillas* or 1 cup masa harina *for tortillas mixed with ½ cup plus 1 tablespoon warm water*

½ cup parsley leaves

½ cup fresh epazote leaves *(see page 336)*

½ cup hierba santa *leaves, ribs removed (about 4 leaves; see page 336)*

Black pepper to taste

In a heavy 6-quart stockpot, heat the oil over high heat. When it smokes, add the pureed green tomato mixture, stirring until heated through, about 10 minutes.

Place the *masa* in a blender with 2 cups of the pork stock. Puree until smooth and add to the green tomato mixture. Heat to thicken, stirring, at least 15 minutes, over medium heat.

Put the parsley, *epazote*, and *hierba santa* in the blender with enough stock to blend well. Add the herb mixture to the green tomato mixture and simmer for 15 minutes over low heat. Add salt and pepper to taste. Add the meat and beans to the green tomato mixture and adjust the salt. Thin with at least 1 cup of the pork stock, as needed. The sauce should be thick enough to coat a spoon, no more.

Return the pork ribs and meat to the stock and heat through.

Serve each person one piece of pork rib and one piece of boneless pork shoulder topped with lots of sauce and beans. Serve with fresh corn tortillas.

Hint: You can substitute chicken (with chicken stock) or whole filleted fresh fish (with fish stock) for the pork.

MOLE AMARILLO DE POLLO
Yellow Mole with Chicken

This mole is one of the most versatile of the seven moles. You can use pork, beef, or vegetables instead of chicken. While the chicken is always seasoned with hierba santa, *the pork is seasoned with cilantro and the beef with* pitiona *(a local herb with tiny purple flowers). The vegetarian version usually has* chepil *(a local herb), fresh corn slices, and squash vine tips. Any variety can use dumplings called* chochoyones, *made from dried corn dough, or fresh* masa.

MAKES 6 SERVINGS

4½ cups or more chicken stock (page 343)

1 chicken (3–4 pounds), cut into 6 pieces, skin removed (optional), back and neck reserved for stock

Salt

½ pound small new potatoes (6–8), scrubbed

½ pound green beans, cut diagonally into 3-inch pieces

1 chayote, peeled and cut into 2-inch cubes (see page 326)

6 chiles chilcostles (about ½ ounce), or chiles chihuacles amarillos (about 1 ounce), or 6 chiles guajillos (about 1 ounce), stemmed, seeded, and deveined (see pages 330 and 331)

2 chiles anchos (about 1 ounce), stemmed, seeded, and deveined (see page 330)

5 chiles costeños amarillos (less than 1 ounce) or chiles de onza amarillo (less than 1 ounce), stemmed, seeded, and deveined (see page 330)

3 whole cloves

3 whole allspice

3 black peppercorns

1 teaspoon dried Oaxacan oregano (see page 336)

1 pound tomatoes (2 medium–large round or 8–10 plum)

5 large tomatillos (6 ounces total), husked (see page 327)

1 medium white onion, cut into chunks

In a heavy 4-quart stockpot, heat the chicken stock, add the chicken pieces, cover, lower the heat, and cook until tender, about ½ hour. Add salt to taste. Remove the chicken pieces from the stock and cook the potatoes, green beans, and chayote in the stock, each one separately, until each vegetable is just done. Set aside. Reserve the stock.

Bring 2 cups of water to a boil. On a 10-inch dry *comal*, griddle, or in a cast-iron frying pan over medium heat, toast the outer skin of the chiles until they start to blister and begin to give off their aroma. Remove chiles from the *comal* and soak in the hot water for 20 minutes. Drain the chiles and reserve the water. Place the chiles in a blender with 1½ cups of the chile water and grind until smooth. Pass through a sieve or food mill to keep chile skins from going into the dish. Set aside in a bowl.

On the *comal*, toast the cloves, allspice, peppercorns, and oregano until they give off their scents. Remove and place in a blender.

In a 2-quart saucepan, boil the tomatoes and *tomatillos* in 1 cup of water until the *tomatillos* just change color, about 10 minutes. Skin the red tomatoes and discard the skins. Add the tomatoes with the *tomatillos*, onion, garlic, and 1 cup of the reserved stock to the blender and blend until smooth. Pass through a sieve or food mill to remove the seeds. Set aside in a bowl.

In a heavy 4-quart stockpot, heat the lard until smoking. Fry the chile puree over medium heat, about 15 minutes, stirring constantly. Add the tomato mixture and spices to the chile mixture and fry together about 15 minutes.

Put the *masa* and 1 cup of the stock in a blender and blend well. Add to the tomato and chile mixture. Allow to thicken, about 15 minutes, stirring constantly. Add 1 tablespoon of salt or more to taste. Thin the *mole* with 2 to 2½ cups of stock, or more if needed. It should be thick enough to coat the back of a spoon. Add the whole *hierba santa* leaves to the *mole*. Keep warm.

½ head of garlic, cloves separated

1 tablespoon lard, sunflower oil, or vegetable oil

4 ounces prepared masa for tortillas, or ½ cup masa harina for tortillas mixed with ¼ cup plus 1 tablespoon warm water

2 large or 3 small hierba santa leaves (see page 336)

For the chochoyones:

8 ounces prepared corn masa for tortillas, or 1 cup masa harina for tortillas mixed with ½ cup plus 2 tablespoons warm water

1½ teaspoons lard or corn oil

½ teaspoon salt, or more to taste

FOR THE *CHOCHOYONES*:

In a small mixing bowl, mix the *masa* with the lard or oil until well mixed. Add salt. Make 18 balls about the size of a walnut. With your finger, make an indentation in each. While the *mole* is simmering, add the dumplings one by one and allow them to cook for 5 minutes.

Return the chicken and vegetables to the sauce. Adjust the seasoning and serve hot, with plenty of fresh corn tortillas.

Hint: You can make the sauce a bit thicker by adding more *masa* to the sauce for *Empanadas de Mole Amarillo* (page 229). These are filled with chicken, covered with the *mole* sauce, then cooked on the *comal* and are a popular snack eaten in outdoor stalls.

POZOLE "MIXTECO"
Spicy Red Mole over Herbed Hominy

This pozole dish is one of the best uses for mole rojo *that I have found, other than the Oaxacan-style enchiladas that you can make with either this sauce or the* mole coloradito. *The mole is fiery hot, from the* chilhuacles rojos, *but combined with the layer of aromatic pozole cooked with* hierba santa *and the nuttiness of the sesame seed topping, the intensity is less overwhelming. Some people put chocolate in their* mole rojo, *making it a bit richer and sweeter, but I wouldn't do it for this dish. If you can't find the dried pozole or hominy, use packaged prepared* pozole *and omit the pozole directions.*

MAKES 8 SERVINGS

For the pozole stock:

1 small white onion, chunked

½ head of garlic

1 teaspoon salt, or to taste

1 pound pork ribs, cut Chinese style
into 2-inch pieces

For the pozole:

¾ pound (about 3 cups) pozole
(see page 320), or 2 quarts
canned hominy

3-inch chunk of cal dissolved in
1-quart water (see page 320)

2 medium leaves hierba santa (see
page 336)

For the mole stock:

Seasoning ingredients for chicken
stock (page 343)

1 small chicken (about 3 pounds),
cut into 8 pieces, skin removed if
desired

1 pound boneless pork loin, cut into
2-inch cubes

For the mole rojo:

9 chiles anchos rojos (3 ounces),
stemmed, seeded, and deveined
(see page 330)

15 chiles chilhuacles rojos
(3 ounces) or 50 chiles
costeños rojos (2 ounces) (see
page 330)

4 black peppercorns

3 whole cloves

2 whole allspice

2 sprigs Oaxacan oregano, or 1 teaspoon dried (see page 336)

FOR THE *POZOLE* STOCK:

In a 6-quart stockpot, heat 4 quarts of water over high heat
and add the onion, garlic, and salt. When it comes to a boil,
add the pork ribs. Cover, lower the heat, and simmer 1 hour
or until the ribs are almost soft. Strain and save the stock. Set
aside the ribs.

FOR THE *POZOLE*:

Clean the *pozole* and bring to a boil in a 2-quart saucepan
with the *cal* water. (Do not use the thick lime that has settled
to the bottom.) Cook until corn is soft and peels easily,
about ½ hour. Remove from the heat and allow to cool.
When it cools, wash the corn several times. Peel off the
skins and pick off the head of each kernel. The *pozole* should
be white.

In a heavy 4-quart stockpot, cook the *pozole* with 2 quarts
of the reserved pork stock, the pork ribs, and the *hierba santa*
leaves, covered, over medium to low heat for about 3 hours.
Add more stock as needed. The *pozole* will "flower" or burst
open a bit. Continue to cook over low heat until it dries out,
almost to the consistency of rice, about 20 to 30 minutes
more. Set aside.

FOR THE *MOLE* STOCK:

In a large stockpot, bring 4 quarts of water and the seasoning ingredients to a boil as directed on page 343. Add the
pork loin and the chicken; skim off the foam that appears on
the surface and discard. Cover and cook over a low heat
until meat is soft—the pork loin and chicken should cook in
about the same time, 30 to 45 minutes. Don't overcook.
Add salt to taste. Remove the meat and chicken and set
aside. Remove the pot from the heat and strain the stock to
remove the vegetables. Reserve the stock.

FOR THE *MOLE ROJO*:

Bring 1½ quarts of water to a boil. Toast the *chiles anchos* and
chilhuacles rojos on a dry *comal*, griddle, or in a cast-iron frying
pan over medium heat for about 3 minutes or until the chiles
start to blister and brown and give off their aroma. Remove
the chiles from the pan and place in a medium bowl, pour
the hot water on top, and soak chiles about 20 minutes.

1 pound ripe tomatoes (2 medium–
  large round or 8–10 plum)

1 medium white onion, quartered

½ head of garlic, cloves separated

1 tablespoon plus 2 teaspoons sunflower or vegetable oil

¼ cup plus 3 tablespoons sesame
  seeds

10 pecan halves

8 almonds

2 tablespoons lard, sunflower oil,
  or vegetable oil

1½ tablespoons salt, or to taste

Carlotta Santos making mole

On the same *comal*, frying pan, or griddle, toast the pep-percorns, cloves, allspice, and oregano. Remove and set aside, and then grill the tomatoes, onions, and garlic until cooked through, about 15 minutes.

In an 8-inch cast-iron frying pan over low heat, heat 1 tablespoon of oil and fry ¼ cup sesame seeds lightly, stir-ring until they start to brown. Add the pecans and almonds and keep stirring until they brown nicely. Remove them from the pan and cool. Brown the remaining 3 tablespoons of sesame seeds in the frying pan in the remaining 2 teaspoons of oil and reserve them for the garnish.

In a blender, grind and blend the chiles, adding only enough soaking liquid to turn the blades of the blender. Pass the puree through a sieve or a food mill to remove the skins. Place in a separate bowl. Blend the tomatoes, onion, garlic, and spices with 1 cup of reserved stock. Grind the sesame seed mixture bit by bit in a spice grinder, *mol-cajete*, or *metate*. (They will not blend smoothly in a blender, but you can do this if you must and pass them through a foodmill afterward.) When everything is well ground, heat the lard until smoking in a large *cazuela* or heavy pot. Add the chile puree and stir with a wooden spoon until well seasoned, about 20 minutes. Add the tomato puree and spices. Keep stirring, for at least 15 minutes, until it dries out. Add the ground sesame seeds and stir well to incorporate them into the sauce. Add 4 cups of the stock to thin the sauce so it just coats the back of a spoon. Continue to simmer 20 minutes. Add the salt, pork, and chicken and heat through.

TO SERVE:
In each shallow soup bowl, place a serving of *pozole* with a piece of pork rib and make a well in the middle. Ladle a serving of *mole rojo* with a piece of pork loin and chicken in the well, and garnish with sesame seeds. Serve with plenty of fresh corn tortillas.

CHICHILO OAXAQUEÑO
(Mole Stew

The seventh and most unusual mole gets its color and flavor from the burnt tortilla and blackened seeds of the Oaxacan chiles chilhuacles negros and guajillos. The combination of beef, pork, and vegetables gives it a rich flavor and heartiness, while the anise flavor of the avocado leaves and the final garnish of lime-spiked onion and chile bring it over the top! It is common in Oaxaca to have Chichilo *served with* chochoyones *(page 323). Add them if you like.*

MAKES 8 SERVINGS

For the meats and vegetables:
Seasoning ingredients for beef stock
    (page 344)
1½ pounds boneless stewing beef,
    cut into 2-inch chunks
1 pound pork ribs or backbone
    (espinazo), cut into 2-inch
    slices
Salt to taste
2 chayotes, cut into long slices (see
    page 326)
1 pound small potatoes (6–8)
½ pound green beans, trimmed and
    cut into 3-inch slices

For the mole:
5 chiles chilhuacles negros
    (about 1 ounce), seeded,
    stemmed, and deveined; save the
    seeds (see page 330)
6 chiles guajillos (about
    1¼ ounces), seeded, stemmed,
    and deveined; save the seeds (see
    page 331)
1 tortilla

FOR THE STOCK:
In a 6-quart stockpot, bring 5 quarts of water and the seasonings for beef stock to a boil following the directions on page 344. Once boiling, add the beef chunks and return to a boil. Skim off the top when foam appears and discard. Cover the pot, lower the heat to a simmer, and cook about 1½ hours. Add the pork ribs and continue to cook 1 hour more, or until the meats are soft. Add salt. Remove the meat from the stock. Cook the chayotes, potatoes, and beans in the stock, each separately, until done. Remove the vegetables and set aside. Reserve the stock.

FOR THE *MOLE:*
Bring 2 cups of water to a boil. Toast the chiles on a 10-inch dry *comal*, griddle, or in a cast-iron frying pan over medium heat until they start to blister and give off their aroma, about 4 minutes. Soak the chiles in the hot water for 20 minutes, or until soft. Drain the chiles, reserving the water. Blend the chiles in a blender, using as little of the chile water as needed to turn the blades of the blender. After blending the chiles, pass them through a strainer or food mill to remove the skins. Set aside.

On the same *comal* over low to medium heat, toast the tortilla until it browns on both sides. Then place the reserved chile seeds on top of the tortilla and blacken them well, about 30 minutes. (We usually ignite the seeds and let

2 pounds ripe tomatoes (4 medium–
    large round or 16–20 plum)
2 ounces tomatillos (about
    3 medium), husked
1 small white onion, chunked
1 head of garlic, cloves separated
1 tablespoon sunflower or vegetable
    oil
2 tablespoons raisins
2 tablespoons almonds
2 whole allspice
1 tablespoon cumin seeds
1 whole clove
1 piece of Mexican cinnamon,
    2 inches long (see page 337)
1 sprig Oaxacan oregano, or
    ½ teaspoon dried (see page 336)
1 sprig thyme, or a pinch of dried
1 sprig marjoram, or ½ teaspoon
    dried
2 tablespoons lard, sunflower oil,
    or vegetable oil
4 ounces prepared masa for
    tortillas, or ½ cup masa harina
    for tortillas mixed with ¼ cup
    plus 1 tablespoon water
1 tablespoon plus 1 teaspoon salt
3 avocado leaves, fresh or dried
    (hoja de aguacate; see
    page 338)

For the garnish:
1 medium white onion
2 chiles de agua or other fresh
    green chiles, roasted and peeled
    (see page 328)
1 teaspoon dried Oaxacan oregano
    (see page 336)
2 limes, juiced
Salt to taste

them burn out.) Place the blackened tortilla and chile seeds in 3 cups of cold water to soak, about 15 minutes. Strain the tortilla and seed mixture and discard the water. Add fresh water to cover, then soak the seed mixture again for 10 minutes. Grind the seed mixture separately in the blender until smooth, using only enough water to turn the blades of the blender. Strain the mixture through a fine-mesh strainer and set aside.

On the *comal*, grill the tomatoes and *tomatillos* over medium heat until soft, about 15 minutes. Set aside. Grill the onion and garlic until clear, about 15 minutes. Puree tomatoes, onion, and garlic in a blender with ½ cup of reserved stock and pass through a food mill or sieve to remove skins and seeds. Set aside.

In an 8-inch cast-iron frying pan over medium heat, use the tablespoon of oil to fry the raisins, almonds, allspice, cumin, clove, cinnamon, oregano, thyme, and marjoram about 10 minutes, until a nutty brown. Grind the spice mixture in a blender with ½ cup of stock.

Heat the lard in a heavy 6-quart stockpot, and fry the chile puree well, about 15 minutes, until it "dries out" a bit. Add the tomato mixture and spice mixture and fry well, about 15 minutes. Add 2 cups of stock to thin the sauce, now referred to as *"mole."* Add the *masa* and 2 cups of stock to the blender and blend well; add to the *mole* and cook, stirring, 20 minutes. Add salt.

Toast the avocado leaves over the flame of a gas stove or in a hot dry frying pan until they give off their aroma and add them, whole, to the *mole*. Stir the seed mixture into the *mole*. Add 1 cup more of the stock and stir in. Simmer the *mole* for 30 minutes. Add the cooked vegetables to the *mole*. Then add the pork and beef pieces and heat through. Adjust the salt to taste. If it gets too thick, add more stock so the *mole* just coats the back of a spoon, no more.

FOR THE GARNISH:
Cut the onion in half. Place on a cutting board and cut lengthwise strips of onion. Slice the roasted and peeled *chiles de agua* into ¼-inch lengthwise strips. Place in a small mixing bowl, add the oregano, and cover with lime juice. Add salt.

(continued)

Serve a spoonful on top of each serving of *mole*, or put the bowl on the table to let each person serve themselves. Serve with plenty of fresh corn tortillas.

Hint: You can substitute chicken for the beef and pork with good results.

Adapted from Celia Acevedo de Torres

MANCHAMANTELES OAXAQUEÑO
"Tablecloth Stainer"

This tropical mole *has the addition of ripe plantains and pineapple, which add a wonderful contrast of chile heat and fruit sweetness. Substitute chiles chilhuacles rojos if you don't have chilcostles, or add more chiles guajillos in place of these native Oaxacan chiles. You can add pork meat to this dish also, as is traditionally done in other parts of Mexico.*

MAKES 8 SERVINGS

7–8 cups chicken stock *(page 343)*
1½ chickens *(about 4–5 pounds), cut into 8 pieces, skin removed if desired*

For the mole:
13 chiles anchos rojos *(about 4½ ounces), stemmed, seeded, and deveined (see page 330)*
11 chiles guajillos *(about 2 ounces), stemmed, seeded, and deveined (see page 331)*

In a heavy 4-quart stockpot, heat the chicken stock. Place the chicken pieces in the stock and poach over low heat, covered, for 35 to 45 minutes or until cooked through and the juices run clear when pierced with a fork. Remove from the stock, and strain the stock to remove the vegetables. Reserve the stock. Set chicken aside.

FOR THE *MOLE*:
In a 3-quart saucepan, bring 2 quarts of water to a boil. Toast the chiles on a dry *comal*, or griddle, or in a cast-iron frying pan over medium heat until they start to blister and give off their aroma. Place in a medium mixing bowl, pour the boiling water over them, and allow them to soak 20 minutes. Using tongs, place the chiles in a blender and add as little of the chile water as needed to turn the blades of

4 chiles chilcostles (about
  1 ounce), stemmed, seeded, and
  deveined (see page 330)
1 pound tomatoes (2 medium–large
  round or 8–10 plum), quartered
2 tablespoons sunflower or vegetable oil
½ cup sesame seeds
1 small white onion, quartered
¼ cup almonds
1 tablespoon pecans
¼ cup raisins
5 garlic cloves
2 whole cloves
2 black peppercorns
1 whole allspice
1 piece of Mexican cinnamon,
  1 inch long (see page 337)
2 sprigs Oaxacan oregano, or
  ½ teaspoon dried (see page 336)
2 tablespoons lard, sunflower oil,
  or vegetable oil
2 ripe plantains, sliced (about
  2 cups)
2 big slices of fresh pineapple,
  chunked (about 2 cups)
1 tablespoon salt, or to taste

the blender. Grind, then blend well. Pass the blended mixture through a sieve or food mill to remove skins. Set aside.

Cook the tomatoes well in a dry frying pan over medium
heat for 10 to 15 minutes. They will give off their juices,
then dry out. Blend the tomatoes well, then pass through a
sieve or food mill to remove their skins. Set aside in a bowl.

In an 8-inch cast-iron frying pan, heat 1 tablespoon of the
oil over low to medium heat. Add the sesame seeds and fry,
stirring constantly. (If the seeds jump around too much, add
a pinch of salt.) Keep stirring until the seeds reach a brown,
nutty color, about 8 minutes. Set aside.

In another 8-inch cast-iron frying pan, heat the remaining
1 tablespoon of oil. Fry the onion over medium heat until
clear, about 3 to 5 minutes. Add the almonds, pecans,
raisins, garlic, cloves, peppercorns, allspice, cinnamon, and
oregano and fry until browned and aromatic, stirring constantly. Puree the mixture in a blender with 2 cups of the
reserved stock until smooth, about 3 minutes.

Grind the sesame seeds separately in a *molcajete*, *metate*, or
spice grinder because they don't grind well enough in the
blender.

In a heavy 6-quart stockpot, heat the lard until smoking.
Add the ground chile mixture and fry well, stirring constantly. This may splatter about in the beginning, but will
stop with the stirring of the chile mixture. When the mixture dries out, after about 20 minutes, add the blended
tomatoes and continue to fry and stir, about 15 minutes.
Add the ground sesame seeds and the nuts, raisins, and spice
mixture, stirring to incorporate both well. Fry this mixture
10 minutes more. Thin with 4 cups of stock, then add the
plantain and pineapple pieces and cook through, about
20 minutes. Add salt. Thin with another cup of stock, if needed.
The *mole* should be thick enough to coat the back of a spoon.

Reheat chicken in the stock.

Place the chicken in a wide bowl and ladle the *mole* over
it. When serving, make sure to give pineapple and plantains
to each person. Serve with a lot of sauce and plenty of fresh
corn tortillas.

MOLE EN PASTA
Reconstituted Mole Paste

Going through the markets in Oaxaca, you will pass piles of seasoning pastes in var-ious earthy colors and flavors. Instead of having to spend days in your kitchen, you can reconstitute mole paste and make this ceremonial dish in less than an hour. Serve it with a generous portion of chicken, turkey, pork, or a combination of the three, and plenty of sauce. Although some stalls sell many kinds of pastes, the most popular are rojo, coloradito, and the king of them all, mole negro.

MAKES 6 SERVINGS OR
6 CUPS *MOLE* SAUCE

3 cups chicken stock (page 343)
1 chicken (about 3 pounds), cut into 6 serving pieces, skin removed if desired
Salt to taste
1 pound tomatoes (2 medium–large round or 4–5 plum), cut into quarters
½ pound tomatillos (5–6 medium), husks removed and cut into quarters (see page 327)
1 tablespoon sunflower or vegetable oil, or lard if desired
1 pound mole negro paste

In a heavy 4-quart stockpot, heat the chicken stock over high heat. Add the chicken pieces, lower the heat, add salt, and cover. Poach the chicken for about 30 minutes, or until the juice runs clear when pierced with a fork. Remove the chicken from the stock and set aside. Strain the stock, skim-ming off the fat.

In a dry 8-inch cast-iron frying pan, fry the tomatoes and *tomatillos* until they give off their juices, 10 to 15 minutes, depending on the tomatoes, then let the mixture dry out somewhat. Puree the mixture in a blender, adding up to ½ cup stock to help release the blender's blades. Strain through a food mill or strainer.

In a heavy 4-quart stockpot or clay *cazuela*, heat the oil, then add the *mole negro* paste and fry well over medium heat, stirring constantly with a wooden spoon. When the paste is very hot, after 5 minutes, slowly add the tomato and *tomatillo* puree. Stir until well incorporated, about 10 min-utes. Thin with the remaining stock, letting it reduce a little, about 20 to 25 minutes. It should be thick enough to just coat the back of a spoon.

Reheat the chicken in the stock.

Place a cooked chicken piece on each plate or wide soup bowl. Ladle a good amount of *mole* to cover the chicken. Serve immediately with a stack of fresh corn tortillas or use to make *Enmoladas de Mole Negro* or *Tamales Oaxaqueños* (page 261).

Hints: Turkey or boneless pork shoulder can be substituted, or any combination of the three.

This recipe can be used for *mole coloradito* or *mole rojo* paste with the elimination of the *tomatillos*.

PAN DE MUERTO
Egg Bread for Day of the Dead

The traditional pairing of bread and chocolate for the Mexican table is never more apparent than in the celebration of Día de Muertos. Throughout the fiesta, people are always served the "offering" of large bowls of foaming chocolate with slices of bread to dunk in it. Every year, the men in our village rent time in the village bakery to make massive amounts of Pan de Muerto for their brood, using their own family recipes. At first the dough is very sticky, so it must be kneaded a long time to turn it into the soft dough that is characteristic of this bread.

MAKES TWO 8- TO 9-INCH
BREADS

4 cups all-purpose flour
2½ tablespoons active dry yeast
½ cup sugar
¼ teaspoon salt
½ tablespoon aniseeds
3 eggs
¼ cup lard or vegetable shortening, softened
2 tablespoons butter, softened
1 tablespoon sesame seeds

In a large bowl, mix the flour, yeast, sugar, salt, and aniseed with your fingers until well incorporated. Make a well in the center. Add the eggs, lard, butter, and 1 cup water and mix to make a sticky dough. Knead for 15 minutes or until the dough is soft. (We say 15 minutes and 9 beads of sweat.) The dough should not stick to your hands at the end of the kneading process.

Put the dough in a greased bowl. Spread the top of the dough with a little lard or oil so it will not dry out. Cover with a damp cloth and put in a warm place. Let the dough rise until doubled in size, about 45 minutes.

Punch down the dough, knead it a few minutes, and divide it into 2 balls. Form round loaves, then place them on a piece of waxed paper or a floured baking sheet, allowing space for the bread to increase in size. Wet the sesame seeds with a little water, drain them, and place them in a shallow bowl. Dip your fingers into the seeds and then pat them on top of each bread. Allow the dough to rise for 15 minutes, then cut a slit in the top, using a sharp knife or a razor blade. Allow to rise 15 more minutes.

Preheat the oven to 350°F.

Bake for 45 minutes or until nicely browned and the bread has a hollow sound when tapped. Allow to cool completely before you cut it, or it will smush down and won't rise back up again. It is a very soft bread, so don't stack them, either.

Hint: The breads will keep for weeks wrapped in a cloth in a plastic bag. Here we keep them in a basket lined with cloth. The bread is traditionally dipped into a bowl of hot chocolate, so it doesn't matter if it dries out like a biscuit. It is also great used for French toast. Without the aniseeds, it is called *pan de yema*.

This recipe is inspired by Romero González Ortiz, Galdino Larraro, and German Castro Santiago, who taught me over the years.

CALABAZA EN DULCE
Pumpkin Squash in Syrup

For Día de Muertos, Mexican families make altars to honor the saints, their ancestors, and friends who have died. The altar is decorated with photos, flowers, chocolate, bread, and other special foods to entice the dead to come back for the fiesta. Seasonal fruits and vegetables are made en dulce, or sweetened to preserve them, and placed on the altars, then given out to relatives after the final church bells ring, signaling the end of the fiesta. In Oaxaca, this recipe is commonly made with the native tamala squash, but I have used the North American pumpkin here.

1 pound piloncillo or 2½ cups
  brown sugar (see page 348)
3 pounds pumpkin, cut into
  12 2-inch wedges, seeded and
  peeled
1 piece of Mexican cinnamon,
  3 inches long (see page 337)

Place the *piloncillo* or brown sugar in 3 cups of water in a
2-quart saucepan or clay *cazuela* with a lid and bring to a
boil. Cook over high heat for 10 minutes.

Add the pumpkin wedges and cinnamon stick, cover the
pot, and cook over medium heat for 50 minutes. Remove
the cover and simmer for another 30 minutes to reduce the
liquid to a syrup.

Serve at room temperature with coffee.

CHOCOLATE DE AGUA
Hot Chocolate Made with Water

*One of Mexico's most important gifts to the world, with the biggest impact, is the
cacao bean to make chocolate. Legend has it that the God of Light, Quetzalcoatl,
brought it down to the Toltecan people and taught them how to cultivate it. It
was a special offering and was considered "food of the gods." It has retained its place
among the most cherished foods in Mexico. The tradition is that chocolate is made
only by the hands of a woman, whipped into a foamy mixture, and always served
with Pan de Muerto (page 279).*

MAKES 4 CUPS

4–5 ounces first-class Mexican
  chocolate (depending on your
  preference), broken into pieces

In a 2-quart *jarra* or saucepan, bring 4 cups of water to a boil.
Just before it starts boiling, add the chocolate pieces.
Remove the pan from the heat. With a *molinillo* (see
page 351) or a wire whisk, whip the chocolate continually
until the pieces melt. When the chocolate has a thick layer
of foam on top, serve in ceramic bowls or mugs with *Pan de
Muerto* on the side.

Hint: You can make *chocolate con leche* by substituting milk
for the water and increasing the chocolate to 6 ounces.
Champurrado can be made by adding 6 ounces of chocolate
to *Atole de Maíz* (page 160) and more sugar, if needed.

CHAPTER ELEVEN

Traditions Evolve
(Las Tradiciones Evolucionan)

Eric and the children (Gretchen Wirtz)

Overleaf: Rancho Aurora (Gretchen Wirtz)

When I first came to Oaxaca I was really intrigued by Oaxacan cooking because it was so different from any Mexican food I had when I was growing up in the States. It is kind of like playing jazz: you have to learn the basic notes first and then you can branch off and be creative. In Oaxaca I learned the basics and then started to experiment with some of the flavors that I missed from my childhood and from past experiences as a chef.

When I moved to Oaxaca, I had more than fifteen years

of cooking background—French, Cajun, Mexican American, and Asian. I wanted to utilize the best of these methods and to blend them into the cooking style that was now my main focus. For instance, when women here make a stock, they use only water, a bay leaf, some onion, and meat or fish. I had worked with chefs who taught me the essence of stock making, which is the backbone of soups and sauces. My rule of thumb is to never use water if I can help it! I strive to respect rather than defy such bits of culinary knowledge. In other chapters of this book, I subtly incorporate some of my basic techniques, but in this chapter I show the evolution of my personal food world. Contained here are recipes that have been in my family (natural or adopted), in which I approach the typical uses of ingredients in new and inspiring ways.

In my Cajun restaurant in New York, Bon Temps Rouler, I made jambalaya every day. Here in Mexico, I took the "holy trinity" of the Cajun kitchen (onions, peppers, and celery) and, because I didn't have the tasso ham or the andouille sausage, I added a trio of the Mexican kitchen: *chile poblano*, squash flowers, and garlic. Taking it a step further, I added chicken stock and short-grain brown rice, which imparted a nutty flavor. I named this new Mexican dish *Arroz Criollo Mexicano*, or Mexican Jambalaya (page 299).

For dessert, bread pudding is one of the most popular Louisiana sweets. After years of eating bread pudding every day at my restaurant in New York, I resurrected it for fund-raising events and special occasion dinners here in Oaxaca. Using the crusty *pan bolillo* and the local orange *tamala* squash, I paired it with rum sauce in place of whiskey. *Budín de Tamala y Pan* (page 308) is just as popular in its transformation as it has always been.

Another example of fusion food is *Plátanos Fritos con Crema de Jengibre y Jalapeño*, or Fried Plantains with Ginger Jalapeño Cream (page 291). The fried plantains, a popular Mexican dish, are served with a savory, cream cheese sauce, rather than a sweet sauce, as a Mexican would expect. However, the sweetness of the plantains offers a good contrast to the hot, gingery, garlicky sauce of my concoction. This dish has even evolved a step further. After making it in many cooking classes, we now use the leftovers as the filling for an omelet.

Some traditional family recipes are included here with a new presentation. The traditional turkey dinner of my mother, Melanie Chavana Trilling, has been transformed to a spicier, Mexican version. Originally, the turkey recipe contained a bread stuffing, but now I've added different herbs, chiles, fruits, and fruit juices to bring us closer to the time of the first Thanksgiving, when Mexico and the present United States were still one country. And the turkey dinner wouldn't be complete without creamed onions on the side. My mom made hers with frozen onions and peas in a cream sauce topped with fried onion rings. One of my passions in Mexican cooking is the grilled onions cooked directly on hot coals. These white onions become clear and translucent, bringing out the sweetness of the vegetable. Adding corn and squash flowers in a traditional béchamel sauce completes my new version.

When I was growing up, my Aunt Renee's gelatin mold was served at every Trilling family fiesta, including the holiday dinners. Many of the fiestas given at the Rancho are for children, and the Trilling tradition continues since their most request-ed dish is *gelatina*. In Mexico, *gelatinas* are transformed into true works of art and presented as healthy desserts—or could even be on the breakfast menu (*Gelatina de Tía Renne*; see page 313).

My grandmother, Marie Antoinette Chavana Flores, has influenced my cooking a great deal. Her outstanding homemade desserts and preserves, made from fruit of the trees in her yard, were ever present in her kitchen. Her orange cake was simple and straightforward; mine (*Pastel de Naranja de Mi Abuela;* page 311) is more elaborate, rolled with cream and fruit. The flavor of the orange is reminiscent of Tampico, the area where my grandmother was born, which in spring is filled with the intoxicating aroma of orange blossoms.

My almost mother-in-law, Phyllis Gosfield, who, with her husband, Gene, owned the Under the Blue Moon Restaurant in Philadelphia, has also had a tremen-dous impact on my cooking life, but in a more professional way. She has always been a mentor, not only in introducing me to foods from all over the world but also in sharing her love of cooking and her zeal for life. Her contribution is a torte transformed into *Pastel de Nuéz con Chocolate* (page 309). I have adopted that cake as our traditional family birthday cake, using almonds and pecans which grow nearby.

I met Eric, my husband, when a friend brought him to me to interview for a cooking job. Previously he had cooked in a curry house in Australia and owned his own restaurant in Spain. For years after that, he was the cook in the galley of various fishing boats. His specialty is making something from nothing in a very short period of time. Since we have been together, this talent has gone into hibernation, but it comes out once in a while when he makes a great curry or the tomato soup (*Sopa de Tomate con Albóndigas;* page 287) included here. The use of the leeks in the recipe comes from his Dutch heritage, the love of which was handed down from his mother, Toos. Also, because he is a tomato farmer here in the valley, we take advantage of the harvest to make tomato puree from his every crop.

Once you come to understand the Oaxacan ingredients and cooking methods, encourage your own cooking traditions to evolve. If you can't find the exact ingre-dient, experiment with another. The most important thing is to get into the kitchen and cook, and let your own spirit and creativity unfold.

IN THIS CHAPTER

SOPA DE AJO CON FLOR DE CALABAZA
Garlic Soup with Squash Blossoms

Chicken soup is known as "Jewish penicillin," and this soup has all the makings of a Mexican version. It includes enough garlic to kill all of the bacteria in your system, while the chile de árbol opens your sinuses and heats your chest. My addition of squash blossoms and the licorice-smelling hierba santa gives it a distinctive Oaxacan flare. The optional poached egg creates a dish hardy enough for a cena (evening meal), although I've eaten it for breakfast many times.

MAKES 8 SERVINGS

1½ tablespoons butter

1½ tablespoons olive oil

2 heads of garlic, cloves separated and thinly sliced

16 fresh squash flowers, cleaned, with sepals, stems, and pistils removed

2 medium hierba santa leaves, rib removed and cut into strips (see page 336), or ½ bunch water-cress with a nice shot of Pernod or anisette

1 chile de árbol or chile japonés (see pages 330 and 331)

1 bay leaf

8 cups chicken stock (page 343)

Salt and black pepper to taste

1 bolillo (see page 347) or other bread, cut into 1-inch square chunks to make 2 cups croutons

5 sprigs flat-leaf parsley, stems removed and leaves finely chopped

¼ pound quesillo, manchego or Muenster cheese, cut into ½-inch chunks (see pages 345 and 346)

In a heavy 4-quart stockpot over low heat, melt the butter and olive oil together and sauté the garlic slowly, stirring so it does not brown, for about 15 minutes or until soft and translucent. Add the squash flowers and *hierba santa* or watercress and sauté 3 minutes longer, stirring lightly, taking care not to break up the squash flowers. Add the chile, bay leaf, and chicken stock. Simmer, covered, for 45 minutes.

Meanwhile, toast the bread cubes in a hot 400°F oven or in a dry frying pan until brown.

Five minutes before serving, season soup with salt and pepper and add parsley.

In the bottom of each soup bowl, place 5 bread cubes and 5 cheese cubes. Ladle the soup over the bread and cheese, sprinkle with Parmesan cheese, and serve. Or, if serving the eggs, carefully break open the eggs, one at a time, on a flat plate and slip them into the hot broth. Spoon a poached egg into each serving bowl, add the cheese and the bread cubes, ladle the soup over all, and sprinkle with the Parmesan cheese. Serve immediately.

4 tablespoons freshly grated
    Parmesan cheese
8 eggs (optional)

SOPA DE TOMATE CON ALBÓNDIGAS
Tomato Soup with Meatballs

This soup is a classic in our household and was created by Eric with the puree we make from each tomato crop he harvests. He loves a good beef stock, which is the backbone of the soup, and he uses leeks, which show his Dutch heritage. His mother was always making soups and stews in Holland to ward off the cold, dreary days of winter, and these are the foods he likes the best. It's best if you can use puree from your summer tomato crop, but if you can't, use a good store-bought substitute.

MAKES 6 TO 8 SERVINGS

For the meat:
Seasoning ingredients for beef stock
    (page 344)
2 pounds beef bones

For the meatballs:
1¼ pounds ground sirloin
1 teaspoon freshly ground black
    pepper
½ teaspoon salt
¼ cup sunflower or vegetable oil

For the soup:
1½ medium white onions, finely
    chopped
1 large leek, halved and thinly
    sliced
1 tablespoon finely chopped garlic
1½ teaspoons ground black pepper

FOR THE MEAT:
In a 6-quart stockpot, bring 4 quarts of water and the seasoning ingredients to a boil following the instructions on page 344. Once the water is boiling, add the beef and return to a boil. Skim off the foam that appears on the surface and discard. Lower the heat, cover, and cook the meat 2H–3 hours or until tender. Strain the stock and reserve.

FOR THE MEATBALLS:
In a medium bowl, mix the ground beef with the pepper and salt. Shape the meat mixture into tiny meatballs the size of black cherries. In a heavy 4-quart stockpot, heat the oil over medium to high heat and brown the meatballs on all sides, for about 2 minutes, bit by bit in the oil without crowding them. Remove from the pan and set aside.

FOR THE SOUP:
If there is extra grease in the stockpot, remove it, leaving 2 tablespoons. Fry the onions and leek until they are soft over medium heat, 4 to 6 minutes. Add the garlic and season with the pepper and bay leaves. Add 4 cups of the reserved

3 bay leaves

5 cups thick tomato puree (see Hint)

1½ teaspoons salt, or to taste

1 tablespoon finely chopped fresh parsley

1 tablespoon finely chopped garlic chives or chives

beef stock, the tomato puree, and the meatballs. Lower the heat, cover, and cook for 1½ hours. Add the salt, parsley, and chives and cook 5 to 10 minutes longer. Serve with garlic toast. The soup tastes even better the next day and freezes very well.

Hint: To make your own tomato puree, peel and seed 7 pounds of plum tomatoes, then puree them in a blender. This should yield about 10½ cups of tomato puree. Cook the puree over low heat for 1 to 1½ hours, until reduced to 5¼ cups of thick tomato puree, stirring occasionally. The puree freezes well. We don't season it so we can use it with any type of food.

Lider and Serafin (Eric Ulrich)

PLÁTANOS FRITOS CON CREMA DE JENGIBRE Y JALAPEÑO

Fried Plantains with Ginger Jalapeño Cream

This is an appetizer from my New York City days after I had come back from Thailand and was cooking a blend of Thai-Mexican food. The sauce was inspired by my old friend Sarah Gross, and it works well with the sweetness of the ripe plantains. One discovery made here in Oaxaca was having the leftovers from cooking classes for omelet fillings. The combination of ginger and egg is more Thai than ever and is worth making extra just to have left over!

MAKES 6 SERVINGS

For the sauce:

1-inch piece of fresh ginger, peeled and finely chopped

3 garlic cloves

3 chiles jalapeños en escabeche, stemmed and seeded (see page 333)

½ bunch parsley, leaves only

½ pound cream cheese, softened

½ cup sour cream, or ¼ cup milk (optional)

Salt and white pepper to taste

For the plantains:

6 ripe plantains (but not real black), peeled

Sunflower or vegetable oil, for frying

FOR THE SAUCE:

Put ginger, garlic, *jalapeños*, and parsley leaves in the bowl of a food processor and pulse until it is all finely chopped. Add the cream cheese and blend well. Add enough sour cream or milk to bring to the consistency of a dip. Add salt and white pepper. Chill for at least 15 minutes.

FOR THE PLANTAINS:

Cut the plantains on an angle into slices about ¾ inch thick. In an 8-inch cast-iron frying pan, heat the oil. When the oil is hot, fry the plantain slices until golden brown, about 3 to 5 minutes. Remove from the oil and drain on paper towels. Arrange on a serving platter and serve immediately, with the sauce.

Hint: For unripe plantains, cut them diagonally into thick pieces and fry. Remove from the oil and drain. When all are cooled, smash each piece with a mallet or the side of a chef's knife or cleaver. Fry again quickly, drain, and salt lightly.

JALAPEÑOS RELLENOS CON QUESO CREMA Y PESCADO AHUMADO

Stuffed Jalapeños with Smoked Fish Cream

This is a fun appetizer to serve at a cocktail party or as part of a cold botanas platter. The chiles are very picante, so they have to be soaked in salted water for 30 minutes to cut some of the heat. If your chiles are not spicy, omit this step. The chiles should have a bite, particularly after eating a whole one. This is a tribute to the Jewish food from my father's side of the family in Philadelphia and the Mexican food we ate in Texas visiting my mother's family.

MAKES 10 STUFFED CHILES

3 ounces queso crema *(see page 346)*
  or cream cheese, softened
3 ounces smoked lisa fish *(see*
  page 345), or smoked sable or
  salmon, boned and finely shredded
2 tablespoons finely chopped onion
3 garlic cloves, finely chopped
2 tablespoons finely chopped
  parsley leaves
¼ teaspoon Worcestershire sauce
½ lime, juiced
Pinch of salt
Pinch of ground white pepper
10 fresh or pickled chiles
  jalapeños (see page 329)
2 tablespoons pecan pieces

With an electric mixer, beat the cream cheese until light and fluffy. Add the smoked fish and continue to beat. Add the onion, garlic, and parsley and mix in well. Season with Worcestershire sauce, lime, salt, and white pepper. Chill the cream in the refrigerator, about 30 minutes.

With a sharp knife, make a slit down each *jalapeño* from the stem to the point. Carefully remove the seeds from each. In a bowl with 2 cups of salted water, soak the *jalapeños* for ½ hour. (If your *jalapeños* are not hot [there are some mild varieties grown in the United States], or you really like your food spicy, or you are using pickled *jalapeños*, omit this step.) Remove the chiles from the water and drain. Use a piece of paper towel or a light cloth to dry the inside of each chile.

Place the cream in a pastry bag or take a tablespoon of the mixture and fill each chile. The filling should be mounded out of the top. Place on a serving platter.

On a 10-inch dry *comal*, griddle, or in a cast-iron frying pan, toast the pecans until brown and giving off their scent. Allow them to cool, then chop them finely. Sprinkle the toasted pecans over each *jalapeño*. The nuts should cover the cheese filling. Serve chilled.

FLOR DE CALABAZA RELLENA DE REQUESÓN
Squash Flowers Stuffed with Farmer Cheese

This dish is wonderful served as an appetizer for a fancy meal or as a botana or appetizer with the sauce served out of a hollowed-out small pumpkin or squash and the flowers piled up on the sides. We also eat it at home, serving the flowers on a bed of white or chepil-flavored rice and the sauce lightly drizzled over all. If squash flowers are out of season, you can substitute small zucchini or yellow squash and bake instead of sauté them. If you don't have the chile pasilla oaxaqueño, *substitute the more readily available* chile chipotle, *but the* pasilla *is well worth looking for in your mail-order catalogue!*

MAKES 12 SERVINGS OF 2 FLOWERS EACH AS AN APPETIZER, OR 6 SERVINGS OF 4 FLOWERS FOR A MAIN COURSE

For the corn stock:

1 ear of corn, kernels cut off and cob reserved (about ½ cup kernels)

1 sprig epazote (optional; see page 336)

For the flowers and vegetable filling:

24 squash flowers

3 tablespoons olive or sunflower oil

½ medium white onion, finely chopped

½ pound criolla squash (see page 325) or zucchini, finely chopped

¾ cup finely chopped mushrooms

7 garlic cloves, finely chopped

¼ cup hulled pepitas (about 1 ounce), toasted (see page 338)

3 black peppercorns

1 whole allspice

FOR THE CORN STOCK:
Put the corn cob, *epazote*, and 2 cups of water in a medium saucepan and bring to a boil. Cover, lower the heat, and simmer for at least ½ hour to make corn stock. Strain and reserve the stock.

FOR THE FLOWERS AND VEGETABLE FILLING:
Wash and clean the squash flowers carefully, removing the stamen inside and the sepals from the outside, keeping the flowers and stems intact. Allow them to soak in a bowl of water for 5 minutes, then dry carefully in a dish towel. Set aside.

Heat the oil in a deep sauté pan over medium heat. Add the onions and fry until clear, about 3 minutes. Add the squash and the corn kernels and sauté 10 minutes. Add the mushrooms and garlic and sauté 5 minutes longer. Set aside.

On a 10-inch dry *comal*, griddle, or in a cast-iron frying pan, toast the *pepitas* over medium heat, stirring, until they puff up and have a nutty brown color, about 5 minutes. When they are all puffed, remove from the pan and allow to cool.

Add the peppercorns and allspice to the *comal* and toast until they give off their scent, about 2 minutes. Add to the *pepitas* and grind in a *molcajete* or blender to a medium grind, not a powder.

Add the seed mixture to the vegetable mixture, stirring well. Add the *jalapeño* juice and 1 cup of the reserved corn

1 tablespoon chile jalapeño *juice,*
   from chiles jalapeños en
   escabeche *(page 333)*

½ *teaspoon salt*

10 epazote *leaves (see page 336) or*
   4 sprigs cilantro, finely chopped
   (2 tablespoons)

For the cheese filling:

½ pound requesón *(see page 346),*
   farmer cheese, or fresh ricotta

¼ *teaspoon Mexican cinnamon*
   pieces, toasted and ground (see
   page 337)

2 *eggs*

¼ *teaspoon ground black pepper*

1 *tablespoon finely chopped*
   cilantro leaves

1 *tablespoon* chepil *leaves (or omit*
   and double the cilantro)

Salt to taste

For the caldillo de chile pasilla con
   tomate:

2 *pounds ripe tomatoes*
   (4 medium–large round or
   16–20 plum)

2 *large* chiles pasillas
   oaxaqueños, *stemmed, seeded,*
   and deveined (see page 331)

2 *tablespoons sunflower or vege-*
   table oil

½ *medium white onion, finely*
   chopped

7 *garlic cloves, finely chopped*

Salt and pepper to taste

To finish and serve:

½ *cup all-purpose flour mixed with*
   ½ teaspoon salt and ½ teaspoon
   pepper, for dredging the flowers

½ *cup sunflower oil, for frying*

stock. Cover and simmer for 20 minutes over low heat. Add salt. Turn off the heat and add the *epazote* or cilantro.

FOR THE CHEESE FILLING:
In a medium mixing bowl, place the cheese, cinnamon, eggs, pepper, cilantro, and *chepil* and whip with a whisk or fork for about 5 minutes. Add salt.

FOR THE *CALDILLO DE CHILE PASILLA CON TOMATE*:
In a 2-quart saucepan, bring 1 quart of water to a boil. Make an x in the bottom of each tomato. Add the tomatoes to the boiling water and boil them 3 minutes. Remove the tomatoes from the water, reserve the water, and set tomatoes aside to cool.

On a 10-inch dry *comal*, griddle, or in a cast-iron frying pan, toast the chiles on both sides until they blister and give off their scent. Remove from the *comal* and place in the hot tomato water and soften for 20 minutes.

Peel the tomatoes and put them in a blender together with the chiles; blend them until smooth.

Heat the oil in a heavy frying pan, add the onion, and fry until clear, about 5 minutes. Add the garlic and sauté for 1 minute more. Strain the tomato and chile mixture, and add to the vegetable mixture. Cover and simmer for 20 minutes over low heat. Add salt and pepper.

TO FINISH AND SERVE:
Carefully open each squash flower and put 1 tablespoon of the vegetable mixture in each flower and follow with 1 tablespoon of the cheese mixture on top. Enclose the cheese mixture with the petals. Heat the oil in a large frying pan over medium heat. Dredge the stuffed flowers in the flour and shape each flower in the palm of your hands. Shake off excess flour. Place the flowers in the oil about 3 or 4 at a time, and fry on both sides, turning once, until golden brown, about 4 minutes. Remove the flowers and place them on paper towels to drain. Continue until all the flowers are fried.

To serve, ladle ¼ cup of the tomato sauce onto each plate and place two of the flowers on top. Garnish with squash leaves or parsley.

MIGAS
Fried Tortillas in Eggs

It's funny how recipes evolve. Twenty years ago, when I was living in Austin, Texas, one of the best things to do on a Sunday morning was eat Migas at La Reyna Bakery—what I considered real Mexican food. Migas is the Tex-Mex cousin of chilaquiles; it's based on old tortillas but has the addition of chopped vegetables. Also, the eggs are cooked in, not served on top. Here on the ranch, we make it frequently for almuerzo or midmorning brunch and a taste of American food. Always fond of the Italian frittata, I combined the Migas ingredients with the oven cooking method to make it easier and to free up my hands to make a platanada or to mash the beans served alongside. I taught this to my assistant, Irene, who now makes Migas better than I do!

MAKES 8 SERVINGS

¼ cup sunflower or vegetable oil, or more if needed to fry the tortillas

6 corn tortillas, 8 inches in diameter, cut into 1-inch squares or triangles

1 cup finely chopped onion

1½ tablespoons finely chopped garlic

¾ pound tomatoes (1½ medium–large round or 6–7 plum), finely chopped

½ pound tomatillos, husked and finely chopped (see page 327)

2 chiles jalapeños, finely chopped (see page 329)

9 eggs, beaten

1½ teaspoons salt, or to taste

1 teaspoon ground black pepper

4 ounces queso fresco, crumbled (see page 346), or manchego or Gouda Cheese, grated

½ cup chopped cilantro

Preheat the oven to 375°F.

In a 3-inch-deep, 8-inch-wide heavy frying pan that is ovenproof, heat the oil over high heat. Add the tortillas and cook for 3 minutes or until browned. Remove and drain in a colander. Add the onion to the frying pan and cook for 5 minutes or until translucent. Add the garlic, tomatoes, *tomatillos*, and chiles. When the mixture is well fried, add the tortilla squares and mix carefully.

In a mixing bowl, beat the eggs with ¼ cup water, the salt, and pepper. Add to the tortilla mixture. Cook for 5 minutes, moving the eggs away from the sides of the frying pan to set them a bit. Bake the mixture in the oven for 15 minutes. Remove and place under the broiler for a few minutes to set the top. It should rise up and start to brown. Sprinkle the cheese and cilantro on the top, then return to the broiler for a minute to melt the cheese. Serve immediately with black beans and hot *bolillos*.

Hint: Although I personally like this as a vegetarian dish, you can put any leftover meat in the vegetable mix. Sometimes I add sausage to the mix, layer cream cheese or sour cream on top, and place it under the broiler until it bubbles.

ENSALADA DE BETABEL BENDITO
Blessed Beet Salad

Every year on Palm Sunday, the agricultural pueblo of San Antonino Castillo Velasco bursts with excitement. Starting before dawn, the villagers congregate in the cemetery with the best of their harvest to donate to a large float for Saint Antonino. The biggest fruits and vegetables are chosen and made into a large tower, with the saint on top, that takes six strong men to carry through the village. Everyone gathers for a big Mass and the blessing of the fruits, vegetables, and donations. After the Mass, the fruits and vegetables are auctioned off at one of the most animated auctions I've ever attended. I was lucky enough to get the beets off the float, hence the name—Blessed Beet Salad.

MAKES 6 SERVINGS

For the greens:

1 pound beet greens, spinach leaves, or Swiss chard, rinsed well

2 garlic cloves, finely chopped

1 tablespoon fresh lime or lemon juice

2 tablespoons good olive oil

Pinch of salt, or to taste

¼ teaspoon ground black pepper

For the salad:

½ cup fruit or red wine vinegar

¼ cup olive oil

7 garlic cloves, finely chopped

½ teaspoon aniseed

¼ teaspoon ground black pepper

2 tablespoons lime juice

3 cups whole beets, cooked, peeled, and cut into ½-inch cubes

2 oranges, peeled and cut into wedges

1 tablespoon sliced green onion (white part only)

1 tablespoon finely chopped parsley leaves

FOR THE GREENS:

If the greens are really big leaves, roughly cut or tear them. Steam the greens for 10 minutes over 2 cups water. Drain for 20 minutes, then place the greens in a medium mixing bowl.

In a small mixing bowl, mix the garlic, lime juice, oil, salt, and pepper. Pour over the greens and toss well.

FOR THE SALAD:

In a small mixing bowl, mix the vinegar, oil, garlic, aniseed, pepper, and lime juice. Add the beets and allow to marinate.

At serving time, lay the greens on a platter. Spoon the beet cubes on top and top with orange wedges, green onion, and parsley.

ENSALADA DE PIÑA, JÍCAMA, Y AGUACATE

Pineapple, Jicama, and Avocado Salad

The key to this refreshing salad lies in the toasting of the pecans and the use of perfectly ripe fruit. Because fruit is allowed to vine or tree ripen in Mexico, there is a lot of aroma, flavor, and juice released from a pineapple as you cut it. If you find you don't have any juices running from your pineapple, add 1 to 2 tablespoons of canned or bottled juice. The cream cheese and avocado should remain in chunks or small pieces throughout the salad. Don't stir it into oblivion!

MAKES 8 SERVINGS

2 cups cubed ripe pineapple, in
½-inch pieces (reserve 1–2 tablespoons juice)

1 small–medium (about ½ pound)
jicama, peeled and cut into
½-inch cubes

2 ripe avocados, Haas or other
native type, peeled and cut into
1-inch cubes

½ small red onion, thinly sliced

3 ounces softened queso crema
(see page 346)

¼ cup vinegar (mixed fruit, pineapple, or apple cider vinegar is
best)

¼ cup olive oil

4 sprigs parsley, finely chopped

4 sprigs cilantro, finely chopped

Salt and pepper to taste

½ cup pecan halves, toasted

Place the pineapple, jicama, avocados, and onion in a medium bowl. Cut the cream cheese into chunks and add to the mixture.

In a small bowl, mix the reserved pineapple juice, the vinegar, oil, parsley, and cilantro. Add salt and pepper. Toss the pecans into the salad. Pour the dressing over the salad and toss very lightly, to keep the cheese in chunks. Serve immediately.

CEBOLLAS ASADAS CON CREMA

Creamed Roasted Onions

This is a different twist on the traditional creamed onions served at Thanksgiving dinner. The onions are grilled directly on the coals or on a griddle to bring out the sweet onion flavor. During the rest of the year, they can be served with Arroz con Chepil (page 52) and a roasted chicken or Asado de Venado Enchilado (page 178).

MAKES 8 SIDE-DISH
SERVINGS

3 pounds small Texas white onions (about 1 ounce each)

2 cups chicken stock (page 343) or corn stock (page 293)

2 cups corn kernels, fresh or defrosted frozen

3 tablespoons butter

2 tablespoons finely chopped garlic

3 tablespoons flour

2 cups milk

1 tablespoon brandy or port

1 tablespoon Worcestershire sauce

½ teaspoon finely grated nutmeg

2 tablespoons finely chopped parsley leaves

Salt and white pepper to taste

5 ounces flor de calabaza squash flowers (about 30), stems, stamens, and pistils removed (optional; see page 326)

Prepare a charcoal grill. When the coals are white, place the onions directly on the coals (if possible) or on a griddle and grill all the way through, turning slowly, until clear and transparent, about 10 to 12 minutes. Remove the onions and peel off the black outer layer. Set aside.

In a medium saucepan, bring the chicken stock to a boil, add the corn, cover, and lower heat to medium. Cook until tender, about 3 to 10 minutes, depending on the variety. Set aside.

In a heavy 4-quart saucepan, heat the butter over medium heat and add the garlic. Sauté slowly until clear, about 1 to 2 minutes. Add the flour and make a light roux, stirring, for at least 5 minutes. Slowly add the hot chicken or corn stock mixture and whisk in well. Add the milk and continue to cook for about 15 minutes. Add the brandy and Worcestershire sauce. Grate in nutmeg. Add parsley and salt and pepper. Add the grilled onions and the squash flowers, stir gently, and simmer at least 30 minutes, covered.

Hint: This is good topped with *queso fresco* and baked in a 350°F oven for 15 minutes.

ARROZ CRIOLLO MEXICANO

Mexican Jambalaya

This aromatic rice is a crossover from my earlier days of cooking Cajun food at my restaurant Bon Temps Rouler in New York City. In Oaxaca, I combine the Cajun ingredients with the Mexican ones to make a vegetarian version of jambalaya without the shrimp or ham. I particularly like the nuttiness of the short-grain brown rice, which is usually transported here by friends or students. If I don't have brown rice, I substitute white rice and lower the amount of chicken or vegetable stock in the recipe to make the ratio 2:1, liquid to rice. Serve by itself as a sopa seca, *or with* Estofado de Pollo *(page 33),* Liebre en Adobo *(page 176), or* Albóndigas Estilo Ejutla *(page 29).*

MAKES 8 TO 10 SERVINGS

1½ tablespoons butter or olive oil

2 medium white onions, chopped

1 red bell pepper, chopped

5 celery ribs, chopped

2 chiles poblanos, *roasted, peeled, and chopped (see page 329)*

12 flor de calabaza *(squash flowers), cleaned with pistil removed (see page 326)*

½ head of garlic, *cloves separated and finely chopped*

1 tablespoon cumin seeds

1 tablespoon black peppercorns

3 bay leaves

1 chile de árbol *(see page 330)*

Salt to taste

5 cups chicken or vegetable stock *(page 343)*

2 cups short-grain brown rice

¼ cup cilantro leaves, finely chopped

¼ cup parsley leaves, finely chopped

In a heavy 4-quart stockpot with lid, heat the oil, then sauté the onions, red pepper, and celery until soft. Add the *chiles poblanos*, squash flowers, and garlic and sauté a few minutes longer, stirring gently.

On a 10-inch dry *comal*, griddle, or in a cast-iron frying pan, toast the cumin seeds and peppercorns until they give off their scents and are slightly browned. Grind them in the *molcajete* or spice grinder. Stir the ground spices, the bay leaves, *chile de árbol*, and salt into the vegetables. Add the stock and bring to a boil. Add the brown rice, stirring well. Bring it to a boil, then lower the heat, cover tightly, and simmer 55 minutes. Lift the lid quickly, taste for salt, add the cilantro and parsley, and replace the lid. Continue to cook the rice 5 minutes more or until all the broth is absorbed. Serve.

Hint: You must taste for salt after adding the rice to make sure the jambalaya is well seasoned before cooking it through.

POLLO ASADO CON SALSA DE PAPAYA Y CHIPOTLE
Grilled Chicken with Papaya and Chipotle Sauce

This chicken is delicious served right off the parrilla *(grill). Usually we make it as part of a* botanas, *or assorted appetizer platter, but many evenings we cook outside and serve it with rice and a fresh green salad. You can substitute* chile pasilla oaxaqueño *for the chipotles by toasting and soaking them in water to reconstitute them.*

MAKES 8 SERVINGS AS AN APPETIZER, 6 SERVINGS AS A MAIN COURSE

For the marinade:
7 garlic cloves, finely chopped

½ medium white onion, finely chopped

2 teaspoons chiles chipotles en adobo *(page 332) or finely chopped* chiles pasillas oaxaqueños *soaked in hot water for 10 minutes (see page 331)*

½ pound tomatoes (1 medium–large round or 4–5 plum), finely chopped

2 teaspoons red wine vinegar

1 tablespoon lime juice

1 teaspoon freshly ground pepper

Salt to taste

2 pounds whole chicken breasts, boned and skin removed

3 tablespoons olive oil

For the salsa:
1½ tablespoons chiles chipotles en adobo *(page 332) or* chiles pasillas oaxaqueños, *stemmed (see page 331)*

FOR THE MARINADE:
Place the garlic, onion, *chile chipotle en adobo*, and tomatoes in a medium bowl. Add the vinegar, lime juice, pepper, and salt.

Cut the chicken cutlets into 2-inch strips for *botanas* or in ½-inch strips for a main course and place them in the marinade. Add the olive oil to coat the chicken pieces well. Marinate the chicken for ½ hour or more.

FOR THE SALSA:
Put all the ingredients except the crème fraîche and seasonings in a blender or food processor and pulse, leaving the sauce chunky. You can chop the ingredients by hand if you want more of a relish. If the flavor is too strong, add the crème fraîche. Season with salt and pepper.

TO FINISH AND SERVE:
Prepare a charcoal fire. When the coals are white, grill the chicken pieces for about 5 minutes on each side or until nicely browned. The meat should remove easily from the grill when cooked.

Serve salsa in a bowl along with the chicken or spoon on top if serving as a main course.

Hint: This recipe can be adapted for baby lamb chops to grill over applewood chips.

1 cup papaya pulp (mamey variety
    is best), cut into ½-inch cubes
    (see page 340)
1 tablespoon Dijon mustard
1 tablespoon fruit vinegar or cider
    vinegar
7 garlic cloves, finely chopped
¼ cup crème fraîche or sour cream
    (optional)
Salt and pepper to taste

CAMARONES ASADOS CON SALSA DE GUAJILLO

Grilled Shrimp with Guajillo Sauce

This shrimp dish is great as an appetizer or a main course, if you like. I have been serving it for over twenty years with a variety of sauces and condiments. The shrimp goes nicely with salsa de chile guajillo *as a dipping sauce or drizzled over. Often I serve this with* Bocadillos de Papa y Chorizo *(page 227) or leftover* Tamales de Chepil *(page 151) that are reheated on the* comal *in their husks, so they are toasted and a bit charred around the edges. They are dipped into the same guajillo sauce.*

MAKES 3 TO 4 SERVINGS

1 pound shrimp (about 21–25)

For the marinade:
1½ cups olive oil, or ½ cup olive oil
    and 1 cup blended oil
1 medium white onion, sliced
11 cloves garlic
12 whole peppercorns
5 bay leaves
5 chiles de árbol (see page 330)

Peel, clean, and devein the shrimp. Save the shells and set shrimp aside.

FOR THE MARINADE:
In an 8-inch cast-iron frying pan, heat the oil over medium heat and add the reserved shrimp shells, onion, garlic, peppercorns, bay leaves, *chiles de árbol,* and allspice. Cook for 15 minutes over low heat until the shells change color, turning golden brown, and are crispy. Strain through a sieve and mash down to extract all the oil. Allow oil to cool in a medium bowl. Discard shells and seasoning.

Add the lime juice, Creole seasoning, Worcestershire

1 whole allspice

Juice of 2 limes

1 tablespoon Creole or Cajun dry seasoning (optional)

1 tablespoon Worcestershire sauce

1 tablespoon Salsa Valentina (page 331)

1 bunch green onions, green parts only, thinly sliced

7 sprigs parsley, leaves only, finely chopped (¼ cup)

7 sprigs cilantro, leaves only, finely chopped (¼ cup)

Salt

For the salsa de guajillo:

7 tomatillos (about ¾ pound)

1 medium white onion, chunked

3 garlic cloves

2 chiles guajillos, stemmed, seeded, and deveined (see page 331)

Salt to taste

1 teaspoon red wine vinegar

To serve:

Greens to line serving platter and lemon or lime wedges to garnish

sauce, *salsa valentina*, green onion, parsley, and cilantro to the oil. Add salt to taste, whisking well. Add the shrimp and stir well. Leave shrimp to marinate at least 1 hour, or overnight if desired.

FOR THE *SALSA GUAJILLO*:

In a small saucepan, bring 1 cup of water to a boil. Place the *tomatillos* on a 10-inch dry *comal*, griddle, or in a cast-iron frying pan and cook over medium heat for about 10 minutes. Add the onion and garlic and cook for 3 minutes more. Then add the chiles and cook for another minute, being careful not to burn the flesh of the chiles. The garlic will cook faster than the rest, so remove it first, turning the onion and chiles on both sides. Remove the chiles from the *comal* and soak in the boiling water until soft, about 20 minutes. Remove the onion and *tomatillos*.

In a blender or *molcajete*, grind the chiles and garlic with a little salt. Then add the onion and *tomatillos* and blend until smooth. Add the vinegar and more salt to taste. Chill until ready to use.

TO FINISH AND SERVE:

Soak mesquite or pecan wood chips in a little water. Start a charcoal fire. When the coals are very hot, place the wood chips on the coals and, when there is aromatic smoke, place the shrimp on the grill. Cook until just done, grilling on both sides, about 3 minutes each side.

Place the shrimp on a serving platter lined with the greens. Serve with *salsa de guajillo* and lemon wedges on the side.

Hint: If you don't have a grill, you can broil the shrimp or cook them on a hot *comal* or in a cast-iron frying pan. You can also use the marinade for chicken breasts or mushrooms to get a "shrimpy" flavor. After soaking the chicken or mushrooms for at least ½ hour, grill and serve alongside the shrimp or use in a layered *torta* with avocado and tomato slices.

MEDALLONES DE LOMO DE PUERCO CON SALSA DE TUNA
Pork Loin Medallions with Cactus Fruit Sauce

This recipe is a hit with my children, whose idea of a great time in the summer is to walk around with a big stick of carrizo *and knock down the* tunas *growing on cactus.* Tunas *are the fruit of the prickly pear cactus and they come in various forms and colors ranging from dark to bright reds or greens.* Tunas *are usually made into ices or flavored waters, or just enjoyed with chile powder, salt, and a squirt of lime. If you can't find* tunas, *substitute kiwis, which have a similar texture and flavor, but the sauce will be green, not the reddish purple from the* tunas. *Serve this with roasted potatoes and Chayotes Asados (page 236) or Arroz con Chepil (page 52).*

MAKES 6 SERVINGS

2 pounds boneless pork loin, cut into 12 ½-inch-thick slices

¼ cup flour mixed with ½ teaspoon salt and ½ teaspoon pepper

2 tablespoons butter, or more as needed

2 tablespoons olive oil, or more as needed

2 small white onions, finely chopped

1½ tablespoons finely chopped garlic

2 tablespoons flour

2 cups pork stock (page 344), made with pork ribs or bones instead of boneless pork shoulder

½ pound ripe, red tuna, pitaya (see page 340), or kiwifruit, peeled and pureed (1 cup)

¼ cup medium sherry

1 sprig thyme, or ¼ teaspoon dried

Dip the pork into the flour mixture, then shake off excess flour. In a heavy 10-inch frying pan, fry the pork in the butter and olive oil until brown, about 7 to 10 minutes on each side. You will have to do this in batches; don't crowd the pan. Remove from the pan, place slices in a baking pan, and cover and place in a warm oven.

Add the onions to the frying pan (there should be butter and oil remaining; if not, add 1 tablespoon of each) and sauté until transparent, about 3 minutes. Add the garlic and cook until soft, another 2 minutes. Add the 2 tablespoons flour and whisk well. Cook the roux for 5 minutes, stirring constantly. Add 2 cups of the pork stock and cook for 10 minutes. Add the *tuna* puree and sherry and whisk in. Add the thyme, salt, pepper, parsley, and orange peel. Cook over medium heat, allowing the mixture to thicken slightly, stirring. If your sauce gets too thick, add a touch more stock. Be careful not to let it dry out.

Ladle 4 to 6 tablespoons of the sauce on each plate and place a slice of pork on it. Lay an orange slice on top, slightly overlapping. Add another slice of pork on the orange slice, slightly overlapping it to one side. Sprinkle the parsley in a line across the top and serve immediately.

Salt and pepper to taste

2 tablespoons finely chopped
   parsley leaves

1 teaspoon finely grated orange peel

For the garnish:

1 eating orange, peeled and sliced
   into 6 rounds

1½ teaspoons finely chopped
   parsley leaves

Hint: This sauce is excellent with chicken or fish, changing the stock as needed.

Inspired by Jonathan Barbieri

GUAJOLOTE RELLENO ENCHILADO AL HORNO

Baked Stuffed Turkey Rubbed with Chile Paste

Every year since I've been living in Mexico, we have celebrated Día de Gracias, or Thanksgiving. It's been fun having our Mexican friends eat the ritual dinner for the first time and see their approval of Norteamericano-style turkey with all the trimmings. Over the years, the guests have changed and now we have a mixed group of friends who eat a potluck Thanksgiving dinner. I always do the turkey, and I grow fennel in my garden in anticipation of the bread stuffing. The traditional glaze has become spicier and more Mexican influenced. I do use commercial roasting turkeys, though, as we learned that the free-range turkeys here are much too tough and stringy to bake, though they are great stewed.

MAKES 12 TO 16 SERVINGS,
WITH LEFTOVERS

For the stuffing:

7 cups cubed whole wheat bread or
   bolillos *(see page 347)*

2 chiles poblanos *(see page 329)*

¾ cup (1½ sticks) butter

FOR THE STUFFING:

Preheat the oven to 400°F.

   Place the bread cubes on a baking sheet and bake for 10 to 15 minutes or until dry. Remove from the oven and cool, then place in a large bowl. (If you are using day-old bread and it is dry, omit this step.)

   On a 10-inch dry *comal*, griddle, or in a cast-iron frying pan or over an open flame, roast the *chiles poblanos* until they

2 tablespoons olive oil

1 large white onion, chopped

1 large leek, cleaned well and
    thinly sliced

1 red bell pepper, chopped

1 cup chopped celery

1 small fennel bulb, sliced (with
    ¾ cup stem and leaves)

1½ tablespoons finely chopped
    garlic

2 large Rome apples, cored and
    coarsely chopped

2 Anjou pears, cored and coarsely
    chopped

½ cup prunes, pitted and halved

½ cup black figs, crystallized or
    dried

1 teaspoon cumin seeds

1 teaspoon black peppercorns

1 tablespoon grated orange rind

2 teaspoons salt, or more to taste

½ cup finely chopped parsley leaves

½ cup garlic chives or chives

3 eggs, beaten

For the turkey:

1 large turkey, 15 to 20 pounds,
    neck and gizzard reserved

Seasoning ingredients for chicken
    stock (page 343)

3 chiles pasillas oaxaqueños or
    chiles chipotles, stemmed,
    seeded, and deveined (see
    pages 330 and 331)

½ cup finely chopped garlic

1 teaspoon salt

1 tablespoon black peppercorns

¼ cup orange juice

1 tablespoon good olive oil

1 tablespoon honey

Port or red wine, for deglazing

blister, turning to roast all sides. Place in a plastic bag to "sweat" for 15 minutes. Peel and remove stems and seeds. Chop the same size as the vegetables.

In a heavy 4-quart stockpot, heat the butter and olive oil. Add the onion and leek and cook until transparent, about 3 minutes. Add the red pepper, celery, and fennel, and cook until soft, another 5 minutes. Add the garlic, *chiles poblanos*, apples, and pears and cook for 10 minutes. Stir in the prunes and figs.

In a small, dry frying pan, toast the cumin seeds and peppercorns until brown and they give off their scent. Grind them in a *molcajete* or spice grinder and add to the vegetable mixture along with the orange rind. Add salt. Add the parsley and chives, and heat through.

Add the sautéed mixture to the bread cubes and carefully mix in. Let the mixture cool. Add the beaten eggs and mix in. If the mixture is too dry, add another egg to the mixture. Adjust the salt and pepper. Allow the stuffing to cool *completely* before putting it in the turkey cavity. It's best made the day before.

FOR THE TURKEY:
Preheat the oven to 400°F.

Put the seasoning ingredients in a 6-quart stockpot, following the directions for making chicken stock on page 343, substituting the turkey neck and gizzard for the chicken parts. (Do not use the liver in the stock.) Cover and simmer gently for 1½ hours, while you make the turkey. Strain the stock and reserve for later use with the gravy.

Bring 1 cup of water to a boil. Toast the *chiles pasillas* on a 10-inch dry *comal*, griddle, or in a cast-iron frying pan until they puff up and give off their scent. Soak them in the hot water for 15 to 20 minutes. In a *molcajete* or blender, grind the garlic in the salt until pasty. Add the peppercorns, then the *chiles pasillas* and continue to grind. Add the orange juice, olive oil, and honey until you achieve a thick, but wet mass. Set aside.

Turn the wings back and tuck under the turkey. Dry the turkey thoroughly. Rub salt and pepper on the inside of the turkey. Carefully stuff both ends of the bird and skewer shut. (If you have stuffing remaining, bake it in a buttered

For the gravy:

1 medium onion, finely chopped

½ cup finely chopped celery

2 tablespoons finely chopped garlic

½ cup unbleached all-purpose flour

4 to 6 tablespoons good port or red wine

½ teaspoon freshly grated nutmeg

Salt to taste

1 teaspoon ground black pepper

2 tablespoons finely chopped parsley leaves

Susana in her kitchen, Rancho Aurora, Oaxaca (Marcela Taboada)

baking dish on the side, covered, for 1 hour.) Rub the chile mixture on the turkey skin on all sides.

Place the bird breast side up on a rack in an oval roasting pan and put in the oven. Cook for 15 minutes, then lower the heat to 300°F and cook for 30 more minutes. If you wish you can make a collar of heavy-duty aluminum foil around the baking rack, and remove the turkey from the pan to baste it. Turn the turkey over breast side down on top of the foil collar and continue to roast. (I have had very good luck with this method and the breast stays very moist. Sometimes, however, it doesn't always look picture-perfect and the breast gets a little smashed.) Cover turkey with a buttered piece of foil and continue to bake 3¼ to 5 hours (depending on size, calculating 20 minutes per pound from the beginning). Baste every 30 minutes or so until cooked all the way through.

Turn the turkey breast side up on a cutting board and let rest for 15 to 20 minutes, covered with foil. Deglaze the roasting pan with the wine, stirring for about 5 minutes over high heat. Remove the liquid from the roasting pan and strain to remove particles with a fine-mesh strainer. Place the basting liquid in the freezer for about 10 minutes. When it congeals, scrape ½ cup of the turkey fat off the top; reserve the bottom juice for the gravy.

FOR THE GRAVY:

In a medium saucepan, fry the onion in the turkey fat until opaque, about 5 minutes. Add the celery and garlic and continue to cook. Add ½ cup flour and stir in well with a whisk. Cook at least 5 minutes, then slowly add 4 to 5 cups reserved turkey stock, whisking and cooking, letting it thicken, 15 to 20 minutes. Add the wine, nutmeg, salt, pepper, and parsley. Finely chop the turkey giblet and add to the gravy. If the gravy gets too thick, add more stock.

TO SERVE:

Scoop out the stuffing, slice the turkey, and serve with gravy and *Cebollas Asadas con Crema* (see page 298).

FILETE DE RES CON NANACATES

Beef Tenderloin with Wild Mushrooms

This dish is particularly good in the rainy season when the orangey yellow or pale brown nanacates, or wild mushrooms, are brought down from the mountains. Sometimes I make the dish with the small wild mushrooms we gather in the hills behind our ranch, using them whole in the sauce. You can substitute portobello mushrooms for the nanacates, and sirloin tip for the tenderloin.

MAKES 4 SERVINGS

1 pound beef tenderloin, cut into
  4 portions

1 pound nanacates (see page 327),
  or 4 large portobello mushrooms, stems removed

2 tablespoons Cajun seasoning

3 teaspoons Worcestershire sauce

3 tablespoons butter or olive oil, or
  a combination

1 small white onion, halved and
  thinly sliced

1 tablespoon finely chopped garlic

1–2 chiles costeños rojos or
  chiles de árbol, stemmed,
  seeded, deveined, and thinly
  sliced (see page 330)

4 tablespoons Hornitos tequila (see
  page 349)

4 tablespoons fresh orange juice

1 teaspoon Oaxacan oregano
  leaves, fresh or dried (see
  page 336)

½ teaspoon salt, or more to taste

½ teaspoon freshly ground black
  pepper

2 tablespoons finely chopped
  parsley leaves

Season each beef portion and the mushroom caps on both sides with the Cajun seasoning. Put the Worcestershire sauce on a plate. Dip each piece of meat and mushrooms in the sauce on both sides.

In a large 10-inch frying pan, heat the butter or olive oil until it starts to sizzle, then sauté the beef filets about 10 to 15 minutes or until browned on both sides and rare in the middle, or as you prefer. Remove from the pan and keep warm.

In the same frying pan, fry the *nanacates* in the same manner, turning to cook them on both sides, about 3 to 4 minutes. (If you need more butter or oil, add a little.) When the mushrooms are cooking on the second side, add the onion and fry until clear, about 3 minutes. Add the garlic and chile slices. Sprinkle on any remaining Worcestershire sauce. Add the tequila and flame. After flames subside, add the orange juice, oregano, salt, pepper, and parsley. Reduce the sauce over high heat for at least 5 minutes or until it starts to thicken.

Place some *nanacates* on each plate and lay a filet on top. Spoon the sauce over the top and serve with rice or potatoes.

BUDÍN DE TAMALA Y PAN
Bread Pudding with Pumpkin

This is a favorite Cajun recipe from New Orleans that I adapted when I moved to Oaxaca. It is most certainly a crowd pleaser, and I have made it for special occasions such as Christmas or for Piña Palmera fund-raisers, to satisfy the sweet tooth and to be served before the auction begins. It is a good keeper and actually gets better after a day or two. Both the pudding and the sauce should be served hot. You can gild the lily by adding fresh or whipped cream on the top. Serve with coffee, tea, or Mexican chocolate.

MAKES 8 TO 10 SERVINGS

For the bread pudding:
4 cups milk

½ cup (1 stick) butter

2 tablespoons rum

½ cup raisins

4 eggs

1½ cups sugar

1 teaspoon ground nutmeg

1 teaspoon Mexican cinnamon (see page 337)

2 teaspoons vanilla extract

¼ teaspoon salt

2½–3 bolillos, cubed (see page 347), or 6 cups stale bread cubes

1 cup calabaza tamala *squash or pumpkin, cut into 1-inch cubes (see page 325)*

For the rum sauce:
½ pound piloncillo (see page 348) or 1¾ cups tightly packed brown sugar

¼ cup rum

½ cup (1 stick) butter

FOR THE BREAD PUDDING:
Preheat the oven to 350°F.

In a 2-quart saucepan, bring the milk to the scalding point. Add the butter to melt, then allow the mixture to cool for 10 minutes.

In a small saucepan, heat the rum, 2 tablespoons water, and the raisins. Simmer over low heat for 10 minutes.

In a large mixing bowl, mix the eggs, sugar, nutmeg, cinnamon, vanilla, and salt. Then add in the milk mixture, whisking all the while so as not to cook the eggs. Mix well for about 5 minutes. Drain the raisins and add to the egg mixture. Reserve the rum for the rum sauce.

Add the bread and squash cubes, and stir to coat. Pour into a buttered 3½-quart casserole and bake for 1¼ hours or until a knife inserted comes out clean.

FOR THE RUM SAUCE:
Put all the ingredients plus the reserved rum in a 2-quart saucepan. Bring to a boil and cook over high heat, uncovered, about 5 minutes. Serve the sauce over individual servings of pudding and top with whipped cream, if desired.

½ cup heavy cream

¼ teaspoon salt

2 cups heavy cream, lightly
   whipped and slightly sweetened
   and flavored with Mexican
   vanilla (optional)

PASTEL DE NUÉZ CON CHOCOLATE
Pecan Torte with Chocolate Glaze

*This is my favorite cake of all time. I originally ate it made with hazelnuts and wal-
nuts at Under the Blue Moon, the restaurant of my first mentor and almost mother-
in-law, Phyllis Gosfield. I use the local pecans from our neighbor's trees and almonds
that are easily available here and I roll it up. Its light texture, with the whipped cream
and simple chocolate glaze, makes it so scrumptious that you can always find room
for a piece, even if you are stuffed from a wonderful dinner. I change the fruits with
the season and flavor the cream with various flavors of crema de mezcal that our
friends make in the valley of Tlacolula.*

MAKES 8 TO 12 SERVINGS

For the cake:

7 large eggs

1¼ cups pecans (5 ounces), toasted
   and finely ground

1¼ cups almonds (6 ounces),
   toasted and finely ground

¼ cup fine bread crumbs (whole
   wheat is best)

½ teaspoon salt, or more as needed

1 teaspoon baking powder

1 cup granulated sugar

1 teaspoon vanilla extract

FOR BAKING THE CAKE:

Preheat the oven to 375°F. Grease a jellyroll pan with oil or
line it with waxed paper oiled on both sides.

Separate the egg yolks and whites into two medium
bowls.

In another bowl, mix the pecans, almonds, bread crumbs,
salt, and baking powder. With a mixer, beat the egg yolks
until they are light and lemon colored. Slowly adding ½ cup
of the sugar, mix the yolks to a thick mass, 15 to 20 minutes.
Add the vanilla and beat 3 minutes more. Add the nut mixture to the egg yolk mixture and stir well.

With a mixer, whip the egg whites with a pinch of salt
until soft peaks form, about 10 minutes. Add the remaining
½ cup of sugar to the egg whites, 2 tablespoons at a time,
beating until stiff peaks form, about 4 minutes more. Fold

For the filling:

2 cups whipping cream

1 teaspoon vanilla extract, or orange-flavored mezcal, or other liquor of your choice

2 tablespoons–¼ cup confectioners' sugar

2 cups cubed fresh strawberries, guavas, blueberries, bananas, mangoes, peaches, or a mixture of any two, in 1-inch pieces

For the chocolate glaze:

½ pound semisweet chocolate (see Hint)

4 tablespoons brewed strong coffee

Tiny pinch of salt

6 tablespoons unsalted butter, softened

the egg white mixture into the egg yolk mixture, one-third at a time, until well incorporated. Pour the batter into the greased and papered pan. Bake for 25 minutes or until the cake separates from the sides of the pan.

FOR THE FILLING:

Whip the cream with the vanilla until soft peaks form, about 7 minutes.

Sift the confectioners' sugar to remove the lumps and add it to the whipped cream (see Hint) and continue to whip until stiff peaks form, about 3 minutes more. Fold the cut fruit into the cream and set aside.

FOR THE CHOCOLATE GLAZE:

Melt the chocolate slowly in the top of a double boiler over low heat. Add the coffee and salt and whisk well. Add the butter bit by bit, whisking constantly until a sheen appears on the chocolate.

TO ASSEMBLE THE CAKE:

Let the cake cool for 20 minutes, then invert onto a sheet of waxed paper or a tea towel that has been dusted with confectioners' sugar (see Hint). Take a damp cloth and lightly rub the top of the waxed paper that is adhered to the cake. Carefully peel the paper off the top and dust off the crumbs. Spread the filling over the cake, leaving a 1-inch border on all sides. Roll the cake lengthwise and place it seam side down on a serving platter. Pour the chocolate glaze over, allowing it to drop over the sides. Garnish with a fresh bougainvillea spray or other edible flowers and serve.

Hints: I used to be a real snob about chocolate, when I had every imaginable kind available in New York City. My favorite was Callabaut semisweet from Belgium. Now I feel lucky if I can get Turín, a semisweet with very little butterfat, which is the best local chocolate to cook with. Use the best-quality chocolate you can find. It will really make a difference.

The cream in Oaxaca is fresh and sours very quickly, becoming like crème fraîche. You have to adjust the confectioners' sugar to taste according to your local cream.

You can wait until the next day to fill the cake if you

roll the warm cake in waxed paper or tea towels that have been dusted with confectioners' sugar and store it in a dry, airtight plastic bag.

PASTEL DE NARANJA DE MI ABUELA
My Grandmother's Orange Cake

I found this recipe in a pile of notes that my grandmother still has in her files. I can recall eating this delicious light tube cake in her kitchen when I was a child visiting her in San Antonio. The memory of eating a slice topped with her homemade orange marmalade and freshly whipped cream can make me hungry even today. This cake can be made in a jellyroll pan and filled with the whipped cream and cut fruit. For a lighter version, make this cake in a tube pan, top with fresh fruit, and dust with confectioners' sugar. Here in Oaxaca, I can step outside my kitchen door and pick fresh oranges for the juice and rind. ¡Qué rica es la vida! (How rich is life!)

MAKES 8 TO 12 SERVINGS

For the cake:
6 large eggs, at room temperature
    for 1 hour
1¾ cups all-purpose flour
½ teaspoon salt
1½ cups granulated sugar
6 tablespoons fresh orange juice
    (about 1 orange)
1 tablespoon grated orange rind,
    using the small side of the grater

For the topping or filling:
1 pint whipping cream
1 teaspoon Mexican vanilla (see
    page 338)

Preheat the oven to 375°F. Oil a standard 10-inch tube or jellyroll pan. Line the jellyroll pan with waxed paper and turn the paper so that both sides are oiled well.

Separate the eggs into two medium bowls.

In a third bowl, measure the flour and sift it with the salt. With a mixer on high, beat the egg yolks until thick and lemon colored, about 15 minutes. Gradually beat in 1 cup of the sugar and, when it is incorporated, continue to beat for 3 minutes more. Slowly add the flour mixture and the orange juice alternately, beginning and ending with the flour. Mix in the orange rind.

Whip the egg whites on high speed until they form soft peaks, about 5 minutes. Add the remaining ½ cup sugar and beat constantly until stiff peaks form, 5 to 8 minutes. Fold the egg whites into the batter, one-third at a time, using a rubber spatula.

¼ cup confectioners' sugar, plus extra for dusting cake

2 cups cubed fresh mangoes, strawberries, guavas, or other fruits

FOR TUBE PAN:

Pour the batter into the prepared pan. Spread it evenly to reach the edges of the pan and bake for 35 to 40 minutes. Let the cake cool in the pan for 20 minutes before turning it out onto a cake platter.

Whip the cream with the vanilla until soft peaks form. Add the confectioners' sugar and continue to whip until stiff peaks form. Sprinkle the top of the cake with confectioners' sugar. To serve, top a slice of cake with a dollop of whipped cream and add the fruit.

FOR JELLYROLL PAN:

Pour the batter into the prepared pan, spreading it out evenly to reach the edges of the pan, and bake for 35 minutes. Let rest for 5 minutes, then remove from the pan and

invert the cake onto a clean tea towel that has been dusted with confectioners' sugar or a fresh piece of waxed paper. Remove the waxed paper by rubbing the surface of the paper with a dry towel and then peeling off the paper. Cover the cake with another clean tea towel and roll up lengthwise in the towels, like a jellyroll, while the cake is still warm.

Whip the cream with the vanilla until soft peaks form. Add the confectioners' sugar and continue to whip until stiff peaks form. Fold the fruit into the whipped cream, unroll the cake, spread a thin layer of the fruit and cream mixture on the cake, and reroll. Place seam side down on a platter and dust with confectioners' sugar.

Given by Marie Antoinette Chavana Flores

Susana's grandmother, Marie Antoinette Chavana Flores (Lewison Studio, San Antonio Texas)

GELATINA DE TÍA RENEE
Aunt Renee's Gelatin Mold

I always say that the national dessert of Mexico is flan or gelatina. *It is served daily with the* comida corrida *at local restaurants. It is often sold in the mornings in little cups of various flavor combinations with fruit inside and is popular with young and old alike. This recipe of my Aunt Renee is a family favorite for special occasions, especially when turkey is served. She uses sweet black cherries, which we can't find here, but I substitute the small native peaches that come from the nearby Sierra Juárez. This is better made a day before serving.*

MAKES 8 TO 12 SERVINGS

2 (6-ounce) packages black cherry Jell-O

1½ pounds peaches, peeled and halved, or 2 cans (16 ounces each) peaches or black cherries in light syrup, reserving the juice

2 (3-ounce) packages lime Jell-O

6 ounces cream cheese, softened

In a medium bowl, mix one package of the cherry Jell-O with 2 cups boiling water and 1½ cups cold water, or the reserved fruit juice.

Arrange half of the peach halves in the bottom of a greased 6-cup ring mold or Bundt pan. Add enough cherry Jell-O to barely cover the peaches, and chill until firm. Chill the remaining Jell-O until syrupy and add to the jello mold when the first layer is firm.

In another medium mixing bowl, mix the lime Jell-O with 1 cup boiling water and 1 cup cold water. Chill until syrupy. With a blender or hand beater, blend in the softened cream cheese. Add to the mold after the first two layers of cherry Jell-O are very firm.

Repeat the first step with the second package of cherry Jell-O. Chill until syrupy. When the lime layer is firm, add the remaining peaches and pour the cherry Jell-O over the peaches. Chill until firm. To serve, invert and center the jello mold on a large, wet plate. Rub a tea towel soaked in hot water over the top of the mold. Gently lift the mold off the gelatin. Arrange cut flowers in the middle of the gelatin and serve.

Hint: If you make this a day ahead, keep the mold in the refrigerator wrapped in plastic until ready to serve.

TAMALES DE CHOCOLATE

Mexican Chocolate Tamales

I first made these tamales *when our friend and teacher Elaine González was coming to town to lead one of her famous chocolate tours on the uses of cacao in Oaxacan culture. Elaine is always pampering us with chocolate treats, so we try to return the favor. As always, she is a big inspiration to me and for these* Tamales de Chocolate.

MAKES 22 TO 24 *TAMALES*

3 packages dried cornhusks (24 per package)

For the masa:

1½ pounds prepared masa *for tamales or 2⅔ cups* masa harina *for tamales*

1 cup grated Mexican chocolate (about 4 ounces; see page 349)

2–4 teaspoons salt

2 teaspoons baking powder

1 cup (2 sticks) butter

½ cup plus 2 tablespoons sweetened condensed milk

1 cup pineapple or other fruit juice

½ cup pecan pieces, toasted

½ cup raisins

½ cup diced pineapple

Soak the cornhusks in water to cover for ½ hour to soften.

Put salted water in a *tamalera*, fish poacher, or pot with a steamer rack and bring to a boil.

FOR THE *MASA*:

If using prepared *masa*, break up the *masa* in a medium to large mixing bowl. If using *masa harina*, place it in a bowl and add 1 cup plus 2 tablespoons warm water to make a soft dough. Allow to rest for 15 minutes.

With either *masa*, mix in the chocolate, salt, and baking powder with your fingers. Put the butter in a mixer and whip until fluffy. If you have a heavy-duty mixer like a KitchenAid, add the *masa* mixture and beat well. If you don't, add the whipped butter to the *masa* in your bowl and work it in with your hands, mixing until thoroughly incorporated.

Add the condensed milk and pineapple juice and beat for about 10 minutes, or until smooth. Stir in the pecans, raisins, and pineapple pieces. Check for salt and add more if needed. The *masa* should have a slight salty taste at the back of your mouth, no more. If there is not enough salt, they won't taste like anything!

Remove the cornhusks from the water. Dry them with a towel. Line the steamer rack with some cornhusks.

Fill each cornhusk with ¼ cup of the *masa* (see Hint) and roll up. Fold over and put into the steamer. Steam for 1 hour. Serve hot.

Hint: You can eliminate the chocolate from the recipe and use ½ cup red sugar to tint the *tamales* pink; the pink ones are eaten when a girl is born. Chocolate *tamales* are for little boys.

AGUA DE HOJA DE LIMÓN
Iced Lime Leaf Tea

Before Eric finished building our home, we planted a huerta, or grove, of citrus trees on both sides of our driveway. Now several years later, they are established and producing lots of fruit. I particularly love the days when the rains start. All the trees flower at once and the perfume is an aphrodisiac. I use all parts of the tree for drinking—limeade from the fruit, hot aromatic tea from the flowers, and this house specialty from the leaves.

MAKES 12 CUPS

2½ cups (1½ ounces) lime leaves
   (see page 339)
¼–½ cup sugar, or to taste

In a blender, combine the lime leaves with 1½ cups of water. Blend well. Strain the mixture through a sieve into a large pitcher. Add 10 cups of water and the sugar. Add ice and serve.

AGUA DE PEPINO, APIO, Y PIÑA
Cucumber, Celery, and Pineapple Drink

The very first person I met in Oaxaca city upon my arrival from Piña Palmera was Edith López Cortez. She and her son Beto were the owners of Chips cafeteria, which served the best cappuccino in town, hot or frozen, as well as other fruit drinks and concoctions. We became good friends. One Sunday afternoon, while visiting our ranch, she taught me this healthy, cleansing drink.

MAKES 2 QUARTS

2 cups chunked pineapple
1 cup peeled and chunked
   cucumber
1 cup diced celery
2 tablespoons lime juice
¾ cup sugar, or to taste

Put the pineapple, cucumber, celery, and 2 cups of water in a blender. Blend well. Pour the liquid through a sieve to strain out the pulp, then pour into a large pitcher. Add 6 cups of water, the lime juice, and sugar. Mix well.
   Serve well chilled.

CHAPTER TWELVE

Essential Ingredients

Ollas, Sierra Mixe (Alfredo Díaz Mora)

Overleaf: Esteban Espinoza preparing lisa fish to smoke, San Blas Atempa, Isthmus of Tehuantepec (Alfredo Díaz Mora)

Years ago I met a food writer in Austin, Texas, who encouraged me to write a book about Oaxacan cooking. My response was "There are no Oaxacan ingredients in the United States and the food is unique; it could never translate to the American kitchen." But inspiration and teaching outside of Oaxaca over the years have changed my tune, and now I see it as a challenge to find ingredients stateside and make substitutions whenever possible. Of course, some specialized dishes could never make it into this book, but there are so many wonderful dishes in the state of Oaxaca that I now feel I am presenting only the tip of the proverbial iceberg.

I think the major differences in Mexican and U.S. ingredients are the ripeness at harvest and the freshness of ingredients, two factors that affect overall flavor. The varieties of foods differ, too—for example, the *criollo* corn that we grow in Oaxaca is comparable to the field corn in the United States. The lack of availability of ingredients has been taken into consideration, and I have put substitutions in the recipes where possible. If you can't find the ingredients in a Mexican specialty market, I encourage you to look in Asian markets. Beans, nuts, and seeds can be found in their natural state in health-food stores. I also suggest you purchase seeds or root stock and try to grow your own herbs. (Look in the Sources at the back of the book for listings.) Of course, the best thing to do is to come to Oaxaca, visit the markets, and take back the dried herbs and chiles you need to re-create the magic and *sazón* of Oaxaca in your home.

This chapter serves as a reference point for information on the ingredients for the Oaxacan kitchen. Because many items may be unfamiliar, I have described what they look like and how to handle them. Even in Mexico, names of herbs and chiles change from region to region, so they may be difficult to identify by name only.

Since the size of ingredients can be so different in Mexico and the United States, I suggest you weigh ingredients whenever possible. A kitchen scale is an invaluable item—every kitchen should have one! All the baking times have been tested at sea level, but baking times may vary somewhat. Likewise, if you don't have the exact kitchen tool to make a dish, do it the Mexican way and be creative: invent a different way to get to the same end. The important thing is to try the dishes.

CORN

Of all the ingredients in the Oaxacan kitchen, corn is at the heart of the *comida* (meal). The year revolves around the cycle of corn, which is planted in the same fields as beans and squash to make a perfect growing environment. The cornstalk grows, the bean plant crawls up the corn, and the squash vine sprawls out and shades the ground to keep it moist. The beans add nitrogen to the soil that the corn uses up. Some of the corn is harvested in August and eaten fresh, while the rest is left on the stalks to dry. All parts of the corn plant are used—kernels, husks (for *tamales*), cobs (pig feed), and stalks (cow feed). The dried corn is stored and used in many ways throughout the year.

FRESH CORN

CHILEATOLE: Fresh corn *atole* (see below) with hot chile added.

ELOTE: Fresh corn, roasted or boiled whole. It is also used cut into rounds or as kernels cut off the cob.

ESQUITES: Soup of corn kernels served with mayonnaise, lime, salty cheese, and chile.

HUITLACOCHE (CUITLACOCHE) (*USTILAGO MAYDIS*): Corn fungus that is considered a delicacy of the rainy season. Spores attack the corn and mutate the kernels, causing them to enlarge and burst open the green husks that normally enclose them. *Huitlacoche* is gray on the outside and inky black on the inside. Traditionally eaten in tacos, contemporarily eaten in soups, sauces, and crepes. Best eaten fresh, it can be frozen or is available canned, in Mexican specialty markets.

MILPA: Cornfield.

PAN DE ELOTE: Originally from the Isthmus of Tehuantepec, bread made from fresh corn, baked in adobe ovens.

TAMAL DE ELOTE: Fresh corn *tamal*, usually sweetened, wrapped in fresh green cornhusks.

DRIED CORN

ATOLE: Hot gruel drink made with different textures and flavorings, usually made with corn, but can be made with wheat, oats, or sesame seeds.

CAL (*CALCIUM HYDROXIDE/OXIDE*): Slaked lime. Used in cooking water to soften corn kernels. Available by mail order or in specialty stores.

MAÍZ: Dried white, red, yellow, or black corn.

MAÍZ PALOMERO: Corn for popping. Popped corn is called *palomitas*.

MASA: Corn cooked in slaked-lime water and ground into a soft, smooth-textured dough. It can also be made from *masa harina* and water, and is used for making tortillas, *tamales*, dumplings, empanadas, and countless other dishes. Also used as a thickening agent in sauces and bean dishes. The word *masa* means any type of dough.

MASA HARINA: Dehydrated corn flour. Comes finely ground for tortillas and coarsely ground for *tamales*.

NIXTAMAL: Dried corn that has been soaked and boiled in slaked-lime water and that will be ground to make *masa*; see recipe on page 322.

POZOLE: Large-kernel corn used to make a soup with aromatic spices and pork; also served topped with *mole rojo*, or in a sweet version combined with *calabaza en dulce*.

SEGUEZA: Pre-Hispanic toasted corn stew, served with rabbit, pork, chicken, or beans.

TOTOMOXTLE: Dried cornhusks used as *tamal* wrappers. The cornhusks available in the United States are cut on both ends, unlike the ones in Mexico. To make *tamales*, I suggest using two cornhusks, wide ends overlapping. Spread the *masa* in the center and place the filling in the middle. Roll up or fold the edges of the husk and secure with ties made from strips of shredded cornhusk. To make ties: soak cornhusks in warm water until soft and pliable. Shred them to make ⅛- to ¼-inch strips. Tie two together to make longer strips.

TORTILLAS

BLANDA: Soft hand-made tortilla.

ENCHILADA: Folded tortilla dipped in *mole coloradito* or *mole rojo*, garnished with *queso fresco*, white onion, and parsley.

ENFRIJOLADA: Soft tortilla dipped in a black bean sauce seasoned with *poleo* or avocado leaf and *chile de árbol*, topped with cheese, white onion, and flat-leafed parsley.

ENMOLADA: Folded tortilla dipped in *mole negro* sauce garnished with *queso fresco*, white onion, and parsley.

ENTOMATADA: Folded tortilla dipped in tomato sauce garnished with *queso fresco*, white onion, and parsley.

TLAYUDA: Large, well-cooked, crispy tortilla sold plain or topped with *asiento*, bean paste, cabbage, meat, and salsa.

TORTILLA: Flat, unleavened corn disk baked on a *comal* over a wood fire.

TORTILLA DE PLÁTANO: Corn and green plantain tortilla.

TORTILLA EMBARRADA: Tortilla smeared with a black bean sauce.

TOSTADA: Dried or fried, crispy tortilla.

TOSTADA DE COCO: Crispy tortilla of corn and coconut.

TOTOPO: Thin, crispy corn tortilla cracker from the Isthmus of Tehuantepec that has holes in its surface and is baked in a sunken clay oven called a *comiscal*.

TORTILLAS DE MAÍZ
Corn Cortillas

MAKES 4 POUNDS OF *MASA*;
OR 16 (9-INCH) *BLANDAS* OR
12 (11-INCH) *TLAYUDAS*

⅓ cup (3 ounces) cal *(see page 320)*
2 pounds dried corn, or 7 cups
   masa harina *for tortillas*
   (page 320)

If using dried corn, in a 4-quart stainless steel stockpot or clay *olla*, bring 2½ quarts of water to a boil.

In a plastic container or bowl, crumble the *cal* in 1 cup of water and stir until it totally dissolves. Allow this mixture to settle, about 5 minutes. There will be sediment at the bottom and milky water at the top.

Put the corn into the boiling water and add the milky *cal* water (not the sediment). Bring to a boil, cover, and cook for 40 minutes over medium heat. When the corn is cooked, it will be slightly yellow and you will be able to bite into a kernel. Drain and rinse the corn.

Use a hand grinder or a grinding attachment for a mixer to grind the corn into a smooth dough. You may have to repeat this several times to obtain a smooth texture. (For most *tamales*, you need a coarser dough, so grind it only once or twice.) Place the dough in a medium bowl and cover with a damp cloth.

If using *masa harina*, mix the *masa harina* with 4½ cups warm water in a large mixing bowl. Cover with a damp cloth and allow to sit for 15 minutes.

TO MAKE TORTILLAS:
Divide the dough into 12 or 16 pieces, depending on which size tortilla you are making. Roll them into balls and cover with a damp cloth. Press the *masa* balls out on a tortilla press between two sheets of plastic. Remove the top sheet of plastic from the tortilla. Lay it gently on top of the tortilla and invert the tortilla with the plastic on both sides. Peel off the plastic on top and invert the tortilla onto your hand. Remove the remaining piece of plastic. If you don't have a tortilla press, put the ball in between two pieces of plastic. Pat out the tortilla shape with the heel of your hand on a table.

For *blandas*, lay the tortilla in the center of a 12-inch dry *comal* over high heat (see Hint) and cook it for 1 minute. Then turn it over and cook it for another minute over medium heat. Turn it over again and cook for another minute.

For *tlayudas*, lay the tortilla in the center of a 12-inch

dry *comal* over medium to high heat (see Hint) and cook it for 1 minute. Then turn it over and cook it over medium heat for 3 minutes. Turn it over again and cook for another 3 minutes.

Hint: In place of a *comal*, use 2 large frying pans or a long griddle. Set one burner on high heat, the other on medium.

DISHES MADE WITH CORN MASA

ANTOJITOS: "Little whims." A variety of snacks.

BODOKE: Dumpling made of *masa* and green plantains or bananas.

CHALUPA: Crispy corn tortilla "boat" layered with beans, cheese, and tomatoes.

CHILAQUILES: Recycled tortilla pieces bathed in a sauce and topped with cheese, onion, and cream.

CHOCHOYONES: Also called *chochoyotes* or *chochos*. Small *masa* dumplings kneaded with lard or oil and cooked in soups or *moles*.

EMPANADA: Filled turnover made of corn or wheat *masa*, filled with sweet or savory stuffings that are baked or fried.

ITACATE: Little dishes of taco fillings that you would eat in the *campo*.

MA'ACH: Ceremonial dish that, by village law, must be eaten on August 1 of every year in Tamazulapan, Mixe, to ward off hunger.

MEMELA: Also called *memelita*. Oval tortilla with fluted edges that is smeared with *asiento* and/or beans, and garnished with cheese, salsa, and other toppings.

MOLOTE: Torpedo-shaped *masa* fritter filled with potato and chorizo, topped with salsas and cheese, and served on lettuce leaves.

PANUCHO: Stuffed fried tortilla with a spicy chicken topping.

QUESADILLA: Corn turnover stuffed with *queso fresco*, *quesillo*, *epazote*, and often squash flowers.

TACO: Soft or fried rolled tortilla filled with potato, pork, beef, *chicharrón*, refried beans, *chiles poblanos*, etc.

TAMAL: Corn dough whipped with or without lard and steamed in *totomoxtle*, corn leaves, or banana leaves filled and flavored with salty or sweet ingredients. To reheat *tamales*, leave them in their wrappers and steam them in a *tamalera* or a steamer until heated through, or toast them on a *comal* or dry griddle, covered, over medium heat. Turn occasionally to reheat evenly, letting the wrappers scorch slightly for a toasty flavor.

TETELA: Triangle made of corn dough filled with red bean paste, from the Juxtlahuaca area, Mixteca.

BEANS AND LEGUMES

Beans, along with corn, are a principal staple of the Oaxacan diet. They are eaten both fresh and dried all year. There are as many varieties of dried beans as there are microclimates that they grow in. Beans are seasoned simply, always a bit soupy, and almost always cooked with *epazote*. They are either served in a bowl as the main meal (with tortillas and salsa) or made into a variety of dishes.

FRESH BEANS

AYOCOTE: Small red flower of the scarlet runner bean plant, often used in egg dishes or *moles*.

EJOTE *(PHASEOLUS VULGARIS)*: Green beans, runner beans. Cooked in soups, *moles*, and egg dishes, and used in salads.

FRIJOLÓN *(PHASEOLUS COCCINEUS)*: Large scarlet runner beans.

HABA *(CANAVALIA ENSIFORMIS)*: Fava bean usually used in soup.

MACHÍN: Garbanzo beans toasted whole, green shell and all, on the *comal*, until totally charred, smoky, and nutty.

DRIED BEANS AND BEAN DISHES

CHILAQUILES DE FRIJOL: Fried tortilla pieces smothered with a seasoned black bean sauce topped with cheese, white onion, and cream.

FLOR DE MAYO: Light purplish brown "Flower of May" bean.

FRIJOL ALUBIA: Small white bean from the mature dried green bean. Used in soups, stews, and *mole verde*.

FRIJOL ALUBIA GRANDE: Large white bean.

FRIJOL BAYO: Flat, brownish yellow bean.

FRIJOLES CHARROS: Beans prepared with fried onion, garlic, tomato, chorizo, ham, bacon, green chile, and cilantro.

FRIJOL COLORADO: Dark red bean.

FRIJOLES DE OLLA: Black or pinto beans cooked in a clay pot with herbs.

FRIJOL DE ZATOPE: Medium bean of mixed colors.

FRIJOL DELGADO: Small black bean.

FRIJOL NEGRO: Black bean, turtle bean.

FRIJOL PINTO: Medium speckled bean.

FRIJOLES REFRITOS: Black beans, mashed and fried into a paste in lard or oil.

FRIJOLÓN: Large blue-black bean, usually cooked with *yerba de conejo*.

GARBANZA: Large chickpea. Name used in the Isthmus of Tehuantepec.

GARBANZO: Small chickpea used in soups and sweets.

HABA: Dried fava beans cooked in a clay pot with *hierba santa* and tomatoes. A specialty in Etla.

HARINA DE FRIJOL: Black bean flour used in smooth soups called *cremas*.

HARINA DE GARBANZO: Dried, toasted chickpea flour; used in soups called *cremas* or in sweets.

LENTEJAS: Small brown lentils used for soups and side dishes. They are the small French type and have lots of flavor.

TAMAL DE FRIJOL: A pre-Hispanic *tamal* layered with black bean paste, seasoned with chiles and avocado leaf or *poleo* and large pieces of *hierba santa*.

VEGETABLES

The last part of the "holy trinity" of the Mexican kitchen is the *calabazas,* or squashes of different varieties. Almost all parts of the plant are utilized. The other vegetables mentioned here are generally available in U.S. markets, but I've listed their Spanish names.

ACELGAS (*BETA VULGARIS*): Swiss chard, used in soups and stews.

AJO (*ALLIUM SATIVUM*): Garlic is very important as a flavoring, generally roasted for sauces and used raw in table salsas. It is a heart strengthener and a blood purifier, and is used as a natural antibiotic and antiparasitic. It is thought that if you are traveling and you eat a raw clove of garlic and a fresh lime every day, you'll never get sick. The garlic heads and cloves in Mexico are a lot smaller, but stronger flavored, than the garlic found in the United States. Use the same amount of cloves; they will yield more volume, but the same amount of flavor. One head of garlic has approximately 23 cloves.

CALABAZAS (*CUCURBITA PEPO L.*): Squashes of different types.

Calabacita criolla: Pale green, round squash.

Calabacita cuarentena: Also known as zucchini or Italiana. Long, pale green squash with cream-colored speckles.

Calabaza chompa: Squash used for cow fodder.

Calabaza güiche: One of four native squashes, the type used for *guías de calabaza.*

Calabaza tamala: Orange winter squash; can substitute pumpkin.

Chilacayota (Cucurbita ficifolia): Large, watermelon-shaped squash used to make a fruity drink; can substitute Hubbard squash.

Flor de calabaza: Squash blossom, used in soups and sauces, also stuffed, dipped in batter, and fried.

Guías: Tender, young vines of a native squash plant, harvested fresh and cooked with the young squash, squash flowers, corn, and indigenous herbs.

CAMOTE (*IPOMEA BATATAS*): Sweet potato, yellow-orange or purple, traditionally cooked in sweet syrup.

CEBOLLA (*ALLIUM CEPA*): Onion. In Mexico, the white onion is most common. Sold with its green stem still attached, it is grilled or fried and put in sauces or *moles*. It is also finely chopped for a garnish for *barbacoa*, used in soups or salads or added to salsas, or sliced lengthwise to sprinkle on top of dishes.

CEBOLLA DE CAMBRAY: Small white bulbous onion that is frequently roasted on hot coals. You can also get this roasted effect by grilling or blackening it on a dry griddle.

CEBOLLÍN: Wild onion or bulbous chive.

CEBOLLITA: Small green onion or scallion.

CHAYOTE (*SECHIUM EDULE*): Prickly pear squash. In the southern United States, it is called mirliton squash. There are many varieties and colors, with or without spines. The spiny-skinned ones have much better flavor and texture than the smooth-skinned ones. In markets, they are available boiled in their skins or raw to be used in beef soup or *mole*. The chayote seed is considered a delicacy, and I've been told to make a salad of just the seeds to show someone you love him or her!

COL (*BRASSICA OLERACEA*): Also called *repollo*. Green cabbage, often used as a garnish, pickled in brine, or cooked in soups.

CRIOLLO TOMATE (*LYCOPERSICON LYCOPERSICUM*): Also called *cuatomate*. Tiny, very sweet wild tomato, which appears in the rainy season.

ESPINACA (*SPINACIA OLERACEA*): Spinach.

GUÍAS DE CHAYOTE: Tender vines and leaves of the prickly pear squash.

HONGO: Wild mushroom that grows in the mountain areas. Cooked in soups, *mole amarillo*, or empanadas.

HUAUZÓNTLE (*CHENOPODIUM NUTTALLIAE*): Lamb's quarters. I call this a pre-Hispanic broccoli.

JÍCAMA (*PACHYRRHIZUS EROSUS*): Crisp root vegetable that is a favorite among children; eaten raw and garnished with lime and chile powder; also used in salads.

Small jícamas are used to adorn sugarcane arches and altars made for the Day of the Dead.

JITOMATE OR TOMATE (*LYCOPERSICON ESCULENTUM*): Red tomato. Although the red tomato is a fruit, I include it here as a vegetable. The tomato is a basic ingredient of the Mexican kitchen and is usually dry-roasted to bring out its sweet flavor. The roasting is done directly on the hot coals, on a *comal*, or in a dry frying pan. This blisters the skins, which are then easily removed.

MAGUEY (*AGAVE ANGUSTIFOLIA*): The heart or center of this plant is used in the production of mezcal. The fiber in the leaves is made into rope and other products. The leaves are used for flavoring and serving food (*barbacoa*, for example), the pointy leaf tips are used as pottery tools, and the worms (*gusanitos*) that live inside the plant are extracted for a delicacy.

NANACATE: A wild mushroom, very much like portobello mushrooms, used in empanadas, soups, and *mole amarillo*.

NOPAL (*OPUNTIA SP.*): Cactus paddle. Also called *nopalito*, it is used in soups, salads, stews, egg dishes, and drinks, and can be boiled, fried, or roasted. This cactus grows in the desert and has lots of fiber and vitamins. Medicinally, it is used to control diabetes and can help lower cholesterol. The thorns are carefully removed with a sharp knife, but not peeled. When *nopales* are boiled, they become slimy, so they are cooked alone, rinsed well, and then added to a dish. When roasted they do not need to be rinsed.

OREJONA: Lettuce similar to romaine. Literally means "long ears."

QUELITES (*AMARANTHUS CRUENTUS*): Also called *quintoniles*; wild amaranth. Any nutritious weed found growing wild. Often steamed or boiled and eaten in tacos.

TOMATE SALADETTE (*LYCOPERSICON ESCULENTUM VAR.*): Tomato frequently grown in Oaxaca. Also called *tomate guaje*. This plum variety is considered meatier and packs well to go to market. The best tomato you can use in the United States is the plum variety except in the summer, when juicy round tomatoes are in season.

TOMATILLO (*PHYSALIS IXOCARPA*): This fruit looks like a small green tomato, with a green husk surrounding it, but is actually in the gooseberry family. It is used in soups, salsas, and *moles*. It is generally roasted or boiled until it changes color, then pureed into a sauce. It is slightly acidic and is rarely used raw in Oaxacan cooking.

VERDOLAGA (*PORTULACA OLERACEA*): Purslane. A wild herb with fleshy leaves, said to be a blood purifier and to stimulate growth of red corpuscles. Generally used in soups and stews and as taco filling.

YERBA MORA (*SOLANUM NIGRA*): Wild spinach. Popular for breakfast in Tuxtepec.

CHILES

One of the foods that give spice to life are chiles. Not only are they a great source of vitamin C, but they add excitement to our mouths and taste buds. One bite of a searing hot chile releases endorphins in the brain, giving a feeling of well-being. Ask any chile eater and he or she will tell you that chiles can be rather addicting. What I find interesting about chiles is how different they are from one another and even how different each is depending on how it is prepared. Take the versatile *chile de árbol*, for example. Used whole in soups, stocks, and stews, it warms the diner's chest and releases the sinuses. Once toasted and ground, however, it is very *picante*. If you can't find the exact same chile as called for in a recipe, substitute what I have suggested or use what you have on hand.

When using chiles, please remember that the volatile oils in the pepper will be released on your hands. To avoid burning your eyes (especially contact lens wearers) or anywhere else that the hands may touch, rub a tomato cut in half all over your hands after you are finished cleaning the chiles, and then wash your hands with soap and water. The tomato seems to absorb the oils of the chiles. If you are more sensitive or have to clean a lot of chiles, use rubber gloves.

FRESH CHILES

One of the most classic smells in the Mexican kitchen is that of fresh chiles roasting on the fire. The aroma evokes sweet anticipation of what is to come and always makes my mouth water. I roast fresh chiles by putting them directly on the burner of my gas stove, or directly on the coals if I am using a *comal* with firewood. If I have a lot of chiles to roast, I usually heat a long rectangular cast-iron *plancha*, or griddle, and roast them on that. After they blister and give off their scent, I place them in a plastic bag and allow them to "sweat" for 10 minutes. Then I remove them from the bag and use a sharp knife to scrape off the burned skin. I never rinse them with water, because the valuable oils that give the chile its flavor and heat will be washed away, too.

CHILE BRAVO: Small, 2-inch-long, very hot, blackish green, dark green, or red chile with *picante* flavor. Sometimes called *chile parado* because it stands straight up on the plant when growing, it is frequently served with *Sopa de Guías de Calabaza* (page 116). Can substitute Thai or fresh *chile piquín*.

CHILE DE AGUA: About 5 inches long, 1½ inches wide, color ranges from dark to light green to orange, thin skinned, delicate flesh. This *criollo* chile of Oaxaca has a *picante* flavor and is grown in the Central Valleys. It is used for *chiles rellenos, rajas*, and salsas.

CHILE HABANERO: Small, 1-inch-round bell pepper–shaped, green, orange, red, and sometimes yellow and very hot. From the Yucatán and the Caribbean. Often used to make bottled hot sauces.

CHILE HUACHINANGO: Large (about 3 inches long) *chile jalapeño*, green, very *picante*, thick skinned. The Mitla variety has lines or cracks in the skin, like fish scales. In the United States, you can substitute the *chile jalapeño* available locally. About 12 per pound.

CHILE JALAPEÑO: About 2 inches long, 1 inch wide, tapering to a round point, *picante,* thick skinned, green color; also sold pickled. Often called *chile gordo*. In recipes, fresh *jalapeños* are used unless pickled are specified. About 28 per pound.

CHILE MANZANO: About 4 inches long, apple shaped, yellow, red, and green color, very *picante* with small black seeds inside. Sometimes called *canario*. Grown primarily in the Cañada and Cuicatlán regions, it is often used when cooking with *nopales*.

CHILE POBLANO: About 5 inches long and 2½ inches wide, it tapers down to a point. Dark green with thick flesh, milder, depending on the variety and soil. From Puebla. Used for stuffing, for making *rajas*, in *cremas*, or in combination with corn and squash. About 6 chiles per pound.

CHILE SERRANO: Mountain grown, 2 to 2½ inches long and ½ inch wide, dark green color, medium hot, sometimes eaten raw as garnish, pickled, or roasted for salsas. A pickled canned variety is called *chiles serranos en escabeche*. About 120 chiles per pound.

CHILE TUXTA: Small, pointy, 1½ inches long and about ½ inch wide, ranges in color from green to purple, red, orange, yellow. From the mountain areas near the Pacific coast, medium to hot in taste, used in salsas.

CHILITO VERDE: Another name for *chile serrano*, used in Tuxtepec.

DRIED CHILES

Dried chiles are usually rinsed lightly and wiped with a damp cloth, then stemmed, seeded, and deveined. It is important to remove the ribs in the chiles, because they can cause a bitter taste. The chiles are generally toasted on the clay *comal*, dry cast-iron frying pan, or griddle. In some recipes the chiles are toasted both on the inside and outside. For many recipes they are soaked in hot water for smoother blending. Sometimes chiles are dry ground, such as when making a dry *chile de árbol* and salt powder to sprinkle on fresh fruit. Generally I soak the chiles in boiling water and allow them to soften. The chile water is often used to grind the chiles, but the rule of thumb is to use only as much as is needed to turn the blender blades. I strain the chile purees so that there are no small bits of skin in the sauce. Again, use the cut-tomato method (see above) to clean your hands, because dried chiles are just as hazardous as fresh.

Although these are not all the chiles available in Mexico, these are the chiles available in Oaxacan markets.

CHILE ANCHO NEGRO: Another name for *chile mulato*.

CHILE ANCHO ROJO: About 4 inches wide, tapering to a point, mildly *picante*, has a sweet, rich flavor and thick skin. This is what I call the raisin of the chile family. Usually used in combination with hotter chiles, this is a dried *chile poblano*. From Zacatecas. About 80 chiles per pound.

CHILE CHILCOSTLE: Dark red chile, 4 to 5 inches long, 1¼ inches wide, sharp flavor, thin skin, from the Cañada Chica region of Oaxaca.

CHILE CHILHUACLE AMARILLO: About 2½ inches long, 1½ to 2 inches wide, tapering to a rounded point, yellow-orange-red color, sharp *picante* taste, thin skin; from the Cañada Chica region.

CHILE CHILHUACLE NEGRO: From 2 to 3 inches long, about 6 inches in diameter, blue-black color, round in shape, sharp *picante* taste, thin skin, from the Cañada Chica region. About 84 chiles per pound.

CHILE CHILHUACLE ROJO: About 3 inches long, 2½ inches wide, tapering to a point, dark red color, sharp flavor, thin skin, from the Cañada Chica region.

CHILE CHILTEPEC: About ¼ inch wide and 2 inches long, orange colored, stemless, aromatic, fruity flavored, also called *chile seco*, from the Tuxtepec region.

CHILE CHIPOTLE: From 2 to 3 inches long, about 1 inch wide tapering to a rounded point, reddish-brown color, *picante,* thick, wrinkled flesh; this is a smoked *chile jalapeño*. From Veracruz. About 400 chiles per pound.

CHILE CHIPOTLE MECO: From 2½ to 3 inches long, ¾ to 1 inch wide, brown-gray color, *picante,* smoky flavor, wrinkled flesh; this is a smoked seedless *chile jalapeño*. From Veracruz.

CHILE COSTEÑO AMARILLO: About 2½ inches long, 1 inch wide, tapering to a point, yellow color, *picante* flavor, thin skin, from the Jamiltepec area of the Coast.

CHILE COSTEÑO ROJO: About 2½ inches long, red chile, 1 inch wide, tapering to a point, very *picante* flavor, thin skin. From the Jamiltepec area of the Coast, it is the favored chile of the Mixtecan people. About 1,000 chiles per pound.

CHILE DE ÁRBOL: Red, thin, about 3 inches long, ¼ inch wide, *picante*, thin skin, used whole in soups and stocks, ground for salsas, stews; name translates as "tree chile."

CHILE DE ONZA AMARILLO: About 3 inches long, yellow, about ½ inch wide, tapering to a rounded point, thin skinned with little flesh, and is grown in the mountains.

CHILE GUAJILLO: From 4½ to 6 inches long, dark red, 1½ inches wide, tapering to a rounded point, sharp fruity flavor, thin skin, used in many sauces and salsas. About 136 chiles per pound.

CHILE JAPONÉS: About 2 inches long, ¼ inch wide, generally very hot, imported from Asia. Thai chiles are the most commonly imported.

CHILE MORITA: About 1 inch long, ½ inch wide, tapering to a point, a small smoked chile from Veracruz. About 880 per pound.

CHILE MULATO: Black color, 4 to 5 inches long, 3 inches wide, tapering to a wide point, sharp, rich flavor, thick skin. Also called *chile ancho negro*, this is a dried variety of *chile poblano*. Grown in Zacatecas.

CHILE PASILLA MEXICANO: From 7 to 8 inches long and 1 inch wide, sharp flavored, used for *moles* and sauces, grown in Central Mexico. About 140 chiles per pound.

CHILE PASILLA OAXAQUEÑO: Variably sized, largest 3 to 4 inches long, 1 inch wide, tapering to a point, dark reddish black in color, smoky flavor, medium thick skins, smoked over open fires in the Sierra Mixe region. About 160 chiles per pound.

CHILE PIQUÍN: Tiny, ¼ to ½ inch long, about ⅛ inch wide, very hot, used fresh and dried in sauces, grown all over the United States and Mexico.

CHILE SECO: About 2 inches long, ¼ inch wide, reddish-orange colored, stemless, aromatic, fruity flavored; also called *chile chiltepec*, from the Tuxtepec region.

BUFALO SAUCE: A bottled chile sauce.

SALSA VALENTINA: A bottled chile sauce.

A FEW CHILE RECIPES

Preserving chiles has always been popular in Mexico. Smoking and drying chiles is done commercially, but here I include some other methods of preserving them. They can be used in salsas, soups, and various dishes, or simply served as a condiment to enhance the meal. They can be made in large quantities and kept in glass jars in the refrigerator or can be pressure canned. Follow manufacturer's instructions.

CHILES CHIPOTLES EN ADOBO
Chipotle Chiles in Chile Sauce

I have been buying canned chipotles en adobo for many years, with Don Alfonso's being my favorite recipe. Recently, my friend Eliseo showed me some fresh chipotles that had just arrived from Veracruz. Inspired, I bought them and returned home to experiment. After a few tries we came up with this recipe, and now have included this in our cupboard for use in sauces, marinades, and soups and stews. Serve as a garnish or use in Sopa de Tortilla (page 13), in salsa de papaya y chipotle (page 300), or in Lenguado a la Talla (page 213).

MAKES 2 CUPS

60 chiles chipotles *(4 ounces; see page 330)*

1 chile ancho *(about ½ ounce; see page 330)*

8 ounces ripe tomatoes *(1 medium–large round or 4–5 plum)*

7 garlic cloves

½ white onion, *chunked*

1 piece of Mexican cinnamon, *about 1 inch long, toasted (see page 337)*

1 teaspoon fresh Oaxacan oregano leaves *(see page 336)*

1 teaspoon fresh thyme leaves

2 tablespoons sunflower or vegetable oil

½ cup cider vinegar

1 tablespoon piloncillo *or brown sugar (see page 348)*

2 bay leaves

½ tablespoon salt, *or to taste*

Bring 3 cups of water to a boil. Remove the stems, seeds, and veins from 5 *chiles chipotles* and the *chile ancho.* Toast all the chiles on a hot *comal* or dry frying pan until they give off their scent and blister, about 2 minutes, turning once. Place the 5 *chiles chipotles* and the *chile ancho* in a small bowl. Pour 1 cup of the hot water over them and allow to soak for 10 minutes. Place the rest of the *chiles chipotles* in a bowl and pour the remaining 2 cups of hot water over them. Allow them to soak for 20 minutes.

In a medium saucepan, bring 2 cups of water to a boil, add the tomatoes, and cook about 5 minutes. Drain and cool.

When the tomatoes are cool enough to handle, remove the skins and discard them. Place the skinned tomatoes in a blender. When the chiles are soft, put the 5 stemmed *chiles chipotles* and the *chile ancho* in the blender. Add the garlic, onion, cinnamon, oregano, and thyme. Blend until smooth, using a little chile water if necessary. Pass the whole mixture through a food mill or sieve for a very smooth puree.

In a large frying pan, heat the oil until smoking hot and add the chile puree and fry until well seasoned, about 10 minutes. Add the vinegar, *piloncillo,* and bay leaves, lower the heat to a simmer, and cook, covered, for about 10 minutes longer. Add the remaining chiles and their soaking liquid, and cook 10 minutes more. Add salt to taste. Allow to cool. Fill sterilized jars and refrigerate.

CHILES JALAPEÑOS EN ESCABECHE
Pickled Jalapeño Chiles

Although chiles jalapeños en escabeche *are available everywhere, it's also fun and easy to make your own. Irma Moguel de Sorroza makes pickled vegetables, chiles, and pig's feet to sell at her stall in Mercado de Abastos and inspired me to make them. You can add potatoes and cauliflower to this pickle to make it sweeter. Use these* jalapeños *as a condiment, in salsas, and many other dishes calling for* jalapeños.

MAKES 2 QUARTS

2 cups white vinegar

1½ cups cider vinegar

2 teaspoons dried Oaxacan oregano
  (see page 336)

1 teaspoon dried marjoram

½ teaspoon dried thyme

2 bay leaves

1½ teaspoons black peppercorn

1 whole clove

1½ teaspoons salt

Pinch of sugar

1 pound chiles jalapeños (see
  page 329)

6 tablespoons olive oil

1 medium white onion

½ head of garlic, cloves separated
  and sliced lengthwise

¼ pound carrots, peeled and diagonally sliced

¼ pound green beans, cleaned

¼ pound new potatoes, peeled and
  cut into quarters (optional)

¼ pound cauliflower, broken into
  small pieces (optional)

In a medium saucepan, combine the vinegar and add the herbs and spices. Bring to a boil over medium heat, then reduce heat and simmer for 30 minutes.

Cut an x at the tip of each chile. In a 10-inch frying pan, heat the oil over low heat. Sauté the onions and garlic until clear, not brown, about 5 minutes. Transfer to saucepan with the vinegar mixture.

Add all the remaining vegetables to the vinegar and cook until vegetables are soft, about 30 minutes. Fill sterilized glass jars and refrigerate.

Ajo *(Barbara Lawton)*

CHILES PASILLAS EN VINAGRE
Pickled Chiles Pasillas

My comadre and friend Carlota always has these pickled chiles available in her little fonda in San Lorenzo Cacaotepec. She also makes pickled mangoes and potatoes in the same manner. She offers them at the table with the wonderful food that she serves daily.

MAKES 2 QUARTS

25 chiles pasillas *(see page 331)*

1 quart fruit or cider vinegar

1 head of garlic, cloves separated

1 whole allspice

1 whole clove

1½ large white onions (12 ounces), cut into slices

1 teaspoon salt

1 tablespoon piloncillo *(see page 348) or brown sugar*

4 sprigs fresh thyme, or ¼ teaspoon dried

2 tablespoons dried Oaxacan oregano *(see page 336)*

In a medium saucepan, bring 5 cups of water to a boil. Make a slit in the side of each chile. In a medium bowl, pour the hot water over the chiles and soak them for 15 minutes. Drain and allow the chiles to cool.

In another medium bowl, mix the vinegar, garlic, allspice, clove, onion slices, salt, and *piloncillo*. Add the drained chiles and thyme. Rub the oregano in your hands and sprinkle over the top of the mixture. Mix well. Sterilize two 1-quart jars and fill with the mixture. Refrigerate. Leave for 3–5 days before using.

Hint: Serve as part of a *botana* platter, with grilled meats or with *bolillos* and butter as an appetizer.

Gudelia Santiago Rosales and her nopales, El Gramal, Oaxaca (Barbara Lawton)

CHINTESTLE
Smoked Chile Paste

Chintestle *is a product of the Mixes in the Sierra Norte region of Oaxaca. I learned
this recipe from the village* cocineras *of Santa María Tlahuitoltepec. It is a
very simple paste used by the people to spread on tortillas or as a soup or sauce base.
It is an instant meal for the* campo *or while walking the many miles in between
villages. In the Sierra Sur,* chintestle *is made with ground dried shrimp heads
and pumpkin seeds.*

MAKES 1½ CUPS

½ *pound* chiles pasillas oaxaqueños *(see page 331), stemmed
and seeded*
11 *garlic cloves*
½–1 *teaspoon salt, or to taste*

In a small saucepan, bring 2 cups of water to a boil. On a
10-inch dry *comal*, griddle, or in a cast-iron frying pan over
low heat, toast the chiles for about 2 to 3 minutes, turning
them often. They should brown and give off their scent.
Remove the chiles to a bowl and pour the water over them.
Soak for 15 minutes.

In a blender, grind the chiles and garlic to make a thick
paste. Do not put in extra water unless needed to turn the
blades. Do this in small batches and blend until smooth.
Remove the paste from the blender and stir in the salt. This
should be very hot! Allow to cool completely and store in
plastic bags, removing as much air as possible. Refrigerate.

Hint: A favorite recipe of mine is grinding garlic, salt, *chintestle*, honey, orange juice, and a little olive oil in a *molcajete*
to make a runny paste. I smear it all over a chicken and roast
it in a 400°F oven for 10 minutes, then reduce the temperature to 350°F and roast for 50 minutes.

HERBS

The state of Oaxaca is said to have more endemic herbs than any other Mexican state. I hope more of these herbs will become available in the United States, but I have given substitutes in recipes when possible. If you are not able to find the herbs, look in Mexican groceries, but I urge you to experiment and grow your own herb garden.

CHEPICHE (*POROPHYLLUM TAGETOIDES*): Long, rounded grasslike plant with blue flowers and a bright pungent taste, eaten raw or in rice dishes. Here, they are eaten with beans.

CHEPIL (*CROTOLARIA LONGIROSTRATA*): A fresh herb that grows wild in the rainy season; used in soups, *tamales,* and rice dishes.

CILANTRO (*CORIANDRUM SATIVUM*): Coriander. Used in salads or to garnish soups, stews, and *antojitos.*

COLCAMECA VINE (*ARISTOLOCHIA LAXIFLORA*): Tropical vine used in Tuxtepec and Yalalag for making a ceremonial drink with cacao.

EPAZOTE (*CHENOPODIUM AMBROSIOIDES;* new name *TELOXYS AMBROSIOIDES*): Wormseed used as a flavoring in beans and many other dishes. It is an antiparasitic herb; used as a tea for stomach ailments.

HIERBABUENA (*MENTHA SPICATA*): Spearmint, used as a flavoring in tea or a variety of dishes and for upset stomach.

HIERBAS DE OLOR: "Aromatic herbs"—oregano, thyme, marjoram, and sometimes bay leaf, sold in tiny bundles.

HIERBA SANTA (*PIPER AURITUM*): Native plant with heart-shaped leaves, used as an anise-flavored seasoning. Also called *hoja santa, yerba santa.* Used in *moles,* stews, and *tamales*, and to wrap chicken and fish when they are steamed.

JAMAICA FLOWERS (*HIBISCUS SABDARIFFA*): Dried flowers used to make a dark red drink called *agua de jamaica,* or sorbets.

LAUREL (*LITSEA SP.*): Bay leaf, used in stocks, soups, stews, and pickling brines.

MEJORANA (*MARJORANA HORTENSIS*): Marjoram, used in sauces, soups, stews. Part of the *hierbas de olor* bundle.

OAXACAN OREGANO (*LIPPIA SP.*): Local type of oregano, part of the bundle called *hierbas de olor.* You can substitute marjoram or European oregano for this herb, but use a little less.

PEREJIL (*PETROSELINUM VAR. NEAPOLITANUM*): Flat-leaf Italian parsley used for flavoring soups and sauces. Leaves are used to garnish dishes such as enchiladas, *entomatadas,* and salads.

Pericón (*Tapetes lucida*): Mexican tarragon, used medicinally.

Pitiona (*Lippia alba*): Flavorful herb with purple flowers, used in *mole amarillo* with beef.

Poleo (*Satureja oaxacana*): Also called *hierba de borracho*, used as a tea for hangovers; also given at *fiestas* for welcoming guests. It is a savory, like summer savory.

Tomillo (*Thymus vulgaris*): Thyme. Used in soups, sauces, and marinades, it is part of the *hierbas de olor*.

Yerba de Conejo (*Tridax corono piifolio*): "Rabbit herb" used for making *frijol* dishes.

SEEDS, NUTS, AND SPICES

Achiote (*Bixa orellana*): Seeds from the annatto tree are used to make a paste for flavoring and coloring (red-orange) food. Grows in the states of Oaxaca, Yucatán, Campeche, Quintana Roo, and Tabasco.

Almendra (*Rosaceae family*): Whole almond meats, used in *moles*, stews, desserts.

Anis (*Pimpinella anisum*): Aniseed, used in baking and sauces or dressings.

Amaranto (*Amaranthus hypochondriacus l.*): Amaranth. Highly nutritional grain used for cereal, candies, and desserts.

Cacahuate (*Leguminosae family*): Peanut. Used as a snack, or ground into salsas, stews, or *moles*.

Cacao (*Theobroma cacao*): Cacao beans are used to make chocolate and other ceremonial drinks and as an ingredient in *mole*.

Cacao Pataxtle (*Theobroma bicolor*): Calcified cacao. The cacao beans are soaked in water for 5 to 7 days and then buried in a pit during the full moon. They ferment in the pit for four or five months. When they are dug up, the inside of the bean has a pure white chalky texture. This is used for *chocolate atole* made with cacao *pataxtle*, cinnamon, sugar, and wheat berries, rice, or corn.

Canela (*Cinnamomum cassia/zeylandicum*): Cinnamon bark, from Sri Lanka, used to flavor chocolate, soups, stews, and desserts.

Chocolate de la Casa: Family recipe handed down and made for *fiestas* and special occasions.

Clavo (*Eugenia aromatica*): Clove, usually toasted whole, then ground into sauces, stews, *moles,* and sweets.

GUAJE *(LEUCAENA ESCULENTA)*: Seeds and pods from the hoaxin tree eaten as a snack. Wards off parasites and amoebas, and aids in digestion. The name Oaxaca is derived from *guaje*, "place of the *guajes*." Dried seeds are ground into sauces.

HOJA DE AGUACATE *(PERSEA AMERICANA)*: Avocado leaf, used as a seasoning. The *criolla* variety is preferable, which has a subtle anise flavor. The leaves are used to flavor *tamales*, bean pastes, *barbacoa,* or sauces.

HOJA DE POZOLE: A leaf used in Tuxtepec for wrapping *tamales*.

NUEZ *(CARYA ILLINOENSIS)*: Pecan eaten as snacks, used in *moles*, desserts, and cakes.

PEPITAS *(CURRCURBITA PEPO L)*: Inner green part of the pumpkin seed, used whole, toasted, or ground into a sauce called *pipián*.

PIMENTA GORDA *(PIMENTA OFFICINALIS)*: Allspice, toasted whole, ground, and used in sauces, stews, *moles,* and sweets.

TAMARINDO *(TAMARINDUS INDICA)*: Seed pod of the tamarind tree. The pod has a soft, brown shell with an acidic sticky pulp inside. It is used for *agua de tamarindo* or for candies, mixed with salt, sugar, and chile.

VAINILLA *(VANILLA PLANIFOLIA)*: The processed bean of the vanilla orchid, used whole or made into extract.

Susana's Formula for Making First-class Oaxacan Chocolate

1½ ounces Mexican cinnamon sticks, broken (see page 337)

2 pounds first-class fermented cacao beans

2½–3 pounds finely granulated sugar

On a 10-inch clay *comal*, toast the cinnamon sticks until browned and giving off their scent. You must do this quickly and constantly move the cinnamon around, so it will not burn. Remove it from the *comal* and set it aside.

Add the cacao to the *comal* and toast the beans, moving them constantly with a *comal* brush or a wooden spoon, until the beans snap and puff up from a flat reddish bean to a rounded darkened one. Allow the cacao beans to cool, then peel off the shells and discard them.

METATE METHOD:

Grind the cinnamon until fine and remove it from the *metate* to a bowl. Then continue by grinding the cacao on the *metate* two times. Mix in the cinnamon and then grind once more.

Stir in the sugar slowly with a wooden spatula or a knife, adding as much sugar as the mixture can absorb, but no more than 3 pounds. Grind it again two more times to make it a shiny and smooth consistency.

MOLINO OR MILL METHOD:

Put the cinnamon and cacao in the mill. Put the sugar in the bottom, reserving some to scrape out the machine later. Grind the cinnamon and cacao together. Mix in the sugar well, using the reserved sugar as an abrasive element to clean any of the cacao mixture that may be sticking to the machine. Grind it all together for the second grind.

TO SHAPE:

On a large cutting board, pat out the chocolate mixture in a rectangle ¼-inch thick until smooth and shiny. Slide a large chef's knife underneath the mass to release it from the cutting board, turn it over, and pat out the other side. Cut pieces about 4 inches long by 1 inch wide. Place two of these together and join the 4-inch sides together to make a double bar of chocolate. (You can also roll these out into balls or fill disk-shaped chocolate molds.)

Place the bars on a banana leaf or a piece of waxed paper to dry. These will harden in 2 hours or so, depending on the humidity. Store the bars in plastic bags or an airtight glass container. The bars weigh 2 ounces each.

FRUITS

AGUACATE (*PERSEUS AMERICANA*): Avocado. Soft, creamy, exquisite fruit that comes in many varieties.

AGUACATE CRIOLLO (*PERSEUS AMERICANA VAR.*): The small native avocado measures 3 inches in length with soft black skin that is edible and anise flavored.

CHICOZAPOTE (*ACHRAS SAPOTE*): Fruit of the chicle tree, with a thin, light brown skin. Flesh is soft, textured, with a honey flavor. Used for drinks, ices, and fruit salads.

GUAYABA (*PSIDIUM GUAJAVA*): Guava. The small, hard seeds are removed to make candies, drinks, conserves, and a paste called *ate*. The leaf is often used in tea to treat diarrhea.

GRANADA (*PUNICA GRANATUM*): Pomegranate.

HOJA DE PLÁTANO (*MUSA ACUMINATA*): Fresh banana leaf used as *tamal* wrapper, for lining baking pans, and wrapping chicken or fish.

LIMA-LIMÓN (*CITRUS LIMETTA*): Sweet lime. Grown in central Mexico, it is a citrus fruit like a sweet aromatic lime.

LIMA (*CITRUS LIMETTA*): Sour lime; a small, light green lime that has a very aromatic rind.

LIMÓN (*CITRUS AURANTIFOLIA*): Small key lime, used in drinks and ices and as garnish for many foods.

MAMEY (*CALOCARMUM SAPOTA*): Football-shaped brown-skinned fruit with soft orange flesh. The large pit inside is used to make *tejate*. Also the name of a color.

MANGO (*MANGIFERA INDICA*): Soft, fibrous, luscious fruit with large pit that comes in many varieties. Often eaten unripe with chile powder.

NANCHE (*BYRSONIMA CRASSIFOLIA*): Tiny, yellow, cherry-like fruit that is often brined in vinegar and is a specialty of the Isthmus of Tehuantepec.

NÍSPERO (*ERIOBOTRYA JAPONICA*): Loquat.

PAPAYA (*CARICA PAPAYA*): Yellow variety is large with gray seeds inside; the mamey variety is smaller and elongated and is a salmon color. There is also a smaller salmon-colored papaya called Maradol that originated in Cuba and is very popular here.

PITAYA (*STENOCEREUS GRISEUS*): Fruit of an organ cactus used in sauces or eaten fresh.

PLÁTANO: Eating banana.

PLÁTANO MACHO (*MUSA CAVENDISHII*): Plantain used for cooking, green or in various stages of ripeness. Plantains are ripe when they start to turn black—not completely black, but yellow with black spots on them. They should be softer to the touch than the greener, starchy, unripe plantains. When a plantain has gone completely black it gets very soft, sweet, and translucent inside and is eaten raw and considered a delicacy by some.

PLÁTANO MORADO (*MUSA SAPIENTUM VAR.*): Banana with maroon-colored peel, used for eating or frying. This is one of many varieties available in Oaxaca.

SANDÍA (*CITRULLUS LANATUS*): Watermelon. Eaten fresh or made into drinks and ices.

TEJOCOTE (*CRATAEGUS PUBESCENS*): Hawthorn berry. Used in *ponche* and candied.

TUNA (*STENOCEREUS STELLATUS*): Fruit of the prickly pear cactus, used in drinks and sorbets.

ZAPOTE NEGRO (*DIOSPYROS DIGYNA.*): Round green-skinned fruit with black custard-like flesh, used for ices and drinks and eaten like pudding.

VINAGRE DE FRUTAS
Fruit Vinegar

MAKES 1 GALLON

Peel of 1 ripe pineapple
3 cones pineapple pineapple *(6 ounces each;*
see page 348) or 3 cups brown
sugar

The night before, place the peel on a plate outside to let it catch the morning dew. In the morning, place the peel in a 1-gallon container that has a tight-fitting lid. Add the *piloncillo* and fill with pure water. Cover the container and let sit in a dark place for about 2 weeks. A "mother" will form in the bottom of the container that will look like thick white skin. Strain the vinegar into a bottle and cork. Replace the water in the container, add more *piloncillo* to the "mother," and start again. It keeps indefinitely and is used for marinades, pickling brines, salads, and salsas.

NIEVE DE SANDÍA
Watermelon Ice

MAKES 2 QUARTS

⅔ cup sugar
½ cup orange juice
⅔ cup light corn syrup
2 tablespoons lime juice
8 cups chunked watermelon

In a 2-quart saucepan, place the sugar, orange juice, and corn syrup over medium heat and bring to a boil, stirring occasionally. Simmer for 5 minutes without stirring, then add the lime juice. Allow it to cool. Put the watermelon chunks in a blender and puree until smooth. Strain and add to the cooled sugar syrup.

Put the mixture into a shallow pan and cover with plastic wrap. Freeze until firm, 3 to 6 hours. Spoon into a food processor and beat quickly. Pour back into the pan and freeze until firm. Serve.

MEAT

ASIENTO: Lard drippings from *chicharrón* preparation, used to flavor *antojitos*.

BARBACOA: Meat baked in an underground pit. For *barbacoa roja*, the meat (usually butchered on the spot: goat, lamb, pork, or beef) is rubbed with *adobo* paste. A large soup pot of water, giblets, and vegetables is placed in the bottom of the pit. A grill is placed over the pan, which is covered with avocado leaves. The meat is stacked on top of the grill and then covered again with more avocado leaves and finally some huge maguey leaves and a few sealed bottles of mezcal. The pit is then covered with a metal sheet and soil and left to bake for 6 or 7 hours. The grease from the meat drips into the soup pot and becomes the broth. The pit is unearthed to the accompaniment of much music and fireworks; the ones who encounter the hot mezcal bottles are in charge of offering rounds to the crowd.

BISTEK: Steak, usually cooked as a *guisado*.

CARNITAS: Seasoned pieces of pork, fried in lard.

CECINA: Thin slices of pork cut in the same manner as *tasajo*. *Cecina blanca* is pork seasoned with salt. *Cecina enchilada* is pork smothered with an *adobo* paste.

CHAPULINES: Fried grasshoppers.

CHICHARRÓN: Pig skin fried in lard.

CHORIZO: Sausage made from minced pork and flavored with herbs, spices, and chiles. Oaxacan chorizos are small and round and tied in long strings.

CONEJO: Rabbit, cooked in *moles*, *tamales*, and stews.

ESPINAZO: Pork spine, backbone.

GUAJOLOTE: Wild turkey.

GUSANITOS DE MAGUEY: Also called *gusanos de maguey*. Worms from the maguey plant that are dried and smoked. They are used as seasoning in salsas and mezcal or ground with chile and salt to make *sal de gusano*.

HIGADITOS: Chicken or pork livers. This is also the name of a festival egg dish.

JABALÍ: Wild boar.

LIEBRE: Hare.

MANTECA: Lard or rendered pork fat.

PICADILLO: Meat shredded into very fine pieces and mixed with chiles, herbs, spices, raisins, and almonds and used as stuffing for tacos, *chiles rellenos,* and stuffed plantains.

POLLO: Chicken.

TASAJO: Cut of beef, thinly sliced with the grain until almost the end, then turned and sliced again, pulling on the sliced piece to a longer and longer strip of meat. The beef is then salted and either sold fresh or hung above the butcher's counter to dry to the very leathery jerky stage, which takes weeks.

TESPESCUINTLE: Wild agouti eaten in Tuxtepec.

VENADO: Deer.

CALDO RECIPES

CALDO DE POLLO
Chicken Stock

MAKES 8 CUPS

3½ pounds chicken parts
    (including necks, backs, and
    feet), or 1 whole chicken, cut up
1 large white onion, studded with
    1 whole clove
2 celery ribs with leaves, or 1 celery
    heart with leaves
½ large or 1 small head of garlic
2 carrots, peeled and thickly sliced
1 bay leaf
1 chile de árbol or chile japonés
    (see pages 330 and 331)
3 black peppercorns
1 sprig thyme, or pinch of dried
1 whole allspice
Salt to taste, approximately
    1 tablespoon

In a heavy 6-quart stockpot, place the chicken backs, necks, and feet in enough cold water to cover, about 3 quarts. Add the onion, celery, garlic, carrots, bay leaf, *chile de árbol*, peppercorns, thyme, and allspice and bring to a boil. Cook covered, over medium heat, at least 15 minutes. Add the rest of the chicken parts or the whole chicken and continue to simmer, covered, over low heat for ½ hour, or until juices run clear when the dark meat is pierced with a fork. Add salt. Remove the chicken and strain the stock. Discard the seasonings. Cool the stock and then skim the fat off the top.

Hint: You can treat yourself to the carrots that were poached with the chicken. This stock freezes well and keeps up to 6 weeks in your freezer.

CALDO DE PUERCO
Pork Stock

MAKES 8 CUPS

1 medium white onion, thickly
    sliced
1 head of garlic
1 carrot, peeled and thickly sliced
3 celery ribs, with leaves
1 bay leaf
1 whole allspice
1 chile de árbol (see page 330)
5 black peppercorns
2 pounds pork ribs, bones, or
    boneless pork shoulder
Salt to taste

In a heavy 6-quart stockpot, bring 3 quarts of cold water to a boil (see Hint). Add the onion, garlic, carrot, celery, bay leaf, allspice, *chile de árbol,* and peppercorns. Boil for 15 minutes, then add the pork and lower the heat to a simmer. Cook, covered, until tender, about 1 hour. Add salt. Remove the meat from the pot and set aside.

Reduce the stock by simmering, uncovered, for 10 minutes more over high heat. Strain the stock and discard the seasonings. Allow to cool and skim the fat off the top.

Hint: If you are using pork bones to make the stock, start by putting the bones in cold water and bring to a boil with the vegetables. This enables the bones to give off their juices.

CALDO DE RES
Beef Stock

MAKES 8 CUPS

1 tablespoon sunflower or
    vegetable oil
2 pounds beef bones or shank
1½ medium white onions
3 carrots, cut into large chunks
3 celery ribs, with leaves
1 head of garlic
5 bay leaves
½ teaspoon dried thyme
15 black peppercorns
1 whole allspice
1 chile de árbol (see page 330)

Preheat the oven to 400°F.

In a heavy 6-quart stockpot or Dutch oven, heat the oil over high heat. Add the beef and bones, onions, carrots, celery, and garlic. Cover. Place the pot in the oven and roast for 45 minutes.

Take the pot out of the oven and put on the stove top. Add the bay leaves, thyme, peppercorns, allspice, *chile de árbol,* and 4 quarts of water. Cover and cook for 3 hours over low heat. Let cool, then skim off fat and strain.

FISH AND SEAFOOD

BACALAO: Dried codfish. *Bacalao de cazón*, dried shark meat now used for economic reasons.

BARRILETE: Small tuna from the Pacific Ocean.

CAMARÓN: Shrimp.

CAMARÓN SECO: Salted dried shrimp.

CAMARONCITO SECO: Minuscule salted, dried shrimp.

CHARALES: Also called *charalitas*. Little silver dried fish.

HUACHINANGO: Red snapper; also a local name for large *chile jalapeño*.

LISA: Mullet, a fish that inhabits the lagoons and rivers near the Pacific coast. Mostly found smoked or salted and dried.

MARISCOS: Seafood such as crab, shrimp, mussels, lobsters, oysters, octopus.

ROBALO: Snook.

CAZÓN: Shark.

PULPO: Octopus.

CHEESE AND DAIRY PRODUCTS

The cheeses of Oaxaca are made from cow's milk and are made primarily in the valley of Etla, where Rancho Aurora is located. Almost everyone in our village raises dairy cows milked for cheese production. The land around us is green with alfalfa, corn, or sorghum, which is grown for fodder. There still is not enough milk produced here in the valley to support the cheese makers, so large milk tanks bring additional milk down from Puebla each day.

CREMA: Thick, dairy cream, like crème fraîche.

CUAJO: Rennet, or cow's stomach, that is dried and preserved with salt and lime. It is soaked in whey to release the enzymes and added to the fresh unpasteurized milk to coagulate it.

MANTEQUILLA: Butter. All recipes in this book use unsalted butter.

QUESILLO: White string cheese, also called *queso de hebra*, used extensively in the Oaxacan kitchen. Fermented curds are placed in hot water and stirred with a wooden mallet to make what looks like a giant wad of chewing gum. When the cheese can be handled, long threads are pulled and then salted. The strings are wound into balls.

QUESO AÑEJO: Aged, dry, hard, salty cheese used for grating.

QUESO COTIJA: Another name for *Queso Añejo.*

QUESO CREMA: Cream cheese.

QUESO FRESCO: Fresh salted curds that are formed in molds. This cheese has a slightly acid taste and crumbles easily. This is what I call the "mother cheese." It is used for *quesadillas* and *salsa de queso* and crumbled over myriad Oaxacan dishes.

QUESO MANCHEGO: Light yellow semisoft cheese with a very mild taste. You can substitute Gouda, Edam, or Muenster.

QUESO PRENSADO: Fresh cheese that has been formed in a woven straw mold *(petatito)* and pressed until most of the moisture is removed. It can be aged uncovered on a small wire rack in the refrigerator. A yellow crust will form.

QUESO RANCHERO: Ranch cheese. This dry white cheese is used for crumbling on top of dishes. It is made in large wheels, found in Tuxtepec.

REQUESÓN: Literally means "re-cheesed." Soft cheese made from the leftover whey in the making of *queso fresco.* Often used like ricotta or farmer cheese.

MOLES

AMARILLO: Yellow *mole,* one of the seven *moles* of Oaxaca, that may contain either *chiles chilhuacles amarillos* or *chiles costeños amarillos* combined with other chiles, tomato, and *tomatillo.* It is thickened with *masa* and flavored with *hierba santa,* cilantro, or *pitiona,* depending on the meat used.

CHICHILO: Unusual *mole* that gets its smoky flavor from burnt seeds and tortillas that are ground into the sauce. It is frequently made with beef and pork, potatoes, chayotes, and green beans resulting in a stewlike *mole.* It has a special topping of marinated *chile de agua,* onions, and lime.

COLORADITO: Brick-red *mole,* one of the two *moles* that contain a small piece of chocolate as one of its many ingredients. This sauce is used to make enchiladas.

MANCHAMANTELES: Literally meaning "tablecloth stainer," this *mole* is sweet and has a fruity, tart flavor owing to the pineapple and plantains that are two of the ingredients.

MOLE PASTE: All the prepared ingredients of a *mole,* except the tomato and *tomatillo,* are reduced to a paste by frying until dry. This concentrated paste is reconstituted with tomatoes, *tomatillos,* and broth.

NEGRO: King of *moles.* It gets its black color from toasting the chiles until dark and burning their seeds. It has over twenty-five ingredients and is one of the two *moles* that contain a small piece of chocolate. It is made for the Day of the Dead and other fiestas. This sauce is used to make *enmoladas*.

ROJO: Originally called *tlemole (clemole)*, this *mole* was recorded when the Spanish came to Mexico and is one of the spiciest. It is used in *Pozole Mixteco* (page 271) and enchilada sauce.

TESMOLE: Thin *mole* from the Cañada region.

VERDE: Fresh, herbal *mole* made with green chiles, green tomatoes, herbs, and *tomatillos*. It is frequently made with pork and white beans and is thickened with *masa*.

BREADS

BOLILLO: Crusty bread rolls, similar to French bread, popular for *tortas*.

HOJALDRA: Inflated flat bread of salted yeast dough, sprinkled with red sugar, made into shapes such as bunnies, rounds, or pretzels, from Etla in the Central Valleys.

MARQUESOTE: A sweet, light bread made with beaten egg whites, traditionally eaten in the Tlacolula valley.

MOLLETES: Bread sweetened with *piloncillo* and topped with sesame seeds, made in Etla.

PAN: Wheat bread of all types.

PAN AMARILLO: Inflated flat bread of salted yeast dough sprinkled with sesame seeds.

PAN GUAPA: Sweet bread made with *piloncillo* in the Isthmus of Tehuantepec.

PAN DE MANTECA: Bread made with lard.

PAN DE MUERTO: Egg bread in rounded shapes, flavored with anise seeds and adorned with tiny *caritas*, or faces. Made especially for the Day of the Dead, they are placed on the altar, and served with hot chocolate.

PAN DE YEMA: Round egg bread with sesame seeds on top, served with hot chocolate.

PAN DULCE: A variety of sweet bread eaten in the morning or at night with coffee or *atole* as a light meal.

PAN RESOBADO: Yeasted sweet bread in an oval shape.

PIEDRAZOS: Dried bread soaked with pickled fruit, vegetables, and chiles.

REGAÑADA: Yeasted, thin, flat bread made with lard and sprinkled with sugar.

TORTA: Sandwich often made from crispy *bolillo* roll, one half smeared with bean paste and mayonnaise and then stuffed with meat or *quesillo* and pieces of tomato, avocado, and chile. Also the name for an egg omelet.

SWEETS

Acitrón: Crystallized cactus pieces.

Alegría: Sweet made with amaranth seeds and *piloncillo*.

Arroz con Leche: Rice cooked with milk and cinnamon to make a sweet, custardy dessert.

Ate: Concentrated fruit paste of various flavors—quince, guava, pineapple, cherry, lime.

Borracho: Bright red cake soaked in mezcal or rum syrup.

Buñuelos: Thin flour tortillas fried and soaked with syrup.

Calabaza en Conserva: Pumpkin squash that is peeled, perforated with a fork, soaked in *lejía* (lime water), and boiled with *piloncillo*. This treat keeps well.

Calabaza en Dulce: Pumpkin squash that is boiled in *piloncillo* syrup.

Capirotada: Lenten bread pudding with dried fruit, nuts, cheese, and a sweet, savory sauce.

Casquito: Meringue in a cookie crust topped with coconut.

Cono de lechecilla: Pastry cone that is filled with custard.

Dulce: Sweet, candy.

Empanadas: Turnovers filled with *lechecilla*, coconut, pineapple, or *calabaza en dulce*.

Gelatina: Gelatin. These range from very simple to very elaborate concoctions.

Jamoncillo: Sweet made from *piloncillo* and coconut from the Juquila area.

Lechecilla: Egg yolk and milk custard.

Nenguanitos: Small fried cookies that are stacked five high, each layer bathed in sugar syrup.

Nicuatole: Pre-Hispanic corn gelatin made with milk, sugar, and cinnamon. Today it is often seen with a sprinkle of red sugar *(carmín)* on top.

Panela or Piloncillo: Extracted sugarcane juice, boiled for hours and then poured into forms. It is sold in dark cones, bricks, or half-moons.

Panqué: Rectangular sweet bread, like a pound cake.

Panquecito: Pound cake muffin, with raisins or pecans.

Pepitoria: Bar candy made from pumpkin seeds with *panela* or *piloncillo*.

Postre: Dessert.

Tecuta: Little tarts filled with *chilacayota* or coconut paste.

Tortitas de Piña: Little pineapple cakes made especially for Lent.

DRINKS

AGUARDIENTE: Sugarcane liquor.

AGUA DE CHILACAYOTA: Drink called "hair of angels" for the fibrous consistency of the cooked, sweetened *chilacayota* squash that's beaten by hand. It has lime peel, pineapple chunks, and lots of ice added.

AGUA DE SABOR: Also called *preparado de frutas*; a drink made of fruit, water, and sugar. Examples are *agua de sandía* (watermelon), *agua de melon* (cantaloupe), *agua de limón* (lime), *agua de tuna* (cactus fruit), and *agua de papaya*. Flower infusions, such as *agua de jamaica* (hibiscus flower) and *agua de tamarindo* (tamarind seed pods), are also popular drinks.

ATOLE: Hot drink made from ground corn.

ATOLE DE GRANILLO: A variety of *atole* made with crushed corn.

ATOLE DE PANELA: Corn *atole* sweetened with *panela* or *piloncillo*.

BOLIS: Flavored ice balls made from *agua de sabor*.

CAFÉ (*COFFEA ARABICA*): Coffee. Beans are grown in the Sierra, Cañada, and Coastal regions. Pluma is the coffee grown at altitudes above 9,000 feet. Pergamino is a variety of coffee that has a protective casing around the bean.

CHILEATOLE: Corn drink made with fresh corn, *epazote,* and chile.

CHOCOLATE ATOLE: Ceremonial drink that is very frothy, made of corn and white chocolate.

CHOCOLATE DE AGUA: Hot chocolate made with water.

CHOCOLATE DE LECHE: Hot chocolate made with milk.

CAFÉ DE OLLA: Coffee boiled with sugar and cinnamon in a clay pot.

CHAMPURRADO: Combination of *atole* and chocolate.

HORCHATA: Blended rice drink flavored with cinnamon and sugar, served with diced cantaloupe and pecans.

HORNITOS TEQUILA: Liquor of Jalisco state that is made from an agave plant.

JUGO: Juice.

LICUADO: Drink made with fresh fruit and milk.

LIMONADA: Limeade.

MEXICAN CHOCOLATE: Mixture of dried toasted cacao and Mexican cinnamon sticks ground with sugar by hand on the *metate* or in a mill. It is then made into tablets or balls and whipped to a froth in a special clay pot with a *molinillo* (wood beater). One variety called *almendrada* contains almonds.

MEZCAL/MEZCALITO/CREMA DE: Liquor distilled from the maguey (agave) plant. In Oaxaca they also make *cremas de mescal* with flavors such as orange, coffee, and almond.

PONCHE: Mulled drink made with fruits for the Christmas season.

POPO: Ancient drink of the Chinantla region made with cacao, corn, sugar, and *colcameca* root, which are whipped to make pure foam and drunk from gourds.

REFRESCOS: Soda pop.

ROMPOPE: Liquor much like eggnog, reputedly made by nuns.

ROSITA DE CACAO (*QUARARIBEA FUNEBRIS*): Aromatic flower used as an ingredient for *tejate*.

TEJATE: Pre-Hispanic beverage made from corn cooked with wood ash (*conesle*), plus cacao beans, *rositas de cacao,* and mamey pits that have been toasted. This mixture is ground on a *metate* to make a *masa*. The *masa* is hand-beaten in a clay bowl by the *tejatera* until a certain sound is heard, then cold water is added in a stream until foam appears on the surface. This high-calorie, high-fiber drink is drunk out of gourds and is an energizer.

TEPACHE: Pineapple beer served at village parties.

COOKING TERMS

ADOBO: A seasoning paste made from dried chiles, vinegar, and salt.

AL MOJO DE AJO: Cooking style meaning "soaked in garlic," often appropriate for fish and seafood.

ASADO: Grilled.

BORRACHO: Food soaked in liquor, literally meaning "drunk."

BOCADILLO: Snack, literally meaning "mouth filler."

BOTANA: Cocktail snack served on trays, cold or hot.

CALDILLO: Sauce with the consistency of thin soup.

CALDO: Broth, stock.

CONSOMÉ: Meat or seafood broth.

CREMA: Cream soup or bisque.

DORADO: Browned.

ENCHILADA: Smothered in chile paste or chile sauce.

EN DULCE: Sweetened, candied.

Opposite: Outdoor kitchen at Seasons of My Heart Cooking School, Rancho Aurora (Stephen Honeybill)

ENTOMATADA: Tortilla or meat dipped in spicy tomato sauce.

ESCABECHE: Chiles, vegetables, or pig's feet pickled in fruit vinegar.

ESTOFADO: Stew.

FRITADA: Italian baked egg omelet.

GAJOS: Wedges.

GUISADO: Meat, chicken, or fish cooked in a sauce.

MIGAS: Egg dish made of fried tortillas with onions, tomato, and chiles.

MOLITO: A sauce mixture similar to *mole*.

PICANTE: Spicy.

RAJAS: Roasted chiles that are cut into strips, then sautéed with onions and used in a variety of dishes. Made from *chile de agua*, *chile poblano*, or *chile jalapeño*.

RELLENO: Filled or stuffed.

REMOJADO: Soaked.

SOPA AGUADA: Soup.

SOPA SECA: Dry soup, usually rice or pasta served before the main course.

TORTITA: Fritter.

VINAGRE: Vinegar. Here in Oaxaca, fruit vinegars are usually made from pineapple or apple rinds or *tejocotes* (see page 340).

KITCHEN EQUIPMENT

ANAFRE: A portable charcoal grill.

CAJETE: Round ceramic bowl used in cheese making.

CAZUELA: Large clay cooking casserole.

CAZUELITA: Small clay cooking casserole.

CHIRMOLERA: A ceramic *molcajete* used for making salsas.

COMAL: Flat, round griddle made of unglazed pottery used to bake tortillas and to dry-roast or toast spices. To season a clay *comal*, mix a piece of *cal* with water and stir to dissolve. With a *comal* brush (or any type of brush), paint the surface of the cold *comal* completely with the *cal* water. Allow to dry. The *comal* surface will be white.

COMISCAL: A round sunken clay oven for baking *totopos*.

HORNO: Oven, either adobe or in a stove.

HORNO MÁGICO: Steam oven used on top of stove.

JARRA: Jug or pitcher.

JICALPAXTLE: Elaborately painted gourd used as a bowl to hold fruit, vegetables, candies, or tortillas.

LEÑA: Firewood.

METATE: Pre-Hispanic grinding stone with three legs; still in use today.

MOLCAJETE: Stone grinding bowl for chiles, spices, and salsas. To season a *molcajete*, grind dry corn in the *molcajete*, then discard. Grind rice in the *molcajete* until fine; discard. Continue grinding corn and rice in turn until the rice grinds to a clean white powder with no traces of gray stone. Wash the *molcajete* well, and it is ready for use.

MOLINILLO: Wooden whisk for whipping chocolate.

MOLINO: Mill. A wet *molino* is used for grinding corn, chiles, beans, or rice drinks. A dry *molino* is used for grinding chocolate or flour.

MANO: A stone rolling pin–shaped utensil used with the *metate* to grind seeds, tomatoes, chiles, etc.

OLLA: Clay pot or stockpot.

PARILLA: Grill.

TAMALERA: Pot for steaming *tamales*.

TEJOLOTE: Handheld grinding stone used with the *molcajete* or *chirmolera*.

TENATE: Palm basket used for carrying *nixtamal*, *masa*, and tortillas.

GLOSSARY OF SPANISH WORDS

ADELANTE: Come in! Farther, ahead, forward.

ADOBE: Sun-dried bricks made of mud mixed with horse manure or hay.

ALMUERZO: Late breakfast or early lunch.

AMATL: Tree bark used as an early form of paper.

AMIGAS(OS): Friends.

APROVECHAR: To take advantage of.

BORRACHO: Drunk.

¡BUEN PROVECHO!: Enjoy! Digest it well.

BUEN SAZÓN: Having a good taste bud or palate, or a good hand at seasoning.

CALENDA: Procession, parade.

CAMPESINA(O): Farmer, country folk.

CAMPO: Field, countryside.

CANTERA: Green or pink stone quarried locally.

CARBÓN: Burned wood used in a grill like charcoal.

CARRIZO: Bamboo-like reed that is used for baskets and for building.

CELEBRACIÓN: Celebration.

CENA: Light evening meal (soup, *antojitos*, tamales, or *pan dulce*).

CHICÁL: Large calabash container hollowed out and hung over a wood fire to darken color.

COCINERA(O): Cook.

COLECTIVO: Group taxi.

COMEDOR: Dining room, restaurant, café.

COMIDA: Food, large midday meal.

COMIDA CORRIDA: Menu of the day, "food on the run."

COPAL: Incense made of tree resin; burned in churches and on personal altars.

CRIOLLA(O): Native to the area.

DÍA DE MUERTOS: Day of the Dead.

DÍA DE PLAZA: Day of the market.

DOÑA: Madam, Mrs., also title of respect.

DONAJI: Zapotec princess.

DULCE: Sweet, candy.

EJIDO: Communal land that was divided into individual parcels during the *reforma agraria* after the Mexican Revolution.

ENCINO: Type of oak wood used for cooking.

FANDANGO: Collective party or *fiesta*.

FARMACIA: Pharmacy.

FERIA: Fair.

FINCA: Property, piece of real estate.

FIESTA: Holiday, celebration.

FONDA: Small restaurant or inn.

FUERZA: Strength.

GUEZA: Spontaneous gift giving.

HIJA: Daughter.

HUARACHE: Sandal.

HUERTO: Large vegetable garden.

HUESERO: Native chiropractor, bone manipulator.

HUIPIL: Native woman's tunic.

JARIPÉO: Rodeo with bareback bull riding.

JEFE(A): Boss, leader, manager.

LANCHA: Boat, motor launch, motorboat.

LIENZO: Fragment of codex.

LIMPIA: Clean, spiritual cleansing.

MAESTRO: Master, chef, teacher.

MARIACHIS: Band of musicians who perform a rousing type of Mexican music.

MARIMBA: Band of musicians who play music featuring a wooden instrument similar to a xylophone.

MAYORDOMIA/MAYORDOMO: Host family or host of a village *fiesta* honoring a saint.

MERCADO: Market.

MERCADO DE ABASTOS: "Market of supplies." The name of Oaxaca's largest market, which is both wholesale and retail.

MILPA: Cornfield.

MUERTEROS: Band of dancing men wearing masks and dressed as women who travel from house to house during the *Día de Muertos fiesta*.

MOTO: Motorcycle.

NACIMIENTO: Creche scene or *fiesta* on Christmas Eve.

NOCHE DE RABANOS: Large festival on December 23 in Oaxaca where local artisans carve giant radishes into three-dimensional displays that are part of a competition.

NOVIA(O): Girlfriend, boyfriend, fiancé(e).

OTRO LADO: The other side (of the border), the United States.

PADRINO/MADRINA: Godfather or mother of a child or a sponsor of an item at a *fiesta*.

PALENQUE: Home factory where small quantities of mezcal are produced.

PAISANO: Countryman.

PALAPA: Thatched-roof beach structure.

PARQUE DE LLANO: A city park in Oaxaca.

PETATE: An all-purpose woven palm mat.

PLATO FUERTE: Main dish.

PUEBLO: Village.

PUESTO: Stand or stall.

QUINCEAÑOS: Fifteenth birthday of a young girl. A large celebration or coming-out party to present the young woman to society.

REBOZO: Wrap, shawl.

SEÑORA: Madam, Mrs., title of respect.

SABROSO(A): Delicious, tasty, savory.

SALUDOS: Greetings.

SOMBRERO: Hat.

SIERRA: Mountain.

SERRANO: From the mountains.

TEJATERA: Woman who makes *tejate*.

TEMPORADA DE LLUVIAS: Rainy season.

TÍA: Aunt; also title of respect.

TORTILLERAS: Women who make tortillas for sale.

TRAPICHE: Sugarcane mill.

TURISTA: Tourist; also slang word for intestinal illness.

VELA: Ceremonial dance in the Isthmus of Tehuantepec where the women come together to show their beauty and grace.

VIGILIA: Lent.

YUNTA: Team of oxen that draws carts or plows the fields.

ZÓCALO: Picturesque central square found in most Mexican towns and cities.

SOURCES

MEXICAN INGREDIENTS AND UTENSILS

Unless otherwise noted, all of these suppliers have a retail store or sell by mail order.

ADRIANA'S CARAVAN
409 Vanderbilt Street
Brooklyn, New York 11218
800-316-0820
718-436-8565
Web site: http://www.adriannascaravan.com
CHILES: They stock most chiles.
SPICES: Over 400 spices, including Mexican oregano, *epazote*, *poleo*, Mexican cinnamon, dried avocado leaves, *achiote* paste, annato seeds.
OTHER: Black, red, and scarlet runner beans, *moles*, tortillas, *masa*, *masa harina*, *pozole*, blue and white corn flour, cornhusks, Mexican chocolate, *nopalitos*, *piloncillo*, *huitlacoche*, pumpkin seeds, banana leaves, tortilla presses, *molcajetes*.

AURORA EXPORTS
A.P. Postal 42, Admon. 3
Oaxaca C.P. 68101, Oaxaca
Mexico
Tel./Fax: 011-52-951-87726
Cell phone: 011-52-954-83115
E-mail: seasons@antequera.com
Oaxacan specialty items, including *mole* pastes.

AZTEC FOODS, INC.
5005 S. Nagle Avenue
Chicago, Illinois 60638-1491
708-563-6600
Web site: http://www.Aztecafoods.com
A variety of Mexican specialty items.

THE CHILE GUY
206 Frontage Road
Rio Rancho, New Mexico 81244
800-869-9218
505-891-0291
Wholesale only.

THE CMC COMPANY
P.O. Box 322
Avalon, New Jersey 08202
800-CMC-2780
Fax: 609-861-0043
CHILES: A variety of dried chiles, such as *ancho*, *mulato*, *pasilla oaxaqueño* and *mexicano*, *guajillo*, *de árbol*, *chilhuacle*, *negro*, *morita*, and *chipotle*.
SPICES: Mexican oregano, *epazote*, *canela*, and dried avocado leaves.
OTHER: *Nopalitos*, *piloncillo*, *achiote* paste, *huitla-coche*, pumpkin seeds, *pozole*, and dried cornhusks. They also have kitchen items: *molcajetes*, tortilla presses, and *comales*.

COYOTE CAFE GENERAL STORE
132 West Water Street
Santa Fe, New Mexico 87501
800-866-HOWL
Fax: 505-989-9026
CHILES: *Ancho negro*, *de árbol*, *mulato*, *guajillo*, *japonés*, *chilhuacle rojo*, *pasilla mexicana*, *piquín*, *chipotle*, *chipotles en adobo*.
SPICES: *Epazote*, *achiote* paste.
OTHER: *Masa*, *masa harina*, *pozole*, blue corn flour, cornhusks, Mexican chocolate, tortilla presses, *molcajetes*.

FRIEDA'S, INC.
P.O. Box 58488
Los Angeles, California 90058
800-241-9477 and 800-241-1771
Fax: 714-816-0273
E-mail: mailorder@friedas.com
An extensive Web site lists exotic fruits and vegetables, including *La Cocina Frieda*, featuring vegetables, chiles, spices, and other ingredients used in Mexican cooking.

HARBAR CORPORATION
17-25 Broad Street
Quincy, Massachusetts 02169
617-769-0023
Fax: 617-769-0400
White and blue corn tortillas, white flour, whole wheat, and flavored (spinach, tomato, and chile) tortillas.

HERBS OF MEXICO
3903 Whittier Boulevard
Los Angeles, California 90023
213-261-2521
Wide variety of herbs, *achiote*, *epazote*, avocado leaves, *poleo*, *hierba santa*.

KITCHEN MARKET
218 Eighth Avenue
New York, New York 10011
212-243-4433
CHILES: *Ancho, pasilla, chilhuacle negro* and *rojo, guajillo, onza, chilcostle, pasilla oaxaqueña, chipotle, mora, costeño, de árbol.*
SPICES: *Piloncillo, achiote,* avocado leaves, *canela, epazote, hierba santa,* Mexican oregano.
OTHER: *Moles, masa harina,* cornhusks, *huitlacoche, pozole, nopales,* slaked lime, *jamaica* leaves, *molinillo,* tortilla presses.

LOS CHILEROS DE NUEVO MEXICO
P.O. Box 6215
Sante Fe, New Mexico 87502
505-471-6967
Fax: 505-473-7306
CHILES: *Ancho negro, ancho rojo, de árbol, mulato, guajillo, japonés, piquín, chipotle, chipotles en adobo.*
OTHER: *Masa harina,* blue corn flour, *pozole,* cornhusks.

MO HOTTA-MO BETTA
P.O. Box 4136
San Luis Obispo, California 93403
800-462-3220
Fax: 805-545-8389
Lots of hot sauces from all over the world. *Achiote,* cornhusks, *epazote, masa harina, nopalitos,* Mexican oregano, *piloncillo,* pumpkin seeds.

MOZZARELLA COMPANY
2914 Elm Street
Dallas, Texas 75226
800-798-2954
Fax: 214-741-4076
Mexican cheeses: *Queso blanco, queso fresco, quesillo,* and Oaxacan string cheese.

NEWBURGH FARM MARKET
555 Broadway
Newburgh, New York 12550
914-565-6666
CHILES: Nearly 20 varieties of fresh chiles.
SPICES: Avocado leaf, *hierba santa, epazote.*
OTHER: *Masa harina, quesillo, queso fresco, queso añejo, requesón, chayotes, nopales.*

THE NEW MEXICAN CONNECTION

2833 Rhode Island N.E.
Albuquerque, New Mexico 87110
800-933-2736
Fax: 505-292-0058

CHILES: *Ancho negro, chilcostle, de árbol, mulato, guajillo, japonés, chilhuacle negro, pasilla mexicana, pasilla oaxaqueño, chipotles,* and *chipotles en adobo.* They also sell chile seeds.

SPICES: Mexican oregano, *epazote, hierbabuena,* cilantro.

OTHER: *Moles, masa harina,* blue and yellow *pozole,* blue corn flour, cornhusks, Mexican chocolate, *adobo* sauce, vanilla.

PENDERY'S

1221 Manufacturing Street
Dallas, Texas 75207-6506
800-533-1870
Fax: 214-761-1966

CHILES: All the chiles except *ancho rojo, chiltepec, chilhuacle amarillo,* and *rojo* (they have *negro*) and *chilitos, chipotles en adobo.*

SPICES: Mexican oregano, *epazote, poleo, canela, achiote* paste, annato seeds.

OTHER: *Masa, masa harina,* cornhusks, Mexican chocolate, pumpkin seeds, tortilla presses, *molcajetes.*

PENZEY'S SPICES

P.O. Box 933
Muskego, WI 53150
414-679-7207
Fax: 414-679-7878
Web site: http://www.Penzeys.com

CHILES: *Ancho rojo, de árbol, piquín, chipotle.*

SPICES: Mexican oregano, *epazote, poleo* (dry), *canela,* annato seeds.

TIERRA VEGETABLES

13684 Chalk Hill Road
Healdsburg, California 95448
707-433-5666

Over 20 varieties of fresh and dried chiles and 7 different varieties of *chipotle,* Oaxacan *chilhuacles,* and *costeño* chiles.

ZINGERMAN'S MAIL ORDER

422 Detroit Street
Ann Arbor, Michigan 48104
888-636-8162
Fax: 734-769-1235

A variety of international specialty items, including *mole* paste.

SEEDS AND PLANTS
(Grow Your Own!)

BILL COLEMAN

P.O. Box 631
Carpinteria, California 93013
805-684-5569

Grows and distributes a wide variety of organic Asian and Latin American herbs and greens.

COMPANION PLANTS

7247 N. Coolville Ridge Road
Athens, Ohio 45701
740-592-4643
Fax: 740-593-5092

An internationally recognized herb nursery that also sells seeds. Amaranth, lamb's quarters, *epazote,* coffee, cilantro, Mexican oregano, sweet marjoram, *tomatillo,* Mexican bush oregano, *chia, hierbabuena,* Mexican tarragon, ginger.

J.L. HUDSON, SEEDSMAN

Star Route 2, Box 337
La Honda, California 94020
No phone, no Web site, no visitors! Write for catalog, $1.00.
Ethnobotanical items, including the Zapotec Collection (collected deep in the Sierra Madre del Sur, in southern Oaxaca), vegetables, herbs, ornamental and medicinal plants. Seeds include *jitomate*, pea (*chicharro criollo*), *epazote*, several types of squash.

GALLINA CANYON RANCH

P.O. Box 706
Abiquiu, New Mexico 87510
505-490-3333
Seeds for all kinds of dried beans.

RICHTERS

Goodwood, Ontario
L0C 1A0 CANADA
905-640-6677
Fax: 905-640-6641
A beautiful and comprehensive collection featuring a variety of rare herbs and plants, including *epazote*, Mexican chile peppers, jícama, purslane, lambs-quarters.

SEEDS OF CHANGE

P.O. Box 15700
Santa Fe, New Mexico 87506-5700
505-438-8080
800-957-3337
Fax: 505-438-7052
Web site: http://www.seedsofchange.com
They have seeds for *costeño amarillo*, *costeño rojo*, *guajillo* chiles, also *epazote*, Mexican tarragon, black and white *alluvia* beans, scarlet runner beans.

SHEPHERD'S GARDEN SEEDS

30 Irene Street
Torrington, Connecticut 06790-6658
860-482-3638
Fax: 860-482-0532
In addition to vegetable, herb, and chile seeds (an extensive selection), they offer some useful cooking items such as the *asador,* a stove-top grill for roasting onions, garlic, and chiles and for toasting tortillas.

Rolando Jiménez displaying ground chocolate at Molinos del Sol, Mercado de Abastos, Oaxaca (Stephen Honeybill)

BIBLIOGRAPHY

Álvarez, Luís Rodrigo. *Historia general del estado de oaxaca.* Oaxaca, Mexico: Carteles Editores, 1996.

Atlás Culturál de México (Flora, Sep, Inah, Planeta), 1987.

Andrews, Jean. *Peppers, The Domesticated Capsicums.* Austin, Tex.: University of Texas Press, 1995.

Bayless, Rick, and D. G. Bayless. *Authentic Mexican Regional Cooking from the Heart of Mexico.* New York: William Morrow, 1987.

Bayless, Rick, D. G. Bayless, and J. M. Brownson. *Rick Bayless' Mexican Kitchen.* New York: Charles Scribner's Sons, 1996.

Bernal Alcántara, Juan Areli. *El camino de añukojm-totontepec y los salesianos.* Mexico D.F.: Talleres Gráficos de Litografica Impro, S.A de C.V, 1991.

Casas, María, ed. *Oaxaca; fiestas y tradiciones del istmo.* Oaxaca: Sedetur. Gobierno del Estado de Oaxaca, 1998.

———. *Oaxaca; pueblos y paisajes de la mixteca.* Oaxaca: Sedetur. Gobierno del Estado de Oaxaca, 1997.

Coe, Sophie D., and Michael D. Coe. *The True History of Chocolate.* New York: Thames and Hudson, 1996.

Cotton Country Collection. Monroe, La.: Junior Charity League, 1972.

Cousineau, Ruth. *Country Suppers.* New York: William Morris, 1997.

Cowl, Scott, and Martin Diskin, eds. *Markets in Oaxaca.* Austin, Tex.: University of Texas Press, 1976.

Flannery, Kent, and Joyce Marcus. *The Cloud People.* New York: Academic Press, 1983.

Fussell, Betty. *The Story of Corn.* New York: Alfred A. Knopf, 1994.

Gónzalez, Alvaro. *La guelaguetza; breve semblanza.* Oaxaca: Instituto Oaxaqueño de las Culturas, 1993.

González de la Vera, Fernán. *La cocina mexicana, a través de los siglos: época prehispánica.* Mexico: Fundación Herdez, 1996.

González, Elaine. *The Art of Chocolate.* San Francisco: Chronicle Books, 1998.

Gran diccionario español ingles. Mexico D.F.: Librairie Larousse, 1983.

Gúzman de Vásquez Colmenares, Ana María. *Tradiciones gastronómicas oaxaqueñas.* Oaxaca, Mexico: Privately published by Ana María Gúzman de Vásquez, 1982.

Green, Judith Strupp. *The Days of the Dead in Oaxaca.* San Diego, 1969.

Hernández Díaz, Gilberto. *La Cañada, nuevos estudios sobre la Cañada.* Mexico D.F.: Inah, 1982.

Jované, Ana, and Carmen Valles Septién. *Mexico's Gift to the World: Plants.* Mexico D.F.: Reproducciones Fotomecánicas, 1994.

Kennedy, Diana. *The Art of Mexican Cooking.* New York: Bantam Books, 1989.

———. *The Cuisines of Mexico.* New York: Harper and Row, 1972.

———. *Recipes from the Regional Cooks of Mexico.* New York: Harper and Row, 1978.

Marcus, Joyce, and Kent V. Flannery. *Zapotec Civilization: How Urban Society Evolved in Mexico's Oaxaca Valley.* London: Thames and Hudson, 1996.

Martínez, Zarela. *The Food and Life of Oaxaca: Traditional Recipes from Mexico's Heart.* New York: Macmillan, 1997.

McGee, Harold. *On Food and Cooking: The Science and Lore of the Kitchen.* New York: Charles Scribner's Sons, 1984.

Nahmad, Salamon. *Los mixes. estudio social y cultural de la región del Zempoaltepetl y del Istmo de Tehuantepec.* Mexico D.F.: Instituto Nacional Indigenista, 1965.

Naj, Amal. *Peppers, A Story of Hot Pursuits.* New York: Vintage Books, 1993.

Novo, Salvador. *Cocina mexicana historia gastronómica de la ciudad de México.* Mexico: Editorial Porrúa, S.A., 1993.

Ortíz, Elisabeth Lambert. *The Book of Latin American Cooking.* New York: Alfred A. Knopf, 1979.

Palomo, Margarita Dálton, Verónica Loera, and C. Chávez. *Historia del arte de Oaxaca: Arte contemporáneo.* Oaxaca, Mexico: Gobierno del Estado de Oaxaca, and Instituto Oaxaqueño de las Culturas, 1997.

Paola y Luna, Ana Rosaurade. *Las recetas de tía rosaura.* Oaxaca, Carteles Editores, 1994.

Pardo, M., and Robledo, H. *Pueblos indigenas de México.* Mexico D.F.: Instituto Nacional Indigenista y Secretaría de Desarrollo Social, 1994.

Pepin, Jacques. *La Technique.* New York: Pocket Books, 1976.

Portillo de Carballido, Maria Concepción. *Oaxaca y su cocina.* Oaxaca, Mexico: Privately published by María Concepción Portillo de Carballido, 1987.

Pueblos indigenas de Mexico, Chinantecos. Mexico D.F.: Instituto Nacional Indigenista, 1995.

Pueblos indigenas de México, Mixes. Mexico D.F.: Instituto Nacional Indigenista, 1995.

Rivera, Guadalupe, and Marie-Pierre Colle. *Frida's Fiestas.* New York: Clarkson N. Potter, 1994.

Rodale's Illustrated Encyclopedia of Herbs. Emmaus, Pa.: Rodale Press, 1987.

Rombauer, Irma S. and Marion Rombauer Becker. *The Joy of Cooking.* New York: Bobbs-Merrill, 1974.

Ross, Gary N. "Night of the Radishes." *National History,* December 1986.

Sahagun, Fray Bernardino de. *Codice florentino.* Florence, Italy: Secretaria de Gobernación, Archivo General de la Nación, 1979.

Sierra Juárez, Trabajo comunitario, identidad y memoria histórica de los pueblos. Mexico D.F.: INI/CEHCAM, 1994.

Sunset Western Garden Book. Menlo Park, CA: Lane, 1992.

Suculentas Mexicanas-Cactáceas. Mexico: Comisión Nacional Para el Conocimiento y Uso de la Biodiversidad, 1997.

Toor, Frances. *A Treasury of Mexican Folkways.* New York: Bonanza Books, 1985.

Velázquez de León, Josefina. *Cocina oaxaqueña.* Mexico: Editorial Universo, 1991.

Whitman, Joan, and Delores Simon. *Recipes into Type.* New York: Harper Collins Publishers, 1993.

. . . Y *la comida se hizo de dulces y postres.* Mexico D.F.: Editorial Trillas, 1990.

Yzábul, María Dolores Torres, and Shelton Wiseman. *The Mexican Gourmet.* San Diego: Thunder Bay Press, 1995.

Zaslavsky, Nancy. *A Cook's Tour of Mexico.* New York: St. Martin's Press, 1995.

INDEX

ABOUT THE AUTHOR

Susana Trilling, international chef and cooking instructor, has had extensive experience with Mexican and international cuisine. Her love of Mexican food was born when her grandmother, from Tampico, Mexico, gave Susana her first *tamales*. Susana began her formal study of Mexican cooking in 1977. Since then she has been a chef, writer, and food consultant and has developed recipes using Mexican food products.

Owner of Seasons of My Heart Cooking School, she has been living in and studying Oaxacan cooking for over ten years. Her classes, culinary tours, and lectures focus on pre-Hispanic foods; traditional culinary, medicinal, and spiritual herb usage; and the Spanish influences on the contemporary Oaxaqueño kitchen. The classes are participation based, and are combined with market tours and demonstrations in local homes and cottage industries to immerse the students into the culture. In the year 2000, Susana will begin offering a special culinary tour of the seven regions of Oaxaca. She will feature actual visits to the regions and cooking and eating specialties of each area.

She has published *My Search for the Seventh Mole: A Story with Recipes from Oaxaca, Mexico*, and has been featured in numerous shows about Oaxacan cooking. Susana and her partner, Eric Ulrich, are the owners of Aurora Exports, a company exporting Oaxacan food products, including *mole* pastes.

She lives with Eric and their sons, Kaelin, Jesse Beau, and Lider, in the foothills of the Sierra Madre outside the city of Oaxaca, Mexico.